Fight Sports and American Masculinity

Fight Sports and American Masculinity

Salvation in Violence from 1607 to the Present

CHRISTOPHER DAVID THRASHER

McFarland & Company, Inc., Publishers
Jefferson, North Carolina

LIBRARY OF CONGRESS CATALOGUING-IN-PUBLICATION DATA

Thrasher, Christopher David.
    Fight sports and American masculinity : salvation in violence from 1607 to the present / Christopher David Thrasher.
        p.   cm.
    Includes bibliographical references and index.

    ISBN 978-0-7864-9704-1 (softcover : acid free paper) ∞
    ISBN 978-1-4766-1823-4 (ebook)

    1. Hand-to-hand fighting—United States—History. 2. Sports—United States—History. 3. Sports—Social aspects—United States—History. 4. Violence in men. 5. Masculinity in sports. I. Title.
    GV1111.T48 2015
    796.80973—dc23   2015017630

BRITISH LIBRARY CATALOGUING DATA ARE AVAILABLE

© 2015 Christopher David Thrasher. All rights reserved

No part of this book may be reproduced or transmitted in any form or by any means, electronic or mechanical, including photocopying or recording, or by any information storage and retrieval system, without permission in writing from the publisher.

Front cover: *There Was a Man: Abe Lincoln Licks Jack Armstrong* (from the Lincoln Financial Foundation Collection, courtesy of the Indiana State Museum and Allen County Public Library)

Printed in the United States of America

McFarland & Company, Inc., Publishers
   Box 611, Jefferson, North Carolina 28640
     www.mcfarlandpub.com

To my wife—I could have done it all without you,
but I am grateful that I did not have to.

Acknowledgments

If I have accomplished anything in life, it is only because people have been nice to me. For anything worthwhile within these pages, I give all credit to my benefactors. All errors are entirely my own.

I am grateful for the priceless archival assistance provided by the entire staff at the H.J. Lutcher Stark Center for Physical Culture and Sports at the University of Texas at Austin.

I would never have been able to finish my doctorate without the guidance and support of my advisors at Texas Tech University. I thank Dr. Gretchen Adams, who provided me with insights into early American history and more importantly into the cutthroat realities of academia. I appreciate the efforts of Dr. Barbara Hahn to help me understand many aspects of Southern, economic, and technological history. If I ever bump into you on Bourbon Street, Dr. Hahn, the drinks are on me. Special thanks go to Dr. Zachary Brittsan, who expressed no hesitation in assisting with a project far outside his area of primary expertise and often provided words of encouragement that meant more than he will ever know.

I express my undying gratitude to my dissertation advisor, Dr. Randy McBee. No scholar could ever ask for a more patient, more kind-hearted, or more unapologetically demanding mentor.

I reserve my deepest thanks for my parents, David and Theresa Thrasher. From the moment of my birth, they indulged my curiosities, encouraged me to fall in love with learning, and convinced me that the answers to life's mysteries lay within the yellowed pages of long-forgotten books.

Table of Contents

Acknowledgments	vi
Preface	1
Introduction: Global Fight Sports from Prehistory to 1607	13
I. "To Cut Out the Tongue or Pull Out the Eyes": Fight Sports in the Americas, 1607–1810	29
II. "A Boxing We Will Go": Boxing Takes Root in the United States, 1810–1915	49
III. "With the Energy of a Trip-Hammer and the Vehemence of a Sioux": Asian Martial Arts Come to the United States, 1850–1941	99
IV. "We Live in Our Heroes": Boxing Reigns Supreme in the United States, 1915–1941	140
V. "Everybody Was Kung Fu Fighting": Asian Martial Arts Gain Unprecedented Popularity in the United States, 1941–1981	166
VI. "We Shall Not Stand by Helplessly": The Birth of Mixed Martial Arts, 1981 to the Present	198
Chapter Notes	237
Bibliography	281
Index	291

Preface

Throughout America's past, some men feared the descent of their gender into effeminacy, and turned their eyes to the ring in hopes of gendered salvation. In 1888, the writer and pugilist Duffield Ossborne ended his defense of the arena with a stirring call to action.

> Come then! Let thinking men who value their manhood set themselves in array, both against the army of those who, unmanly themselves, wish to see all others reduced to their own level, and against the vast following who, caught by such specious watchwords as "progress," "civilization," and refinement," have unthinkingly thrown their weight into the falling scale. Has mawkish sentimentality become the shibboleth of the progress, civilization and refinement of this vaunted age? If so, then in Heaven's name leave us a saving touch of honest, old-fashioned barbarism! That when we come to die, we shall die, leaving men behind us, and not a race of eminently respectable female saints.[1]

Ossborne's comments highlight many of the themes of gender and civilization in this work. In this essay, titled "A Defense of Pugilism," he speaks to "thinking men who value their manhood." He then suggests that these men are opposed by those who "unthinkingly" value a warped sense of civilization which robs men of their masculine identities. He mocks "unmanly" opponents, suggesting that if civilization is now tied to femininity, then men should retain a sense of "old-fashioned barbarism" so that, as he states in his final sentence, "when we come to die, we shall die, leaving men behind us." Ossborne clearly sees manly identity as something under assault, as something more valuable than "civilization"—or at least as some define civilization—and he defends boxing as a force with the power to preserve masculine identities.[2] Ossborne's call was largely reiterated nearly a century later by the sportswriter Curry Kirkpatrick, who presented his appeal in *Sports Illustrated*.

> We shall not stand helplessly by and allow a great American institution to be so threatened by the cottage-cheese mentality pervasive in society. Is Don-

ahuemanology rampant in the land? Is nothing sacred? Let the bleeding hearts trash all the arms sales and rock 'n' roll lyrics they want, but, hey, stay away from violence in sports.... Let's be serious and admit it. We're looking for the wheels to go over the wall. We're waiting for the Blackhawks and the Bruins to take off the gloves and begin socking the "eh's" out of each other. Preferably wade into the stands and molest a few cops, too. We're desperately hoping that the next time John McEnroe and Ivan Lendl scream at each other, they won't meekly appeal to the chair but instead say something like ... "You want some of me?" ... and start duking it out right on Centre Court. We're just praying we're not dealing bridge at the country club the night Mike Tyson rearranges one of his no-talent palooka dance partners into a vegetable. What a guy, Tyson! Once raised pigeons. Now reduces people to pulp. The American Dream.... So raise your hands and be counted. Don't fade into the woodwork.[3]

Kirkpatrick echoes many of Ossborne's themes and demonstrates some of the changes documented in this work. Kirkpatrick calls men to action, urging them to "not stand helplessly by" as feminine rivals attempt to push violence to the periphery. Unlike Ossborne, who sought to defend boxing, Kirkpatrick revels in the much more wide-ranging violence of boxing, hockey, and even tennis while making references to arms sales, rock music, assaults on police, and car crashes. He, like Ossborne, ends on a note of defiance, urging men to "raise your hands and be counted" as supporters of an unashamedly violent masculinity.[4]

This book explains how the salvation-granting fight sports change over time. It argues that the dominant fight sports in the United States change in response to larger societal shifts in American culture, most importantly in popular perceptions of the world beyond the nation's borders. It presents a grand narrative of American history as seen from the bars, gyms, stadiums, and living rooms of the American heartland and demonstrates the agency of ordinary Americans who use their money and their bodies to determine the nation's dominant fight sports and its masculinity. This work shows that popular culture provides a place of cultural negotiation where Americans set boundaries of citizenship, race, and gender. Today, mixed martial arts routinely attracts more viewers than boxing and dominates the younger demographics, with very few viewers younger than age 35 preferring boxing to mixed martial arts.[5] This battle in the war for cultural dominance between boxing and mixed martial arts is only the most recent in a series of conflicts between fight sports.

The present conflict makes sense only when viewed in a broader chronological context. To understand the present we must turn our attention to the past. A study of the past reveals that the debates have always existed. Recent arguments over mixed martial arts are remarkably similar to past debates that have played out in a pattern often more cyclical than linear. In colonial

America, a North Carolinian took humorous pride in the distinctly American love of eye gouging, a practice another American called "madness."[6] After the War of 1812, an American author praised English-style boxing, while a journalist disagreed and condemned the sport as "barbarism."[7] An early 20th-century American sailor denounced his Japanese rival for using "street rules" rather than fighting under the code espoused by Queensbury, which the sailor preferred.[8]

This work provides a needed addition to the historiography. It undermines the economic determinism so prevalent in studies of American fight sports, which are largely unified around an overemphasis on economics as the driving force in the creation and popularization of these sports. Elliot Gorn argued boxing was "a marketplace of violence," which he contextualized as part of larger shifts in American labor.[9] Jeffrey Sammons summarized defenses of boxing based on its role of economic escalation for poor young men.[10] Geoffrey C. Ward presented his biography of famed heavyweight champion Jack Johnson as the story of how Johnson "punched his way up from poverty to wealth."[11] Michael T. Isenberg argued that changes in the sport of boxing were often driven by a desire to "gain money."[12] This economic emphasis extends to studies of wrestling. Scott Beekman argued that American men became wrestlers primarily "to earn large sums of money."[13] In contrast to those works, this book argues that culture and not money was often the primary driving sport in the development of American fight sports. This aspect takes inspiration from Gerald Morton and George O'Brien, who argued that wrestling was a ritual as well as a commercial sport.[14]

This book will also seek to correct the scholarship's myopically domestic focus. While this work is a history of fight sports in America, it demonstrates an unprecedented appreciation for how American fight sports were connected to the rest of the world. Elliot Gorn did an excellent job of explaining how immigrants contributed to a growing 19th-century American boxing subculture, but he did not adequately explain how changes in American perceptions of the world coincided with migrating workers.[15] Jeffery Sammons argued that American nationalism motivated many American men to enter the ring, but he said nothing about how the nationalism of other countries motivated their young men to come to America.[16] Scott Beekman briefly hinted at the idea that race could occasionally trump nationalism among American fighters, but it was only a passing comment that he did not develop.[17]

In contrast to these studies, this work will cast a wider geographic net. It will demonstrate that Americans adopted new fight sports as their opinions of foreign nations shifted, and some American men sought to save their manhood by emulating or besting nations worthy of their admiration. It draws inspiration from Micol Seigel's *Uneven Encounters*, which deemphasized the nation state as a category of analysis and instead focused on identities that are "odd-shaped beasts, neither fully within nor simply larger than their nation states."[18] This book seeks to demonstrate the oddly shaped identities at the heart of fight sports. It also applies the work of Robin Kelley, who argued, "We have much to learn from African American historical scholarship about the international context for American history."[19] This work provides the first introduction of those lessons into the historiography of American fight sports.

Unlike almost every other study of fight sports in America, this book examines many sports rather than a single one. The titles of existing works indicate how each focuses on a single sport: *The Manly Art*; *Bare-Knuckle Prize Fighting in America*; *Beyond the Ring: The Role of Boxing in American Society*; *Ringside: A History of Professional Wrestling in America*; and *Wrestling to Rasslin': Ancient Sport to American Spectacle*. This book adopts a broader approach. Michael Poliakoff argued, "The element of fighting makes combat sports easy to mark off as a group."[20] The present volume provides additional support for his assertion and adopts his method of looking at fight sports as a group of interconnected sports rahser than as separate activities, as most studies of American fight sports have done. This approach is not limited to Poliakoff; other scholars of fight sports in areas outside the United States have also examined a broad range of fight sports. Donald Kyle often grouped fight sports together in his *Sport and Spectacle in the Ancient World*.[21] One of the most exciting works to come out in recent years was Thomas Desch-Obi's *Fighting for Honor: The History of African Martial Art Traditions in the Atlantic World*.[22] Desch-Obi's work, like this book, casts a broad net over geography and interconnected fight sports. While Desch-Obi focuses on the African diasporas, this volume investigates fight sports that came to America from Europe, Asia, and Africa. The many fight sports of America, including boxing, wrestling, kickboxing, and mixed martial arts, all provided refuges for American masculine identities.

Fighting arts provide a rare moment of connection between diverse populations because they offer a primal violence that crosses cultural boundaries more easily than many sports. Physical domination needs far less explanation than more complicated games such as baseball or football. People from enormously diverse backgrounds understand and appreciate it on a very visceral level. Scholars such as Joanna Bourke, in *An Intimate History of Killing*, demonstrated that many men enjoy violence regardless of nationality, even if they hesitate to admit it.[23] Bourke focused on military violence while noting the connections many men felt between violence in war and in sport.[24] The scholar and professional soldier Dave Grossman agreed, citing testimony from soldiers raised in many cultures that violence "gives pleasure and satisfaction."[25] While he, like Bourke, focused mostly on military violence, he notes that violent sports can provide similar pleasures to combat.[26] He also argued that many people, particularly young men, actively pursue physical danger, including violent sports, simply because they find them enjoyable.[27] Andrea Smalley noted that the pleasure of violence even extends across the gendered boundary, with one woman noting, "I just like to kill things."[28]

The most direct explanation of the universal appeal of fight sports comes from two of the most famous fighters themselves. The great 19th-century heavyweight boxing champion John L. Sullivan made observations in his autobiography indicating that people of his time shared a love of violence that spanned boundaries of time and place. Referring to his fans, he claimed, "Men who doze in obligatory pews on Sunday to the soothing accompaniment of a clerical homily, struggle eagerly to see Christians pound each other."[29] Sullivan enjoyed his work—as did the fans—giving up on a promising career as a professional baseball player to pursue boxing. He noted, "Fighting, under the Marquis of Queensbury Rules before gentlemen, is a pleasure."[30] Sullivan's comments stressed the connections facilitated by fighting arts, referring to boxing as "an unbroken inheritance from the ancients" and fondly recounting his boxing tours across Europe.[31] Sullivan was a racist and his racism motivated his refusal to fight Peter Jackson, the black boxing champion from Australia.[32] However, his love of the ring occasionally overcame his racism: his former opponent, the Maori pugilist Herbert Slade, became one of his trusted friends and earned Sullivan's respect as one of the "gamest" men he ever knew.[33] A century later, the globe traveling champion of karate, kickboxing, wrestling, and mixed martial arts, Chuck "The Ice Man" Liddell, explained these ideas even better than his predecessor. He argued, "Everyone can relate to wanting to be tough, to being able to knock someone out, and sometimes, just as important to being able to take a punch." Liddell describes this desire as "a visceral, innate feeling that we pick up as kids and never really let go of." Demonstrating the uniqueness of fight sports, he suggested, "When someone challenges you in a bar, your first instinct isn't, I can take that guy in a game of one-on-one or I can throw a football farther than he can. You're thinking I can take that guy out."[34] Many people share an appreciation for violence and a desire to be tough regardless of language, religion, or race. Fight sports facilitated a cultural interaction more difficult with nonviolent sports that allowed for rare moments of connection between the people of East and West.

American fight sports build on much older traditions. The Introduction will demonstrate that debates about fight sports and alternative visions of masculinity that played out in America rested on a basis as old as humanity. Jacob won the name "Israel" when he wrestled an angel into submission.[35] The ancient Sumerian king Shulgi proclaimed himself master of both the battlefield and the wrestling ring.[36] The Mahabharata offered a ringside perspective to vigorous bouts between men who battled for the delight of spectators.[37] These early accounts demonstrate that every immigrant to America came from a culture with a long history of fight sports. History documents huge diversities of human experiences, but few themes spread more broadly than an insatiable desire to engage in and to witness violence that flows across the spiritual, the martial, and the recreational aspects of life in ways that tear down distinctions between these segments.

The first chapter builds on the groundwork laid in the Introduction, taking up the story with the spread of English colonists to North America in 1607 and tracing the narrative until the first decades of the 19th century. It analyzes the formation of a unique American identity as British subjects adapted their culture and their love of fight sports to new homes. The new land offered a wide array of possible masculinities among Indian warriors, African slaves, and white sailors. In the cities, taverns became social centers where a shared love of violent sport brought rich and poor men together.[38] Colonists wrestled with Indians to prove their strength and demonstrated their mastery over slaves by forcing them to engage in fights for their owners' amusement.[39] Militia members practiced wrestling to improve their capacity to defend their settlements, facilitating the transfer of an English sporting culture to America.[40]

On the early American frontier, reputations became priceless, scars became badges of honor, and brutality became a virtue. Frontiersmen of the lower sort adapted English boxing into the uniquely American fight sport of gouging, which dispensed with any pretense of restraint and encouraged fighters to bite, scratch, and gouge their opponents.[41] Gouging brushed aside the luxury of decorum and embraced mayhem in all of its glorious varieties. Colonial legislators recoiled in horror and passed laws that made gouging illegal, but hardly affected the practice on the frontier.[42] The new art even became a point of pride for colonists who were challenging the British Empire. On the eve of revolution a North Carolina journalist jokingly offered gouging as evidence of colonial superiority. He asked his readers, "Are we not able to slay thousands, yea tens of thousands with our thumb nails?"[43] He took nationalistic pride, demanding to know, "What men of any nation upon earth can cope with us at gouging?"[44]

Gouging faded away as American colonies became an American nation and middle-class reformers, particularly from the East, won with cultural ideals what they could not acquire with legal prohibitions. This text provides additional support for Eric Foner's assertion that some middle-class Americans were uncomfortable with the lifestyles of the lower class.[45] Eliot Gorn argues that the duel became a substitute for gouging, but I disagree, tracing the descendants of frontier gougers to working-class wrestling and boxing rings rather than the dueling grounds of elites.[46] Many Americans looked to ancient Greece for inspiration in the early 19th century, embracing their sports, including wrestling.[47] Citizens of the young nation increasingly embraced a distinct masculinity that traveled a middle path, abhorring the brutality of gouging, but demonstrating strength by physically dominating challengers in a wrestling style with connections to ancient Greece. This book, like Marcus Reddiker's *Between the Devil and the Deep Blue Sea*, will present the 18th-century Atlantic world as a place of new and contested masculinities.

The second chapter shows that wrestlers did not long stand at the pinnacle of American fight sports or masculinity. Boxing replaced wrestling as America's favorite fight sport after a long battle that spanned the 19th century. In this period American cities exploded with immigrants from northern and western Europe. The old economy of master craftsmen suffered numerous setbacks and was largely replaced by a factory system that deskilled the workplace and caused economic upheavals, leaving men disconnected from older masculine ideals and looking for new meanings. The growth of an urban sporting culture in America shifted fight sports away from the wrestling matches of militia musters and toward the boxing ring with its more dramatic violence, which in turn attracted bigger crowds and larger profits for the promoters who increasingly treated fight sports as a business. Scott Beekman argues in *Ringside* that boxers replaced wrestlers as America's favorite athletes, but this book emphasizes the similarities between these sports.[48] Early 19th-century American boxing and wrestling often shared many of their techniques, competitors, and fans in a very fluid sporting culture. A new generation of wrestlers carried on the traditional arts in newly founded collegiate athletic programs and an international sporting culture that included the restoration of the Olympic Games. Some scholars criticize Anthony Rotundo's work in *American Manhood* as presenting simplistic conclusions not fully supported by his evidence.[49] However, this text provides additional support for his assertion that 19th-century America witnessed a shift in the dominant American masculinity from the patriarchal man of republican virtue to the passionate man of industrialized spectacle.[50]

The third chapter covers the first entry of Asian martial arts onto the American fight scene from roughly 1850 to 1941. In this period, Chinese laborers began migrating to the United States. Japan, opened to Western trade by Commodore Perry's artillery, began to spread its fight sports. Americans and Japanese appeared to share little in common, but young men of both nations gloried in recreational violence. American and Japanese fighter squared off in matches that delighted combined crowds of Japanese and American fight fans.[51] Asian martial arts quickly spread across the oceans. Japanese marital artist and educator Jigoro Kano recalled that after inventing judo, it "occurred to me that I should not keep this knowledge to myself alone, but that I should teach it to others worldwide."[52] Like missionaries of violence, Kano and his students exported judo in an effort to educate the world about their nation.[53]

Many Americans of the early 20th century viewed Asians with a sense of racialized revulsion that dated back to the Mongol Invasions of the Middle Ages and proved stronger than Japanese fighters. In 1904, Teddy Roosevelt, who loved fight sports of every variety, invited a delegation of Japanese martial artists to demonstrate their skills at West Point.[54] Unimpressed students challenged the visitors to impromptu fights in which the cadets proved Western martial arts to be the equal of their Eastern counterparts. In 1914, judo expert Ito Tokugoro faced off against the American wrestler Ad Santel. Three seconds into the match Santel threw Tokugoro to the ground with enough force to knock him unconscious and convince spectators that Tokugoro would return home in a wooden box. This was only Santel's first of many, mostly successful, fights against Japanese experts. When the Japanese refused to send additional challengers to America, Santel traveled to Japan in 1921 and defeated fighters on their own ground. His victories made an enormous impression on the Japanese, many of whom began studying Western style wrestling and paving the way for American-style professional wrestling in Japan later in the century.[55]

Asian martial arts proved unable to win over large numbers of American fans before World War II.[56] The success of Western martial arts in the ring led Americans to doubt the viability of Japanese fighting techniques and the masculinity of the Asian men who used them.[57] The slow pace and subtle techniques of judo ensured that boxing retained its dominance in mass spectacles. The biggest problem that faced Asian-influenced martial artists was their emphasis on an "anything goes" approach that accepted any technique that ensured victory.[58] This philosophy ran counter to a 19th- and early 20th-century Western sporting culture increasingly moving toward regulation and sport rather than the "fatal tricks" of Asian arts.[59] While judo players never gained dominance in any aspect of American life, they did find a toehold in the formation of judo clubs and introduction of Asian fighting arts into America.

The fourth chapter covers boxing's brief golden age from roughly 1918 to 1949. Boxing continued to soar in popularity and pugilists became national heroes. Observers on both sides of the Atlantic suggested that America's increasing success in the boxing ring against British opponents provided a symbolic passing of the torch from an aging world power on the decline to its younger successor on the rise. The popular association of American masculinity with whiteness increasingly fractured in response to challenges from abroad as whites decided that nation sometimes trumped race. Threats from a resurgent Germany propelled greater, though still limited, American tolerance for domestic racial differences.[60] Not every white fight fan cheered for Joe Louis over his white competitor, the German Max Schmeling, and Louis's example meant only so much to the millions of African Americans still suffering discrimination across the nation, but his story demonstrates that the nation was making some limited progress. The white faces in the crowds that cheered for Louis stood in stark contrast to the universal white anger at Louis's predecessor Jack Johnson.

The fifth chapter covers the years after World War II when a new wave of fighting arts came to America from Asia. Unlike judo's ambassadors, most of the early proponents of Japanese karate, Chinese Kung Fu, and Korean Ta Qwon Do in the United States were white Americans, freshly returned from military service in East Asia and eager to spread the martial arts they learned while in uniform.[61] Like the judo players who proceeded them, these fighters proved incapable of supplanting existing fight sports, but they refused to fade away, opening schools, spreading their ideas, and building communities. In 1976, Muhammad Ali traveled to Tokyo in search of the largest payday of his life, where he sought to fight Antonio Inoki, a Japanese fighter of mixed Asian and Brazilian heritage skilled in American-style wrestling.[62] Conflicts over the acceptable rules led to farcical restrictions in which neither combatant could shine and the contest ended in a draw. While a competitive joke, the event attracted a huge worldwide audience and demonstrated the potential viability of a fight sport that welcomed competitors from a mix of martial traditions. By the 1970s, Muhammad Ali and Bruce Lee fractured popular ideals of white American masculinity still further with their rise to fame in the ring and on the screen.[63] The rise of Ali and Lee expands on Robert Lee's assertion in *Orientals* by presenting popular culture as a place of gendered as well as racial negotiations.

The final chapter covers the closing decades of the 20th century and the first years of the 21st, a period almost entirely untouched by historians. Beginning in the early 1980s, bored fight fans went in search of new thrills. Some Americans found those thrills in the arms of a lover named "tough man." In 1979, Michigan businessman Art Dore held the first of the tough man contests.[64] The events caught on as the new decade began, providing many men with just the excitement they wanted.[65] The new sport provided a test of old-fashioned toughness, not scientific pugilism.[66] American kickboxing gained some popularity in its pitting of fighters from various martial arts against each other.[67] Fight promoters examined the plethora of fighting arts in vogue and began broadcasting fights between fighters of different styles in an effort to determine the most effective style for the delight of television viewers. These fights offered enormous challenges to fighters and promoters, who confronted the basic riddle of how to pit fighters against each other who disagreed on the most fundamental boundaries of fight sports.[68]

In 1993, the new sport took a huge step forward with the inaugural event of the Ultimate Fighting Championship (UFC) in Denver, Colorado. The promoters invited students of kickboxing, karate, sumo, boxing, wrestling, and the almost completely unknown art of Brazilian jujitsu. The competitors included fighters from the United States and Europe, as well as a skinny 27-year-old martial artist from Rio de Janeiro who needed less than five minutes to destroy his three opponents and win the contest. American fight fans stood in stunned disbelief as the South American fighter dominated American boxers and wrestlers without ever breaking a sweat. Fighters came out of judo clubs, boxing rings, karate schools, and wrestling teams across the world to try their hand at the new contests most commonly called mixed martial arts. The new sport offered a simple challenge to practitioners of every martial art in the world: prove it. It invited them to step into the eight-sided cage and demonstrate the effectiveness of their art in an arena with few rules and many potential paths to victory.

While Japan had already witnessed similar events, the UFC became the most profitable and widely respected mixed martial arts promotion in the world.[69] It held events throughout Europe and the Americas, signed fighters from every corner of the globe, and attracted fans from almost every nation on earth. The organization took advantage of new technologies including home videos, pay per view networks, streaming online video players, and reality shows to spread their products, obtain cultural dominance, and earn huge profits. The final chapter concurs with Micol Seigel's *Uneven Encounters* that identities are "odd shaped beasts, neither fully within nor simply larger than their nation states" and traces the previously ignored and strangely shaped identities of fighters and fight fans.[70]

In the early years of the 21st century, some American men embraced a new global masculinity personified in the champion mixed martial artist Randy Couture, who combines many of the most popular aspects of previous masculinities with traits born of the 21st century. Couture is an army veteran from a working-class background who represents America in international competitions and pummels opponents in movies as well as in the ring.[71] Unlike any of his predecessors, Couture is a global savant who speaks German and French, owns gyms in Canada, frequently travels to Japan, and trains with men from six continents. While Couture primarily identifies himself as a practitioner of Greco-Roman wrestling, he supplements his base by studying Brazilian jujitsu, Japanese judo, and Thai kickboxing. Couture represents a new model of the globalized American man. Like the consumers highlighted in the *Gender and History* article "The Modern Girl Around the World," Couture and the men who admire him embrace a transnational masculinity that borrows from every nation to create an identity which is not purely American, Brazilian, Dutch, Japanese, or a blending of these cultures, but instead an entirely unique identity reminiscent of the transnational masculinities practiced by Roman athletes and documented by Helen Lovatt in *Statius and Epic Games*.[72]

This book does not present mixed martial arts as an inevitable result or a final stage. Every shift in American fight sports grew from the individual choices of countless fans, fighters, and promoters. Their decisions were hardly inevitable, and different choices could have just as easily led to a 21st-century American fight culture dominated by gougers or sumo wrestlers rather than mixed martial artists. The new sport will certainly not be the last. In time, something new and perhaps unimaginable will replace mixed martial arts, just as it recently began replacing boxing in the hearts and minds of American fighters and spectators. Randy Couture will not remain forever as an iconic figure. Already the 47-year-old veteran seems in decline even within his favorite sport. Recently, Cain Velasquez, a 28-year-old son of Mexican migrant farm workers who was educated in Iowa and marches into the ring with a bare chest bearing the tattoo "brown pride," captured the Ultimate Fighting Championship's heavyweight title and the admiration of millions of fans across the globe.

Introduction

Global Fight Sports from Prehistory to 1607

Once upon a time, human beings and spirits were neighbors and had many things in common. One of the bonds holding them together was the annual wrestling contest held in the land of the spirits. This particular annual event was much anticipated by all concerned because each community fielded its best wrestlers. The human society sent six stout men with Akpi as their leader. The special feature of this contest was that any contestant whose back touched the ground died instantly.

Akpi was the one to open the competition; his opponent was a three-headed but one-legged spirit. The wrestlers appeared to be evenly matched. Akpi killed the leader of the spirits and defeated the rest of them, but all his companions were killed. Akpi stole a magic horn from the spirits and restored his men to life, and they fled. Akpi was on the verge of crossing the boundary between the lands of the spirit and human beings when the spirit caught up with him and scratched his back with his claws. This accounts for the man's furrow-behind or the hollow at his back.
—Traditional story from the Igbo people of central Africa[1]

Father Zeus, you who rule over the ridges of Atabyrium, grant honor to the hymn ordained in praise of an Olympian victor, and to the man who has found excellence as a boxer, and grant to him honored grace in the eyes of both citizens and strangers. For he walks a straight course on a road that hates arrogance, knowing clearly the sound prophetic wisdom of his good ancestors. Do not bury in obscurity the shared seed of Callianax.
—Ode of Pindar for Diagoras of Rhodes, 464 BCE[2]

Numerous oral traditions provide examples of fight sports in the dark recesses of the past where lines between history and mythology blur. A legend from central Africa claims that humans once made annual journeys to the spirit world to participate in wrestling tournaments. According to the book of Genesis, Jacob won a divine blessing when he won a wrestling match with God.[3] In India, the God Man Krishna reportedly wrestled with both mortals and gods while ruling over the traditional art of yoga.[4] Chinese myths attribute the origins of fighting arts to conflicts between the Yellow Emperor and Chi You, a six-armed king of barbarian hordes with horns like a bull. Chi You's followers head-butted their opponents to imitate his fighting style.[5] The world's oldest historical artifacts provide more concrete evidence for the ancient history of fight sports.

The people of southern Mesopotamia produced what might have been the world's first civilization and certainly produced some of the oldest evidence for the importance of fight sports. Excavations of a Sumerian temple from 3000 BCE revealed the oldest-known depictions of fight sports. Two boxers face off across a stone relief carving. A bronze sculpture depicts two men forever locked together in a wrestling match.[6] In 2000 BCE, the Sumerian king Culgi proclaimed himself the master of both the battlefield and the wrestling arena.[7] This early claim provides important evidence that even at this early date people engaged in fight sports that were separate from warfare.

Another literary work provided a more detailed testament to the importance of fight sports to ancient people. The *Epic of Gilgamesh* originated sometime around 3500 BCE and is one of the oldest texts in existence.[8] It tells the story of Gilgamesh, a king of the city of Uruk in Mesopotamia, and centers on his interactions with Enkidu, a wild-man counterpart to the civilized Gilgamesh. When Enkidu barred Gilgamesh from entering a room, the king attacked him. The two men wrestled fiercely, shattering the doorway and tearing down walls. Eventually they decided to call it a draw. Enkidu and Gilgamesh kissed, formed an alliance, and became inseparable friends.[9] Their bond ended only with Enkidu's tragic death.[10] In history's oldest document, two men from different backgrounds wrestled and walked away as friends, sharing a bond of mutual respect for the strength and skill that both men demonstrated in a fight. Gilgamesh was just one of many ancient figures who practiced fight sports.

Ancient Africans promoted fight sports to an unprecedented degree. During the Middle Kingdom of 2040–1785 BCE, the Egyptians became the first people to apply systematic training to fight sports.[11] They formalized rules in which wrestlers earned victory by forcing an opponent's back or shoulder to the ground, a standard common in many forms of modern wrestling. The temple paintings at Beni Hasan, Egypt, from around 2000 BCE provide the world's most ancient training manual for fighters.[12] The frescos present a wide array of techniques, including throws, trips, holds, and pins. Captions accompany depictions of wrestling, with referees warning fighters to obey the rules and competitors taunting each other.[13] By 1300 BCE, Egyptians engaged in international wrestling competitions against Nubians and Syrians for the honor of the pharaoh.[14] Many of these competitors were probably soldiers, displaying the skills they learned during their military training.[15]

Similar events played out across Asia at about the same time. The Chinese developed their own distinctive fight sports, which incorporated punches, kicks, and wrestling holds, around 2000 BCE.[16] Some of these arts incorporated techniques inspired by the movements of animals. These styles became highly advanced during the Chou dynasty (1122–256 BCE).[17] Wrestling formed a key component of Chinese as well as Egyptian military training. By 770 BCE, high commanders choose champion wrestlers as their personal bodyguards. Around 209 BCE, a Chinese emperor designated wrestling the official sport of the military, which the Chinese chronicles increasingly distinguished from boxing.[18] Asians, like Africans, performed fight sports for the delight of royalty. The sacred texts of the Hindu faith provide a thrilling account of an event held centuries before the Common Era.

> They gave each other violent kicks. And they struck knee and head against head, producing the crash of one stone against another. And in this manner that furious combat between those warriors raged on without weapons, sustained mainly by the power of their arms and their physical and mental energy, to the infinite delight of the concourse of spectators. And all people, O king, took deep interest in that encounter of those powerful wrestlers who fought like Indra and the Asura Vritra. And they cheered both of them with loud acclamations of applause. And the broad-chested and long-armed experts in wrestling then pulled and pressed and whirled and hurled down each other and struck each other with their knees, expressing all the while their scorn for each other in loud voices. And they began to fight with their bare arms in this way, which were like spiked maces of iron. And at last the powerful and mighty-armed Bhima, the slayer of his foes, shouting aloud, seized the vociferous athlete by the arms even as the lion seizes the elephant, and taking him up from the ground and holding him aloft, began to whirl him round, to the great astonishment of the assembled athletes and the people of Matsya. And having whirled him round and round a hundred times till he was insensible, the strong-armed Vrikodara dashed him to death on the ground. And when the brave and renowned Jimuta was thus killed, Virata and his friends were filled with great delight. And in the exuberance of his joy, the noble-minded king rewarded Vallava then and there with the liberality of Kuvera. And killing numerous athletes and many other men possessed of great bodily strength, he pleased the king very much.[19]

Although separated from the present by thousands of years, this scene provides sights and sounds familiar to modern fight fans. The male competitors used kicks, body slams, and knee strikes like modern mixed martial artists. They pulled and pressed each other in ways that sound similar to those practiced by 21st-century wrestlers. A mass of spectators cheered on the athletes with applause, a familiar sound to modern sports fans. While rarely treated with the same joy shown in this passage, deaths in the arena remain a reality of today's boxing matches.[20]

The Asian love of fight sports was hardly unique. At roughly the same time that Bhima and Vrikodara were thrilling crowds, Europeans were formalizing their own fight sports.

The Greeks did not invent fight sports, but they did advance them to an unprecedented degree. Greek fight sports emerged as a unique variation on older traditions, bearing the imprint of older styles of sport imported from Anatolia.[21] Like their predecessors in Africa, Greek warriors trained in fight sports as part of their military training. The Greeks were the first civilization to hold a regular series of strictly regulated fights for the delight of spectators, which stood in contrast to the sporadic contests held for the amusement of royal audiences across Africa and Asia.[22] They staged far more of these events than any of their contemporaries or predecessors.[23] The most famous athletic Greek festivals were the Olympics, which began in 776 BCE and included fight sports by 708 BCE. Ancient Greeks celebrated competition and institutionalized both the regulations on sport and their rewards. They spiritualized the runner's high and viewed fights as mystical experiences.[24] Sports—and fight sports in particular—provided a focal point for the Hellenic world that bound the Greek city-states together.[25] This bond was rooted in Greek literature. Dating from roughly 800 BCE, Homer's epic poems such as the *Iliad* and the *Odyssey* offer the earliest written descriptions of fight sports in the West.[26] Homer's work refers to boxing and wrestling contests. Most of the athletic events Homer describes take place as part of funeral ceremonies. The practice of fights held in honor of the departed may have grown from older funeral customs of human sacrifice.[27] Greek fighters embraced the erotic as well as the militaristic. Greek athletes trained in the nude, exercising in gymnasiums that were scenes of sexual pleasure.[28]

The arena occupied a place so central to the Greeks' collective imagination that they, unlike many of their contemporaries, allowed women to breach its barriers on occasion. The Athenian philosopher Plato advocated military training, including wrestling, for women so that they could defend their homes if danger threatened while their men were away from home—a rare moment of acceptance for the concept of female soldiers.[29] His fellow Athenians do not appear to have adopted his suggestion. The Spartan emphasis on training women in fight sports was unique, even among the sport-loving Greeks.[30] It grew from Sparta's highly militaristic society, in which leaders expected both men and women to demonstrate strength, vigor, and aggression.[31] The Spartan king Lycurgus the Lawgiver encouraged girls to wrestle as part of an exercise regimen constructed to ensure they survived childbirth. Spartan fathers celebrated the athletic accomplishments of their daughters and erected monuments to memorialize their victories.[32] Female fight sport found critics as well as promoters among the Greeks. The Athenian poet Euripides condemned female athletes as immoral, suggesting that their love of wrestling with men and willingness to display their nude bodies indicated a lack of chastity.[33] Even the Spartans encouraged female athletics only so far. When women became wives and mothers, they typically ended their athletic careers as they turned from the play of childhood to the work of adulthood.[34] This distinguished them from their male counterparts who continued to compete in fight sports as training for warfare, a duty reserved for adult males.

The *Iliad* and the *Odyssey* describe violence both in war and in the arena as a path to glory and immortality for men who demonstrated strength, skill, and bravery. Homer's depictions of fight sports offered a lifeline to subsequent generations of men suffering from a crisis of masculinity. The soldiers of Homer's poems excel in singular combats between aristocrats. While the Greeks continued to admire the individualistic accomplishments of Achilles and Odysseus, the rise of the phalanx, in which soldiers were reduced to cogs in a killing machine, made the old style of combat and its system of individual glory a dangerous anachronism on the battlefield.[35] In response to the announcement of a boxing tournament in the *Iliad*, the pugilist Epeios steps forward, confessing his ineptitude as a warrior but proclaiming his excellence in the arena.[36] Epeios's victory in the ring offers an alternative, although still violent and therefore related, masculine ideal. Long after soldiers became faceless components of great armies, athletes remained as singular heroes. Greek fight sports took on a new focus. No longer simple preparation for combat, they became an alternative path to the masculine glories that had ceased to be available in battle.[37]

The ancient Greeks, unlike other ancient cultures, engaged in three distinct, but related fight sports—wrestling, boxing, and pankration—which they collectively called the *barea athla*.[38] Wrestling differed primarily from the other fight sports in its emphasis on positional dominance, in which fighters typically won by forcing their opponents to the ground three times.[39]

Children wrestled as part of their education and soldiers wrestled during military training. Wrestling, more than any other fight sport, penetrated gendered barriers. The sport provided an experience common to so many Greeks that its imagery infused their language, with the term "three falls" becoming a common expression for defeat.[40] Ancient Greeks appear to have used "three falls" as an expression in a similar fashion to the modern American concept of "three strikes." Greek boxers provided a far bloodier spectacle, with pugilists trading close-fisted strikes to the face until one fighter lay uncurious or conceded defeat with an outstretched finger.[41] The oldest evidence of fighting gloves comes from the aptly named Boxer Vase, an artifact from 500 BCE that depicts Greek boxers using the leather wraps known as *himantes*.[42]

Unlike boxing and wrestling, the Greek sport of pankration had no precedent in the ancient Mediterranean world.[43] The only rules in most pankration bouts were prohibitions against eye gouging and biting. The Spar-

The pankrationist on the right tries to gouge his opponent's eye; the umpire is about to strike him for this foul. Detail from an Attic red-figure kylix, 490–480 BCE. From Vulci, Italy (courtesy Marie-Lan Nguyen and Wikimedia Commons. Published under a Creative Commons License).

tans considered these rules too restrictive and explicitly allowed every possible attack. Common techniques in pankration included punches, kicks, wrestling holds, elbow strikes, and hair pulling.[44] Fighters died during pankration bouts, but most Greeks still considered boxing, with its emphasis on punches to the head, a more dangerous sport. The sport's dangers did not diminish its popularity. Aristotle, Plato, Socrates, and Alexander the Great all commented on their love of the sport. Alexander the Great and Plato even entered the ring and became expert pankrationists.[45]

The Greeks spread their sports as they traveled the world. Alexander the Great took expert pankrationists with him when he set out to conquer the world in 334 BCE. In 327 BCE, he led his armies into India, where his pankrationists may have influenced the development of fight sports in Asia.[46] Greek fight sports took root in some of the areas conquered by Alexander. In 216 BCE, King Ptolemy of Egypt sent his favorite boxer, Aristoikos, to compete at the Olympic Games. Aristoikos faced off against the Theban champion Kleitomachos. Initially, the crowd, which typically sided with challengers, cheered for Aristokos. During a brief pause in the fighting, Kleitomachos scolded the audience for supporting a foreigner. He demanded to know why they wanted an Egyptian, fighting for the glory of Ptolemy, to defeat him who fought for the Greeks and strived to glorify their nation. The speech struck a nerve with the crowd, which began cheering for the Theban—who then proceeded to batter Aristikos into submission.[47]

Romans built on Greek sporting traditions. When Fulvius Nobilior returned to Rome in 186 BCE after his successful campaign in Anitolia, he held games incorporating Greek athletes. In 80 BCE, Sulla held games that included so many Greek athletes that the Olympic Games almost did not take place. Julius Caesar held similar games in 46 BCE. Many of these games included both Greek-style athletic contests and Roman gladiatorial combats.[48] In the Olympic contest between Aristokos and Kleitomachos, boxers represented both themselves and their nations. Roman poets referred to Spartan boxers as beautiful, a veiled reference to the Greek practice of pederasty.[49] Like the Greeks, Romans embraced fight sports for their unique position, as a place where men could prove their skills in singular violence and their virtue when they helped a defeated opponent to his feet.[50] In a search for greater violence, Romans added sharpened metal spikes to the Greek *himantes* and transformed it into a lethal weapon called the *cestus*.[51] The cestus blurred the lines between fight sports and gladiatorial combat. Roman games evolved into something neither historically Greek nor originally Roman, but rather the result of a cultural interaction distinct from both traditions.[52]

Romans, like Greeks, occasionally allowed women to enter the arena.

Many Romans idolized the Spartans as warrior gods. Spartans continued their tradition of women's wrestling while under Roman rule. Many tourists from across the Roman world came to Sparta, enjoying wildly popular female wrestling matches and celebrating the Spartan reputation for strength and ferocity.[53] Spartans responded by encouraging athletics, particularly among women, and enjoying the favorable admiration and profits these events attracted.[54] Sextus Propertius, the great Roman poet of Augustine Rome, praised the female Spartan boxers and wrestlers of his time. He viewed the Spartans' promotion of female athletics as evidence of their national virtue.[55] Propertius suggested approvingly that the sports emphasis on intimate contact between bare bodies made the sports sensual as well as violent.[56] Romans borrowed the Greek practice of holding wrestling contests for female fighters. When female wrestlers began drawing larger audiences than their male counterparts, officials banned them from future games, preserving the ring as a scene of manly virtue.[57]

Asian fight sports developed as the product of very different processes than those at play in the West. Asian fight sports in this period remained closely tied to military training, religion, and personal encounters. They did not develop anything like the mass spectacles of Greece or Rome. The Han Chinese began incorporating the neck and leg throws they learned from nomadic mercenaries into their style of wrestling during the first century of the Common Era.[58] At about the same time the Chinese began spreading their style of wrestling into Korea through their military colonies in the peninsula. Legend claims that the Indian Buddhist monk Bodhidharma arrived in southern China in about 475 CE and took up residence at the Shaolin monastery. Tradition suggests he may have developed a series of exercises, inspired by animal movements, which later fighters codified as the martial art Kung Fu and the fight sport Wushu.[59] Japanese emperors borrowed the concept of large-scale wrestling tournaments from the Chinese. Like their predecessors in Egypt, Japanese wrestlers fought for the entertainment of their ruler.[60]

In Asia, as in Europe, gender and sexuality complicated the ring and how its past is recorded. In 23 BCE, the Japanese emperor Suinin asked the potter Nomi No Sukune to teach humility to a braggart who had proclaimed himself the strongest man in the world. Sukune obeyed his lord's wishes, breaking the braggart's ribs in a hotly contested fight. Some Japanese sources present the encounter as the first sumo match and Sukune as the sport's father.[61] A rival tradition claims that the first sumo match occurred when the emperor Yuryaku overheard a carpenter brag that he never made an error. Yuryaku responded by instructing two of his female servants to strip to their

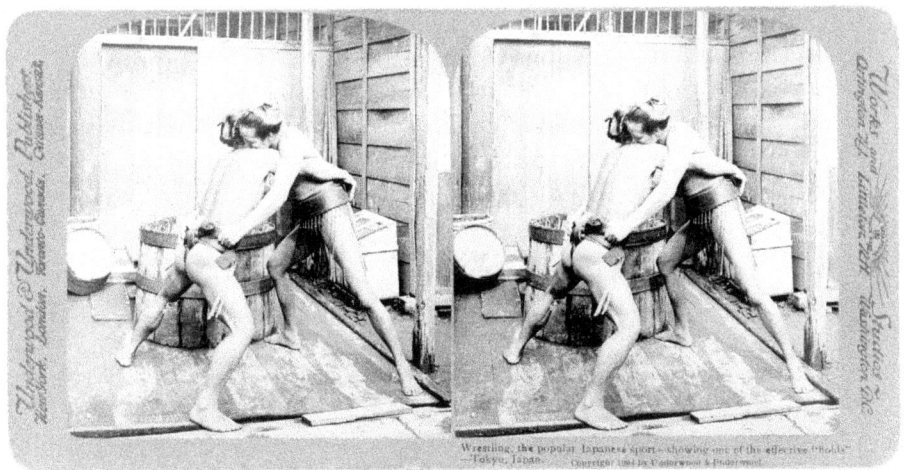

Photographic print on stereo card showing a traditional Japanese sumo wrestling technique. The original caption reads, "Wrestling, the popular Japanese sport—showing one of the effective "holds"—Tokyo, Japan." Published in 1904 by Underwood & Underwood (Library of Congress Prints and Photographs Division).

underclothes and wrestle within sight of the boasting craftsman. After the conclusion of the bout, the aroused carpenter returned to work, no longer able to focus, slipped, and ruined his work.[62] Many authors may omit this story because they are embarrassed by the tale's sexual and gendered overtone, and prefer the story of Nomi No Sukune because it emphasizes the spirituality and masculinity of Japanese fight sports.[63]

Sub-Saharan Africa developed unique forms of fight sports in isolation from Europe and Asia. Wrestling represented the dominant fight sport of West Africa. Many African styles appear very similar to European types, but some Bantu-speaking areas near the coast practiced a unique form in which fighters intertwined their legs with those of the opponent in an effort to trip their adversary and win a fall.[64] In a combination largely unknown in other parts of the world, African fighting, dance, and music were combined into singular shows. Dancers, adorned with bells, entertained crowds before the wrestling matches began.[65] West Africans often wrestled to the music of drummers.[66] This practice later influenced fight sports in the Western hemisphere. For example, the Brazilian sport of Capoeira, growing from a mix of Africa, European, and Native American traditions, features fighters who batter each other to the beat of drums.[67] In Africa, drummers also directed the audience and fighters, playing particular beats to tell the fans when to sit and the fighters when to begin their bout.[68]

Africans practiced unique forms of boxing as well as wrestling. In Nigeria and across much of southwest Africa, distinctly African forms of pugilism dominated. African styles of boxing included dambe, engolo, and kandeka, which became popular no later than the first century BCE.[69] Practitioners of dambe wrapped one fist in a cloth strip called a kara and struck only with the wrapped hand, which they called the spear. The other hand remained bare and served only to block incoming blows, a feature that gave rise to the practice of referring to it as the shield.[70] While the origins of dambe are lost to history, the terms "spear" and "shield" indicate that it may take inspiration from the armed combat styles common in much of Africa.

Women enjoyed greater status in many African societies than in much of the rest of the world, which they lost only after Europeans began imposing their own gendered ideals on Africa many years later.[71] The less stringent gendered hierarchy allowed for a more fluid culture of fight sports. Fight sports possessed the same military connections to military services witnessed in much of the rest of the world. However, unlike in most societies, African women often enjoyed the option of joining men on the battlefield and in their warrior societies.[72]

Similar to the Greeks, many African cultures infused their fighting styles with spiritual meaning. The Igbo people of central Africa always concluded the New Yam Festival, celebrated to ensure the continued fertility of their crops, with wrestling bouts which they believed could magically transfer the strength of competitors to their crops.[73] Women as well as men fought each other at the festivals.[74] Many African fighters carried sacred tokens into the ring at sacred festivals and on other occasions, physically clinging to the mystical aspects of their art.[75] As Africans clung fast to the spiritual aspects of their fight sports, Europeans lost theirs.

The Christianization of Rome pushed fight sports to the cultural periphery of Europe for centuries as spiritual impulses shifted from the embrace to the rejection of fight sports. The Romanized African theologian Quintus Septimius Florens Tertullianus condemned fight sports in his 200 CE treatise *Spectacles*. He argued that boxing, which disfigured the divinely designed human body, angered God.[76] In 394 CE, the Roman emperor Theodosius I banned the Olympic Games as part of a broader campaign against pagan religions.[77] In 500 CE, Emperor Theodoric the Great took it a step further by banning boxing in any form, based on a belief that the sport insulted God by disfiguring human faces, which were the physical embodiment of the divine visage.[78] Church leaders such as Saints Jerome and Augustine approved the ban of sports, which they saw as powerful connections to paganism.[79]

One of Christianity's rivals in the war for souls, however, took a very different view of fight sports. The founders of Islam viewed fight sports with greater acceptance than some of their contemporary Christian counterparts, using them in their conversion efforts. Wrestling often provided powerful imagery for early Muslims. Muhammad (570–632 CE) used references to wrestling in his sermons.[80] Soldiers who served under the prophet followed his strict training regimen of swimming, running, and wrestling competitions.[81] Muhammad even entered the arena to spread the faith. One of the most famous stories in Islamic history reveals his attempts to convert Rukana, a chief of the Quarysh tribe and a champion wrestler. Rukana told the aging prophet that he would accept Islam, if only he knew it as true. Muhammad asked if he could convince the chief by wrestling him to the ground, providing evidence for spiritual truth with physical domination. Rukana accepted the challenge and Muhammad took hold of his opponent, throwing him to the ground with ease. Surprised by his defeat, Rukana demanded another try, and Muhammad immediately tossed him once again.[82] Impressed by Mohammed's skill, Rukana expressed his admiration for the prophet.[83]

In Asia, as in Arabia, leaders promoted fight sports. Asian leaders promoted fight sports as patrons and competitors. The Chinese emperor Zhou Zhong (924–936 CE) enjoyed wrestling and often entered the ring to the delight of spectators. Zhong offered prizes to wrestlers who could defeat him and rewarded a successful challenger by making him the governor of a prefecture.[84] Marco Polo told the story of princess Aiyaruk, daughter of the Mongol king Kaidu. She was a fierce wrestler who refused to marry any man who could not best her in a fight and demanded that any man seeking her hand provide her with 100 horses if she won. After 100 victories, her personal herd numbered 10,000 horses. In 1280 CE, a prince upped the stakes and bet her 1,000 horses that he could emerge victorious. Aiyaruk's father considered the young prince a fine mate for his daughter and begged her to throw the fight. She refused and after a hard-fought battle, Aiyaruk walked away with another 1,000 horses in her stable and an embarrassed suitor on the ground.[85] Legends claim that the "Black Prince" Nareusuen of Thailand defeated a rival noble from Burma in a kickboxing match in 1560, which convinced King Bayinnaung of Burma to abandon his attack on Thailand.[86]

During the 17th century, sumo wrestling became a professional sport in Japan as increasing prosperity and greater urbanization provided fertile ground for the rise of a sporting culture based on mass entertainments.[87] The Tokagawa government initially attempted to ban sumo, but most of the people ignored the prohibitions. Conceding defeat, the government instead regulated sumo to limit the violence and prevent other crimes, such as gambling, among the crowds. The new system gave the old sport a gleam of respectability that secured its enshrined place deep within Japanese culture.[88]

Fighters spread their arts across vast expanses of space and developed hybrid styles from those interactions. Beginning in the seventh century, Indonesians began modifying their traditional styles of fighting in response to techniques brought from India and China by proselytizing Buddhist missionaries.[89] Priests from Tahiti brought the Huna faith to Hawaii in the 13th century. They believed in a duality of spirit in which every faithful follower specialized in nurturing or injuring. Converts who choose to specialize in injury trained in the martial art of lua. This new art encountered older Hawaiian fight styles of boxing and wrestling. Years later, lua began reflecting the influences of karate and jujitsu.[90] In 1392, 36 Chinese families, who included several renowned fighters, traveled to Okinawa as part of a cultural exchange program designed to support a military alliance between the nations. The athletes shaped Okinawan fight sports and helped create hybrid styles.[91]

Early immigrants to the Americas constructed unique versions of fight sports in their new homes. The first Americans probably brought their styles of unarmed combat with them across the Bering Straits. Oral traditions of Native Americans reinforce the long history of fight sports, particularly wrestling, in North America.[92] Members of many North American tribes wrestled from early childhood. The Copper Indians of Canada wrestled to resolve conflicts over women.[93] Some tribes in South America produced unique wrestling traditions, which provided ritual symbolism rather than a method for conflict resolution. The Caraja tribe of modern-day Brazil saw wrestling as the ultimate test of a man and demanded visitors enter the arena.[94] When Columbus's fleet made landfall in the Western hemisphere, a local chief staged a wrestling tournament in the newcomers' honor.[95] While Native Americans certainly engaged in fight sports, they never granted them the same emphasis common across Africa, Asia, and Europe, preferring instead to focus on sports such as lacrosse and foot races.[96] An appreciation of the multiple points of origins for fight sports in America provides depth to the story, but the most influential sporting traditions in American history came from Europe.

During the Renaissance, many Europeans revived the older Greek emphasis on the virtue of sports.[97] Many Europeans admired the ancient Greeks and prized their literature, which provided frequent references to the glories of wrestling.⁹⁸ In Germany, some of the earliest illustrated books taught the finer points of wrestling holds.⁹⁹ Bretons earned fame during the Hundred Years War for their skill as wrestlers and their commitment not to make deals with the devil in exchange for victory.¹⁰⁰ Martin Luther encouraged the faithful to take part in noble exercises such as archery, fencing, and wrestling.¹⁰¹ All of these forces worked together to make wrestling the most popular spectator sport in Europe by the 16th century.¹⁰² While Europeans sought to emulate the Greek emphasis on wrestling, they did not extend this to an embrace of the Spartan acceptance of women in the wrestling ring. In 1528, the Italian Baldassare Castiglione published the widely read *Third Book of the Courtier*, which argued that women should not train with weapons or wrestle, since these activities were the exclusive domain of men.¹⁰³

As part of this larger pattern, sports enjoyed an explosion in popularity in 16th-century England. King Henry VIII (1491–1547) personally enjoyed and encouraged his subjects to engage in vigorous sports including jousting, spear throwing, fencing, and wrestling.¹⁰⁴ Henry was not always the victor in these contests. In 1520, the French king Francis I and Henry VIII witnessed a wrestling tournament held in their honor at a state banquet. When Henry gloated a little too long over the victories of English wrestlers, Francis shut him up by pinning him to the ground with a leg lock.¹⁰⁵ The king's defeat did little, if anything, to diminish the popularity of sport in the British Isles. English writers promoted the classical view of wrestling as a method of building strength and maintaining health.¹⁰⁶ In 1612, the English lawyer Robert Dover attempted to reinvigorate the annual games at Cotsold Hills by turning them into a replica of the ancient Olympic Games.¹⁰⁷ English literature often referred to wrestling, from Beowulf's successful arm lock to the wrestling contest in Shakespeare's *As You Like It*.¹⁰⁸ English parishioners listened to sermons that often expressed theology in terms of fight sports. The story of Jacob's wrestling match with God was a particularly popular source of material for English preachers.¹⁰⁹ Every area of the British Isles produced a unique style of unarmed combat and matches between local champions attracted excited crowds to fairs and festivals.¹¹⁰

The growth of fight sports among the English in the 16th and 17th centuries was largely limited to men. While English women often played cards and bowled, they rarely engaged in fight sports such as wrestling.¹¹¹ English society in this period was extremely patriarchal, even when Elizabeth I sat on the throne. Warfare was accepted as an exclusively masculine activity; wrestling, since it was an aspect of military training, was also deemed unsuited to women.¹¹² As a result, men typically excluded women from the

Two wrestlers demonstrate a hold from a popular European wrestling manual, *Die Ringer-Kunst* ("The Art of Wrestling") by Fabian Von Auerswald, 1539. Notice the leg wrapping technique, which later became unacceptable in many forms of European wrestling.

wrestling rings of fairs and left them to the gender-segregated games of bowling and foot races. Margaret Lucas Cavendish, Duchess of Newcastle (1623–1673), recalled that many English men devoted themselves so thoroughly to wrestling, shooting, and fencing that they seldom enjoyed music or dancing, which they condemned as effeminate."[113]

Not every group in Europe accepted sports unflinchingly. English Puritans engaged in a culture war with their neighbors in which sports were a small, if important, part. Preachers railed against recreations they saw as distractions from religious devotion, tainted with historical connections to pagan festivals and connected to vices of gambling and drunkenness.[114] This view clashed with religious reformers on the European mainland who saw wrestling as a useful method of building boys into vigorous men. In 1583, Puritan writer Philip Stubbes published *Anatomy of Abuses*, which railed against popular sports and the violence that often accompanied them.[115] When King James I visited Lancashire, locals asked him to overrule local Puritan elites who had outlawed sports on the Sabbath. These prohibitions so angered the king that he produced the *King's Book of Sport*, which declared local prohibitions on sports illegal and officially endorsed numerous recreations. The king urged his subjects to work all week, to attend church on Sunday morning, and then spend the rest of the day resting and playing.[116] James's authorization of sports on Sunday, a day the Puritans set aside for serious religious reflection and worship, enraged them.[117] The Norfolk town fathers transformed Sunday sports from a right into an obligation in 1626, when they began requiring their local militiamen to wrestle as part of their military training after Sunday church services.[118]

The Puritans responded by redoubling their resistance to violations of the Sabbath while noting their acceptance of certain sporting activities conducted in ways that did not conflict with service to God. In response to the reassertion of the royal encouragement of sports by King James's successor Charles I, the Puritan lawyer and political theorist William Prynne argued that Puritans took no issue with fun as long as diversions did not occur on the Sabbath or encourage sin. He endorsed several pastimes he saw as particularly healthy, including hunting, fishing, and wrestling.[119]

People from the British Empire, who would begin immigrating to the Americas in the early 17th century, brought with them a sporting culture with contested boundaries. Puritans loved wrestling because it offered a unique cultural space that provided them with a safe middle ground on which men could resolve conflicts violently, for the excitement of spectators, while still limiting the bodily damage common in stick fighting and boxing.[120] They approved of it whole-heartedly as long as wrestlers did not violate the Sabbath or allow it to distract them from their religious duties. Many of their neighbors in England were less restrained. Boxing, with its blood-splattering punches, rapidly grew in popularity as colonization to America began. Many non–Puritan English, including King James, saw no conflict between sports on Sundays and religious devotion.[121] Some of the debates over fight sports are familiar to modern Americans, such as the competing concerns over safety versus excitement that led Puritans to prefer wrestling to boxing or stick fighting. Others—particularly the issue of Sabbatarianism that provided the greatest source of conflict between Puritans and their neighbors—are more alien concepts. Colonists brought controversies over fight sports with them to the Americas, where negotiations over the boundaries of fight sports continued.

I

"To Cut Out the Tongue, or Pull Out the Eyes"

Fight Sports in the Americas, 1607–1810

It shall be Felony to cut out the Tongue, or pull out the Eyes, of the King's Liege People.
—Act of the North Carolina General Assembly, 1749[1]

> Now let us sport us while we may;
> And now, like am'rous birds of prey,
> Rather at once our time devour,
> Than languish in his slow-chapp'd power.
> Let us roll all our strength, and all
> Our sweetness, up into one ball;
> And tear our pleasures with rough strife
> Thorough the iron gates of life.
> Thus, though we cannot make our sun
> Stand still, yet we will make him run.
> —"To His Coy Mistress," Andrew Marvell (1621–1678)

The poor youth was very faint in body, but grew stronger in mind at every contest, and was determined to prevail or perish in the attempt. He exerted his utmost powers, and after the contest he had been continued the usual time, the stranger ceased his efforts, declared himself conquered and said you have wrestled manfully.... Now I will tell you what you must do to achieve your final victory. Tomorrow we will wrestle once more. When you have prevailed over me for the last time, then throw me down and strip off my clothes. You must clean the Earth of roots and weeds and make the ground soft. Then bury me in that very spot, covering me with my yellow and green clothes and then with Earth.
—Origin of Indian corn, by the Chippewa and Ojibwa[2]

He leaped at me—I sprang aside, and he struck the wall with such violence that it stunned him, and he fell at my feet. Impatient I waited his recovery; for I felt that I could easily level him. At length, he gathered himself up, and with curses set upon me—I parried his blows, and gave him two in return—one in the pit of the stomach, and one in the face, that made the blood gush from his nostrils in a steady stream—he staggered against the wall, and stood there retching and panting for more than a minute, with the blood and whiskey running together from his mouth—but the next moment I was under him, as helpless as a babe, stunned and suffocating. Suddenly, I felt his great hand wreathed in my hair, and the thumb approaching my right eye, digging about my temple. I remembered what I had heard—it was gouging—the thought was madness—with one effort I grappled at his throat—I reached it—I seized the loose flesh, and twisted it—he uttered a shriek of agony—his hand fell, and his breath rattled in his throat—I quit my hold, and he rolled from me senseless, black in the face, and apparently dead. I trembled in every joint, shuddered for fear I was a murderer, and fell senseless at his side. I revived—opposite was my antagonist, already recovered, and his comrades. He took me by the hand, and acknowledged himself beat. We spent the day together, and they were ready to worship me—to fight for me, for I had conquered their champion.

—"A Kentucky Fight," *New England Galaxy*[3]

Travelers take their fight sports with them wherever they go, and the early English migrants to North America were no exception. Old World people who came to America to escape religious persecution, to improve their financial position, or because their masters forced them onto the ship at gunpoint all participated in modifying old traditions and creating new ones.

Puritans transferred sporting conflicts to America. They generally accepted sports as long as they did not pollute the Sabbath or disrupt the peace.[4] Colonists across northern North America including Plymouth, Pennsylvania, and New Amsterdam passed laws regulating behaviors allowed on Sundays.[5] On a Christmas Day not long after the founding of Plymouth colony, Governor William Bradford encountered several men playing ball in the street. He told them they could continue as long as they kept to their own homes and clear of the public roads.[6] John Baker dared to venture into public to shoot ducks on the Sabbath and the local judge sentenced him to a whipping.[7] Aristocratic sports such as jousting and fencing that were popular in Europe failed to make it across the Atlantic to any significant degree because of the lack of interest by the middle and working classes that made up the vast majority of immigrants, not due to any official prohibitions.[8] Illicit entertainments such as gambling and cockfights always existed around the fringes of colonial society.⁹ However, the English were not the only people in North America interested in sport.

The indigenous peoples of North America loved their sports and shared them with their new neighbors.[10] Europeans rarely hesitated to deride the natives they encountered as "savages" or "heathens" for their religious practices, economic systems, or methods of warfare. However, European observers typically referred to Indians' athleticism as a virtue and their performance in the wrestling ring as worthy of emotions ranging from admiration to pity, but not disgust.[11] Wrestling provided a place of common ground and cultural interaction between Europeans and Native Americans.[12] French visitors to North America tempered their criticisms of American Indians by noting that they possessed numerous virtues, including the love of wrestling.[13] John Harriot, a British naval officer, admitted that the Indians he met consistently bested him at foot races and climbing contests, but he took pride in his performance as a fighter. He won more wrestling matches than he lost, earning praise from Native Americans. Harriott taught the Indians the sport of single stick, a form of stick fighting commonly used by European sailors to improve their skills with the sword, and impressed them with his performance. He took pride in his ability to hold his own with Indians and claimed that given enough time, he might have become a good Indian.[14] William Wood, a 17th-century English immigrant to New England, was tougher on the indigenous people than Harriot, and proudly proclaimed that the English colonists were far superior athletes to Native Americans who wrestled poorly.[15] The cultural exchange traveled in both directions, and young colonists began adopting a new style of close-contact wrestling inspired by Native techniques.[16]

Fight sports in Europe possessed a dual legacy as sinful celebrations and as a method of transforming men into soldiers. The first legacy made Puritan leaders wary, and the second eventually convinced them to endorse wrestling. The American colonies were a dangerous place for the English, who lived in constant fear of European and Native American rivals.[17] At the conclusion of the Pequot War, the New England colonies began reorganizing their defense forces. In an age before reliable firearms, life and death on the battlefield often came down to close combat. Thus, in 1639, the Massachusetts militia began incorporating wrestling into their training routines.[18] European armies had used similar training techniques dating back to the ancient Greeks and more recently practiced in English militias.[19] Experts pointed to the wrestling programs of triumphant Greek and Roman armies and argued that only wrestling could adequately prepare men for war.[20] Militia leaders avoided theological conflicts by never holding training days on the Sabbath and working to foster an attitude of serious duty, rather than sinful enjoyment.[21] Governor Winthrop proudly reported that 1,200 militiamen who mustered in Boston for a training day in 1641 took their training seriously and avoided mischief.[22] The reformed sporting competitions attracted the attention of clergy, who joined in as spectators and even competitors.[23] Military necessity slowly opened the door for an emerging sporting culture.

Militia days in America began to take on some of the same attributes that Puritans had found so objectionable in England. Serious training evolved into public holidays with the help of a geographic change as the frontier with all of its very real dangers moved ever westward, making danger increasingly remote and training less vital. While not every early migrant to New England was devoutly religious, many were. As increasing numbers of immigrants came to the colony for economic opportunity rather than religious devotion, however, the old commitments to avoid frivolous enjoyment began to fade.[24] Training days began early in the morning as militiamen brought their entire families, including grandparents, wives, and newborn children into town. Around 8 a.m., the militia began parading and drilling in formation to the sound of fifes and drums. These group exercises sometimes climaxed with full-scale mock battles.[25] In the early afternoon, the men took a break for lunch.[26] Women served a feast including biscuits, spare-ribs, pickled cucumbers, and training cake, that glorious dessert made with tantalizing combinations of ginger, cinnamon, sugar, molasses, and nutmeg, and suitable only for special occasions like the militia drills.[27] After lunch, the militiamen entertained the crowds with the horse races, shooting contests, and wrestling tournaments, which authorities initially introduced as serious military training. Winners of the contests enjoyed the applause of the crowd and red ribbons for their hats to mark them as champions of the "Olympiak Games."[28] In the evenings, alcohol flowed freely and a new tradition of drunkenness at militia musters took hold in spite of scolding from religious leaders.[29]

The sporting culture bred in the festive atmosphere of militia days spread through New England society. Weddings witnessed sporting events nearly identical to the militia training, including wrestling matches.[30] Wrestling matches became part of the festivities that accompanied the raisings of buildings. At a raising near Wallingford, Vermont, a "mulatto" wrestler fought a series of bouts against white men, boasting of his skills and ridiculing spectators until a local tailor entered the ring and broke the braggart's arm.[31] In at least one town, amusements completely replaced religion and the townspeople spent their Sundays sleeping, drinking, and wrestling.[32] Taverns often held wrestling tournaments as well as cockfights, races, and shooting contests for delighted patrons.[33] In an odd twist of irony, taverns and the sporting events they sponsored provided a rare area of few class distinctions within Puritan colonies supposedly devoted to a classless society.[34]

The growth of sports in New England resulted from broader societal shifts including the increase and diversification of the population, urbanization, and the rise of businesses dedicated to servicing these populations.[35] From 1660 to 1720, the population of the New England colonies exploded from barely 30,000 to nearly 170,000.[36] Population densities also increased, with the seacoast counties of Massachusetts, for example, increasing from 4.5 persons per square mile in 1650 to 43.8 persons in 1760.[37] Urban areas, such as the rapidly growing cities of New England, provided the scene for an increasingly organized and commercialized sporting culture.[38] New England city dwellers provided both the competitors and the spectators for sporting events.[39] Immigrants to New England increasingly came for economic reasons rather than theological and included non–Puritans from across Scotland and Ireland, which disrupted the spiritual unity of the colonies.[40] New generations born of Puritan parents began to shift their attention away from religion. New Englanders increasingly focused on consumer goods and leisure.[41] All of these changes weakened older patterns of social cohesion. The larger and more concentrated population facilitated greater commercial specialization and businesses opened to provide goods and services. Taverns became increasingly common and often sponsored sporting events to attract patrons.[42]

While the new and newly secular colonists enjoyed many sports, wrestling was always the crowd favorite.[43] It occupied a unique cultural space somewhere between the sacred and the fun. Wrestlers appeared on the village green to fulfill an official obligation to their community, to protect their godly city on a hill from unbelievers who laid in waiting behind every rock and tree plotting the demise of the chosen. Wrestlers strengthened their bodies and honed their techniques to protect their families and ensure that no colonists would ever again die at the hands of raiders as they had outside Fort Saybrook. Preachers urged to men wrestle just as Jacob, their spiritual father, wrestled with the angel.[44] Ministers endorsed wrestling with their actions as well as with their words when they too demonstrated their skills in unarmed combat. The most famous pastor to step into the ring was probably John Wise, a Harvard graduate, respected biblical scholar, and veteran of the Indian wars, who cemented his reputation as a legendary athlete when he responded to a challenge from a local ruffian by slamming his opponent into the ground until the man begged for mercy.[45] Wrestling's constrained violence remained free of the theological problems of competing fight sports such as boxing that disfigured the human face, which had been made in the image of God.[46] All of these factors allowed colonists to enjoy wrestling in good conscience, but people enjoyed the sport primarily because it was enjoyable to play and fun to watch.[47] Wrestling provided a perfect cultural storm of cheerfully dutiful violence among friends and rivals for the delight of an excited crowd with bellies full of good food and homemade beer, with applause and trophies for the winners. The New England colonies shifted gradually away from their old ideals in fits and starts—ideals that remained an important, if marginal, force well into the 20th century.[48]

Migrants to the southern colonies practiced many of the same sports as their northern cousins, but with a different attitude, which led to a different evolution. English settlers who came to the southern colonies tended to be somewhat more secular than the first immigrants to the north.[49] An English colonist encouraged potential immigrants to make the journey, claiming that no people on earth spent more time on recreation than those in Maryland.[50] These settlers saw nothing wrong with King James's promotion of sport and enjoyed numerous recreations with few restrictions. They recreated the culture of English fairs and festivals in their new homes, including the traditional games of shooting, racing, and wrestling. Cudgeling, or stick fighting, which was almost never practiced in the North showed up more frequently in the South, although it remained rare event there until it died out in the 1730s.[51] Virginians even engaged in boxing bouts.[52] People of the time used the term "boxing," but the word's meaning has evolved dramatically over the centuries.

Boxing, in the sense that modern Americans understand it, simply did not exist prior to the late 19th century.[53] Pugilism of the 18th and 19th centuries, in contrast to modern boxing, typically included punching, kicking, wrestling, stomps with spiked boots, and the use of weapons such as knives and clubs.[54] Punches were delivered bare knuckle, without the padded gloves required by modern boxing. Gloved boxers typically keep their hands high, throwing many of their punches to their adversary's head since head shots are most likely to result a knockout, and blocking attacks to their own head with the padding on their own gloves. Experienced bare-knuckle fighters stood and behaved very differently. They kept their hands low. Most of their punches were aimed at the body since bare-knuckle punches to the head are more likely to result in destruction of the relatively fragile bones of the hand rather than the much stronger skull. Fighters tended to block their arms rather than their hands because the more substantial bones and muscles of those areas are tougher than hands.[55] Eighteenth-century pugilism did not just look different than modern boxing; it also occupied a different cultural space.

Boxing suffered from a reputation as a brutal and uncivilized sport dating back to 200 CE and the Roman theologian Quintus Septimius Florens

I. Fight Sports in the Americas, 1607–1810

Advertisement for an 18th-century English boxing school. The advertisement states, "Opened for instructing Gentlemen, on the lowest terms, in the noble Art of Pugilism, …. Such Gentlemen as are prevented by weak constitutions from taking a lesson may be qualified for … polite assemblies with artifical [sic] bloody noses & black eyes." Published for the proprietor by W. Moore, No. 48 New Bond Street, and W. Dickie, No. 195 Strand, Feb. 6, 1788 (Library of Congress Prints and Photographs Division).

Tertullianus, who criticized the sport for disfiguring the divinely designed human body.[56] This stood in stark contrast to various forms of wrestling, which emphasized techniques of control and positional dominance rather than facial mutilation and therefore received praise rather than condemnation from religious authorities.[57] Boxing, though under assault for centuries, never died out in the British Isles, remaining a popular pastime and system of unarmed combat, especially among the working class.[58] The relaxation of civic morality that coincided with the downfall of Puritanism may have allowed boxing to step back into the limelight.[59] Beginning in the early 18th century, entrepreneurs began rebranding boxing in hopes of attracting larger crowds and earning large profits. James Figg, a fighter and boxing coach, appealed to wealthy patrons beginning in 1719 by presenting boxing as a method of self-defense worthy of gentlemen.[60] Although best remembered for his punches, Figg was far better with clubs and blades than his fists.[61] He was not alone. In Britain, during the early 18th century, numerous working-class men and even a few women entered the arena, earning fame as pugilists fighting for the delight of mass audiences and the financial support of wealthy patrons. Rough styles of boxing, popular in Great Britain, quickly spread to the North American colonies.

Southerners faced threats of violence just as serious as those of the northern colonies, fighting a series of wars against Native American tribes and suffering hundreds of casualties in the process.[62] Influential writers, such as John Locke, argued that wrestling provided skills that could ensure victory in life-and-death encounters.[63] When Francis Nicholson, a professional soldier and former lieutenant governor of New York, became lieutenant governor of Virginia, he immediately began preparing the citizens for war, organizing foot races, shooting contests, cudgeling matches, and wrestling tournaments, and offering prizes to the winners.[64] These contests spread throughout the Southern militias, which instituted training programs, similar to those already taking place in the North that included fight sports such as wrestling and cudgeling.[65] As in the Northern colonies, militia musters in the South became festive atmospheres where the alcohol flowed freely.[66]

Southerners displayed a more permissive attitude toward sport than their northern neighbors did, but even they attempted some regulations. Eighty years after Northerners began outlawing sports on the Sabbath, Southern legislatures began passing similar laws. South Carolina became the first Southern colony to limit the sports its residents could practice on Sunday with an act passed in 1712 that prohibited a long list of hobbies including bull-baiting and horse races. In the following years, Maryland, Delaware, North Carolina, Georgia, and Virginia followed suit with a variety of laws that prohibited a wide range of activities.[67] Other constraints were very different from those present in the Northern colonies.

Southern colonial societies sharply divided sporting events based on class. Many wealthy Southerners admired and attempted to emulate the English gentry, particularly their tendency to sponsor social events in the community and on their plantations.[68] Local gentlemen increased their prestige by acting as patrons for the sporting contests that accompanied militia days, providing substantial prizes, including guns and silver buckles, to champion athletes.[69] Sometimes they offered prizes only to competitors from the upper class.[70] The wealthy elites of the Southern colonies made no pretense of creating a classless society and maintained distinctions between themselves and the masses. Elites enjoyed sponsoring wrestling matches for the working class and even participated occasionally, but reserved the sport of horse racing as their exclusive domain. In 1670, the state of Virginia pressed charges against a tailor for enjoying a pleasure beyond his station when he began entering horse races.[71] The upper classes supported the traditional sports of wrestling and cudgeling even if they preferred to compete at horse races.

Southern elites sponsored sporting events among persons of African descent as well as among whites. The first fair ever held in Baltimore, in 1745, included a foot race for slave girls with a white gown as a prize.[72] Other fairs across the South held similar races for slaves. Slave owners often encouraged their servants to spend holidays such as Christmas and New Year's Day playing games and holding foot races.[73] Slaves played team sports, with ball games similar to early forms of baseball being a particular favorite on North Carolina plantations. Southern planters typically rewarded slaves who entertained them with alcohol and small gifts.[74]

Planters promoted fight sports in the colonies. Many Southern planters sent their sons to England for education; while there, the young men became boxing fans.[75] When these slave owners returned home, many of them trained their slaves in pugilism, putting on some of the first boxing matches in America.[76] On Sundays, many plantation owners who did not attend church visited the slave quarters, giving out drinks of whiskey and stirring up disagreements among the slaves in an effort to provoke hostilities. When slaves agreed to fight, white men acted as referees and placed bets on the fights, which were enjoyed by combined crowds of whites and blacks.[77] Other slaves engaged in western-style wrestling contests.[78] Planters wagered huge sums of money on these contests; a few slaves even won their freedom as a reward for victories in the ring.[79]

A few slaves rejected European styles of fighting in these contests. Instead, they preferred to use African techniques including head butts and kicks rarely utilized by whites.[80] The middle passage did not strip many Africans of their unique approach to fight sport, which remained alive up until the 1970s, when European styles of boxing and wrestling finally penetrated the most remote communities of American slave descendants.[81]

Some elites disliked English pugilism's transfer to America and took immediate steps to eradicate it. Surviving records provide only limited glimpses into early American boxing or gouging. The variety of names—including boxing, gouging, "ole Virginny style," and rough and tumble—reveal the sport's diverse nature, which included techniques as varied as punching, wrestling, choking, scratching, biting, and the removal of testicles, noses, and eyes. The only universal prohibition was on the use of weapons. Some fighters even attempted to get around that rule by cultivating fingernails like thorns and filing their teeth into fangs.[82] Unlike modern fighters, gougers did not operate within well-defined guidelines; no patrons ever wrote a rulebook, no national gougers association ever formed, no professional umpires ever stepped into the ring to separate combatants. Competitors gouged for the delight of crowds, to increase their social status, to resolve disputes, and for simple enjoyment, but most of the gougers left no record of their thoughts and their motives remain an eternal mystery. The sport existed for about a century from 1720 to 1820, mostly in remote areas. Unlike wrestling, which many elites took part in as patrons and even competitors, it was a sport almost exclusively of the poor and marginalized. All of these factors ensured that gouging shows up only rarely in the documents, and most of those records originate with elite critics instead of working-class competitors. Some sources use the terms "boxing" and "gouging" interchangeably or describe gouging as a subset of techniques used within otherwise more refined boxing matches, suggesting that these were variations of the same activity. Still others draw hard lines between the two, indicating a widening separation as English boxing became more refined.[83]

The diversity of experiences and the few surviving accounts leave the historian with as many questions as answers. When did gouging begin? When did it end? Where did it reach? What precisely was it? Perhaps the most indefinite question is why? Why did gouging arise whenever and wherever it did? The documents provide no definitive answer and the most likely explanations suggest that the American frontier provided an environment where only the strong and the vicious had any hope of survival. On the sparsely settled frontier, life and death often came down to a man's ability to withstand and deliver punishment and to depend on the man watching his back. In a rough and brutal place, reputations became priceless, scars became badges of honor, and brutality became the highest virtue.[84] Gouging brushed aside the luxury of decorum and embraced mayhem in all of its glorious varieties.

The sources fail to reveal the identity of the first gouger or what gougers were thinking when they pulled out an opponent's eye and began a process that led to transatlantic outrage and governmental action. Gouging must have got its start sometime before 1719, when the colonial legislature of Delaware threatened execution without clerical assistance for anyone who maliciously wounded a subject of the English crown by a variety of methods including putting out an eye.[85] A traveler in South Carolina provided the oldest surviving eyewitness testimony of a gouging match when he observed a 1734 fight in a tavern that concluded when the winner bit off his opponent's nose.[86] The North Carolina legislature followed Delaware's example in 1749 when it denounced the new sport and made it a felony to cut out the tongue or pull out an eye of a British subject.[87] Virginia's 1752 statue took matters a step further, criminalizing a sport it described as a style of boxing often practiced by members of the lower sort and providing penalties not only for people who disfigured the faces and limbs of the king's subjects, but also for anyone who facilitated them, suggesting that the combatants were not the only people involved in these contests.[88] Governor Gabriel Johnston of North Carolina noted that four people had died in fights since the colony passed antigouging legislation. He urged the legislature to take additional actions to promote religious virtue and stamp out the brutal style of boxing common among the lower sort.[89] Although Johnston referred to the fights as boxing, the word possessed a very different meaning in 18th-century America. The Virginia legislature expressed similar frustrations, noting that previous laws against gouging failed to stamp out the activity. In 1772, the legislature increased the penalties and began requiring lashes at the public whipping post for convicted gougers.[90] Elites typically painted gouging in the worst possible light. Philip Vickers Fithian, serving as a tutor on a series of Virginia plantations, referred to gouging as a common and diabolical custom.[91]

In spite of the condemnations, complimentary descriptions occasionally show up as well. One the eve of revolution, a writer looked at the long and glorious martial past of American colonists, contemplated war with Britain, and used a satirical novel to boast;

> Are not we the sons of those warriors who in time of old withstood in bloody conflict the mighty army of the Tryonites, and bade defiance to their general even at the cannon's mouth? And behold, are we not able to slay thousands, yea tens of thousands with our thumb nails; for what men of any nation upon earth can cope with us at gouging.[92]

Some elites attempted to stamp out gouging, even as they occasionally mentioned it in favorable terms, but continued to support wrestling, as an important part of a complete education. The Archbishop of Canterbury, John Potter, wrote several works that praised the Greeks, Lycurgus especially, and his educational system, which used sports, including wrestling, to transform children into vigorous adults.[93] John Locke said that if he had a son, he would want him to learn wrestling.[94] Magazine editors also promoted wrestling, noting that the ancient Greeks and modern Britons both loved the sport.[95] Writers promoted these ideas throughout the larger Atlantic world, not just among the British. Charles Rollin, a French scholar and principal of the University of Paris, wrote books in French that praised wrestling as a method of education, which British publishers later translated into English.[96] The French philosopher, Claude Adrien Helvetius, echoed similar sentiments in his works, which printers picked up and translated into English as well.[97] Eighteenth-century writers also produced books in German that connected education and wrestling.[98] In the English colonies, Benjamin Franklin urged schools to teach wrestling to ensure students grew up healthy and strong.[99]

John Adams argued that when he was young, men improved themselves by running, leaping, and wrestling. They were nothing like the men of his son's generation, who spent all of their time in taverns, smoking, and drinking. Adams blamed schools for failing to teach young people how to behave.[100]

Wrestling became a popular amusement at English schools and then crossed the Atlantic to America's first schools. Oliver Cromwell once remarked that no opposing army ever frightened him on the battlefield the way his opponents had in the university wrestling ring.[101] The faculty of Harvard attempted to define acceptable recreations for their pupils, including specific times for recreation, but in spite of their best efforts, students found ways around the restrictions and frequently engaged in football games, snowball fights, and wrestling matches at whatever times and under whatever circumstances they desired.[102] Students at Yale enjoyed similar amusements.[103] Like their counterparts at Harvard, the administrators of William and Mary College attempted to constrain when their students played sports.[104] Charles Jeffery Smith announced his plans to ban all sports—but especially wrestling—at the academy he was founding at New Kent, Virginia, because he believed they tempted students into immorality.[105] Smith passed away before he could attract sufficient financial support to open his school.

Members of the militia, who wrestled for exercise and recreation, brought the sport with them to war. Sports helped fill the long intervals between battles.[106] Bored with inaction outside Boston in 1775, champion wrestlers from rival Massachusetts regiments fought for the entertainment of a large crowd and the glory of victory. Soldiers held tournaments to find the greatest wrestlers in the armies.[107] These contests were a continuation of the wrestling matches practiced at militia musters for nearly a century. A Massachusetts soldier observed that class divided sporting events, with the officers preferring ball games to the enlisted men's wrestling. While serving in the Continental Army disguised as a man, Deborah Sampson happened past a group of men enjoying a wrestling match who insisted she fight the winner of the current bout. After urgent excuses about why she was unable to fight, comrades shoved her into the ring, where her opponent slammed her to the ground in an instant. The quick victory left her with aching joints, but the limited contact allowed her to maintain the secret of her gender.[108] Legends claim that George Washington responded to mutinous volunteers from Massachusetts by sending one after another hurtling into the ground of the wrestling ring, but the lack of primary sources makes this a questionable claim.[109]

Men also encountered boxing while in uniform, brought to American shores by working-class Irish and English soldiers. Joseph Plumb Martin had heard that boxing was common among low-class Europeans, but he never saw it until one day in camp when one drunk Irishman challenged another to a bout. On the frozen ground, the pair stripped to the waist and banged away for the pleasure of curious onlookers until their blood flowed into the dirt and they agreed to call it a day.[110] An officer from Connecticut joined a curious crowd that gathered to watch a series of boxing matches on Long Island.[111] The British army in North America included many men who loved boxing. Free black men became some of the first professional boxers in America. In occupied New York, the greatest black boxer of his generation, Bill Richmond, fought Irish men in British uniforms for the delight of audiences and the pay of his sponsor General Earl Percy.[112] Descriptions of boxing contests on American soil provide few details, but suggest fights emphasized bare-knuckle punches and wrestling holds, which are illegal in modern boxing. This new wave of 18th-century boxing sat somewhere between the more

A hand-colored etching of a fight between pugilists Spangle Jack the Shewman and Old Price. A well-dressed observer holds out a bottle that appears to be labeled "British Compound" and probably contains liquor. The observer calls out to a battered and bloody Old Price, "Come stand up Old Boy!" Old Price responds, "I will! I will Johny but he hits cursed hard." Published in London by Walker on October 6, 1809 (Library of Congress Prints and Photographs Division).

refined pugilism of the modern world and the rougher styles of boxing popular on the frontier. Exposure to new fight sports ran in both directions. American soldiers got their first glimpse of European boxing while in uniform and expressed curiosity; British soldiers witnessed gouging and expressed disgust.

Observers of North American fight sports frequently unleashed their harshest criticism on lower-class whites rather than slaves or Native Americans. One visitor condemned middle- and lower-class whites in Virginia as barbarians for their preferred style of boxing.[113] Another writer criticized the lower classes of North Carolina, who often gouged out eyes during their boxing matches.[114] Thomas Anburey, who served as an officer with the British army during the revolution, made a distinction between gouging and boxing. He claimed that while English-style boxing was a disgrace to civilized people, its brutality was nothing in comparison to the Virginia style of fighting. He argued that this fighting style was so barbaric that it was beneath even a savage.[115] Anburey noted that before commencing hostilities, competitors agreed on rules. They ran down an informal checklist of possible techniques including biting, attacks on the groin, and gouging, agreeing on the acceptability of each tactic in the upcoming fray. Once the rules were decided, gougers pounced on each other ferociously. Anburey expressed his amazement that even in the heat of the struggle men retained their coolness and restrained themselves from breaking the rules, indicating that gouging was a sport as well as a means of violent resolution to problems.[116] Anburey also provided one of the most detailed eyewitness descriptions of a gouging match.

While in Virginia in 1779, Anburey relaxed in a billiard room with several brother officers and local gentlemen. A man from the lower sort who claimed gentlemanly status entered the room and began playing.[117] Soon, the lower-sort man began to argue with Mr. Fanchee, a respected local surgeon and pharmacist. The lower-sort man insisted on fighting Fanchee. Fanchee asked which rules they would fight under since he was ignorant of boxing, but willing to face his opponent in a gentlemanly like manner. Either this question upset the challenger or he possessed a highly developed sense of ironic humor, because he chose that instant to pounce without warning.[118] Before anyone could react, the assailant pulled Fanchee's eye from the socket so that it dangled down his cheek, with only the optical nerve keeping the eye from falling to the ground. Apparently, the gouger considered this an uncompleted task, because he did not pause and instead pressed his attack trying to sever the nerve and remove the eye entirely. The British officers, men trained in war and no strangers to violence, stood in stunned disbelief.[119] At first Anburey recoiled, and then he condemned.

Anburey called gouging a barbaric custom, embarrassing even to savages, and yet common among Virginians of the lower sort. Although combatants generally discarded their weapons at the start of gouging matches, at least one fighter Anburey knew pushed the boundary by growing his fingernails long and daily hardened them over a candle's flame, transforming empty hands into lethal weapons. While in Virginia, he and his fellow officers lived in fear of gougers and never traveled far without their sidearms. He expressed pity that the barbarians of the lower sort rendered a place ruled by a generous and dignified upper sort almost unlivable.[120] Anburey noted that the colonial government outlawed the practice in an effort to abolish such fights, but these laws had little effect because the lower sort paid scant attention to the government and its laws, particularly on the frontier. Anburey's comments reveal the battle lines in a conflict that ended only years after the guns of the revolution fell silent and newly independent colonists blazed a trail to a unique national identity.

The new nation's leaders continued to support wrestling. Henry Knox, a general during the revolution, attempted to ban all recreations in militia camps during his tenure as Secretary of War (1789–1794), except for the sports of swimming, running, and wrestling—exercises that Knox believed would make men strong, agile, and healthy.[121] Periodical articles that discussed wrestling typically portrayed it in mostly positive terms and described it as the sport of ancient Greece.[122] In the years before the revolution, John Adams lamented the weakness and immorality of young people who preferred drinking in taverns to the wrestling contests enjoyed by men of his own generation.[123] After the war ended, he pondered how to construct a vigorous society. Looking beyond his personal experiences, Adams envisioned sport as a method for building an American nation. He cast his gaze to Lycurgus and recalled how the Spartans transformed their children into strong adults by encouraging them to run, ride, swim, dance, and wrestle. Adams argued that the new nation should immediately make these exercises a required part of their school curricula.[124]

Not everyone embraced wrestling without hesitation. At Harvard, the student body developed a tradition of concluding graduation exercises with wrestling matches between the graduates and the incoming seniors. Some critics questioned the propriety of the custom. *Massachusetts Magazine* published a stirring argument in support of the tradition and of wrestling more generally. The article claimed that wrestling provided a pure expression of gentlemanly virtue that brought men together and earned them the admiration of foreign visitors. The author echoed Adams' ideas of wrestling as a method of building strong citizens and takes the point a step further, arguing that wrestling would help the new nation rise as a new incarnation of Greece and Rome. With his final lines, the author suggested that Harvard would soon produce another Hercules who would teach the entire world the glory of wrestling.[125]

While some elites promoted wrestling, others worked hard to rid the world of the gouging contests still common along the frontier, which were making their way north and beginning to worry Northern as well as Southern elites. Although historians typically view gouging as a Southern art form, it concerned people from other areas as well. Writers in Northern periodicals

A crude portrayal of a fight on the floor of Congress between Vermont Representative Matthew Lyon and Roger Griswold of Connecticut. The row was originally prompted by an insulting reference to Lyon on Griswold's part. The interior of Congress Hall is shown, with the Speaker Jonathan Dayton and Clerk Jonathan W. Condy (both seated), Chaplain Ashbel Green (in profile on the left), and several others looking on, as Griswold (right), armed with a cane, kicks Lyon (left), who grasps the former's arm and raises a pair of fireplace tongs to strike him. Below are the verses: "He in a trice struck Lyon thrice / Upon his head, enrag'd sir, / Who seiz'd the tongs to ease his wrongs, / And Griswold thus engag'd, sir." Print titled "Congressional Pugilists" published in 1798 at Philadelphia, PA (Library of Congress Prints and Photographs Division).

condemned gouging and urged the nation's leaders to take steps to end the practice. A magazine published in Philadelphia related an incident when a man who had agreed to fight under Broughton's Rules violated his promise and gouged out his opponent's eyes, an act the author claimed was as legal as it was immoral. The author argued that gouging was the most disgusting crime in all of history and demanded every state legislature make gouging a felony punishable by execution without benefit of clergy.[126] Another magazine based in Philadelphia told several stories of gouging, a practice the author claimed was common in several of the Southern states and particularly popular at cockfights in some portions of Virginia. The author claimed, "Honor, humanity, and civilization blush, recoil, and shudder with indignant detestation, at such ferocious brutality."[127] A Massachusetts magazine republished an article from a London publication that referred to gouging as a barbaric practice completely unknown in Europe.[128] A British writer claimed that while boxing's rules made it honorable, gouging's absence of regulation made it inhumane. He argued that any government that failed to eliminate gouging in its territory deserved only contempt from its citizens.[129] These comments suggest that some people of the time saw gouging as an entirely unique practice, distinct from boxing.

State legislatures continued passing laws against gouging in the years after the revolution. In 1788, New York provided the death penalty for anyone who maliciously maimed a person by putting out an eye or cutting the face. The act provided the same penalty for anyone who assisted or encouraged these behaviors.[130] New Hampshire passed a very similar law in 1791, but allowed a punishment of no more than seven years imprisonment.[131] In 1795, Pennsylvania continued the trend with a statute that copied the language of New York and New Hampshire almost exactly, with the exception of a unique penalty of two to ten years and a fine of up to $10,000.[132] Kentucky claimed the honor of being the first state that had never been a colony to pass an antigouging law.[133] With no concern for plagiarism, the Kentuckians appear to have copied Pennsylvania's law almost word for word, including the penalty of a term in the penitentiary, an odd requirement since the state passed the act two years before it built its first penitentiary.[134] Legislatures continued to pass laws with Indiana, Louisiana, Tennessee, Georgia, Missouri, Vermont, and finally Illinois passing what appears to be the last gouging law in American history in 1819.[135] State governments enforced these laws, prosecuting gougers and sending them to prison.[136] Gougers also faced military discipline, with at least one officer, South Carolinian Captain Joab Blackwell, losing his commission for gouging out the eye of an enlisted man under his command.[137]

Harsh punishments and threats of execution did not eliminate the practice, however. Gougers continued to rip out eyes in the years after the Revolutionary War. Men missing an eye to the gouger's art were almost as common in some parts of America as men who took pride in their ability to remove one.[138] On the frontier, men gouged out eyes to settle disputes or simply for their amusement and that of spectators who cheered them on to victory.[139] Thomas Ashe, an English traveler and journalist, provided a particularly interesting description of gouging in Wheeling, West Virginia, near the state's borders with Ohio and Pennsylvania. He observed two men, a Virginian and a Kentuckian, quarreling over a recent horse race. A crowd formed around them and demanded to know if the men would fight fair or if they would engage in an "anything goes" match. Both men agreed to a rough-and-tumble fight. The spectators placed their bets and bought food and whiskey from a vendor in the crowd. After some preliminary sparring, the Virginian flung his body at the Kentucky man, tackling him and pinning him to the ground. The Kentuckian struggled violently to escape his opponent. Slowly, the Virginian ran his fingers through his adversary's hair, tracing the outlines of his head and feeling for the eyes. The Kentuckian bucked violently as the Virginian slowly discovered just the right spot on each eye and with a sudden strike pulled both eyes free from their sockets. The thrilled spectators responded with joyous shouts.[140] Blindness did not convince the Kentuckian to give up and seemed only to strengthen him. He grabbed his opponent's nose and snapped it with a vicious twist. The Virginian responded by grabbing the Kentuckian's lip and pulled on it until the skin ripped and blood gushed. Finally, the Kentuckian gave up and the crowd carried the victor away.

As the horse races resumed, Ashe slipped away from the crowd, disgusted by the sports he had witnessed. He sought out a local Quaker he knew and the men enjoyed a meal together. While eating, Ashe shared his experience, but the Quaker expressed no surprise. He claimed that such events took place several times a week. At the horse races every fall and spring, he said, the fights went on continuously for weeks. The Quaker observed that gouging was common everywhere except in the towns populated by the better sort, where the laws were enforced. He foresaw no end to the custom of gouging, which the backcountry people loved and which the authorities were afraid to prosecute.[141] The anonymous Quaker was wrong; while he enjoyed his dinner, gouging was drawing its dying breath.

Gouging died sometime in the first decades of the 19th century, with a death as mysterious as its birth. A Massachusetts author claimed that gouging was becoming less popular in Virginia by 1810.[142] In the same year, a North Carolinian journalist claimed that the state had long ago eliminated gouging from its territory, but legal records reveal that the state prosecuted a handful of gougers as late as 1816 and did not indict its very last gouger until 1840.[143] An American author responded in 1815 to a claim by a British author that the United States was a nation of savage fighters, by arguing that "anything goes" fights were a thing of the past.[144] This timeline finds further support in the fact that 1819 marked the passage of the last antigouging law in American history.[145] The custom continued to show up occasionally on the Western frontier as late as the 1830s.[146]

Gouging died under the weight of a three-pronged assault delivered by Christians, lawyers, and immigrants. Christians opposed boxing as far back as 200 CE, and many developed a particularly antagonistic relationship with gouging. The Southern frontier provided a home for gougers largely because of Christianity's weak influence on the region. Most Southerners were apathetic to Christianity well into the 19th century.[147] Observers argued that gouging existed primarily in the South, where religion exerted only the weakest influence, and rarely in the North, where devout Christians dominated communities.[148] This was particularly true along the Southern frontiers where gouging was the most common.[149] An American author described gouging as sinful and suggested that gougers assaulted God when they disfigured human faces made in the image of the creator.[150] This was consistent with the argument of the Romanized African theologian Quintus Septimius Florens Tertullianus, who argued that boxing's disfigurement of the divinely designed human body angered God.[151] An English visitor argued that Americans engaged in gouging only because their churches were not strong enough to eliminate the practice.[152] Another traveler argued that gougers were openly hostile to religion.[153] Other visitors saw gouging as evidence of a general disrespect for religion and sinful misuse of the sacred Sabbath.[154]

Gouging became weaker when Christianity became stronger. A series of religious revivals often referred to as the Second Great Awakening, which swept the United States from roughly 1790 to 1840, increased religious influences on American life, particularly on the frontier and in the South.[155] One of the primary goals of this movement was to decrease violence of every variety in American society.[156] By 1809, observers noticed changes in the South, claiming that drinking, horse racing, boxing, and gouging declined because of a religious revival sweeping the nation.[157] North Carolina men typically abandoned gouging along with heavy drinking and blasphemy as part of their deeply emotional conversion experiences.[158] Gouging declined in response to the increase in religious influence in Mississippi, with men increasingly embracing a code of honor that valued spiritual purity more highly than skillful violence.[159] The war on gouging was consistent with the revival's emphasis on perfecting society by eliminating the courser aspects of life, including drinking and gambling as well as violence.[160]

Gouging also thrived on lawlessness and died out as local governments exhorted more control over their populations. This fits into a larger pattern in which in the years immediately after the Revolutionary War, state governments in the South were largely irrelevant to people's lives, but began to increase their control in the first years of the 19th century.[161] As governments extended their rule into frontier areas, they passed laws against gouging.[162] Courts enforced these laws, sending some gougers to prison.[163] The newspapers *Raleigh Star* (North Carolina) and *Augusta Sentinel* (Georgia) engaged in a war of words in 1810 that began when the Georgian editor claimed that North Carolinians were all gougers. The *Raleigh Star* editor admitted that gougers were once common in the state, but argued that civilization had long ago come to their land, forcing the gougers to find new homes in the still unregulated wilds of Louisiana and Georgia.[164]

Demographics offers another explanation for gouging's demise. Wrestling, long supported by elites, obtained a boost from increasing numbers of Irish, Welsh, and Scottish immigrants who brought their distinctive and highly effective wrestling styles with them and found receptive students in their new homes.[165] The Irish were by far the most influential of these groups; their communities in Vermont became hotbeds of wrestling that produced America's first professional wrestlers decades later.[166] Increasingly refined versions of boxing also became more popular and took over much of the cultural space gouging once occupied. A new wave of British immigrants brought their love of pugilism across the Atlantic.[167] The introduction of the London Prize Ring Rules in 1838 attempted to reform boxing into something more acceptable to critics, but made only superficial changes.[168] Many Americans fell in love with new varieties of boxing in spite, or perhaps because of, their rough edges.[169]

Gouging died, but the American love of fight sports lived on. With gouging gone and boxing reinforced, the ring was clear for a new contest. The American population continued to expand into the frontier. Larger cities facilitated greater professional specialization. Expanding urban populations provided audiences for mass sporting events and made popular culture into big business. The next round moved from the taverns and militia musters of colonial villages into the arenas and gymnasiums of large cities. Ringed by masses of urban spectators, wrestling—reinvigorated by Irish blood and still champion—began to stare down a new opponent who wielded bare knuckles in the place of sharpened fingernails.

II

"A Boxing We Will Go"

Boxing Takes Root in the United States, 1810–1915

A Boxing We Will Go.
Come move the song, and stir the glass,
For why should we be sad;
Let's drink to some free-hearted lass,
And Cribb, the boxing lad,
And a boxing we will go, will go, will go,
Italians stab their friends behind,
In darkest shades of night;
But Britons are bold and kind,
And box their friends by light.
The sons of France their pistols use,
Pop, pop, and they have done:
But Britons with their hands will bruise,
And scorn away to run.
Throw pistols, poniards, swords, aside,
And all such deadly tools;
Let boxing be the Briton's pride,
The science of the schools!
Since boxing is a manly game,
And Briton's recreation:
By Boxing we will raise our fame,
'Bove any other nation.
If Boney doubt it, let him come,
And try with Cribb a round;
And Cribb shall beat him like a drum,
And make his carcass sound.
Mendoza, Gulley, Molineaux,
Each Nature's weapon wield;
Who each at Boney would stand true,

> And never to him yield.
> We've many more would like to floor
> The little upstart king;
> And soon for mercy make him roar
> Within a spacious ring.
> A fig for Boney—let's heave done
> With that ungracious name;
> We'll drink and pass our days in fun,
> And box to raise our fame.
> And a boxing, &c.
> —"A Boxing We Will Go," popular English song from 1829[1]

> Come then! Let thinking men who value their manhood set themselves in array, both against the army of those who, unmanly themselves, wish to see all others reduced to their own level, and against the vast following who, caught by such specious watchwords as "progress," "civilization," and "refinement," have unthinkingly thrown their weight into the falling scale. Has mawkish sentimentality become the shibboleth of the progress, civilization and refinement of this vaunted age? If so, then in Heaven's name leave us a saving touch of honest, old-fashioned barbarism! That when we come to die, we shall die, leaving men behind us, and not a race of eminently respectable female saints.
> —"A Defense of Pugilism," Duffield Osborne, 1888[2]

> Molineaux, determined to finish the contest, went in with uncommon fury; Blake endeavored to retreat from the violent efforts of his opponent; but was compelled to rally, and who put in a good blow upon the cheek of his opponent. Molineaux returned with a tremendous hit upon Blake's head, that completely took all recollection out of him; the effects of which he did not recover from so as to be ready to time, when Molineaux was proclaimed the conqueror.
> The former slave Tom Molineaux defeats an Englishman, 1810[3]

At the dawn of the 19th century, militia musters retained their historical status as a scene where men engaged in fight sports and formed masculine identities. The militia was the most important organization in the creation and transmission of concepts of masculinity in early America.[4] Wrestling was a common aspect of militia training which high-ranking military and political officials formally endorsed.[5] Critics argued that the militia worked well only on the frontier, where attack was imminent.[6] In more settled areas, it was little more than a men's club devoted to wrestling, drunkenness, and general mayhem. An 1813 article in a New York political journal argued that men who served in the militia were free since they retained the capacity to violently oppose government oppression.[7] Another article in the same issue described

II. Boxing Takes Root in the United States, 1607–1810   51

wrestling, with its emphasis on strength and competition, as a crucial component of militia training.[8] At a militia muster in Kentucky, Micah Taul won an election to the post of captain after demonstrating his particular blend of biting, punching, and head butting for an impressed crowd in a series of brutal fights. Taul's performance was more than entertainment: by demonstrating his capacity to deliver and withstand abuse, he proved himself worthy of a position of leadership.[9] Many 19th-century Americans expected their leaders to prove their leadership by violently dominating their peers. While militia musters remained an important scene of American fight sports, the focus quickly shifted.

During his brief 34 years of life, Tom Molineaux traveled a tortuous path from slavery to international celebrity, before dying in poverty and anonymity. He was born in 1784, a slave on the Virginia plantation of Algernon Molineaux.[10] Tom Molineaux came from one of the first boxing families of America. His father Zachariah Molineaux was a famous pugilist, as were all of his brothers.[11] Tom quickly emerged as the greatest champion in Virginia, surpassing the fame of even his own father. In 1804, Algernon Molineaux granted the young pugilist his freedom as a reward for his victories in the ring.[12] Tom Molineaux traveled to New York where he worked as a laborer and continued to hone his skills in the ring. With limited opportunities for a professional boxer in America, Molineaux took a job as a deckhand on a ship headed for London, the boxing capital of the world. In England, Molineaux proclaimed himself the boxing champion of America, a completely fictional title at this time. He made friends with Bill Richmond, another former slave who began boxing professionally in England during the American Revolution. Richmond, now retired and working as a fight promoter and tavern keeper, took the newcomer under his wing and began coaching him for the challenges ahead.

Molineaux never suffered from a lack of ambition, and he began seeking fights as soon as he arrived on British soil. He proclaimed himself the greatest fighter in the world and dared the legendary champion Tom Cribb to face him in the ring.[13] Richmond may have encouraged Molineaux to make the challenge since Cribb had defeated Richmond years before, denying the former slave the title of English champion.[14] Cribb refused to fight Molineaux, but helped organize a fight between the American and Cribb's protégé, Bill Burrows. With Richmond in his corner, and Cribb in Burrow's, Molineaux stepped into the ring with Burrows on July 14, 1810.[15] For nearly an hour, Molineaux battered his opponent with masterful brutality, turning Burrows' face into a shapeless mass of blood and skin before winning the fight and the admiration of the crowd. The next month Tom Blake, a highly respected

British fighter, took on the now-famous Molineaux. Blake fared no better than Burrows, falling to an irresistible rain of punches from Molineaux.[16] Cribb could no longer avoid Molineaux and he agreed to face the upstart not only for the prize money, but also for the honor of the nation. Members of the British public were outraged at the suggestion that a foreigner, particularly a black one, could wear the boxing crown of England. Cribb was determined to prove such fears unfounded, but Molineaux expressed the highest confidence.[17]

The fight was more than a boxing match: it was a conflict with racial and national significance. The larger issues attracted the attention of many people who typically considered the ring a vulgar place unworthy of their attention.[18] The rival pugilists entered the ring on December 18, 1810. The day was cold, windy, and rainy even by the standards of an English December.[19] A huge crowd of more than 5,000 braved the weather to witness the momentous fight.[20] Cribb was in trouble right away as Molineaux battered the champion and angered the fans. After 19 rounds the spectators took matters into their own hands, rushing into the ring and breaking Molineaux's fingers, before returning to the sidelines.[21] Still the American pummeled the champion, knocking him down in the 28th round. Molineaux should have walked away the victor, but Cribb's supporters intervened again, making baseless accusations that Molineaux was concealing a weapon and giving the champion precious seconds to recover. After 33 rounds, Molineaux was exhausted, cold, and in pain. He conceded defeat, allowing Cribb to retain the title and capture the prize money. One English observer expressed sympathy for the fallen American, lamenting that only Molineaux's race prevented his capture of the champion's title that day.[22]

His unjust defeat on that cold, rainy December day was the high point of Molineaux's career. He demanded a rematch almost immediately, but in the second fight, Cribb won a resounding victory. Molineaux refused to listen to Richmond's advice, abandoned his training regimen, and descended into alcoholism.[23] In spite of Molineaux's flaws and the British press's desire for the boxing title to remain firmly in the hands of a white Englishman, British writers treated Molineaux fairly and often praised his physique, courage, and skills.[24] American journalists, in contrast, showed little interest in the only American competing for a world title and rarely mentioned him.[25] Molineaux concluded his career, traveling to Ireland and putting on boxing exhibitions for masses of Irish fight fans. When he died at the age of 34, probably from tuberculosis, the only people who gathered at his grave were three black friends who had cared for him in his dying days.[26] The first American to challenge the assumption that the greatest boxers in the world were white

Britons passed into dust with little notice. For 50 years no American made a serious attempt at gaining the world title, and it was nearly a century later before a black man won the title denied to Molineaux.

The transoceanic trade in fighters was changed, though not eliminated by the approaching war.[27] During the War of 1812, violent sports provided a rare moment of reasonably friendly interactions between enemies. Along the border of Canada and the United States, American and British soldiers agreed to settle the war with a wrestling tournament. The Americans won, but rival governments failed to recognize the bloodless resolution and the war dragged on.[28] American prisoners of war in Canada filled their days with sporting contests, including boxing.[29] In the lead-up to war on the southern frontier, the famed Creek warrior and chief William Weatherford challenged the notorious gambler and sportsman Wild Bill Thurman to a wrestling match when he discovered Thurman passing through his territory. Thurman repeatedly threw the surprised chief with ease. Weatherford then suggested they try boxing instead. Thurman agreed and proceeded to pummel Weatherford until he conceded defeat. The men emerged from their encounter with friendship born of mutual admiration. They remained friends throughout the war and visited each other many times after the conflict subsided.[30] These interactions demonstrate how shared moments of violence could create oddly shaped connections between men from very different backgrounds.

In the years after Molineaux's defeat, African Americans continued to work as the transnational spreaders of fighting techniques.[31] Black sailors serving with the American Navy practiced an eclectic style of pugilism influenced by concepts from England, the United States, South America, and Africa.[32] They transmitted these styles everywhere they went, and may have even introduced the sport of kickboxing to France during this period.[33] African American sailors imprisoned at Dartmoore Prison in England set up a boxing school where they trained their white comrades. White and black men trained together in the prison and shared daydreams of winning celebrity in the ring.[34] The primary instructor of boxing at Dartmoore Prison, King Dick Crafus, a towering African American sailor with a thickly muscled physique, became the undisputed leader of white and black prisoners of war at Dartmoore.[35] Like Micah Taul on the Kentucky frontier, Crafus appears to have used his capacity for violence as a path to leadership. After the war, Crafus turned his recreation into a profession, setting up a popular boxing school in Boston after the war and spreading knowledge of boxing.[36]

With the close of hostilities between the United States and Great Britain in 1815, the transoceanic exchange of fight sports opened again in earnest, expanding outward from the prisoner of war camps and into the rapidly

Two sailors, tied to a chest suspended between their legs, are about to begin boxing; several other sailors and some loosely attired women observe the match. In the background, a dancing man explains, "I love a bit of hop—Life is ne'ar the worst for it. When in my way to drop—a Fiddle—that's your sort." Meanwhile, a bottle-holding woman encourages one of the fighters to "Rraileup his Peepers." Published in London by Thos. Tegg, July 13, 1812 (Library of Congress Prints and Photographs Division).

growing cities of the United States. Boxing spread to the United States on resurgent transatlantic trade networks that bridged the gaps between the old world and the new.[37] New ideas were transported not only by black sailors such as King Dick Crafus, but also by an emerging sporting press. The English author Pierce Egan was one of the first writers to promote boxing beginning in 1812 with the first edition of his book *Boxiana*.[38] The book began appearing in the United States just a few years after the War of 1812 concluded.[39] British fighters came to America along with British books and set the stage for the birth of formalized boxing in the United States.

On October 15, 1816, two men attempted to settle a quarrel and accidently became two of the founding fathers of American boxing. For reasons lost to history, Jacob Hyer, a bartender from New York, and Tom Beasely, a sailor from England, found themselves in the midst of a conflict which they felt required a violent resolution.[40] The situation was nothing new to the young nation, but their method of violent resolution was unprecedented. They decided to adhere to the Broughton Rules of prizefighting, which were popular in Europe but had been ignored in the United States up to that point. This fight was also unique in that it was one of the first boxing contests in America witnessed by a large crowd who gathered to see the fight.[41] Sources disagree on the outcome: it was either a draw, or Hyer won, or Beasley won, or the two men walked away as friends with no formal resolution to the affair.[42] Few people of the time took notice of the event, and no surviving account gives any indication that anyone present saw it as a momentous event. The fight took on significance only in the decades that followed, as boxing began to emerge from the anonymous periphery of American culture. The contest between Hyer and Beasley matters because the sports fans, competitors, and historians eventually decided that it mattered. They looked back and agreed that this was the moment when boxing took its first steps out of the shadows and began its arduous march toward the spotlight in the United States.[43]

Hyer's fight with Beasley provides a dramatic moment in the advance of boxing, but it was part of a larger pattern of shifts in masculine associations with fight sports. In Philadelphia, a man calling himself simply Mr. Gray began offering courses in fencing, stick fighting, and pugilistic self-defense to "respectable gentlemen" (indicating boundaries both of class and gender) who were worried about their personal safety.[44] Mr. Gray's offer was almost identical to those of British instructors dating back to the legendary James Figg of nearly a century before, which promoted boxing as only one aspect of a blend of fighting arts.[45] In the same city, an author compared various modes of unarmed combat and praised English boxing as a manly and virtuous sport that was conducted under honorable rules, once again connecting gender and honor to fight sports, in contrast to the "anything goes" fights prevalent in America and many parts of Great Britain.[46] American journalists began suggesting that boxing-style training might provide a healthful exercise regimen for men.[47] Boxing also spread to American schools, joining the older recreations of ball games and wrestling.[48] While boxing was making some gains, however, it was still a fringe sport mostly practiced in the nation's few urban areas.[49]

While boxing received unprecedented praise in the years after the War of 1812, it continued to face harsh criticism from critics. The criticisms indicate all indicate that culture—not profit—stood at the center of shifts in fight sports since they based distinctions on masculine ideals and not economics. An article in a Philadelphia newspaper condemned the recent interest in boxing as savage and indecent.[50] John Bristed, writing from New York, took pride in his claim that Americans had largely left the savage sports of cockfighting, bull-baiting, and pugilism behind in Europe, thus identifying a distinctly American culture; he suggested Americans had embraced the more peaceful amusements of dance and music in their place.[51] An encyclopedia published in the United States defined boxing as a barbaric pastime dating back to the Romans and popularized by the English, once again connecting fight sports to national culture.[52] A Connecticut author argued that boxing, while once common in the state, had been entirely eliminated by recent religious revivals.[53] In an attempt to explain his nation to the rest of the world, an American diplomat admitted that North Carolinians enjoyed boxing matches along with cockfights, horse racing, and gambling. However, he argued that even North Carolinians were making progress, becoming more educated and civilized while abandoning the rough practices once prevalent in the state, thereby suggesting that violence and gentlemanly behavior were often perceived as oppositional pursuits.[54] A guidebook for justices of the peace in the same state reminded the reader that boxing and sword fighting were illegal and instructed officials to treat deaths resulting from such contests as manslaughter.[55] In Baltimore, a journalist reported with some disgust that a man had recently died in England in one of the boxing matches held for the delight of the English nobility.[56] These accounts indicate that boxing faced opposition even as its popularity began to build.

Unlike boxing, wrestling received almost universal praise and support from elites and remained America's favorite fight sport in the early 19th century. The American military continued to promote wrestling, requiring soldiers and sailors to wrestle as part of their training. Native Americans enjoyed wrestling, and white observers praised them for their devotion to the art.[57] American physicians explained that wrestling, along with running, leaping, and swimming, offered a healthful exercise regimen. They urged educators to expand school physical education programs.[58] Wrestling—particularly Jacob's biblical wrestling match with an angel—provided a constant source for sermons and religious hymns which reinforced the sport's connection to the divine. Religious officials often encouraged their congregations to wrestle like Jacob, a figure of speech that blurred the lines between spiritual and athletic struggles. All of these influences helped wrestling maintain its cultural dominance. Wrestling's positive cultural connections allowed it to remain a violent outlet that did not jeopardize men's social status. A traveler on the Ohio frontier argued that prizefights were still unknown in much of America in 1817, but stated that wrestling was very popular.[59] In England, in contrast, boxing was well known, but under attack.

Boxing always existed on the rough fringes of British society, and reinvigorated Christianity and class conflicts pushed it even further from the center. Evangelical Christians consistently criticized boxing as a brutal amusement.[60] This was part of a broader trend in which moralizing reformers demanded a rejection of sinful pleasures.[61] In 1820, an Englishman, speaking to an American traveler, claimed that while young British gentlemen had once studied boxing as a method of self-defense, recent improvements in public morality had made those skills unnecessary. Boxing had long offered a rare place of interaction across traditional cultural boundaries dating back at least to the Roman games. Gathered around the ring, upper-class nobles cheered for the working-class fighters they supported financially. English boxing was always an alliance of poor and rich men at its core, but even middle-class lawyers and clerks entered the crowds, rubbing shoulders with people far higher and lower in the social world than themselves. Some members of the increasingly powerful English middle class took offense at the ring's alliance of rich and poor. They also feared that large crowds encouraged violent mobs that might challenge the established social order. One observer candidly suggested that the anonymity of the crowd tended to encourage people to act boldly.[62] In 1821, the Massachusetts Peace Society noted with approval that English members of the upper and middle classes were embracing polite society and leaving boxing to only the lowest class.[63]

A series of scandals in the 1820s assisted in the continuous decline of boxing in Britain. The Prince of Wales, who had long patronized boxing, ended his financial support of boxers in an effort to wash his hands of the sport when he witnessed the death of a man in the ring.[64] John Thurtell, a fight promoter, went to the gallows in 1824, convicted at the conclusion of a widely publicized trial for murdering a gambling associate.[65] Reformers succeeded in passing new laws and encouraging more vigorous enforcement of existing laws.[66] The authorities started breaking up fights and arresting pugilists. Fans, who often walked many miles to attend a fight only to have it broken up before it began, started giving up on the sport.[67] Fighters responded to scandal and persecution by attempting to regulate the sport beginning in the late 1820s, but by this time they had already lost elite support. Lower-class reformers, acting without powerful allies, lacked the legal authority or financial resources to enforce standards.[68]

Under the combined weight of evangelical crusaders, reinvigorated police departments, and a lack of financial support, pugilists found a more receptive populace in rapidly growing American cities. Pugilists traveled to America as part of the larger migration of working-class immigrants from the British Isles.[69] Large numbers of Irish, long known for their love of pugilism, started coming to the United States for the first time in the 1820s.

These poor immigrants with few skills, little money, and few options made new lives in the rapidly growing cities of the United States. Between 1820 and 1830, the population of New York nearly doubled—growing from 123,706 to 202,589.[70] Boston grew at a similar rate, expanding from 43,000 to 61,000 in the same decade.[71] Recent immigrants from England and Ireland made up a large part of the increase in both areas. The new immigrants performed grueling labor for little pay, lived in absolute poverty, and enjoyed alcohol, gambling, and bare-knuckle boxing. These recent arrivals provided a safe haven for pugilists no longer welcome in the old country. By the mid-1830s, New York's large population of immigrant men, and its numerous commercial enterprises devoted to entertaining these men, including sporting newspapers, brothels, and gambling halls, made the city the undisputed center for boxing in the United States.[72] An English newspaper noted with alarm that Americans were developing a taste for pugilism.[73]

Migrating men brought a love of boxing to an America increasingly open to pugilism and British understandings of masculinity. Some British men claimed boxing as the exclusive property of their nation.[74] Nineteenth-century British pugilists saw themselves as ambassadors of a particularly British vision of national pride that reveled in its skill with unarmed combat.[75] Throughout the empire, loyal subjects looked to boxing as a method of proving British superiority.[76] English writers such as the novelist George Borrow promoted this idea in widely read works of fiction.[77] A popular 19th-century song in honor of the English champion Tom Cribb expressed English pride in Britons' identity as boxers. In comparison to Italians, "who stab their friends behind in darkest shades of night," the song exclaimed that "Britons they are bold and kind, and box their friends by light."[78] The song highlighted masculine pride claiming, "Since boxing is a manly game, and Britons' recreation; by boxing we will raise our fame, 'bove any other nation."[79] Thus, as Britons immigrated to the United States, they also exported their art.

James "Deaf" Burke, boxing champion of England, was the most highly regarded fighter to come to America as part of this wave of migration. Born in England to Irish parents, he learned boxing as a young man working on the riverboats of the Thames River.[80] He won the championship title in 1832 after defeating Harry Macone.[81] In 1833, he fought Simon Byrne, a contender from Ireland. As the fight wore on, blood poured from Burke's ear which Byrne had bitten, almost severing it from his head.[82] After over three hours of bare-knuckle, ear-biting mayhem, Byrne lay on the ground and conceded defeat. Byrne died shortly afterward and Burke went to trial for his murder. The jury found Burke not guilty based on the testimony of a surgeon who

Satire on the public conflict between Andrew Jackson and Nicholas Biddle over the future of the Bank of the United States, and the former's campaign to destroy it. The print is sympathetic to Jackson, portraying him as the champion of the common man against the moneyed interests of the bank. In the center, Biddle (left) and Jackson square off. Mother Bank, an obese woman holding a bottle of port, stands beside Biddle. Behind her are Biddle supporters Daniel Webster and Henry Clay. On the right are Jackson's supporters: Martin Van Buren, Major Jack Downing, and "Joe Tammany," a frontiersman in buckskins and raccoon cap. All of the observers make remarks to encourage their champion and demoralize his adversary. The caption below the cartoon states, "Nick's weight of metal was superior as well as his science, but neither were sufficient for the pluck and wind of Hickory, who shewed his through training and sound condition so effectually that in the last round Nick was unable to come to time and gave in." Lithograph published in 1834 by Anthony Imbert (Library of Congress Prints and Photographs Division).

suggested that other factors, in addition to the boxing match, might have contributed to Byrne's death.[83] Ironically, Byrne had killed an opponent in the ring in 1830 and barely escaped the hangman's noose with a verdict of not guilty, thus making Byrne one of only a handful of fighters with the dubious honor of involvement in boxing deaths both as accused murderer and victim.[84] Though he avoided the gallows for Byrne's death, Burke remained a highly controversial figure in England, where he endured police harassment that eventually convinced him to travel to America in 1834.[85]

Burke continued his career in the United States. In addition to prizefights, he engaged in scientific demonstrations of the art of self-defense, similar to the exhibitions James Figg had offered in London during the previous century and to those offered by Mr. Gray at about this same time in the United States. Sam O'Rourke—like Byrne, an Irish champion—sent a letter to one of Burke's events, which publicly challenged Burke to fight him for the title.[86] On May 5, 1837, Burke and O'Rourke squared off in New Orleans for the first world championship fight ever held in the Western hemisphere.[87] Burke initially got the better of his opponent, sending O'Rourke into the dirt during the first round. After seeing their champion absorbing punishment for several rounds, the recent Irish immigrants in the crowd charged the ring. Burke used a butcher's knife to cut his way through the enraged crowd, mounted a horse he found nearby, and fled to New York.[88] Burke returned to Britain several years later, but his departure hardly dampened America's interest in boxing, which was gaining in popularity. American newspapers, such as the *Spirit of the Times*, covered boxing while condemning the sport, explaining that they covered it only as a service to their interested readers.[89]

Not every English fighter and fan responded to religious crusades and police harassment by fleeing for America. Some stayed home and tried to reform and popularize boxing. In 1838, a group of fighters and promoters calling themselves the Pugilists Protective Association published the London Rules in an effort to make boxing safer and more widely accepted.[90] In the same year that the Association introduced its rules, Burke fought Bendigo Thompson in the first championship bout under the new standards.[91] The London Rules were not terribly different from the older Broughton's Rules, but rather served primarily to reinforce and elaborate on them, particularly their prohibitions on kicking, biting, gouging, and striking a downed opponent.[92] They, like the earlier Broughton's Rules, allowed for the possibility of gloved matches, even though fighters almost never utilized the option. They did, however, bring about some unique, if minor, changes. These included the adoption of a standard 24-foot ring and the requirement that fighters stand at center ring after a knockdown to demonstrate their capacity to continue the fight.[93] The London Rules dominated the boxing scene for most of the century in spite of the introduction of the Marquis of Queensbury Rules in 1865; the latter did not become widely used until the end of the 19th century.[94] The London Rules quickly crossed the Atlantic. By 1842, American newspapers mentioned the new rules, referring to their fairness, and some

II. Boxing Takes Root in the United States, 1607–1810   61

boxers fought under their guidelines.[95] Even new rules did not immediately propel boxing into the mainstream, however. It remained an illegal sport at the margin, even if the margin was proving an increasingly viable economic and cultural space.[96]

Boxing gained ground at the urban margins because of unique demographics and geographies. Population density often determined the dominant fight sport in communities. Irish immigrants into New York became boxers rather than wrestlers, almost without exception, while those who made homes in rural Vermont wrestled rather than boxed with even fewer exceptions.[97] Boxing always was, and remains forever, a sport of the city. Population even affected sports within cities. Baseball prospered on the edges of urban areas where open spaces allowed for the construction of baseball fields. In contrast, boxing's minimal space requirements made it an amusement of the most crowded urban neighborhoods. Boxing's embrace of the timed round, its rapid pace, and its highly visible action made it ideally suited to fighters from industrialized workplaces familiar with these realities in their jobs.[98] Crowds of working-class, immigrant, and urban men provided virtually the only islands of rough masculine resistance to the waves of evangelical crusades, known as the Second Great Awakening, which swept the United States and mostly eliminated the already limited practice of boxing in rural areas.[99]

Wrestling, in contrast, was a sport of rural spaces. Across every time and place, wrestling was always an essentially agrarian sport.[100] The sport's traditional emphasis on competition until victory and its subtle techniques only visible to spectators close to the action made it more suited to fighters familiar with working until the work was done and spectators in small groups who could get an up-close view of the action. Wrestling was always a much slower sport in which tired or overmatched fighters could stalemate their opponents, thereby preventing defeat for themselves while boring audiences.[101] Wrestling, unlike boxing, received praise rather than anger from religious officials.[102] Throughout American history, wrestling, even as it made forays into the cities, always radiated out from farming communities—areas where it held out even as the nation as a whole turned to other amusements.[103]

Wrestling's reputation may have benefited from its connections to the masculine virtues of farming. Nineteenth-century journalists held up farmers as "honorable," "patriotic," "useful," "virtuous," athletic," "healthy," "and manly."[104] Thomas Jefferson's writings, including his claims that "cultivators of the earth are the most virtuous and independent of citizens," were repeatedly reprinted during the 19th century.[105] The state legislature of Michigan quoted Benjamin Franklin's declaration that agriculture was an honorable and genteel occupation.[106] Nineteenth-century journals devoted to farming reinforced the connection between agrarian values and wrestling, referring to the sport as respectable and manly.[107] As Americans migrated away from farms and toward the nation's growing urban areas, however, America underwent social upheavals, and the nation's leaders worried that the demographic shift would bring negative changes to the nation.

In last years of the 18th century and the first years of the 19th century, a series of revivals, most often referred to as the Second Great Awakening, swept the United States, creating social movements and shifting masculine identities.[108] The movement encouraged American men and women to abandon earthly pleasures and focus on spiritual perfection. The movement's ideals became highly influential, radiating out from the churches and shaping even the ideals of Americans who rarely attended church. Converts became the nucleus of social reform movements opposing slavery, alcohol, and violence.[109] As part of this shift, men, particularly in the South, were forced to take sides between a fighting masculinity that reveled in violence and a praying masculinity that valued men as sober servants of Christ.[110] Many American men, but certainly not all, became converts to the new movement.[111] The revivals of the Second Great Awakening largely succeeded in eliminating the always controversial styles of rough boxing and gouging from rural America.[112] This allowed wrestling to prosper as the only remaining fight sport with broad support and limited boxing's gains.

Wrestling grew at the same time as boxing and for some of the same reasons. Immigrants—particularly those from Ireland—who made homes in America's expanding cities became boxers and boxing fans. Their counterparts who built lives in rural areas wrestled and helped to popularize distinctly Irish forms of grappling.[113] By 1839, the American press devoted coverage to tournaments of Irish-style collar and elbow wrestling.[114] The Cornish also began to develop a reputation as wrestlers. Wrestling continued to offer a rare point of communion for Native Americans and whites. Stories circulated that some tribes told stories similar to that of Jacob wrestling the angel.[115] In California, the Frazier River Indians earned praise from white settlers for their skills in the wrestling ring and their virtuous tendency to defend themselves violently, in contrast to pacifistic tribes.[116] A biography of George Washington, published in 1833, reinforced the sport's connection to the father of the nation and to the virtue of the founders more generally.[117] On the frontier, wrestling also provided young men with an opportunity for social advancement. In 1832, Abraham Lincoln won his first political victory when he demonstrated his courage and skills in the wrestling ring to a group of young men who helped him win election to the state legislature.[118] The sport began to make some inroads into the cities as well, and gyms offering lessons in wrestling, fencing, and pugilism opened in New York City.[119] Although wrestling never received the same quantity of venom directed at boxing, a few Americans viewed the sport with disdain. At least one physician referred to wrestling and boxing as two examples of English brutality and vulgarity.[120]

Boxing remained primarily the sport of urban, poor, and marginalized men during the mid–19th century. Almost without exception, pugilists came from the ranks of the poorest portions of the working class, and were often recent immigrants.[121] Famine in Ireland during the 1840s convinced millions to depart the Emerald Isle, and the majority of them came to the United States. During the years from 1840 to 1860, 56.3 percent of boxers in New York were born in Ireland, 15.6 percent had parents born in Ireland, and 18.8 percent were born in England.[122] Many of the Irish- and English-born pugilists competed in Europe before coming to America. Observers often described boxers as poor and suggested that promoters used money to lure fighters to commit crimes.[123] Even the most successful boxers found it difficult to make a living in the ring and frequently supplemented their income by working for wealthy, politically connected men who employed them as bodyguards, bouncers, and to intimidate political opponents.[124] When the famous fighter Johnny Broome committed suicide by slitting his own throat at the age of 38, his obituary noted that while he had once earned a significant sum of money, he died penniless after years of suffering from alcoholism and brain damage.[125]

The recent immigrants were not the only poor and marginalized men in American boxing rings; many pugilists traced their lineage to slavery rather than famine. Plantation owners continued to train slaves in boxing. William Johnson, a free black man in Mississippi who kept a diary from 1835 to 1852, reported several public boxing matches in and around Natchez, Mississippi.[126] Similar to the pattern playing out in urban cities of the North, wealthy slave owners in the South used their pugilists as bodyguards and as tools of vengeance.[127] A traveler to Pensacola, Florida, told New York readers of Lorenzo, a free black man respected in the community as a successful merchant and talented pugilist.[128] The presence of some boxing matches in the plantations of rural America does not undermine the vision of boxing as a primarily urban sport, but rather serves to demonstrate that the history of fight sports offers few absolutes. Pugilists of African descent, beginning with Bill Richmond and Tom Molineaux, sought glory in the ring by leaving rural life behind for the boxing cities of New York and London, demonstrating their recognition of the urban space as the pugilist's natural habitat, if not their only possible home. In 1842, two former slaves, Dan Knox and Sam Briggs, faced off in New York under the London Rules for the title of the finest boxer of their race in the state.¹²⁹ An African American fighter known as "Negro Benson" earned recognition for helping to popularize boxing in American cities and praise for his unique system of boxing in which he parried his opponent's blows with his hands, rather than absorb them with his arms like most fighters.¹³⁰ Unlike in England, where men of African descent had fought whites dating back to Bill Richmond during the American Revolution, in America boxers competed only within boundaries defined by race. This practice distinguished American and British boxing life, even as both nations began to embrace some shared ideas on pugilism, including acceptance of the London Rules.¹³¹ American critics of boxing pointed out with disgust that white boxing fans kept company with black men.¹³²

It was not a black man, but rather a globe-traveling Irishman, who arrived in America in 1846, challenged American manhood, and helped popularize boxing as a test of nations as well as of men. James Ambrose, who achieved fame as James Sullivan (one of his many aliases), was born near Cork, Ireland, on April 12, 1813.¹³³ After spending several years as a petty criminal and pugilist in Europe, he traveled to the United States in an effort to elude British authorities. In America, he used his well-developed skills to defeat several top-ranked American fighters.¹³⁴ Observers accused Sullivan of misconduct, and American papers printed claims that Sullivan repeatedly struck a downed opponent in clear violation of the rules—charges that Sullivan adamantly denied. Angered by the newcomer, long-time residents began looking for an American-born fighter to take down the upstart.¹³⁵ The desire for an American to defeat the foreigner played out against a backdrop of nativist sentiments that also included the rise of the Know Nothing political movement. Tom Hyer, son of the well-known pugilist Jacob Hyer and a man widely regarded as the finest boxer in America, agreed to take on the Irishman with the unsavory reputation for the pride of his nation and a $10,000 payday.¹³⁶ The purse of $10,000 was a huge sum in an era when a worker did well to make $300 in a year. To assemble the cash, fighters turned to supporters and patrons who agreed to provide the funds.¹³⁷

Unlike the informal fight Hyer's father got into with a visitor from Europe, the son's bout against Sullivan was a carefully scripted affair. The emerging sporting press, which had proliferated as the new technology of the double-cylinder press decreased publishing costs, helped the fighters agree on conditions and kept them in contact with their fans.¹³⁸ The fighters agreed to use the newest edition of rules published in the book *Fistiana* in the same year.¹³⁹ Journalists visited both men in their training camps and related detailed descriptions of their bodies, diets, and training regimens. Gamblers began placing bets weeks in advance, and the papers dutifully reported on the odds. The *Police Gazette* estimated that $300,000 was on the line for the fight, and the *New York Sun* reported individual wagers as high as $40,000.[140] *The Spirit of the Times* even published a poem that referenced the coming bout.[141]

On February 7, 1849, Hyer, Sullivan, and around 200 fans dodged the Maryland authorities, came ashore in Kent County, and prepared for action.[142] Hyer carried an American flag, while Sullivan waved a banner of green. Hyer won the contest and received the full $10,000 purse.[143] Maryland later convicted Hyer of assault and battery for the fight and fined him $1,000.[144] Patrick Timothy, author of *The American Fistiana*, lauded Hyer as a national champion who demonstrated himself to be the equal of any man in the United States or Britain. He urged Hyer to become an even greater champion by leaving the ring and embracing a life of peace[145]—a suggestion which indicated that even boxing fans considered the sport disreputable. Hyer took that course of action, retiring from the ring and becoming a prominent figure in New York politics with the Know Nothings and then the Republicans, before dying in 1864 at the age of 44.[146]

The contest between Hyer and Sullivan represented an important moment in the history of American fight sports. Unlike the fight between Hyer's father and Beasley, which seemed of little consequence in the moment, people understood the significance of Hyer's fight with Sullivan before it even occurred.[147] It was not just a clash of men, but of nations and ethnicities. Emerging nativists who feared Catholics and foreigners solidly supported the native-born Tom Hyer. His victory made him a national hero.[148] The fight became as well known as the Declaration of Independence.[149] It attracted unprecedented attention from the middle class for the historically working-class sport.[150] The walls of mid-19th-century New York bars were often bare except for mirrors and pictures of Hyer and Sullivan facing off.[151] In 1850, *The Knickerbocker* listed Hyer's bout with Sullivan as one of the four greatest stories of the last few years.[152] The fight, with its nationalistic overtones, increased public interest in boxing to an unprecedented level.[153]

Boxing gained some ground at midcentury in the United States, but the critics never faltered in their condemnation of the sport. As in England, fight fans faced legal problems, and boxing was illegal throughout the United States.[154] Tom Hyer was not the only pugilist who faced conviction: men who entered the ring often endured arrest on an array of charges.[155] Moralizing critics argued that the taverns which held fights were houses of sin, poverty, death, and desperation. They compared prizefighting to the gladiatorial games of ancient Rome and called the sport barbaric. A writer for a religious journal argued that boxing was one of the many evil habits that boys were prone to commit and urged parents to use a hearty dose of Christian discipline to correct their behavior.¹⁵⁶

The reformers faced increasing resistance on the eve of Civil War as proponents of boxing, such as Thomas Hughes in *Tom Brown's School Days*, presented an alternative vision of masculinity and boxing in which pugilism was a sport with the power to improve the minds, bodies, and souls of young Christian gentlemen. Thomas Hughes' work helped to popularize the concept of muscular Christianity on both shores of the Atlantic, promoting an idealized masculinity in which athletics provided a strong body in tandem with a pious soul.¹⁵⁷ Muscular Christianity differed from previous movements, which were largely pacifistic, in its assertion that Christian men could engage in well-regulated violence in support of the national interest in both sport

The familiar metaphor of the presidential contest as a boxing match is invoked once again. The scene is set in an open field, roped off behind to make a ring. Republican candidate Frémont (right) squares off against Democrat James Buchanan (left), after the latter has felled American Party nominee Millard Fillmore. Buchanan warns Frémont, "Look out now Young Mariposa for that hair on your face I will put in the 'Right' when you least expect it!" Frémont replies, "Come to time, Old Buck, I think I can lick a Democrat as old again as you are!" Frémont steps over the fallen Fillmore, who says, "You see, Fremont, I'm down! There must be a good many drops of 'Democratic Blood' in that arm of Old Buck's to strike such a stunning blow!" Buchanan is seconded by an Irishman (far left), who comments, "By Jabbers but Old Bucky knocks 'em." Frémont is supported by a Bowery type (crouching at far right), who urges him, "Go in wooly Hoss don't be afeard." The print was probably issued in summer 1856 or later in the election campaign, after Fillmore's prospects for victory had dimmed (Library of Congress Prints and Photographs Division).

and warfare.[158] An article in the *New York Times* eventually stood against this growing tide and argued that athleticism was fine, but that boxing's inexorable connections to gambling and con artists made it muscular heathenism, not muscular Christianity. The author speculated that historians of the 21st century would find newspapers which printed the names of boxing champions alongside presidents to be very interesting documents, and that those historians would correctly deduce that boxing was a popular sport for many people in both Great Britain and the United States. However, he argued that the public's enthusiasm for pugilism would soon fade before the light of Christianity.[159]

By the time that these predictions were made, the nation's attention was already beginning to turn inward. Stories of conflicts over slavery and sectional conflict appeared next to accounts of championship fights.[160] Stories of the ring gave way to stories of battle, at least for a moment.

After years of sectarian conflict over slavery, trade, and Western expansion, a war broke out in 1861 that eventually resulted in the prohibition of slavery, a renewed sense of American national identity, and increased popularity for fight sports. Wars always bring men together, and this conflict was no different.[161] The Civil War placed large numbers of young men from different races, national origins, regions, and classes in close contact for the first time.[162] The armies provided these men with long periods of boredom, which they often filled with sports. Military leaders, seeking to transform civilians into soldiers, drew on the long historical connections of fight sports as martial training to train men and turn them into soldiers. A lack of trained officers convinced Congress to support the creation of numerous universities, which promoted fight sports as well as education.[163] Observers occasionally compared the war to the ring, borrowing the language of sport to explain the conflict.

Melting pots of young men often result in exchanges of fight sports, and the Civil War was no different. Civil War camps facilitated the flow of sport across regional boundaries.[164] Irish immigrants, recently settled in rural Vermont, brought their distinctive style of collar and elbow wrestling when they rushed to defend the nation.[165] Perhaps their greatest champion was George Flagg of the 2nd Vermont Infantry regiment, a farmer and gifted fighter before the war who quickly established himself as the Army of the Potomac's wrestling champion in a series of hard-fought matches.[166] Many veterans took up the styles of wrestling they witnessed while in uniform and continued to practice them after the conflict.[167] Some pugilists entered the service somewhat more reluctantly than the Vermont Irish, joining the army in exchange for release from jail. Once in uniform, boxers spread their art among their

A pro–Breckinridge satire on the 1860 presidential contest. Republican candidate Abraham Lincoln (right) and Democrat Stephen A. Douglas (left) appear as boxers squaring off in a ring before a small crowd of onlookers. Douglas is seconded by an Irishman (left), presumably representing Douglas's Democratic constituency. Lincoln is coached by a black man, who kneels at right, armed with a basket of liquor bottles, and signifies Lincoln's antislavery leanings. In the background, a third candidate, John C. Breckinridge, thumbs his nose and points toward the White House. He is encouraged on his way by a number of men who cheer and doff their hats to him. Published during the 1860 election, probably in Cincinnati, Ohio (Library of Congress Prints and Photographs Division).

comrades and facilitated its proliferation. Alonzo Hill of the 8th Pennsylvania Reserves noted that sports were extremely common among soldiers; after witnessing a gloved boxing match, apparently for the first time, he decided to try the sport for himself.[168] Gloved pugilism became a fad among bored soldiers of the 149th Pennsylvania Volunteer Infantry in winter quarters before the war's final campaign.[169] A British observer noted that by the end of the war, Union soldiers commonly spent their off-duty hours engaged in rough boxing matches.[170]

Neither the flow of young men into uniform nor the presence of sporting contests in military camps eliminated civilian contests, which continued during the conflict. In 1864, the Cremorne Garden Theatre in New York put on an extravaganza featuring dancing contests, sparring exhibitions, and silver

II. Boxing Takes Root in the United States, 1607–1810   69

Two Union soldiers strike a boxing pose for the camera while other soldiers look on. This image was cropped from an original photograph produced in a federal army camp near Petersburg, Virginia, in April 1865 (Library of Congress Prints and Photographs Division).

cups to the winners of collar and elbow wrestling matches.[171] Newspapers continued to report on boxing matches in England. In January 1864, the *Abingdon Virginian* took a moment away from the quickly deteriorating Confederate military situation to report the victory of the English pugilist Tom King over John Heenan.[172] Weeks later, a Louisiana newspaper, which in 1861 had urged Southern mothers to act like Spartan women, lamented the worthlessness of modern people and declared them incapable of anything approaching the martial virtues of Spartan women who wrestled and boxed like men.[173] In Kansas, a man lost a pugilistic contest to a woman, although the fight was probably more assault than sport.[174] An English war correspondent expressed stunned disbelief that many Americans expressed more interest in reliving the boxing matches than in discussing the war.[175]

Fight sports possess connections to military training dating back to ancient history, and officers drew on these traditions as part of training regimens. The officers of General Hancock's brigade encouraged soldiers to engage in such traditionally military sports as running, leaping, and wrestling.[176] A 72-year-old Mississippi soldier became a camp celebrity by challenging younger men to prove themselves by wrestling him.[177] Wrestling had a long connection to war in the American mind, but the Civil War was the first time many Americans extended that connection to boxing.[178] The ring, like war itself, gave glory to those who demonstrated toughness, aggression, and stoicism.

Leaders worried that many young men of the era would make poor soldiers and began promoting physical education in schools in hopes that future generations would fare better. Congressional leaders supported the creation and expansion of universities, which promoted fight sports as part of a well-rounded education. The 1862 Morrill Act provided support for future athletic and academic powerhouses including Penn State, the University of Michigan, and Ohio State.[179] In 1862, Edward L. Molineaux, a major and inspector in

The American boxing champion John C. Heenan, also known as "The Benicia Boy," knocks an unnamed opponent, who might be the English pugilist Tom Sayers, to the ground while a large crowd looks on. Tobacco promotional image, published in 1860 (Library of Congress Prints and Photographs Division).

II. Boxing Takes Root in the United States, 1607–1810   71

the New York state militia, argued that nations of the strong and vigorous always surpassed the weak. He urged the United States to embrace the trusted wisdom of Rome and Greece and encourage its boys to take up vigorous sports such as wrestling as a patriotic duty.[180] In 1863, John Swett, the superintendent of the Department of Public Instruction, made a similar argument, reporting to the California legislature that the war made the need for school sporting programs obvious. He argued that the Romans and Greeks understood this lesson long ago, turning their boys into men with vigorous exercise programs. Swett urged the legislators to make ball games, jumping, wrestling, and boxing a required aspect of the state's public school curriculum to ensure victory in future wars.[181] Weeks after the war ended, a South Carolina writer agreed, arguing that the authorities should promote fencing, boxing, and wrestling for young men and women while ensuring that no hard liquor was sold within a mile of any sporting event.[182]

Writers often turned to the language of fight sports in an effort to explain the violence of the battlefield. The use of this language indicates the popularity of fight sports, since they obviously assumed their readers would understand the explanations, and helped to solidify connections between the violence born of fun or profit and that flowing from patriotic duty. The *New York Daily Tribune*'s coverage of the battle of Antietam described the armies locked together as wrestlers, pushing, pulling, and straining to exert dominance.[183] A commentator for the *Chicago Tribune* attempted to explain the controversies over the treatment of prisoners of war to his readers by pointing out that war, like wrestling, requires two contestants to play.[184] Years after the conflict, former Tennessee soldier Sam Watkins attempted to describe the war as a gouging match between Jefferson Davis and Abraham Lincoln.[185] At the close of the Civil War, with the game of war over, the men went home and the reinvigorated nation gave birth to a modern sporting culture to rival anything it had known before.[186]

In 1865, two men desperate to save boxing changed it forever. John Graham Chambers and John Shoto Douglas, the 9th Marques of Queensbury, were the owners of a club for amateur pugilists in London. They faced a problem: boxing was a sport on the absolute fringe of British society. Fans and competitors risked the possibility of arrest, robbery, and assault when they came to boxing matches.[187] They also faced condemnation from the many Britons who viewed boxing as immoral and brutal. Douglas and Chambers realized that the sport must change, so they constructed a new set of rules for use in their club, which they hoped would provide a model for other enthusiasts. They differed from the earlier London Rules in several key ways. The Queensbury Rules ended rounds after an arbitrary three-minute time

EMP. NAPOLEON.—*Whip him, Secesh, and when I get Mexico, I'll help you whip him again.*
JOHN BULL.—*Down with him, Secesh—burn his Ships—destroy his Commerce—England has plenty more such clubs for you.*
SECESH.—*I'll fix him—I'll kill him.*
U. S. SOLDIER.—*The flag of my country trampled under foot—the ships of my countrymen burning on the ocean—while I stand here entangled in the coils of this foul Copperhead, and so bound up by Constitutional restraints, that I am unable to put forth my true strength in their behalf.*

limit rather than after a fighter dropped, as earlier rules had done.[188] This made boxing matches uniform and predictable since the clock, rather than the fighters, dictated the pace of work and rest. The new guidelines also forbid all wrestling techniques.[189] The shift away from wrestling once again took control away from the fighters, making it more difficult for them to stalemate as they could in wrestling or in forms of boxing that allowed wrestling techniques. It also made the bouts more conducive to mass spectacles since fans, particularly those with little knowledge of fighting, often found wrestling boring to watch or difficult to discern from distant stands but could more readily see and thrill to punching exchanges.[190]

The final key distinction between the new rules and the old was also the most visible. The Queensbury Rules required that pugilists wear padded boxing gloves at all times.[191] These gloves typically consisted of a leather shell stuffed with several ounces of horsehair.[192] Gloves were nothing new to boxing: ancient Greek and Roman boxers wore various forms of glove-like hand protectors in their boxing matches.[193] James "Deaf" Burke, an earlier boxing champion of England, occasionally wore padded gloves for sparring exhibitions in the 1830s, as did many others.[194] Gloves, more than any other single visual clue, provided a symbolic distinction to competitors and fans that differentiated a rough-and-tumble fight among members of the lower classes from an exhibition of scientific pugilism performed by gentlemen. Gloves also made it more difficult for fighters to grab each other, which helped propel boxing's divergence away from wrestling. Making gloves a required component of boxing matches made it possible for many middle- and upper-class men to enjoy the sport without necessarily damaging their status. In a stroke of genius, Douglas and Chambers created a code of conduct that changed the sport in superficial ways that made it more palatable without altering its

Opposite: **Print published by Oliver Evans Woods in 1863, reflecting grave Northern fears of British and French interference on behalf of the Confederacy in the Civil War. In the center, Jefferson Davis—here called "Secesh"—raises a club labeled "Pirate Alabama" over the head of a brawny Union soldier whose arms are constricted by the Constitution, and around whose waist and legs coils a poisonous snake. Davis tramples on an American flag. At right stands a leering John Bull, who holds a pile of clubs in reserve for Davis. Behind him is a prancing Napoleon III, also watching the contest. In the distance, two ships burn on the ocean. Napoleon: "Whip him, Secesh, and when I get Mexico, I'll help you whip him again." John Bull: "Down with him, Secesh—burn his Ships—destroy his Commerce—England has plenty more such clubs for you." Secesh: "I'll fix him—I'll kill him." Soldier: "The flag of my country trampled underfoot—the ships of my country burning on the ocean—while I stand here entangled in the coils of this foul Copperhead, and so bound up by Constitutional restraints, that I am unable to put forth my true strength in their behalf." The "restraints" mentioned may refer to opposition on constitutional grounds to Lincoln's use of what he considered valid presidential war powers. The cartoon may have been specifically occasioned by the Supreme Court's review in the "Prize Cases" of 1863 of the legality of the Union blockade. "Copperhead" was the derogatory term used for anti–Lincoln or anti–Republican advocates of a negotiated reconciliation with the South (Library of Congress Prints and Photographs Division).**

The Civil War illustrated as a fight between two men. A Union soldier, followed by an African American in broken chains, hurls Jefferson Davis (dressed as a woman), who drops a bag of "stolen gold" over the edge of a cliff; Satan waits below the cliff with a pitchfork. The "last ditch" might have referred to the *New York Herald* headline that announced, in part, of Davis's capture, "He Fails to Imitate Booth and Die in the Last Ditch. His Ignominious Surrender." Lithograph designed by Burgoo Zac and published in 1865 (Library of Congress Prints and Photographs Division).

essential character or its visceral appeal.[195] These reforms were not entirely the product of Douglas and Chambers, but rather a conglomeration and official codification of the rules used for many years in friendly sparring matches.[196] Fighters did not immediately embrace the new rules; change took time. The Queensbury Rules were not widely adopted in the United States for nearly three decades.

Poster advertising a vaudeville wrestling act starring the German American Ernst Roeber. The poster refers to Roeber as "the champion," in reference to Roeber's titles as the heavyweight Greco-Roman champion of the United States, Germany, and Europe. Produced by the U.S. Printing Company in Cincinnati, Ohio, during 1898 (Library of Congress Prints and Photographs Division).

In the post–Civil War years, when professional sports were in their infancy and modern entertainments such as movies, television, and radio remained far in the future, traveling circuses provided Americans with their favorite form of mass entertainment.[197] The nomadic shows combined a diverse array of amusements including animal exhibitions, educational displays of scientific oddities, and the thrilling routines of trapeze and tightrope artists. Circuses also included athletic shows, which featured weightlifters and grapplers. For example, P.T. Barnum—probably the most successful and famous American showman in the 19th century—included wrestlers in his shows. In particular, he hired Ed Decker, a seemingly helpless adversary at only 150 pounds and barely five and a half feet tall. Decker, however, had honed his wrestling skills among the Irish immigrants in Vermont. Barnum offered $100 to anyone who could throw Decker from the ring and $50 to anyone who could remain on his feet for three minutes. The little man never lost and Barnum never paid a cent to a challenger.[198]

Although Barnum promoted wrestling, it remained a very small part of

Fraulein Kussin and Mrs. Edwards touch gloves before engaging in a boxing match, circa 1912 (George Grantham Bain Collection, Library of Congress Prints and Photographs Division).

II. Boxing Takes Root in the United States, 1607–1810 77

his business. The greatest promoter of fight sports in the years immediately after the Civil War was undoubtedly a man from Surrey, England.

During his long life, Harry Hill worked as a horse trainer, pugilist, wrestler, and fight promoter. He was best known for his ownership of Harry Hill's, the most famous sporting venue in North America.[199] Hill attempted to create a neutral ground in the culture wars, inviting upper-class customers to enjoy the sporting life in a place he attempted to keep free from the unsavory realities, such as prostitution and riots, that often accompanied 19th-century sporting culture.[200] He strictly forbid all indecent conduct and did not hesitate to expel violators with a nod to his enforcers or with his own viselike grip.[201] Famous Americans including Mark Twain, P.T. Barnum, Thomas Edison, and many others accepted Hill's invitation and became frequent guests.[202] America's richest men rubbed shoulders with a diverse crowd that included lawyers, bankers, merchants, sailors, clerks, beautiful women, and ruffians. Hill's club was one of the must-see sights in New York City, and on any given night most of the customers were visitors to the Big Apple.[203] They came to Harry Hill's to dance, to drink, to watch comedy shows, and to enjoy the best fights in the city.[204] Wrestling and boxing matches provided Harry Hill's most profitable and most famed performances. Hill pushed the boundaries of sport, hosting fights between women not as raucous titillation, but as serious, if novel, athletic competitions.[205] Many of the greatest fighters in America displayed their talents at Harry Hill's for eager crowds.[206]

Men created masculine identities in the rings and before the cheering crowds of Harry Hill's. By attempting to make his sporting house a bastion of propriety, Hill helped promote a vision of American masculinity that was both tough and respectable. A history of public entertainment, published in 1882, noted the presence of "churchly looking gentlemen" who were enthusiastic spectators at Harry Hill's.[207] An 1883 account suggested the sporting events at Harry Hill's were similar to those presented at the nearby Young Men's Christian Association and the New York Athletic Club.[208] When the New York City police began an investigation of Harry Hill's, thousands of business owners and educated professionals signed a petition in support of the establishment.[209] A visit to Harry Hill's was a rite of passage for many young men visiting New York.[210] A guidebook to New York claimed that the club was a favorite topic of conversation in the countryside since nearly every young man who visited the city spent time in there, only to become minor celebrities when they returned home and shared stories of their visit with eager crowds of other young men, indicating that the singular place exerted influence far beyond its immediate geography.[211] Harry Hill's also exerted its influence by providing the nation with icons of masculinity such as John L.

Sullivan, and William Muldoon, a leading light of muscular Christianity known as "the solid man of sport."

Muldoon, more than any other single person, blazed the trail of the respectable professional fighter. Born in 1845 on a New York farm, he went to war with a Civil War cavalry regiment as a teenager.[212] While in uniform, Muldoon learned French-style Greco-Roman wrestling. After Appomattox, he refused to return to the farm and worked as a bouncer at Harry Hill's before beginning his professional wrestling career in the same establishment.[213] He later joined the New York City police force, rising to the rank of detective and gaining fame as the department's finest wrestler in 1878.[214] Muldoon left the force three years later to devote all of his attention to his professional wrestling career.[215] He took a lesson from the circuses, touring the nation with a troupe of athletes, fighting anyone willing to enter the arena.[216] Some of these matches thrilled spectators, but others elicited only yawns as heavily muscled competitors pushed and pulled at a glacial pace in matches that resulted in stalemates. To keep his fans entertained, Muldoon put on boxing exhibitions, dressed in outlandish costumes, and displayed his impressive physique.[217] When no challengers volunteered to box or wrestle with Muldoon, he put on scripted grappling routines with members of his troupe while billing them as serious competitions.[218] After a series of fights against some of the best in the world, he achieved general recognition as the finest Greco-Roman wrestler in the world in 1882.[219] Muldoon fought not only in his preferred Greco-Roman style, but also in mixed-style matches. He eventually defeated challengers from across the United States, Germany, Spain, and Japan before retiring in 1891 as the undisputed world Greco-Roman champion.[220]

Although a gifted fighter, Muldoon's greatest victories came outside the ring. As a man of the farm and of the 19th-century army, he helped bring wrestling from its rural origins and provide it with a home in the city, if a short-lived one. In an era when many Americans viewed professional athletes, and fighters in particular, with suspicion, Muldoon earned their respect with an impressive resume and his embrace of a respectable lifestyle.[221] His time on the police force suggested his separation from the criminal underworld. Health reformers approved of his dedication to a life of clean living and vigorous exercise, consistent with the highest ideals of muscular Christianity. The press frequently quoted Muldoon's thoughts on health and reported that dignitaries including the Secretary of War and the Army Chief of Staff sought out his expertise.[222] He opened a chain of spas, which were some of the first places offering physical therapy.[223] Many Americans also viewed Muldoon as both a moral and a healthful role model.[224] Temperance reformers reported his lifelong rejection of alcohol.²²⁵ The *New York Times* quoted his calls for moral standards in fight sports.²²⁶ Muldoon's embrace of morality and health fit into a larger movement of Americans who were touting the spiritual virtue of sport and provided them with one of their first heroes.

In the 1880s, increasing numbers of Christians in Great Britain and the United States began to seek connections between the athletic and the divine. The hugely popular 1857 Thomas Hughes novel *Tom Brown's School Days* laid the foundation for a new muscular Christianity, which promoted physical exercise as a path to spiritual perfection.²²⁷ Hughes followed up his success with a more direct promotion of the ideal in his 1880 work *The Manliness of Christ*. Spiritual leaders remained aware of temptations such as gambling, prostitution, and alcohol that swirled around sports, but by the 1880s many saw the softening influence of the city as a greater threat to their young men than the temptations of the gymnasium.²²⁸ A Methodist preacher in Rhode Island hired a professional fighter to provide him and his wife with boxing lessons, much to the surprise of several women of his congregation, who dropped by unexpectedly and discovered the minister and his wife sparring in their library.²²⁹ An 1888 self-defense manual described the devoutly Christian pugilist Arthur Weber as a physical embodiment of muscular Christianity.²³⁰ Weber was just one of many fighters who became widely regarded heroes of sport and religion.²³¹ In 1889, an author proclaimed his time as the era of muscular Christianity when young men had cast aside the effeminacy of their fathers and rediscovered the virtuous pugilism of the ancient Greeks.²³² Even preachers began putting on boxing gloves to teach their children the art of self-defense.²³³

The renewed emphasis on sport quickly spread to American colleges and universities. American schools were always scenes of sporting contests, but the athletic programs grew dramatically after the Civil War's end. Collegiate sports grew largely due to the increasing popularity of muscular Christianity.²³⁴ Famed Presbyterian Reverend Dr. Thomas De Witt Talmage presented sermons in which he praised Princeton's faculty for establishing a gymnasium in an attempt to guide—rather than destroy—men's interest in sport. He argued that young men were wasting away and that only sports could save them. Talmage dreamed of a day when every school founded athletic programs like those of Princeton.²³⁵ Theodore Roosevelt was one of many young men who boxed and wrestled at Harvard in the late 1870s.²³⁶ In 1882, Harvard broke new ground in providing official regulations for sports at the university, with the aim of encouraging athletics while ensuring they never interfered with academics.²³⁷ Billy Frazier, a professional boxer, supplemented his income by teaching college students the manly art.²³⁸ On at least one occasion, he reinforced the image of the boxer as a scoundrel when he disappeared after students paid him in advance for lessons.[239]

Some critics derided the new scholastic interest in sports, arguing that sports transformed college students into little more than common ruffians.[240] College sports also did not always translate into civilian life. Some men who boxed while in college gave up the sport when they came home to communities that still regarded pugilism with suspicion.[241] This indicates that boxing continued to face opposition even as its overall popularity increased.

Men banded together to promoted Christian athletics, transforming old organizations and founding new ones. The Young Men's Christian Association (YMCA) began life in 1844 in England as an alliance for spreading the faith, but by the late 1860s it had turned its attention to sport, building gymnasiums in San Francisco and New York.[242] The New York Athletic Club, founded in 1868, began promoting fight sports in 1878 with competitions in fencing, broadswords, wrestling, and pugilism.[243] The New York police department founded its own athletic club and collaborated with the YMCA and various other clubs to put on exhibitions of acrobatics, fencing, gloved boxing, and Greco-Roman wrestling.[244] Churches also began supporting sports directly, with many large congregations opening gyms and hosting sporting competitions in the 1870s.[245] In 1888, the Amateur Athletic Union built an alliance between 14 amateur clubs across Northern cities to standardize rules and promote healthy athleticism.[246] Within weeks, they organized a wrestling tournament.[247] Local YMCA clubs began applying for membership in the union almost immediately.[248] The theologically minded associations continued to draw a hard line between themselves and the seamier side of sport, denying they had anything in common with saloons.[249] Idealistic members of the Boston Athletic Club, along with men trained at Princeton and Harvard, were eager to represent their nation and sent a team to the first modern Olympic Games in 1896. In that forum, the Americans did well in several sports, but choose not to compete in wrestling.[250] Boxing did not become an Olympic sport until the 1904 St. Louis games, when all the competitors were members of the Amateur Athletic Union.[251]

Clubs did not always remain true to their ideals, however. A sparring exhibition at a Philadelphia athletic club ended in a riot after a spectator bashed a rival fan over the head with a chair.[252] The riot once again demonstrated that boxing had not completely shed its criminal past.

While reformers viewed sports as a method of training young men, the nation's sportswriters saw them as a source of revenue. The American press always devoted some attention to sport, but greatly intensified its coverage in the last decades of the 19th century. American sports and American journalism grew up together. Sports coverage attracted readers to the papers, and athletics grew as the papers spread knowledge about sport. The *Spirit of the Times* covered sports, including boxing and wrestling, beginning in 1831.[253] The *New York Clipper* began publication in 1853 and provided extensive coverage of baseball, and occasionally boxing, in the 1860s and 1870s.[254] The *National Police Gazette* was undoubtedly the most important sporting paper in the second half of the 19th century.[255] It began life in 1845 with the expressed purpose of providing the public with information on unsolved crimes in hopes they could help police bring the guilty to justice.[256] The newspaper languished in obscurity for many years, tottering on bankruptcy before Richard Fox, a writer, editor, and showman from Belfast, Ireland, purchased the paper in 1877. He quickly shifted the journal's focus to sports, particularly boxing, and modeled the reorganized journal on English sporting papers.[257] In 1883, Joseph Pulitzer established one of the first separate departments for the coverage of sport in American history for the *New York World*, and a decade later William Randolph Hearst's *New York Journal* developed one of the first separate sport sections in a newspaper.[258] These papers attracted huge numbers of readers, with the *Police Gazette* alone routinely selling 150,000 copies per issue and with a few special issues hitting 400,000 copies.[259] Journalists wrote books as well as articles. Richard Fox wrote boxing manuals, biographies of athletes, and rulebooks.[260] The development and wide circulation of these materials helped to increase knowledge and acceptance of sports in America. Journalists did not just report on the sporting scene—they also became members of the subculture. Sportswriters and editors often visited Harry Hill's to enjoy the various entertainments and meet with athletes.[261]

Demographics affected the nation's sports and gave the press new opportunities for promotion. Immigrants continued to flow into the United States, but in the last years of the 19th century their point of origin shifted, exposing Americans to different fight sports. As the century wore on, European immigrants increasingly came from south and west Europe, rather than from northwest Europe as they had for most of the nation's history.[262] Several hundred thousand Chinese laborers who immigrated to California between 1849 and 1882 provided the United States with its first significant population of Asian immigrants.[263] Whites were somewhat open to the fight sports of groups they discriminated against, such as southern Europeans, Native Americans, and Asians.[264] China was home to a wide variety of martial traditions, but these styles made little inroads even as Chinese immigrants flooded into America. On at least one occasion, Chinese fighters put on an exhibition of punches and kicks, but the American spectators were bored with what they considered the timidity of the competitors.[265] When the Chinese Exclusion Act of 1882 limited Chinese immigration into the United States, Japanese immigrants filled the gap. Tens of thousands of Japanese immigrants were living in California by the end of the century.[266] The American press praised the Japanese as excellent wrestlers reminiscent of the ancient Greeks and Romans.[267] Style-on-style match-ups in America between fighters of Asian and European ancestry became increasingly common in the final years of the 19th century, although Asian fighters and their arts remained on the fringe of America until well into the 20th century.[268] Fighters of African descent also practiced their distinctive styles in America, as they had for centuries, but these techniques made little penetration into the lives of white Americans, who discriminated against both African fighting styles and the athletes who practiced them.

Demographics propelled changes in wrestling styles. Immigrants from southern Europe helped send Irish collar and elbow style into decline and increase the popularity of Greco-Roman and catch forms.[269] Practitioners of different styles of wrestling frequently fought challenge matches with an array of rule sets. Richard Fox promoted and formalized these contests, inventing a forerunner of mixed martial arts in the process. Since these athletes disagreed on a fight's most basic concepts, Fox constructed his own rules. Rather than combine several rule sets into one all-inclusive system, he opted for a conglomerate approach in which the victory went to the fighter who emerged victorious in two out of three matches, each in a different style. To promote the sport, Fox designed a medal and offered it to the new sport's champion.[270] The rules stipulated that the medal would become the personal property of the first fighter to win three tournaments under these rules. It is unclear if Fox planned to hand out only one medal or if he anticipated that "mixed wrestling champion" would become an ongoing title much as with the heavyweight boxing championship. Whatever Fox's intentions might have been, Duncan Ross, an athlete of Scottish ancestry living in Kentucky, was the first and apparently the only wrestler to win the title.[271] In addition to his fame in the wrestling ring, Ross earned praise as a versatile athlete who excelled at running, boxing, hammer throwing, and dancing. Similar to the problems of indecisive results occasionally faced by Muldoon, at least one of the tournaments on the path to Fox's title bout ended in a draw after 22 minutes.[272]

Fox promoted boxing as well as wrestling, demonstrating that he was more interested in money and fame than in promoting any particular sport. He served as a stakeholder for boxing matches.[273] His decisions to award or withhold the prize money in his care sometimes made him an important arbitrator in controversial fights.[274] He acted as an investor, putting his money

II. Boxing Takes Root in the United States, 1607–1810   83

on the line to set up fights.[275] The *National Police Gazette* sponsored competitions in oyster opening, one-legged dancing, climbing, and many other activities ranging from the absurd to death defying.[276] The paper's most sought-after prizes went to champion pugilists who earned diamond-studded belts, adorned with Fox's visage.[277] The most famous competitor to wear the Gazette's belt was undoubtedly John L. Sullivan, a man immortalized as the Boston Strong Boy, the Great John L, and His Fistic Highness. Sullivan often claimed, "I can beat any sonavbitch in the house," and, almost without exception, he did.[278]

John Lawrence Sullivan traveled from anonymous origins to unprecedented in fame in just a few years. He was born in 1858 in Roxbury, Massachusetts, to working-class Irish immigrants.[279] Initially employed as a plumber, his career ended when he resolved a professional disagreement by breaking his employer's jaw with a heavy-handed punch.[280] Sullivan's first fights came in response to his impromptu announcements in Boston barrooms that he could whip any man in the house—in fairness, he nearly always did.[281] He drifted into baseball, and the Cincinnati Red Stockings offered him a professional contract, which he declined so that he could pursue a career in the ring.[282] His serious pugilistic career began in 1877, when he attended an exhibition held by the famed fighter Tom Scannel. When Scannel called for a volunteer to meet him in the ring, Sullivan accepted. Sullivan attempted to shake hands, but Scannel sucker-punched him. The challenger responded with a single punch that knocked Scannel to the ground.[283] Sullivan's career then began in earnest. He spent the several years obtaining the championship title in a series of hard-fought bouts against the greatest pugilists in the United States and Great Britain.[284]

Sullivan broke new ground as one of the first boxers to borrow a business model from vaudeville and the circus rather than the saloon. In 1883, William Muldoon, the famed wrestler, began working with Sullivan and helped him and his manager Al Smith organize a grand tour, indicating the overlap that often existed between boxing and wrestling.[285] The plan for the tour was essentially identical to Muldoon's successful tour of 1881.[286] Sullivan traveled the country with a troupe of fighters, offering $1,000 to anyone who could last four rounds in the ring with him.[287] Many men entered the arena, most remained conscious only seconds, and none of them lasted the four rounds. When no challenger dared face him, and to fill out the evening after brief bouts, Sullivan and the fighters who traveled with him sparred for the crowds.[288]

The tour provided Sullivan with money and fame, and many Americans from the rural heartland got their first glimpse of an urban man reveling in

Portrait of His Fistic Highness, John L. Sullivan. He often claimed, "I can beat any sonuvabitch in the house," and, almost without exception, he did. Published by William M. Clarke in New York on November 23, 1883 (Library of Congress Prints and Photographs Division).

II. Boxing Takes Root in the United States, 1607–1810   85

the joys of the flesh who provided an alternative masculinity to that endorsed by polite society. Unlike Muldoon, who promoted an image of the moralistic athlete, Sullivan made no pretense of middle-class propriety.[289] He confessed his love of alcohol, joking to journalists that he tried to limit himself to half a dozen glasses of ale during the day and a bottle for dinner.[290] Sullivan's humor came at just the wrong time for many Americans who were fighting an increasingly popular war against alcohol.[291] He was a regular at sporting houses and saloons, where stories of his barroom brawls and drunken sprees became legendary.[292] Reformers saw nothing amusing about Sullivan's habits and condemned him as an inhuman monster and a drunk.[293] When a political candidate received Sullivan's endorsement, the startled politician wrote the *Washington Post* to distance himself from the pugilist and condemn Sullivan as an irreligious, uncivilized disgrace to humanity.[294] Not everyone found Sullivan repulsive, however. His celebrity grew not only because of his athletic accomplishments, but because some men genuinely admired his determination to live life by his own rules.[295]

Sullivan, like Muldoon, faced the problem of satisfying spectators while on tour, but unlike Muldoon, Sullivan's problems were legal rather than structural. Wrestling, particularly Greco-Roman style, with its prohibition of holds below the waist, often moved slowly. To liven up the action, grapplers sometimes resorted to scripted routines. Boxing was an exciting and fluid sport, but pugilism walked a fine legal line in this period. Prizefighting was illegal in every state in the union in the 1880s.[296] Fights took place by avoiding the authorities or under the legal exemption for displays of sparring techniques.[297] The distinction between prizefight and exhibition was often razor thin and hung on the perceived aggression fighters demonstrated, the damage they inflicted on each other, how much they excited the audience, and the subjective interpretations of local police.[298] When referees ended rounds early to limit the damage Sullivan inflicted on an opponent in an 1884 bout, the crowd hissed their disapproval. Sullivan addressed the audience directly, explaining that he put on the best show the law would allow.[299] For his next great fight, he cast aside legal restrictions and ignored reforms within the sport itself.

In 1888, John L. Sullivan agreed to fight Jake Kilrain, in a fight that became the last significant bout of the bare-knuckle era.[300] The pugilists choose the wrestling and bare knuckles style of the old London Rules,[301] despite the increasing popularity of the newer Queensbury Rules. To prepare for the fight, Sullivan turned to an old friend and fitness expert, William Muldoon, who helped him get into peak condition.[302] After a flurry of threats from governors and police officials, the parties eventually decided to hold

John L. Sullivan (left) fights Jake Kilrain in Richburg, Mississippi, on July 8, 1889. This was the last major fight of the American bare-knuckle boxing era (Library of Congress Prints and Photographs Division).

the fight in remote Richburg, Mississippi.[303] On July 8, 1889, the fighters entered the arena surrounded by 3,000 fans, most of who came by train from New Orleans.[304] Kilrain was in trouble from the fight's first moments. He seemed frightened of Sullivan and spent most of his effort running and dodging. After 43 rounds of "hide and go seek," the crowd's anger with Kilrain was matched only by Sullivan's. Kilrain's corner conceded defeat and Sullivan walked away with another victory.[305] The state of Mississippi did not consider the matter settled, however, and worked to bring the fighters to justice. The champion was arrested and found himself charged with violating Mississippi's anti-prizefighting statute.[306] Sullivan's legal battles cost him far more than he won for his pugilistic victory, and he vowed to never again engage in a bare-knuckle prizefight, a development that demonstrated how political elites shaped fight sports by shifting their economics.[307] Sullivan did not fight again for three years, choosing instead to make his living on the stage, where he acted and gave people a chance to meet the Boston Strong Boy.[308]

Sullivan's adamant refusals to fight men of African descent demonstrate that the boundaries of fight sports were often more about culture than economics. Early in his career, Sullivan refused to meet the top African American challenger, C. A. C. Smith, flatly admitting that Smith was perfectly qualified

II. Boxing Takes Root in the United States, 1607–1810   87

to fight him aside from his race and giving no indication that he was unhappy with the fees offered to fight Smith.[309] The champion's racial policies were not entirely consistent or easily understood. Sullivan gladly fought Herbert Slade, a dark-skinned native of New Zealand, and later welcomed Slade into his troupe of traveling fighters. In Sullivan's autobiography, the Boston Strong Boy compared Slade favorably to Hercules and the Roman gladiators.[310] Sullivan was not so kind to Peter Jackson, a dark-skinned challenger from Australia. Jackson won the heavyweight boxing championship of Australia in 1886. In 1889, he won the Colored Heavyweight Championship of the World by defeating George Godfrey in San Francisco. Jackson then traveled to Britain, where he defeated the English champion.[311] Sullivan repeatedly refused large sums of money to face Jackson in the ring.[312] Sullivan claimed to draw the color line because not doing so would compromise his character.[313] The African American press mocked him for his refusal, suggesting Sullivan was not "a true man."[314] In spite of his occasional vacillations or contradictions, Sullivan generally maintained the color line and refused to fight black opponents. Today the policy stains his legacy and begs questions about how he might have fared against excellent black pugilists such as Jackson, Smith, and Godfrey. Nevertheless, his position was entirely consistent with the views of most white Americans in the late 19th century and did nothing to diminish his popularity with white men while he was an active fighter.[315] While Sullivan dodged black contenders in favor of an acting career, America was changing.

By 1890, the United States was far more urban and more industrialized than ever before, which propelled changes in the nation's fight sports and masculine identities. Modern American sporting culture is the product primarily of cultural changes caused by urbanization, which put large numbers of people in small spaces who provided ready-made audiences for sporting events, and industrialization, which facilitated the cultural connections of urban centers with each other and their penetration into the countryside.[316] After the Civil War, Americans from the eastern half of the country spread West in record numbers in search of economic opportunity.[317] Railroad mileage in the United States doubled in the years 1878 to 1890.[318] This change facilitated the movement of people to the West and reduced shipping costs from roughly 1.925 cents per ton per mile in 1865 to only 0.941 cent per ton per mile in 1890, which in turn accelerated economic expansion and migration across the nation.[319] Entertainers such as P. T. Barnum and William Muldoon used the rail lines to further their own successes, traveling the nation and entertaining crowds.[320] John L. Sullivan used the rails as well, which allowed him and his troupe to extend boxing westward into areas previously outside the reach of pugilism.[321]

In 1860, the United States lagged behind the industrialized nations of Germany, Britain, and France; by 1890, it was the world's largest producer of manufactured goods, with an output that exceeded that of the three former leading nations combined.[322] Both farm and nonfarm workforces increased dramatically from the end of the Civil War to 1890, but nonfarm workers increased at a faster pace so that by 1890 farmers made up a minority of the workforce for the first time in the nation's history.[323] In that same year, the Census Bureau announced that the frontier was gone. The West was no longer an untamed wilderness, but rather a scene of growing towns and cities such as San Francisco, Salt Lake City, Los Angeles, and Denver.[324] The cultural centers of America continued their shift away from rural life and toward urban venues, with more than one third of Americans living in cities for the first in time in 1890.[325] Boxing thrived in urban spaces, and as they expanded, so did pugilism.[326]

Changes in demographics and labor propelled changes in masculinity. Beginning in the early 19th century, American men celebrated a vision of self-made manhood that defined men in terms of their ability to make money.[327] As the century ended, men looked at their bodies and worried that business careers were making them effeminate. Economic uncertainty further undermined the idea that men could prove their worth in the marketplace. It made sense, then, that many workers turned to a more elemental concept of manhood, one they could demonstrate during the leisure hours.[328] Increasing numbers of men began embracing a new vision of passionate masculinity that encouraged men to demonstrate their manhood by building strong bodies and proving themselves as athletes, soldiers, and lovers.[329] Students and clerks flooded into new athletic clubs, stepped onto baseball diamonds, and learned the art of pugilism.[330] In 1888, a boxing fan argued, "This vaunted age needs a saving touch of honest, old-fashioned barbarism, so that when we come to die, we shall die leaving men behind us, and not a race of eminently respectable female saints."[331]

America's boxers personified these changes in American masculinity. In 1892, John L. Sullivan reigned supreme as pugilist and masculine icon, but a young challenger arose in the West to contest his domination. His career demonstrated how boxing was changing from a sport of felonious brawlers to a pastime for respectable, middle-class men. James "Gentleman Jim" Corbett lived very different life from Sullivan, both inside and outside the ring. Both Sullivan and Corbett came from Irish stock and became great boxers, but they shared little else. Corbett was born in San Francisco on September 1, 1866, the son of solidly middle-class business owners.[332] He experienced a very different childhood than the working-class, Roxbury, Massachusetts, upbringing of Sullivan.[333] Corbett grew up in relative comfort, completed high school, and took college courses before beginning work as a bank clerk; Sullivan, in contrast, worked as plumber.[334] Corbett began his boxing training with the support and encouragement of his boss, under the famous English boxing instructor Walter Watson at the Olympic Club.[335] Sullivan, in contrast, broke his employer's jaw and learned to box in barroom brawls.[336] Unlike Sullivan, who was known for his power and aggression, Corbett prided himself on his scientific style of boxing, which emphasized precision, agility, and athleticism rather than brute force.[337]

Corbett's reputation was as different from Sullivan's as was his fight style. Commentators consistently presented Sullivan as a drunken, immoral ruffian.[338] They called Sullivan a brute even when they congratulated him on his victories.[339] Corbett's reputation, however, was nearly spotless. Journalists referred to him as a well-educated gentleman from a good family.[340] They praised his elegant manners, handsome appearance, and gentlemanly behavior.[341] The press called him "Gentleman Jim" and described him as a dutiful son who used prize money to pay off his parents' mortgage.[342] In contrast to Sullivan's open enjoyment of alcohol, Corbett made a point of refusing liquor and proclaiming his fondness for milk.[343] His reputation did not suffer when he fought a draw with a black man, Peter Jackson—the same Australian champion whom Sullivan declined to fight.[344] When Corbett challenged Sullivan to fight him for the heavyweight title, the Californian received a rare rebuke. A writer for the *Washington Post* told Corbett that his confidence was prideful and foolish. The author praised Corbett as a fine fighter and admitted that years of debauchery and self-indulgence might have finally brought Sullivan down to Corbett's level. Even in a much-deteriorated state, however, Sullivan was still a dangerous man, too dangerous to justify Corbett's confidence.[345] Sullivan agreed that Corbett was in danger, publicly claiming that he could easily knock out his younger rival within four rounds.[346] The sporting public agreed: in the lead-up to the fight, the betting odds ran four to one in favor of Sullivan.[347] Corbett never flinched as he calmly placed his body into the path of His Fistic Highness.

The fighters entered the fateful arena on September 7, 1892. Consistent with Sullivan's vow to never again fight bare knuckled, and with Corbett's preference for the new style of boxing, the fighters agreed to fight under the Queensbury Rules.[348] The bout took place in the Olympic Athletic Club of New Orleans, which had recently obtained official permission to host gloved matches.[349] More than 8,000 fans crowded into the stands, which surrounded a sturdy arena with ropes to keep the fighters in and barbed wire to ensure the spectators stayed out.[350] Corbett moved with his characteristic speed and agility, but also displayed aggression as he peppered Sullivan with stinging punches that the old champion was unable to return or long endure. After a hotly contested bout, Corbett won. The news quickly spread across the nation. Fans in Eastern cities were initially incredulous, sure that it was some mistake and that no man could best their hero Sullivan. Once they realized that Corbett's victory was real, they joined in unanimous cheers for the Californian.[351] A writer for the *Washington Post* painted an especially stark contrast between the fighters as they left New Orleans, describing Corbett as intoxicated by victory and Sullivan as simply intoxicated.[352] In the fight's aftermath, the press continued to present Corbett as the gracious, middle-class gentleman and Sullivan as the ill-mannered, working-class ruffian.

When fight fans embraced Corbett, they embraced a new American masculinity and a new vision of America.[353] The fight was not just between Corbett and Sullivan, but between the models of manhood they represented. It was the triumph of the Corbett's Apollonian manhood of virtue over the Dionysian masculinity of self-indulgence and excess embraced by Sullivan.[354] Men loved and admired Sullivan not simply because he was a great fighter, but because they admired his rejection of middle-class respectability and his determination to live by his own rules.[355] Sullivan was an unapologetically rough, working-class man who scorned middle-class respectability as he openly professed his love of alcohol and violence.[356] He represented a violent rebellion to the wage labor system and the domestication of the American male, having unapologetically broken his employer's jaw before turning to a career where he battered strangers for profit and soaked himself in alcohol.[357] Corbett offered a more subtle, if no less vigorous masculinity, which his fans celebrated as much as his victories in the ring.[358] Corbett was a solidly middle-class man. Born a decade after Sullivan, he benefited from the American middle class's increasing embrace of muscular Christianity and its tendency to encourage violent sports, as long as they were carefully regulated.[359] Unlike Sullivan, who ended his plumbing career with punch to his employer's jaw and fought in saloons, Corbett learned to box in an athletic club, with the support of the man who owned the bank where he worked as a clerk.[360] Unlike Sullivan, the unapologetic lover of strong drink, Corbett denounced alcohol and upheld middle-class respectability.[361] Many American men admired "Gentleman Jim" Corbett because he was able to pummel the famed John L. Sullivan into submission while never losing his devotion to the manners, economic stability, and morality that made him a member of the American middle class.

The ring and the press did not provide Corbett with his only stage, as he became one of the first fighters immortalized on film. In 1891, inventor

Thomas Edison told the *Washington Post* that he was quickly perfecting a new invention that would allow sporting enthusiasts to watch prizefights in their own homes.[362] After several failed attempts, Edison succeeded in capturing the much-anticipated 1897 heavyweight championship bout between Jim Corbett and Bob Fitzsimmons. The film was a huge success that helped popularize both movies and pugilism.[363] It brought boxing to people previously isolated from the ring owing to their homes being in remote towns, their unwillingness to expose themselves to the dangerous conditions of the boxing arena, and even their gender. A writer for the *New York Times* suggested that even the most disapproving critics of the prize ring secretly harbored a desire to see the celebrated fighters in action. Fight films made it possible to realize those dreams without ever visiting a fight in person or risking its dangers.[364] In many parts of the country, and for many Americans, film replaced the arena as a safe and more readily accessible version of the ring, even as it provided substantial profits for promoters.[365] Sixty percent of such films' viewers were women curious about the manly art and eager to see nearly nude male bodies on display.[366]

Even as boxing's popularity grew, it continued to face controversies that limited its acceptance. A writer for the *New York Times* noted that good people objected to boxing even when promoters claimed that their events were contests of scientific skill rather than prizefights.[367] In Boston, a journalist claimed that most of the city's residents considered boxing brutal in all its forms, and did not approve of the sport in spite of recent reforms.[368] Physicians opposed pugilism on medical grounds, noting deaths in the ring and arguing that the sport was both brutal and dangerous.[369] In 1897, the leaders of the 300,000-member Woman's Christian Temperance Union publicly urged the nation's governors and President William McKinley to outlaw fight films, which they feared would expose unprecedented numbers of Americans to the prize ring and what they saw as its barbaric influence.[370]

Corbett's victories in the ring and on the screen accelerated the construction of alliances between politicians, fighters, promoters, and fans that eventually brought boxing into the mainstream, albeit in a process that often took one step back for every step forward.[371] In 1890, New Orleans's new mayor, the long-time fight enthusiast and boxing referee John Fitzpatrick, gave the city's athletic clubs official permission to hold gloved sparring matches. This made the city an attractive destination for fights such as Corbett's 1892 contest with Sullivan.[372] The sanctioned fight brought to the city thousands of visitors who behaved well and spent lavishly.[373] The permissive atmosphere, however, did not sit well with many of the state's residents who wanted to banish boxing from Louisiana regardless of profit.[374] Politicians in

New York, long a stronghold of boxing, took note of the wealthy patrons flocking to the Crescent City and began allowing politically connected promoters to hold prizefights, even though they were still illegal.[375] In 1894, hometown hero Andy Bowen died from injuries suffered in the ring of the New Orleans Olympic Club, turning public opinion firmly against boxing and convincing the courts to outlaw prizefights in the state.[376] Boxing in New York obtained official endorsement with the 1896 Horton Law, which left the prizefighting laws in force, but made an exception for gentlemanly gloved fights held in private clubs.[377] The letter of the law was rarely enforced by the authorities, such as Police Commissioner Theodore Roosevelt, who preferred to ignore infractions and allow prizefights to take place with little interference.[378]

Nevada politicians turned to boxing in a desperate bid to rebuild the state's economy, which was collapsing with the tapping out of many mines in the state.[379] In 1897, the state's legislature formally legalized gloved boxing contests and repealed all previous laws that might have conflicted with the new statute.[380] The welcoming legal climate quickly made Nevada a prime destination for boxers and their fans.[381] California followed suit in 1899, passing a law, similar to the Horton Law, which maintained the criminality of prizefights while making an exception for gloved sparring exhibitions in licensed clubs.[382] The new law made California, particularly San Francisco, a major center for boxing.[383]

As in Louisiana, legal boxing matches did not last long in the Empire State. In 1900, the New York state legislature repealed the Horton Law and replaced it with the Lewis Law, which allowed boxing only for recognized members of sanctioned clubs.[384] The new law severely curtailed boxing matches in New York, although some clubs and saloons continued to host surreptitious bouts.[385]

In spite of the setbacks, boxing stood on far firmer legal ground in 1900 than it had ever enjoyed before. Traditional homes in Louisiana and New York were largely inhospitable, but those evictions were more than made up for by the new homes among westerners who welcomed pugilists and their fans with open arms.

Boxing received another boost as officers made pugilism a mainstay of the nation's military. Collegiate sport programs and the glories of the prize ring influenced American military training. Before 1890, boxing in the American military often suffered from official policies that ranged from apathy to outright hostility.[386] This changed in the aftermath of Sullivan's defeat by Corbett, when Lieutenant Colonel A. A. Woodhull, a surgeon, argued that the historic fight demonstrated the importance of agility and speed in the ring. Woodhull urged the army's high command to make boxing a key part of military training, suggesting it would help make soldiers more efficient fighters.[387] Years later, Woodhull wrote a textbook for the education of undergraduates in which he provided a further endorsement of boxing, arguing that every man should possess the capacity to defend himself with nothing more than his body, and that boxing provided those skills.[388] Major John Brooke argued the army should emulate civilian universities, which used sports to make young men strong and vitreous.[389] In 1892, an expert in physical education from Yale instructed cadets at the Naval Academy in football, running, jumping, baseball, fencing, wrestling, and boxing.[390] In the same year, West Point greatly expanded its physical training program under the guidance of an instructor of physical culture, Colonel Herman J. Kohler, who was a star athlete and graduate of the Milwaukee Normal School of Physical Training. Kohler trained cadets in sports including running, jumping, fencing, wrestling, and boxing. Kohler's program later came to the attention of President Theodore Roosevelt, who made it mandatory for all cadets.[391] In 1896, an army officer revealed to a journalist that while some civilians still found boxing offensive, soldiers and sailors harbored no such feelings. He indicated

Members of the Newsboys' Protective Association practice fighting techniques in hopes that a little barbarism will keep them safe on the streets of Cincinnati, Ohio. Photograph produced by Lewis Wickles Hine in August 1908 (Library of Congress Prints and Photographs Division).

that boxing provided men of the army and navy with their most popular pastime, and that some soldiers were talented enough pugilists to hold their own with any professional fighter.[392] The young officer may not have considered it at the time, but the West held no monopoly on fighters.

Men, according to commentators of the times, were hardened by their resistance to feminine influences. British educators argued that the poor performance of American high school students was due to the large numbers of female teachers in the United States.[393] President Theodore Roosevelt urged male students to embrace fight sports as a way to protect themselves from feminizing influences.[394] Journalists generally approved of female involvement in sports and even encouraged schools to hire them as physical education teachers, as long as women steered clear of violent sports such as boxing and wrestling.[395] Advice columnist Arthur Dean promoted exercise for men and women, as long as the gendered boundary was maintained, with fight sports remaining solely within the male domain.[396]

Elite attempts to promote fight sports were hampered by problems within the sports themselves. The first decade of the 20th century witnessed a series of scandals involving fixed fights and prearranged outcomes in wrestling and boxing. This was nothing new. In an effort to excite crowds, both Muldoon and Sullivan put on exhibitions with members of their own troupes that walked the line between demonstrations and fixed fights in their late 19th-century tours.[397] In an effort to attract larger audiences, who were often bored by slow-moving wrestling bouts, wrestlers displayed an increasing willingness to choreograph their fights. By 1905, experts estimated that 90 percent of wrestling matches concluded with prearranged outcomes.[398] Newspapers explained in detail how wrestlers worked together to provide matches that appeared completely authentic even though they were entirely scripted.[399] Journalists rarely approved of worked matches, but they did admit that when wrestlers did not choreograph their routines and fought authentically, the resulting bouts were universally boring.[400] Fixed boxing matches were also common in the first years of the 20th century.[401] Boxing was inexorably linked with gamblers who bribed fighters to throw fights, tarnishing the sport's reputation.[402] In 1900, Joe Gans, a lightweight and the first African American to win a world boxing title, met Terry McGovern in Chicago for a fight that lasted barely two rounds.[403] Gans later confessed that he threw the fight in exchange for a bribe, earning public ridicule and condemnation in the press.[404] The scandal provided a major boost for the sport's opponents, who passed legislation outlawing pugilism in Illinois.[405] The damage done to boxing by Gans was somewhat mitigated by an emerging champion—one who never took a dive.

The nation's next African American champion rose to a position of fame and fortune unimaginable to his predecessors. Jack Johnson was born to former slaves in 1878 near Galveston, Texas. With few opportunities in his future, Johnson left school at a young age and began spending his days at the docks, working as a laborer and learning pugilism. While still a teenager, he began boxing professionally and left Texas in search of better opportunities in California.[406] In 1903, he bested Ed Martin and took the black heavyweight title in a bout a journalist called one of the most skillful, prettiest, and obviously authentic fights in history.[407] Johnson immediately began campaigning for a shot at the heavyweight title—an opportunity almost never before granted to a black man. The reigning champion, Tommy Burns, did not want to fight Johnson, but relented to fan pressure and the promise of a big payday.[408] Going into the fight, the betting odds favored Burns, and the fighters' contracts ensured that win or lose, the champion would earn far more than the challenger.[409] Burns and Johnson entered the ring to the cheers of an excited crowd. Johnson quickly demonstrated his mastery and by the 11th round, he proved the odds makers wrong. The first black man to engage in a heavyweight title fight earned the coveted crown, but his greatest challenges were still ahead.

By the early 20th century, the man who wore the heavyweight boxing crown was the "emperor of masculinity," in the words of boxing writer Gerald Early and in the minds of many men around the world, which created a problem when the crown came to rest on a black head.[410] The existence of a black emperor led to reexaminations of American manhood. Peter Jackson's victories had earlier enraged many white men.[411] Jack Johnson's victories dealt a devastating blow to the ideology of manhood possessed by American whites and led them to oppose him at every opportunity.[412] Racism convinced many men to overlook nationalistic boundaries. When American men cheered for the white Canadian Tommy Burns in hopes that he would destroy their dark-skinned countryman, they provided evidence of the oddly shaped nature of identities.[413] Franklin F. Johnson, writing for the *Afro-American* newspaper in 1914, pointed to Johnson as an example for African Americans: "We have grown a manhood sterling, stalwart, and grand, a manhood that has competed with the Anglo-Saxon."[414] Johnson was aware of his status as a masculine icon, explaining his preference for white women as an expression of his masculinity.[415]

Johnson's personal victories as a man created problems for the sport he dominated and demonstrated once again that masculine identities rather than economics dictated the shape of American fight sports. The author Jack London led a chorus of voices demanding that Jim Jefferies, who had retired

Jack Johnson poses with rival pugilist Marty Cutler. Johnson knocked out Cutler in the sixth round of their bout (Library of Congress Prints and Photographs Division).

as the reigning heavyweight champion, come out of retirement to rescue the dignity of white men.[416] Jefferies answered the call, and on July 4, 1910, before film cameras and thousands of fans, Jack Johnson knocked another white man to the canvas.[417] The fight threw salt in racial wounds, with white Americans reacting very differently to the news than their black counterparts. In

Jess Willard stands over a knocked-out Jack Johnson, who is being counted out by the referee in the 26th round of an outdoor boxing match that took place on April 5, 1915. Published in 1915 by the American Photo Co. (Library of Congress Prints and Photographs Division).

the white press, Johnson was a villain, "the Smoke Nuisance" or "Little Arthur" who proved that boxing was barbaric.[418] Whites condemned Johnson as an immoral wretch prone to heavy drinking and assaults on the disabled.[419] Observers were particularly critical of Johnson's open fondness for white women—an affection that was typically mutual.[420] Boxing critics hoped that Johnson had dealt a fatal blow to his sport since Johnson's victories supposedly made it impossible for white men to enjoy pugilism. They predicted that Nevada would soon repeal its prizefighting laws and whites would abandon boxing for intellectual pastimes where they still demonstrated racial superiority.[421] These predictions proved false. Johnson's career actually stimulated white interest in boxing, as the search for the Great White Hope became an obsession for many men.[422]

For all their venom, even whites recognized that Johnson was immensely popular with members of his own race.[423] Many members of the black community and their newspapers embraced Johnson as a hero, a black man who struck back violently at the oppressor and brought glory to their race.[424] They presented him as a virtuous man who taught Sunday school, loved his mother, and rescued the victims of an automobile accident.[425] Men who opposed Johnson did so in spite of his ability to generate revenue for the sport. As Gail Bederman argued, white men hated Johnson because his victories dealt a devastating blow to the masculine identities of white American men.[426]

Since Johnson proved invincible in the ring, his critics defeated him outside the arena. Films of his fights against Jefferies and Burns spread Johnson's fame and made money for promoters, but anger over his victories and fears of social upheaval led to new legislation outlawing boxing films in many states and a federal ban on transporting the movies across state lines.[427] In 1912, the courts found Johnson guilty of transporting a woman across state lines for immoral purposes and, therefore, violating the Mann Act. Sentenced to a year in prison, Johnson fled the country first for Canada and then for Europe.[428] In 1915, an aging, tired, and overweight Johnson proved a shadow of his former self, falling unconscious in a hotly contested championship fight with Jess Willard.[429]

The reign of the first African American heavyweight champion was over, but America's attention did not remain on the fight for long. The storm clouds of war that covered Europe were rapidly moving across the Atlantic. American men, both white and black, turned their focus to the new and unimaginably more violent challenge of World War I that awaited them far from the ring.

American fight sports had changed dramatically from 1810 to 1915. Boxing had taken up firm roots in the cities and begun spreading into the countryside, propelled by immigration, the birth of a commercial leisure industry, and evolving notions of masculinity. The dominant view of American masculinity shifted from the patriarchal man of republican virtue to the passionate man of mass industrialized spectacle.[430] The racial aspects of American masculinity were questioned and rebuilt as a son of former slaves became the world's emperor of masculinity. In spite of its increasing popularity, boxing's success was tenuous, as it struggled to hold its ground against angry reformers and spectators who remained open to other fight sports.[431] Boxing stood at center stage, but on wobbly legs—legs that could not hold the sport's weight forever.

III

"With the Energy of a Trip-Hammer and the Vehemence of a Sioux"

Asian Martial Arts Come to the United States, 1850–1941

During the fights the participants and spectators yell like wild Injuns, their eyes gleam, and the whole face is very much like that of a rat driven into a corner. With a short iron bar and razor-edged hatchet, John pounds and chops away with the energy of trip hammer and the vehemence of a Sioux.
        —1876 account of fights between rival Chinatown gangs[1]

Chicago, Jan. 28.—An exciting contest with incidents bordering on the sensational was witnessed by a large audience at Central Music Hall, in the wrestling match between Matsada Sorakichi, the Japanese athlete, and Evan Lewis, of Madison, Wis. The terms were $250 a side and 75 per cent of the gate receipts to the winner: best three in five falls: catch as catch can. Frank Glover, the pugilist, acted as referee. Sorakichi was hardly a match for Lewis in point of strength, but as to quickness and agility there could be no choice, and in skill the Jap was a trifle the superior man. The first fall was won by Lewis in exactly two minutes and a half. There had been a couple of moments' preliminary skirmish in which Sorakichi appeared to decided advantage. With a rush Lewis secured a hold on his opponent's legs, and lifting him high in the air, threw him squarely on his back. In the second bout Lewis got a terrific neck hold on the Jap and was choking him with deathlike grip [when] Sorakichi, with a sudden jerk, pitched Lewis headforemost off the stage. The Jap profusely apologized and Lewis and he shook hands.
Again the wrestlers grasped each other's shoulders. Quick as a flash

the form of Sorakichi went straight over the footlights and sprawling below the reporters' chairs. The referee, without hesitation, declared this action by Lewis willful, and gave the fall to Sorakichi. Both wrestlers eyed each other wickedly, and in the third bout Lewis succeeded in getting his favorite too feeble to resist. Sorakichi at once declined to wrestle the remaining bouts, declaring the chock process unfair. Lewis offered to leave it out, but the Jap feared to trust the Wisconsin man, and firmly refused to proceed. At 9:45 p.m. Lewis was declared the winner.
—American wrestler Evan Lewis defeats Japanese opponent Matsada Sorakichi in 1886[2]

Asian immigration into the United States began shortly after Americans declared their country's independence. The new immigrants' presence added further nuance to an already diverse racial hierarchy in the young nation. A small number of Chinese immigrants came to the United States through ports on the Eastern coast at the end of the 18th century as part of an emerging trade with Asia.[3] With the end of the African slave trade at the beginning of the 19th century, workers from China began to fill the void in the labor market.[4] At least one writer at the time claimed that the African slave trade ended only because slave traders were able to substitute Asians for Africans.[5] Many Asians left behind the famine, poverty, and civil unrest of their homeland for better wages in America.[6] More joined them with the California gold rush in 1849.[7] Consistent with their role as replacements for slaves, Chinese workers faced widespread racial discrimination. European immigrants, particularly the Irish, who were still securing their claim to whiteness, worked to exclude the Chinese from the ranks of skilled trades in an effort to reinforce their own status.[8] American regulations and customs encouraged migration of males rather than females, due at least in part because women could give birth, and children born on American soil might claim citizenship and improve the status of the Chinese in America—a prospect that worried many Americans.[9] As a result, workers from China were overwhelmingly men. During the 19th century, 95 percent of Chinese immigrants into the United States were male.[10] The increasing number of Chinese immigrants led to the first anti–Chinese backlash in American history, which began around the same time. As Chinese immigrants flooded into California, an anti–Chinese movement began to gather steam and the American press took an increasing interest in Chinese visitors and their homeland.

The American press devoted extensive coverage to British domination of China beginning in the 1820s. Trouble began brewing between the British and the Chinese in 1793, when British envoy Lord George McCartney refused to bow to the Qianlong emperor of China, a custom generally accepted by

III. Asian Martial Arts Come to the United States, 1850–1941   101

nations doing business with the Chinese.[11] In the 1820s, the British began selling opium, produced in their Indian territories, to the Chinese.[12] Opium addiction became an epidemic in China, and the Chinese government outlawed importation of the drug.[13] British merchants ignored Chinese law, lured by large profits, emboldened by a belief in their racial superiority, and encouraged by the support of high-ranking British officials.[14] In 1839, the conflict erupted into war.[15] American observers had few compliments for either side in the conflict. They condemned the British as immoral imperialists, selling their souls for cash and interfering with China's right to protect its own citizens from the ravages of a dangerous drug.[16] They also derided China as a weak nation that relied on an inferior military equipped with anachronistic weapons and completely unprepared for war with the British.[17] The war ended in 1842, with a British victory.[18] As part of the peace treaty, China ceded control of Hong Kong to the British and opened its borders to Western influences, including the Christian missionaries it had long resisted.[19] An American political journal attributed the Chinese defeat to the fact that they were a scholarly race that valued education while ignoring athleticism and aggression, claiming that violent encounters were very rare among the Chinese.[20]

American perceptions of the Chinese nation spilled over into their understandings of Chinese masculinity and Chinese immigrants into the United States. During the mid–19th century, American publications typically treated China and Chinese immigrants with contempt and derision. They were particularly unimpressed with Chinese masculinity. A writer for the *New York State Mechanic* reflected on Chinese immigrants and evaluated them in light of their nation's inability to resist British domination. The author concluded that while the British were villains for their treatment of China, the Chinese were even worse.

> We cannot much pity the Chinese, we despise them so much. Had they shown signs of manhood we would honor them and grieve them. Brave men, lavish of blood, and fierce in fight for native land, have our sympathy in triumph or defeat: but for the poltroon and the imbecile, let him take care of himself. Let him sink unless he has the spirit to swim.[21]

An article published in an American military journal argued that the Chinese military failed on the battlefield because the national culture did not value martial prowess.[22] An American traveler in China dismissed the Chinese as unwilling to defend their women and incapable of appreciating the noble concept of chivalry.[23] The *New York Times* published a letter from an observer of the civil unrest wrecking China in 1853, who referred to the imperial soldiers as cowards.[24] Another journalist claimed that the Chinese were a ridiculous people who fled like sheep from violent confrontations.[25] A missionary referred to his Chinese traveling companions as cowards too frightened to even follow him up a steep incline.[26] Americans' low regard for China and Chinese men was both racial and gendered, suggesting that the Chinese men were not masculine because their race was incapable of appreciating masculine virtues. American observers were somewhat less insulting to Chinese athletes.

Chinese immigrants came from a culture with a long history of martial arts. The Chinese developed their own distinctive fight sports, which incorporated punches, kicks, and wrestling holds, around 2000 BCE.[27] Some of these arts incorporated techniques inspired by the movements of animals. These styles became highly advanced during the Chou dynasty (1122–256 BCE).[28] Wrestling formed a key component of Chinese military training. Indeed, by 770 BCE, high commanders often chose champion wrestlers as their personal bodyguards.[29] Around 209 BCE, a Chinese emperor designated wrestling the official sport of the military, which the Chinese chronicles increasingly distinguished from boxing. In the Han dynasty, Chinese athletes began incorporating the neck and leg throws they learned from nomadic mercenaries into their style of wrestling during the first century of the Common Era. At about the same time, the Chinese began spreading their style of wrestling into Korea through their military colonies in the peninsula.[30] Legend claims that the Indian Buddhist monk Bodihidarma arrived in southern China in about 475 CE and took up residence at the Shaolin monastery. Tradition suggests he may have developed a series of exercises, inspired by animal movements, which later fighters codified as the martial art Kung Fu and the fight sport Wushu.[31] Japanese emperors may have borrowed the concept of large-scale wrestling tournaments from the Chinese. The Chinese emperor Zhou Zhong (924–936 CE) enjoyed wrestling and often entered the ring to the delight of spectators.[32] Zhong offered prizes to wrestlers who could defeat him and rewarded a successful challenger by making him the governor of a prefecture.[33]

Chinese martial arts lost official acceptance in the 13th century and never fully regained their former status. China fell to foreign domination in 1215, leading to a succession of ruling Mongol and Manchu dynasties that lasted until 1911. These rulers feared rebellions from their subjects and discouraged the Chinese people from practicing martial arts, which they saw as an activity that promoted nationalism and military preparedness.[34] The foreign rulers encouraged the Chinese people to direct their energy into science, spirituality, and art, rather than the martial arts.[35] In contrast to the case in many nations that were not dominated by foreigners and that offered paths to fame and power through martial prowess, almost the only path open to ambitious Chinese was scholarship, as demonstrated in the civil service examinations that granted government jobs.[36] The Chinese military became a separate class, closed off to most Chinese, isolated on the northern frontier, and dominated by military families with foreign roots.[37] The military, and the arts connected with it, became a fringe experience in China, neither understood nor valued by most of the population. Most Chinese abandoned martial arts, with only isolated groups such as the military families on the frontier and bandits keeping the arts alive.[38] This convinced many Chinese that martial arts were dishonorable, fit only for criminals and barbarians.[39] The emperors so feared rebellion among their own population that they eventually decided to surrender to the British rather than allow mass enlistments of their own population into the army.[40] There is no indication that the Chinese who came to America immediately abandoned this view when they crossed the Pacific.

An American journalist noted that the most popular pastimes among the Chinese included kite flying, boat races, and gambling. He expressed admiration for Chinese performers who calmly juggled dangerous weapons.[41] Vigorous sports were not nearly as popular in China as they were in the West. In contrast to the views of noble athletes common to the traditions of Greece, Rome, and England, most Chinese considered strenuous athletics disreputable activity, fit only for foreigners and criminals. The popular perception of Chinese men as weak while in their own nation extended to Chinese immigrants to the United States, whom the press typically dismissed as weak and cowardly.[42]

American perceptions of the Chinese were mostly negative, particularly regarding their ability to demonstrate manly virtues; however, American observers occasionally complimented them. These compliments indicate a belief that spirituality and commerce could bring people of the East and the West together. Some of the few compliments American observers bestowed on Chinese immigrants during the mid–19th century indicate that Americans were open to the idea that men from China possessed potential as workers, Christians, and even Americans. In Baltimore, a journalist informed readers that immigrants into California from China were hard working and polite. He argued that the Chinese and whites could learn from each other.[43] Other papers endorsed this vision, reprinting the article without comment.[44] The Reverend Henry M. Field argued that the Chinese were hard-working people who were beginning to convert to Christianity in large numbers.[45] He predicted that the Chinese people who had lived in America would soon become vital allies for missionaries spreading Christianity into Asia, suggesting that religion could bring people of East and West together.[46] A scholar, recently returned from the California gold fields in 1852, suggested that the Chinese were industrious gold miners who were eager to convert to Christianity; he suggested that by working in America and studying the Bible, they would quickly become Americanized.[47] Even these compliments were often backhanded, however. A visitor from California praised the hard-working Chinese on the West Coast in 1851, explaining that the Chinese men living in California were excellent laundresses."[48] The author's decision to diminish Chinese manhood even as he praised their industriousness indicates the racist derision the Chinese faced even at this early date. Many Americans viewed the Chinese immigrants as effeminate because they engaged in jobs typically seen as belonging to women.[49] The irony is that the Chinese men typically took these jobs because European immigrants successfully barred Asians from other, more prestigious forms of work.[50]

American observers were far more impressed when they encountered men from a different part of Asia. A combination of luck and geography allowed Japan to avoid foreign domination and retain a militaristic culture. Japan sits on a chain of islands that are separated from the Asian mainland by the Sea of Japan, a watery obstacle that often protected Japan from foreign invasion.[51] In 1274, a Mongol army attempted and ultimately failed to conquer Japan after facing determined resistance led by the samurai, Japan's elite warriors.[52] A typhoon sank the Mongol invasion fleet of 1281, a storm which became the divine winds or *kamikaze* of Japanese legend.[53] During the 1540s, the Japanese began trading with Europe.[54] Western influence spread through the nation, particularly in the form of missionaries, and resulted in a failed rebellion launched by Japanese Christian peasants in 1637 and brutally crushed by samurai loyal to the government.[55] The Japanese government then expelled all Europeans, except for a small number of Portuguese whom they allowed to continue trading through Nagasaki, demonstrating their ability to dictate control of their own territory and interact with the rest of the world only on their own terms.[56] Unlike in China, which was ruled by foreigners and martial artists dispatched it to the disrespected fringes of society, Japanese martial artists remained at the center of national culture as embodiments of the masculine virtues admired by the Japanese people.[57]

In 1852, Commodore Mathew Perry led an expedition to Japan to open the door for trade between the United States and Japan, and fight sports slipped in with the diplomats and peddlers. A writer for the *Albion* argued the Japanese were courageous and fascinating.[58] Perry's sailors put on a boxing exhibition and a minstrel show for the Japanese. The Asians responded by holding a sumo contest in honor of their visitors. Both sides observed the very different bodies of their counterparts. Western sailors described the sumo wrestlers as very fat. Japanese artists, in turn, depicted their muscular wrestlers as providing the thin, starving visitors with gifts of rice.[59] Observers from the United States described the particular style of Japanese wrestling as entertainment and preparation for war in great detail. They commented favorably on the Japanese love of the sport, comparing them to the ancient Greeks and Romans.[60] The American consul described the Japanese as a serious people who allowed themselves few entertainments except for wrestling.[61] A traveler from the United States noted that many of the poorest Japanese men made a living as professional wrestlers.[62] Many Americans described the Japanese a manly race owing to their love of wrestling, but still considered themselves superior, noting that American fighters consistently bested the Japanese experts, even when the Americans were far smaller than their opponents.[63] The Japanese nation was generally eager to engage the West and possessed a confidence born of its identity as an independent and powerful nation.[64] Japan had defeated the Mongols, remained independent as neighboring nations fell to Western imperialists, engaged Western missionaries on its own terms, and felt as if it had little to fear and a great deal to gain from engaging the West.[65] The Japanese actively interacted with the West, attempting to export their own culture while learning from foreigners.[66]

As Japan opened to the West, its people began traveling the globe, encountering a global community that often welcomed them as the representatives of a free and independent nation. Once again, visitors to America from Asia enjoyed a status born of their nation's relationship to the rest of the world and their occupations. The first Japanese visitors to America were upper-class diplomats from a fiercely independent nation rather than the working-class laborers from a subjugated China.[67] The *New York Times* scolded American bureaucrats who failed to sufficiently prepare for the arrival of high-ranking Japanese guests.[68] When a diplomatic delegation from Japan arrived in New York, the American press treated them with respect, referring to them as "great men."[69] An English traveler, writing for an American audience, provided approving descriptions of a wrestling exhibition between Japanese females he witnessed in a Stockholm theater.[70] A minister scolded Americans for encouraging drunkenness among the normally sober Japanese visitors, suggesting that the Japanese visitors were morally superior to many Americans.[71]

Japanese acrobats and circus performers followed closely on the heels of more official travelers, providing another moment of connection between the people of East and West.[72] Many American made their first contact with Japanese culture through the acrobats who toured the nation beginning in the 1860s.[73] A New York journalist's account of 1867, reprinted in Chicago, praised the troupe of Japanese performers he met as excellent entertainers who demonstrated intelligence and charm in social settings.[74] Later the same year, the *New York Times* reported the rapid recovery that a Japanese acrobat was making after falling during a performance due to an equipment failure. The account suggested his rapid healing was proof that his physical training had rendered him nearly indestructible.[75] When a reporter for the same paper interviewed members of a Japanese acrobatic troupe in 1871, the account praised the foreigners as gentlemen with excellent manners.[76] The Japanese performers became a sensation across the West, earning praise from numerous American observers.[77] Some of these examples may seem exaggerated, but the evidence clearly indicates that many Americans respected and admired the Japanese. Nevertheless, even as Americans generally welcomed the Japanese and enjoyed their presence as performers and honored guests, Americans sometimes displayed racial prejudice against them.

American observers often described Japanese male bodies in feminine terms. One writer suggested the typical Japanese military officer was a small man with feminine facial features.[78] An 1868 eugenics study of the Aino people, living on islands off the coast of Japan, argued that the Aino men's beards and large chest muscles gave them a masculine appearance as opposed to the more effeminate Japanese.[79] A journalist explained that Japanese men's bodies looked female and that only their shorter hair styles indicated their gender.[80] Benjamin Smith Lyman, an American engineer who worked in Japan, suggested that Japanese men looked feminine because they lacked the facial hair common among Western men.[81] Even American praise for Japanese bodies was somewhat tempered. A reporter described a famous acrobat as small and boyish rather than in unambiguously masculine terms.[82] Another reporter described a Japanese performer by noting he was far stronger than his feminine physical appearance had initially indicated.[83]

Other insults revealed a belief that the Japanese were more primitive than persons of European ancestry. In the same year that Perry landed in Japan, a journalist described Japanese-style writing as ugly and suggested the Japanese people were too primitive to have adopted the superior Roman alphabet.[84] Also in 1852, the *Democrat's Review* analyzed the Japanese and concluded that while the Japanese embodied many admirable virtues, their government was sorely lacking; according to this source, the Japanese were controlled by an autocratic and primitive government.[85] The next year, a more in-depth analysis of Japan concluded that the Shinto religion was primitive and the Japanese political and economic systems were like those of long-departed feudal Europe. In remarks similar to the statements made by Rudyard Kipling half a century later, the author argued that the West had a duty to educate the Japanese in modern-style commerce, government, and Christianity, even if the Japanese were not interested in the lessons.[86]

Many American observers were quick to discuss varieties of Asians, often comparing the newly contacted Japanese with the more familiar Chinese. Americans made these comparisons while operating within a complicated understanding of race that was radically different from the more simplistic black-and-white binary accepted by many Americans today. They approved of the Japanese attempts to embrace the West and argued that alliances with them were far more promising than those with any other Asian nation.[87] A journalist noted that the bodies of the Japanese looked more masculine and rugged than those of the Chinese.[88] An evaluation of the military capacity of the two nations concluded that the Japanese were better soldiers and more dangerous on the battlefield.[89] A writer for the *Southern Planter* argued that China had an effeminate culture that prided itself on scholarship and hard work. In contrast, the Japanese were less intelligent, simple, often violent, and manlier.[90] A visitor to Asia compared the two nations and told the readers of the *Spirit of the Times* that what Great Britain was to the West, Japan was to Asia—that is, an island nation of manly virtues and martial prowess. He argued that Japan was nothing like China, with its emphasis on scholarship and distaste for war.[91] An article from the *Edinburgh Review* that was reprinted in New York dismissed the peoples of India and China as racially inferior before proclaiming that the Japanese people's ability to retain national independence made them racially superior to their Asian neighbors. However, the praise for the Japanese as first among the Asians was tempered by derision born of religious intolerance, as the writer dismissed the dominant Shinto religion of Japan as a primitive form of spirituality.[92] As with the Catholic Irish, religion helped define racial boundaries.[93] Animosity between the Japanese and the Chinese also complicated and reinforced racial distinctions between the two peoples. Japanese immigrants expressed anger when Americans confused them with the Chinese, for whom they openly expressed hatred.[94] These intra–Asian racial conflicts grew from territorial economic and political conflicts between the nations of China and Japan.[95]

Demographics and labor provided another point of contrast between the Chinese and the Japanese. During the 19th century, far more Chinese newcomers came to the United States than Japanese immigrants.[96] By 1867, the Chinese lived in constant fear of assault and riots initiated by the Irish immigrants who competed with them for work.[97] While many Chinese were laborers excluded by European immigrants from all but the most low-paying and poorly esteemed trades, Japanese immigrants were typically middle- or upper-class business owners.[98] Some of the first Japanese families arrived in California in 1869, with all of the plants and equipment they needed to expand their silk production businesses into America.[99] Americans regarded silk growers as skilled workers, with expertise largely unknown in the West, and the California legislature paid Japanese silk experts to settle in the state.[100] In 1869, Charles Adams, a member of the American Social Science Association, expressed fears at the association's annual meeting that Japanese immigrants might turn New York into a Japanese city.[101] A writer for the *Independent* dismissed the scholar's fears, arguing that New York would benefit from the transformation.[102] It does not appear that any significant labor disputes occurred between Japanese immigrants and other groups in the United States before 1870. This is probably a result of the small number of Japanese immigrants and the fact that they typically engaged in trades, such as silk production, that other workers lacked the skills to undertake. In contrast, the Chinese immigrants' large numbers and presence in the unskilled labor market led to bloody conflicts with European immigrants. In 1870, which was the first year the United States Census Bureau compiled numbers for both Chinese and Japanese immigrants living in the Unites States, 64,565 Chinese lived in the United States, compared to only 73 people from Japan.[103]

The Japanese engaged the West in a more open and welcoming fashion than many of their Asian neighbors. In an attempt to survive the tide of Western imperialism, the nation's political, cultural, and intellectual leaders attempted to build relationships and alliances with Western nations.[104] The Japanese also tried to learn from the West in an effort to strengthen their nation.[105] Consistent with this pattern, Japanese fighters eagerly interacted with Westerners, actively engaging them in an effort to build cultural relationships and share knowledge.[106] This attitude stood in contrast to that displayed by visitors from other parts of Asia. Fighters from the Philippine islands kept their martial arts a secret from Westerners. They practiced within their own communities, but protected them from prying Western eyes, afraid that foreigners who uncovered their secrets would become more dangerous adversaries.[107] Chinese fighters also considered their martial arts secrets to conceal from Westerners.[108] A Chinese American man named Lo Yung Fat gave Kung Fu lessons in San Francisco's Chinatown during the 1870s. His students included at least one Chinese immigrant who worked for the San Francisco police, but there is no indication that he ever accepted students who were not of Chinese ancestry.[109] Chinese fighters feared that if foreigners learned Chinese martial arts, they would use the knowledge against them.[110]

Urban geography strengthened the divide between the Chinese and other Americans by adding a spatial component to the existing cultural and racial gulf.[111] Facing racial discrimination and open hostility from both Americans and other Asians, Chinese immigrants, like members of many ethnic groups, congregated in homogeneous enclaves in an effort to protect them-

III. Asian Martial Arts Come to the United States, 1850–1941   109

selves.[112] They were under pressure from European immigrants, who competed with them in the unskilled labor market and occasionally assaulted and rioted against the Chinese as early as the 1860s.[113] Beginning in the mid-19th century, almost every major city in the United States included a Chinatown.[114] The largest Chinatowns were in San Francisco, Los Angeles, and New York.[115] The term "Chinatown" as a description for these ethnic enclaves shows up in American newspapers by the 1860s.[116] Within their enclaves, Chinese workers toiled in laundries, barber shops, restaurants, and garment factories.[117] Economic desperation often leads people to engage in illegal enterprises to survive,[118] and Chinese immigrants were no different. They provided access to opium, which was made illegal in some American cities as early as 1875; gambling, also criminal in many 19th-century American cities; and prostitution, illegal in many parts of 19th-century America, but often ignored in exchange for bribes to police or local politicians.

Most Chinese immigrants into the United States were male.[119] Not surprisingly, so were most residents of American Chinatowns. As a result, these communities became places where Chinese men developed a unique Asian-influenced bachelor subculture.[120] These communities often paralleled and interacted with the European and African American bachelor subcultures. Commercialized sex, gambling, and intoxicants were common themes among the bachelor subcultures of Asian, African, and European Americans[121] and, in fact, represented key aspects of bachelor life for American men of every race. Most large cities included a separate vice district for blacks.[122] By the mid-19th century, prostitution was a staple of bachelor-dominated urban life in America.[123] New York's Chinatown, where most prostitutes were white women providing services for Chinese men, served as one of several clusters of commercialized sex in the city.[124] In San Francisco, things worked a bit differently. Most prostitutes in that Chinatown were Chinese females living in conditions of virtual slavery, imported specifically to provide sexual services to Chinese men.[125] Chinese immigrants enjoyed intoxicants, but preferred opium to the alcohol that flowed so freely among white and black men.[126] Gambling was another popular pastime of young bachelors. European and African American enjoyed English-style card and dice games.[127] Chinese immigrants also loved to gamble, but preferred games such as baakgaap and fan tan, which they brought with them from China.[128] In white neighborhoods, Anglo, Irish, and Italian criminals organized to control these illegal enterprises.[129] Chinatown produced its own version of organized crime. The gangsters contributed to the popular perception that Chinatowns were dangerous, but the danger did not always deter visitors.

Americans noted the rise of Chinatowns, studying them with fascina-

An advertisement for the popular musical comedy, *A Trip to Chinatown*. The play centers on two young men who seek love and adventure in Chinatown but end up proving their manhood when a fight breaks out over dinner. Published during 1900 by the U.S. Printing Co. of Cincinnati and New York (Library of Congress Prints and Photographs Division).

tion. Chinatowns possessed competing reputations as a scene of the exotic but moral as well as the illicit and dangerous. The presence of numerous brothels, opium dens, and gambling houses in Chinatowns gave the enclaves a reputation as vice districts, which, along with reports that diseases flourished in the areas, convinced many non-Chinese Americans to avoid Chinatowns.[130] This strengthened the racial divide and impeded the possible flow of fighting arts to and from the Chinese. However, a few visitors braved the sordid reputations and threats of disease in Chinatowns and reported their findings. In 1863, the health officer of Sacramento claimed in an official report that his greatest challenge was found in Chinatown, battling against the unsanitary conditions of Chinese immigrants. He described the city's Chinatown as a dangerous and filthy place responsible for 95 percent of Sacramento's deaths due to unknown diseases.[131]

In 1869, Annie Morris and several companions visited San Francisco's Chinatown and explained to the readers of the *American and Continental Monthly* that the area was so foreign that she often forgot she was only a few blocks from her own home. She described the fascination she felt with the area and admired the exotic fabrics, foods, and glassware available for purchase.[132] She praised the Chinese as among the most hard-working and moral people in the city and as being master cooks and skilled laundrymen. She noted the presence of opium, but did not comment on the drug.[133] Her observations indicate that commerce, like fight sports, could bring the people of East and West together.

In 1870, a journalist claimed that walking the streets of San Francisco's Chinatown provided the illusion of an overseas visit even in the midst of his own nation.[134] Later that same year, Auber Forestier explained to the readers of the *Saturday Evening Post* that he traveled to Grass Valley's Chinatown in hopes of finding something unique among the shops and street performers.[135] A Boston crowd eagerly listened as a visitor from California described the exotic trinkets he saw produced in Chinatown.[136]

Not every visitor to Chinatown came in search of clean laundry or exotic trinkets, of course. Many sought the illicit entertainments, including opium, prostitutes, and gambling, that gave Chinatowns their reputations as vice districts.[137]

Chinese immigrants moved into Chinatowns in hopes of protecting themselves from violence born of racial and economic hostilities, but in the 1870s a rising wave of anti-Chinese anger swept the nation and placed the Chinese in greater peril. In the early 1870s, the United States fell into a deep depression caused by crop failures and banking scandals.[138] Many workers, who had occasionally harassed, assaulted, and rioted against the Chinese for years, developed a newfound animosity for Chinese immigrants.[139] Many European American workers believed that the Chinese willingness to accept lower wages and worse working conditions decreased wages and diminished working conditions for all workers.[140] In Massachusetts, a coalition of Irish and French Canadian immigrants drove most of the Chinese from the state.[141] Los Angeles's Chinatown erupted in violence in 1871 as a result of long-standing animosities when a mob of native-born Californians stormed Chinese homes and attempted to burn down an entire city block. The Chinese fought back with hatchets and pistols, but the mob overpowered them, lynching 16 Chinese men.[142] Chinese miners in Oregon fared little better, suffering assaults and arson.[143] In San Francisco, a portion of the 10,000 workers assembled to discuss labor concerns wrecked a Chinese-owned laundry, set fire to it, and cut fire hoses to prevent the firefighters from extinguishing the blaze.[144] In his work *The Indispensable Enemy,* Alexander Saxton demonstrated that this violence was so common that perpetrators treated it as routine.[145] The violence widened the racial gulf, but did not completely erase the Chinese influence on Americans.

When Chinese immigrants continued to come to the United States in spite of the campaign of violence, European American workers increasingly sought a political solution.[146] The economic depression led to increased unemployment, and many unemployed and underemployed workers began to agitate for wider changes.[147] Emerging labor unions and trade guilds sought to create a coalition of immigrants from Europe that excluded non–Europeans, particularly the Chinese.[148] In 1870, the San Francisco Labor Union adopted a resolution arguing that Chinese immigrants polluted America.[149] Sue Fawn Chung argued that by the end of the 1870s, the anti–Chinese movement was a unifying sentiment among many diverse aspects of the growing American labor movement.[150] In 1880, the San Francisco Board of Health condemned the local Chinatown as a nuisance and called for its destruction.[151] Its decision met with the approval of workers who had threatened to riot if the city's officials refused to act.[152] American politicians across the nation, including both Republicans and Democrats, seized on the anti–Chinese sentiment in an effort to gain votes.[153] One of the few voices of support for the Chinese came from the American author John Jennings, who lamented in his extraordinary book from 1882, *Theatrical and Circus Life,* that the expulsion of the Chinese workers would virtually shut down the entertainment industry in many American cities.[154] Jennings' observations indicate that, like the popular Japanese circus performers, theaters provided a place of positive cultural interaction between people from the East and West. The anti–Chinese movement won its biggest victory in 1882, when Congress passed the

Chinese Exclusion Act.[155] The legislation did not remove the Chinese from America or even end all immigration, but it did prevent the entry of Chinese laborers who had never before been in America and, as a result, froze the existing bachelor culture in place.[156] Against a backdrop of increasing hostility, a particular type of Chinese man began to push out of the bachelor enclaves.

Expanding from the vice districts of Chinatowns, some Chinese immigrants built a reputation as dangerous members of organized crime syndicates that controlled the trade in prostitutes, intoxicants, and gambling. In 1873, the San Francisco police announced that Chinese secret societies, known as Tongs, were conducting criminal operations in the state.[157] An article in the *Los Angeles Times* warned the public that the Tongs worked with the support of dangerous criminals called the hatchet men, so named for their weapon of choice.[158] In 1876, a journalist described the hatchet men in a hearing held by the California state legislature. He argued they were fighting men who killed without hesitation.[159] The same year, the *Chicago Tribune* painted a picture of hatchet men as ferocious fighters who "yell like wild Injuns" and attack "with the energy of a trip-hammer and the vehemence of a Sioux."[160] The racialized imagery indicates an attempt at categorization, placing the hatchet men into the same racial space as Native American warriors. The hatchet men earned praise in the press for the bravery they displayed during brutal street fights in Portland, Oregon.[161] Their violence took on a mystical component, as hatchet men preparing for confrontations ate the hearts of wild cats, believing that they would provide them with magical strength.[162] Fredric J. Masters, writing for the *Chautauquan*, described the violent work of the Chinese gangsters. He argued that hatchet men were eager to kill, ignored pain, and remained aggressive while absorbing gunfire that would force most Europeans to retreat. According to Masters, the bravery that Chinese gangsters displayed in street fights conclusively disproved the commonly held belief that all Chinese men were cowards.[163]

While it is possible that observers exaggerated the dangers posed by Chinese criminals as part of a wider effort to slander the Chinese, the hatchet men were clearly a real, if exaggerated, phenomenon. Thus, a century before Bruce Lee began selling out movie theaters, journalists suggested that an entire group of Chinese men—their names largely forgotten—displayed manly virtues of bravery, fearlessness, and stoicism. They argued that the Chinese were capable of masculinity. Violence, first demonstrated to further criminal enterprises, poured into the arena.

Chinese immigrants, including members of criminal organizations, put their bodies to the test in the athletic contests. The *National Police Gazette*, that eminent journal of the emerging sporting scene, announced that two rival enforcers for the Tongs introduced a new and brutal fight sport to Pittsburgh. The men fought for a large and enthusiastic audience assembled in a Chinese laundry. The bout included the use of kicks delivered with sharpened spurs, a technique unknown in the West.[164] Another pair of Chinese fighters put on an exhibition of punches and kicks in California, but the American spectators were bored with what they considered the timidity of the competitors.[165] They were more impressed with two Chinese immigrants in Montana who squared off for the delight of their audience, each with a hatchet in one hand and a knife in the other.[166] Witnesses reported that the fight proceeded ferociously until blood flowed and police intervened.[167] The *National Police Gazette* reported what it claimed was the first gloved boxing match between Chinese men. This observation once again highlights the problematic comparisons of Eastern and Western techniques. A careful examination of the account reveals a fight with little connection to traditional Western-style boxing bouts, even though the *Gazette*'s reporter called it boxing. The fighters kicked each other and wrestled on the ground in spite of the referee's demands that they limit themselves to boxing techniques.[168] An account of a wrestling bout between Chinese men in New York held before a crowd of immigrants included a stylistic observation that the Chinese fighting arts held technique in higher regard than brute strength, an observation consistent with comments by Japanese fighters about their arts and indicating a possible common theme in Asian-style martial arts.[169]

When the Chinese Exclusion Act of 1882 severely limited Chinese immigration into the United States, the Japanese, many of whom were fleeing upheavals caused by their nation's attempts to modernize, helped fill the gap. Tens of thousands of these individuals were living in California by the end of the century.[170] In 1880, before the passage of the Chinese Exclusion Act, the U.S. population included 104,468 Chinese-born residents and only 401 Japanese-born residents.[171] By 1900, the numbers were somewhat more balanced, with 81,534 Chinese-born and 27,788 Japanese-born persons in the United States.[172] Many of the Japanese worked as farm laborers, particularly in the emerging California sugar beet industry.[173] These Japanese workers inherited some of the discrimination aimed at their Chinese predecessors as they began filling a somewhat similar niche in the labor market.[174] Even as religion, trade goods, and fight sports provided moments of connection between East and West, labor disputes pushed them apart. By the end of the century, an anti–Japanese movement began taking shape along the same lines as its predecessor anti–Chinese movement.[175]

Japanese immigrants practiced their martial arts in the United States, earning praise from many Americans, even the ones who bested the men

III. Asian Martial Arts Come to the United States, 1850–1941   115

from across the Pacific. Style-on-style match-ups in America between fighters of Asian and European ancestry became increasingly common in the final years of the 19th century. Ever since Perry's expedition had made landfall in the land of the rising sun, fighters from the United States and Japan had learned from each other. As the 19th century progressed, exchanges between fighters of East and West became commonplace.[176] Japanese sailors serving on American ships often transmitted techniques, just as their African American predecessors did earlier in the century.[177] Some American fighters admired their Asian counterparts and complimented them publicly, but they showed little interest in adopting their arts, which seemed incapable of demonstrating any clear advantage over more familiar styles.[178]

Japanese fighters looked on Western fight sports with more open minds. Born in 1860 into a family of wealthy merchants, Jigoro Kano earned a doctorate and became a respected educator. Kano embraced the West, traveling though the United States and Europe, and learning from Western sports even as he became a master of traditional Japanese jujitsu.[179] In 1882, he founded a new art he called judo or "the gentle way," a term he used to distinguish his almost muscular Christian emphasis on athleticism and morality from the often unapologetically brutal practices of traditional Japanese arts.[180] Judo was a middle way, a compromise that incorporated many ideas from both the East and the West.[181] It reinforced the duality of Japanese martial arts as both sport and self-defense. Kano's ideas proved to offer an excellent physical education program for students by formalizing the new fight sport of judo and opening up a tantalizing toolbox of violence for fighters. Sport added realism to training, and Kano encouraged students to learn self-defense techniques including the use of clubs and swords, which were not allowed in the sporting contests he sponsored.[182] By 1900, Japanese educators had made judo a required activity for all students.[183] While securing a monopoly on the domestic market, Kano got into the export business.

In the first decade of the 20th century, judo experts fanned out across the globe like missionaries of well-mannered mayhem bringing humanity the good news of bone-shattering salvation. Years later, Kano reflected on his life, recalling that after inventing judo he felt a need to share it with the world.[184] Kano and his students exported judo in an effort to educate the world about their nation.[185] The cultural outreach paved the way for improved national relationships. Koizami Gunji brought judo to Europe, where it became a craze across the continent, particularly in France and Great Britain.[186] Ground-fighting expert Mitsuyo Maeda spread the good word to several nations before settling in Brazil, where he became a celebrity and patriarch of Brazilian fight sports.[187] These arts spread to women as well as men, with London becoming the European capital for female martial artists.[188] A British fitness magazine featured a cover story on the female jujitsu expert Frances Weste, who studied under Japanese masters before launching her jujitsu school for women.[189] British female police volunteers also adopted the art to keep them safe while on patrol.[190] Jujitsu then spread from the police to militants. The oppressed attempted to learn martial arts as a tool of resistance. Sylvia Pankhurst urged her supporters to learn jujitsu and carry clubs to rallies so they could defend themselves against baton-armed police who knew jujitsu, and she called for anyone with knowledge of the martial arts to contact her and offer their expertise.[191] Some suffragettes became known as dangerous characters who would not hesitate to use their martial arts skills to punish rude men.[192] One expert suggested that jujitsu became popular in the United States, largely because Americans wanted to emulate Europeans who practiced the art.[193]

Traveling Japanese experts found fertile ground in an America with a newfound appreciation for athleticism. Both Japanese athletes and their muscular Christian counterparts in America celebrated a union of the athletic and the spiritual.[194] Within the world of sports, the Japanese people once again engaged the West on their own terms, working with foreigners rather than suffering under racist domination. The YMCA recognized the similarities as well as the differences and partnered with leaders in the Japanese sporting community.[195] Fight sports provided a point of connection between the men of East and West since it was an activity men with a shared appreciation for violence but widely different technical backgrounds could agree on. Sam Brown, head of the YMCA in Tokyo, became a jujitsu student during his time in Japan.[196] William Muldoon, an American army veteran turned wrestling champion, was a leader in the American muscular Christianity movement.[197] Muldoon fought challenge matches against Japanese rivals and praised their skills even when he defeated them.[198] Although Christianity is sometimes associated with pacifism, many participants in the muscular Christianity movement saw nothing wrong with violence as long as it was the limited violence of the arena or the properly directed battlefield.[199]

Of the numerous Japanese fighters who crisscrossed America fighting challenge matches, none was more famous than Sorakichi Matsuda. Matsuda was probably the first professional fighter from Asia to work in America, and he was certainly the first to achieve any measure of fame.[200] Unlike the highminded purist Jigoro Kano, who proclaimed his desire to spread Japanese arts as a form of cultural outreach, Matsuda's career demonstrated far greater flexibility. In Japan, he worked as a juggler as well as a professional athlete.[201] He came to America in 1883 as a circus performer, but quickly abandoned

III. Asian Martial Arts Come to the United States, 1850–1941   117

Editorial cartoon titled "The Suffragette That Knew Jiu-Jitsu. The Arrest." Produced by Arthur Wallis Mills. Published in *Punch* and *The Wanganui Chronicle* in 1910 (Wikimedia Commons).

peaceful pursuits for the life of a professional fighter.[202] Matsuda's first bout was an 1884 Greco-Roman bout against Carl "The German Giant" Abs that ended in one of the draws that so often plagued wrestling matches. Next, the Japanese fighter won a victory over James Quigley, the New York Police Department wrestling champion, when Quigley forfeited the match shortly after it began.[203] His defeats of the highly regarded wrestlers James Daly and Edwin Bibby provided more convincing displays of his prowess. Matsuda met his first defeat at the hands of the mixed wrestling champion Duncan Ross in 1884, but Ross expressed tremendous respect for his opponent, complimenting his skill, his physique, and his race.[204] Later the same year Matsuda faced William Muldoon in a mixed-style match similar to those sponsored by the *Police Gazette*. The men fought four rounds, two under the rules of Japanese wrestling and one each according to the rules of Greco-Roman and catch wrestling. Muldoon won the fight easily, three rounds to one. Observers noted that the international bout attracted few customers and barely covered the event's expenses.[205] The remainder of Matsuda's career witnessed a lackluster series of fights in which he experienced more defeats and draws than victories.[206] The few accounts of his fights offer little detail for stylistic comparisons of Eastern and Western techniques or Asian bodies. A rare exception was one observation that Matsuda was not tall enough to do Greco-Roman wrestling.[207] He never made much money wrestling. His European American wife left him after he spent all of her money, threatened to hit her, and moved his Japanese girlfriend into their home.[208] Matsuda died alone and in poverty in 1891 at the age of 32 from illnesses that might have resulted from injuries he suffered in the ring.[209] In an interview, Matsuda once expressed his admiration for John L. Sullivan, the great pugilistic champion, and declared his intention to take up boxing at some future date that Matsuda never lived to see.[210]

While American fighters bested Matsuda in the ring, opponents from another corner of Asia proved more dangerous opponents on distant battlefields. In the final years of the 19th century, Chinese nationalists lashed out after half a century of foreign domination. The Opium Wars of the mid–19th century had left European nations with considerable control over China.[211] The British occupied Hong Kong in 1841. The Chinese faced further humiliations with defeat in the 1894–1895 Sino-Japanese War. In 1897, Russia and Germany pressed their claims in China, securing important strategic ports at the expense of the Chinese. Also in 1897, the British expanded their rule by occupying Weihai and the French seized Zhanjiang. Many Chinese were upset over cultural as well as military domination, and began expressing their anger with Christian missionaries.[212] America's open door policy of 1899 asserted the right of any foreign power to establish a sphere of influence in China while offering nominal support for the Chinese people's authority over their territory; it provided the final straw for some Chinese nationalists.[213] By the spring of 1900, many Chinese were fed up with foreign domination and their government's inability or unwillingness to provide effective resistance. They began lashing out at foreign influences in an uprising known as the Boxer Rebellion.[214]

A group of nationalistic, mystical martial arts experts led the uprising. They called themselves by Chinese terms, which linguists have translated into a variety of English phrases, including "The Society for Unity and Righteousness," "The Righteous Harmonious Fists," "The Society of Harmonious Fists," "The Fists of Patriotic Union," and most commonly, "The Boxers."[215] All of these variations shared references to the movement's emphasis on martial arts.[216] The Boxers initially promoted martial arts as a method of exercise and self-defense from criminals.[217] The group claimed that the spirits of ancient warriors returned from the dead to teach them martial arts.[218] They quickly evolved into a political and military organization. The Boxers put their martial arts knowledge to work during the uprising, sending foreigners

III. Asian Martial Arts Come to the United States, 1850–1941 119

scrambling for defensible positions where they could await reinforcements.[219] A British diplomat, quoted in the *Chicago Daily Tribune,* praised the Boxers' bravery.[220] American Marines under siege in Peking reported the Boxers attacking with furious aggression.[221] Some Chinese immigrants in the United States urged restraint in dealing with the uprising, blaming arrogant missionaries for the conflict.[222] After some initial successes, a coalition of forces from the East and West put down the rebellion, further humiliating Chinese nationalists and widening the gulf between China and the rest of the world.[223] Americans viewed the failed rebellion as further proof that China was a weak nation, incapable of controlling its own territory or resisting foreign domination.[224]

The Boxers sparked a renewed martial arts renaissance in China. Chinese martial arts became an anti-imperialist art form in the Boxers' empty hands.[225] The Boxers also represented a reawakening of the Chinese martial spirit long buried by half a millennium of rule by foreign dynasties that had attempted to divert the Chinese into exclusively peaceful pursuits.[226] For the first time in centuries, masses of Chinese men rose up against their oppressors, enlisted the ghosts of their ancient ancestors, and attempted to make up for a lack of modern weapons with deadly martial arts techniques honed in combat against bandits. Inspired by the extraordinary bravery of the Boxers, many Chinese intellectuals put aside their books, began studying martial arts, and took newfound racialized pride in the violent past they had almost forgotten.[227]

While some American soldiers fought against Chinese nationalists, others entered battle against nationalists from nearby islands. In 1898, the United States went to war with Spain in what is descriptively, if unimaginatively, known as the Spanish–American War. The conflict ended after less than a year of fighting in 1898. Soon after it ended, nationalists in the Philippines, a chain of islands off the coast of Asian mainland ceded to the United States by Spain as part of the peace treaty, launched an uprising against their new overlords in 1899.[228] The United States declared victory in 1902 with the surrender of the last Filipino general, but sporadic violence continued until 1913.[229] The campaign pitted well-equipped American soldiers against insurgents who, like the Boxers, relied on their courage and their knowledge of traditional martial arts.

In the Philippine jungles, American soldiers encountered fierce guerrilla fighters who, like the Boxers, attempted to make up for a lack of modern weaponry with martial arts.[230] Filipino martial arts were mostly focused on the use of weapons including daggers, clubs, and machetes.[231] Each region in the Philippines produced its own variation of the very similar and closely related martial arts, with northerners calling their form *arnis*, residents in the central regions preferring the term *escrima*, and southerners calling their style *kali*.[232] All of the arts shared a common lineage of techniques borrowed from Malaysia, India, and Spain as well as indigenous Filipino techniques.[233] Americans recognized their opponents' skills and referred to the Filipinos as dangerous foes and capable fighters.[234] Indeed, they considered the typical insurgent a dangerous animal.[235] American combat veterans reported that the insurgents used firearms, but did their most lethal work during silent ambushes launched with knives.[236] American war correspondents, traveling with American soldiers, described the Filipino insurgents as remarkable men who continued to charge even as they absorbed multiple bullets.[237] Dissatisfied with their handguns that were unable to stop the charging insurgents, the American army switched from a .38 to a heavier .45 caliber sidearm.[238]

Filipino martial arts were unable to bridge the gap between East and West in spite of the somewhat flexible racial relationships at play. The Filipinos understood that Americans of African ancestry faced discrimination in the United States and attempted to make common cause with them against whites.[239] These efforts rarely succeeded: only about a dozen black soldiers chose to fight with the Filipinos.[240] Nevertheless, race and nationality made for complicated identities during the insurgency. One African American soldier explained that while his racial sympathies rested with the Filipinos, he was incapable of turning his back on his own nation.[241] While it is possible that some of the dozen men who fought with the rebels might have learned martial arts from their new allies, no records of such lessons remain. An exchange of martial arts knowledge would have been hampered by the tendency of Filipino fighters to treat techniques as carefully guarded secrets, refusing to share their knowledge even with Filipinos from other areas, giving rise to the regionalized variations of their arts.[242] Many fighters were even more secretive and shared knowledge only within their own families.[243] While martial arts knowledge does not appear to have crossed the racialized and nationalized divide during the conflict, at least not in any significant or long-lasting way, it did solidify American understandings of the Filipinos as skillful warriors.[244] This understanding laid the groundwork for American willingness to eventually embrace Filipinos as worthy allies half a century later during World War II.[245] The divide that prevented the transmission of martial arts began to change only many years later, during World War II when Americans and Filipinos worked together as allies rather than adversaries.[246]

Japanese martial artists, in contrast, were eager to share their arts with Westerners, and sources provide ample evidence of Americans learning Japanese arts. Westerners who traveled to Japan for a variety of reasons became

III. Asian Martial Arts Come to the United States, 1850–1941   121

students and teachers of martial arts during their stay. An American military officer, Hubbard Wigmore, applied to the Tokyo Martial Art Society in hopes of learning jujitsu and Japanese-style fencing.[247] The famous American novelist Harrie Irving Hancock also studied Asian martial arts while in Japan.[248] Sam Brown, the head of the YMCA in Tokyo, spent three hours each day training in jujitsu while living in Asia.[249] D. T. Weed, professor of English at Keio University in Tokyo, became the first American to earn a black belt in a Japanese martial art.[250] The American boxer A. M. Loughney studied jujitsu and gave boxing lessons while in Japan.[251] He argued the Japanese took to boxing quickly because, in his opinion, they were natural-born fighters.[252] This contrasts with Hancock's claim that Japanese fighters dismissed Western-style boxing as shockingly brutal, which once more highlights the problems with making definitive comments on style preferences.[253]

Japanese fighters and Asian admirers began increased promotion of Asian arts in the Unites States in the first decade of the 20th century. Jujitsu practitioners began touring on the vaudeville circuit.[254] Judo experts began giving classes in New York, Washington, and Boston.[255] Judo clubs also formed in Seattle, Hawaii, and Los Angeles, locations of the nation's largest populations of Japanese immigrants.[256] Esa Sugizaki, a veteran of the United States Navy, founded a Japanese club in Brooklyn that began teaching jujitsu, Japanese fencing, and Western-style boxing.[257] The Nippon Athletic Club in Atlanta emphasized athleticism in the judo lessons it gave to local men and women who trained together.[258] Chinese and Japanese fighters entertained large crowds as part of style-on-style matches that included punches and grappling.[259] Madison Square Garden hosted a bout in which an Icelandic wrestling champion bested a Japanese jujitsu expert.[260] When American wrestlers pointed out that Japanese experts failed to demonstrate a significant superiority in the ring, Japanese fighters replied that many of the most devastating jujitsu tricks were lethal and not permitted in sporting fights.[261] Lethal techniques sounded awfully appealing to some Americans more interested in survival than sport.

In 1902, Sam Hill, a wealthy American businessman living in Seattle who witnessed a judo demonstration while traveling through Japan, invited the judo expert professor Yoshiaki Yamashita to come to America and teach his son, whom he considered weak and effeminate, the art of judo in hopes of salvaging his masculinity.[262] Yamashita accepted the offer. Shortly after arriving on the West Coast, he proved his skills by soundly defeating a well-regarded English boxer. The judo expert then abandoned Hill, without ever giving a single lesson to his son, and began a very popular tour of the United States in which he gave demonstrations, taught classes, and fought challenge matches.²⁶³ Yoshiaki Yamashita often shared the stage with another judo expert, his wife Fude.²⁶⁴ He gave demonstrations at Harvard, the U.S. Naval Academy, and West Point.²⁶⁵ In Washington, D.C., Professor Yamashita gave private lessons to long-time fighter President Theodore Roosevelt and his two sons.²⁶⁶ The president befriended Yamashita and hired him to teach at the Naval Academy.²⁶⁷ When naval officers questioned whether Japanese arts could offer them anything of value, Roosevelt proposed a fight between Yamashita and the best fighter at the academy. The navy accepted, sending 32-year-old Lieutenant George Grant, who stood at 6'9" and weighed 320 pounds to face the 41-year-old Yamashita, who was barely 5'7" tall and tipped the scales at a mere 150 pounds. After two minutes of combat, Grant lay on his back, turning blue from lack of oxygen as Yamashita choked the life from his body. The naval officer surrendered, the American high command apologized to the president, and Yamashita became the newest member of the academy's faculty.²⁶⁸

Sam Hill spent the rest of his life denouncing judo, telling anyone who would listen about Yamashita's desertion, and using his considerable influence to help ensure that, at least in Seattle, the racial divide remained and white men rarely practiced Japanese arts.²⁶⁹ In spite of Hill's anger, another judo expert, Professor Tomet, came to America and gave demonstrations at West Point. When Tomet called for volunteers to fight him, Cadet Tipton, a star football player, stepped forward and repeatedly pinned and threw Tomet.²⁷⁰ American and Japanese newspapers proclaimed the fight a defeat for the Japanese nation and race.²⁷¹

American police departments began teaching Japanese martial arts to their officers early in the 20th century. Many such departments had established boxing and wrestling programs in the mid–19th century.²⁷² By the early 20th century, the police boxing programs faced mounting pressure from increasingly active reformers who still associated boxing with corruption and vice, in spite of the attempts at reform by boxers.²⁷³ Wrestling faced little direct opposition from reformers, but Western wrestlers such as the New York Police detective William Muldoon worked with Japanese fighters and modified their systems under Asian influences beginning in the 1880s.²⁷⁴ New York City Police Commissioner McAdoo invited Higashi, a jujitsu expert, to demonstrate Asian style arts for the city's police force in 1904.²⁷⁵ Higashi repeatedly embarrassed the police, throwing and pinning them with ease and laying the foundation for a police jujitsu program.²⁷⁶ The police in Connecticut adopted jujitsu, believing it would help small officers subdue much larger criminals.²⁷⁷ New York Patrolman Henry Seligman earned praise when he used his jujitsu skills to subdue a criminal attempting to force his way into

III. Asian Martial Arts Come to the United States, 1850–1941   123

This illustration shows President Theodore Roosevelt and the Democratic nominee for president, Alton B. Parker, as boxers in a boxing ring, shaking hands before the start of the match. Uncle Sam, as the referee, stands in the background. Published on the cover of *Puck* magazine, July 20, 1904 (Library of Congress Prints and Photographs Division).

A policeman and a policewoman practice self-defense techniques in a photograph taken sometime between 1909 and 1932 (Library of Congress Prints and Photographs Division).

a woman's apartment.[278] Jujitsu became part of the training regimen for Chicago policewomen after British policewomen demonstrated its effectiveness.[279] The New York police incorporated jujitsu competitions into their annual charity carnival.[280] In Providence, Rhode Island, police officers provided jujitsu exhibitions as part of a community outreach program.[281]

American racial prejudice impeded the flow of martial arts knowledge from Asia into the Unites States. The idea that racially distinct bodies functioned differently was a fundamental assertion of the various eugenics movements.[282] A 1911 study claimed Japanese people had superior feet to Europeans since they were able to grip and manipulate objects with their toes, an ability they shared with Egyptians.[283] The *New York Times* suggested that there was no harm in jujitsu training for the police, but the classes were unlikely to change much in the field since Americans would never fully master the art. The journalist argued that jujitsu was ideally suited to the smaller bodies and more cunning instincts of the Japanese, but not to the brute strength of Americans.[284] A journalist in upstate New York agreed, arguing that while the police might obtain some small benefit from studying jujitsu, white men would never master the art because it required tremendous strength, flexibility, and agility that only the Japanese possessed.[285] These descriptions demonstrate a racialized understanding of the world in which Japanese and American men possessed different bodies that prevented them from excelling at the same fighting arts. Any men who accepted the advice of these prominent newspapers would be unlikely to take up jujitsu or to engage in it enthusiastically if they believed their non–Asian bodies were incapable of ever mastering the martial arts. The articles show how even complimentary racial perceptions—for example, the idea that the Japanese were exceptionally agile—created barriers to cultural transmission and impeded the flow of martial arts from Asia into the United States.

Police officers took up jujitsu for many reasons, all of which stemmed from its dualistic reputation as both a dangerous art filled with techniques too dangerous for the arena and a humane approach to physical confrontations when martial artists demonstrated restraint and limited themselves to less dangerous techniques. The New York police began training in jujitsu only after a Japanese expert physically dominated members of the force, thereby convincing police officials that jujitsu offered a superior capacity for physical domination compared to traditional Western arts.[286] A Milwaukee journalist reported that policewomen studied jujitsu because the art's dangerous techniques allowed women to subdue much larger and stronger male adversaries.[287] The *National Police Gazette* suggested that police studied jujitsu because the Japanese open-handed chop was a more lethal blow than the boxer's punch.[288] Other sources indicate police interest in jujitsu was born of a desire to limit violence. New York Deputy Police Commissioner Godley referred to his department's new jujitsu program as a more humane method of subduing criminals.[289] He may have made this comment, at least in part, because the New York police department was under fire at this time for brutalizing suspects.[290] A New York police officer who subdued a resisting criminal with a jujitsu submission hold, rather than club him, won praise in the *New York Times* for his restraint.[291]

Police and military martial arts programs found additional support from an emerging English-language literature on Asian arts. In the first decade of the 20th century, the American novelist and judo enthusiast Harrie Irving Hancock published some of the first English-language manuals for Asian martial arts. Hancock had initially studied jujitsu in Japan, and later continued his studies when Japanese experts began teaching at clubs in the United States.[292] Hancock claimed that jujitsu was a superior art of unarmed combat.[293] He argued that the Western ideals of limited violence were anachronistic and suggested that Americans should instead emulate the Japanese, who believed in the acceptability of any technique that brought victory.[294] Hancock devoted one of his books to promoting jujitsu classes for children, claiming that the Asian arts would make them strong and healthy.[295] He wrote a separate volume for women, which encouraged them to take up martial arts and offered practical advice. According to Hancock, jujitsu training made Japanese women the strongest and happiest women on earth. His work attempted to push the boundaries of gender roles as well as ideas related to violence. He argued that old-fashioned ideas of frail women were out of date, and suggested that women should practice jujitsu as part of a healthy exercise regimen.[296]

Hancock was hardly alone in suggesting that women could benefit from sports, and his ideas fit into a larger pattern of increasing acceptance of athleticism for women at the dawn of the 20th century.[297] Catherine Beecher, an early advocate of female education, founded the first women's physical education programs during the early 19th century.[298] In 1900, the first female competitors took part in the Olympic Games, representing nations from across Europe and including the United States, although they were restricted to golf, sailing, tennis, and croquet.[299] Margret Abbot became the first female American Olympic champion when she took the gold medal for the ladies golf competition, a triumph the American press barely mentioned.[300] By the first decade of the 20th century, many women's colleges included athletic programs for women, often directed by female educators.[301] These programs indicated progress for female athletes, but they typically operated within the fundamental gendered assumptions that women were in need of protection and restriction from sports that might cause injury.[302] While Hancock fit into this larger pattern, he was unique both in his suggestion that women should engage in violent sports in an era when most Americans believed even the pole vault was too physically demanding for female bodies and in his advo-

This illustration demonstrates a jujitsu expert's defense against a boxer. Photograph from H. Irving Hancock, *Jiu-Jitsu Combat Tricks: Japanese Feats of Attack and Defense in Personal Encounter* (New York: G.P. Putnam's Sons, 1904), 40 (courtesy of Cornell University Library).

cacy of jujitsu for women based not on an assertion that it was consistent with traditional views of frail women, but because it would allow women to break out of those anachronistic restrictions.[303]

Hancock's books received favorable attention in the press, even though his ideas on gender roles did not immediately take hold. The *Independent* told its readers that Hancock's first manual was well written and interesting.[304] *Outlook* named Hancock's book on jujitsu for children a book of the week and encouraged teachers to use it as a guide for physical education courses.[305] The *Critic* urged readers to purchase Hancock's manual for women, which it claimed was a valuable source of knowledge.[306] The *Critic*'s review also noted the book's high-quality illustrations of beautiful women demonstrating the techniques, perhaps suggesting that the book might arouse as well as educate.[307] A review of Hancock's books in the *New York Times* argued that his works were useful and informative.[308] The paper urged its readers to purchase the books as a source of knowledge about jujitsu and for more general insights into the Japanese people.[309]

American women, some of whom learned jiujutsu from manuals such as Hancock's, joined men in martial arts classes.[310] Teiichi Yamagata, writing for *Leslie's Monthly*, argued that jujitsu was an ideal art of self-defense for women because its emphasis on skill and agility made it possible for women to overcome men who relied on brute force.[311] In contrast to Hancock, who encouraged women to practice jujitsu to break out of traditional gender roles, Yamagata encouraged female study of the art while still accepting the underlying gendered assumption that women were weaker than men and attractive targets for crime. Yamagata noted that many upper-class Japanese women were experts in the art.[312] Several women's colleges, including Vassar, began offering jujitsu classes.[313] Other schools offered coed classes in which men and women trained together.[314] Within the first decade of the 20th century, some women knew enough jujitsu to make them capable of holding their own in violent encounters with men.[315] Concepts of race and gender combined when a white woman used her jujitsu skills to subdue an African American mugger until police arrived. When the policeman expressed surprise that she was able to defend herself from the assailant, the woman suggested that she would never run from a black person of either gender.[316] A 10-year-old girl made headlines when she physically dominated a burly police sergeant during a Pittsburgh jujitsu exhibition.[317] U.S. Army jujitsu expert Alan Smith argued in his jujitsu manual that women who trained in jujitsu had nothing to fear from male aggressors.[318] A popular book encouraged women to take up jujitsu to improve their health, make them beautiful, and keep them safe from male attackers.[319]

Female athleticism was controversial at this time, and women in the early 20th century who tried to take up traditional Western fighting styles of boxing and wrestling became objects of mockery, anger, and titillation. As American and British men proclaimed the boxing ring their exclusive domain, they opposed women who attempted to enter this sacred space. An American journalist contemplated women in the boxing ring and exclaimed outrage after arguing that they were far too weak, vain, and cowardly to participate in such sports.[320] In 1907, another author referred to boxing as the ultimate test of manhood and cited bouts between women as bad for boxing and worse for women.[321] In the same year, a lawyer argued against women in the legal profession by proclaiming that women were no more suited to the courtroom than to the boxing ring.[322] When Grace Mayfield, a female wrestler, pinned a male fighter in front of a Los Angeles crowd as part of an exhibition that included boxing matches, a writer for the *LA Times* referred to it as humorous and attributed the loss to her opponent's refusal to give her the beating she clearly deserved.[323] Other women who wrestled for spectators wore bathing costumes and sexually excited male spectators.[324] The perception that women could train in Japanese martial arts, but not Western-style fight sports, was consistent with the widespread understanding of Japanese bodies as smaller and more feminine than those of Western men.

Even as women joined jujitsu classes, the Japanese art remained closely tied to warfare and masculinity. The Russo–Japanese war made headlines in the United States, convincing many Americans of the superiority of Japanese manhood over that of the Russians. Many Americans sympathized with the Japanese in the conflict and considered them more heroic than their Russian adversaries.[325] A newspaper account explained an early Japanese battlefield success by arguing, "The Japanese are applying the principles of jujitsu to the art of war."[326] After a brief and hotly contested campaign, the Japanese military emerged victorious, wining increased international prestige for their nation.[327] A writer for the *Washington Post* argued that the Japanese won the conflict, at least in part, because warfare was ultimately a test of national virtue, and the Japanese were simply superior.[328] An editorial in the *New York Observer and Chronicle* noted the Japanese love of manly sports and claimed that the war between Russia and Japan was nothing more than a boxing match between the rival nations.[329] One observer argued that the Japanese emerged victorious because they understood that war is not fought under Queensbury Rules and that the Japanese, like great warriors of antiquity, had no inclination to adhere to the rules of war.[330] At least one manual of Japanese martial arts saw the military victory as evidence of jujitsu's superiority.

> The Japanese soldier, sailor, and policeman take a compulsory government course in jiu-jitsu. The physical performances of the Japanese in their war with Russia should be sufficient to establish even seemingly extravagant claims for the value of jiu-jitsu as the best system of bodily training in the world.[331]

In reality, the Japanese victory was primarily due to Japan's superior technology and more modern army.[332] However, as a side effect of the conflict, jujitsu achieved greater notoriety in the United States.[333]

As Japan proved its power on the battlefield, Asian immigrants in the United States faced mounting discrimination. The anti–Chinese movement persisted, albeit in somewhat less explosive form after passage of the Chinese Exclusion Act of 1882.[334] The anti–Japanese movement of the first decade of the 20th century was largely a continuation and a reinvigoration of the existing anti–Chinese movement.[335] Japanese populations in the United States grew during the 20th century while the Chinese population declined. In 1900, the United States contained 24,788 Japanese-born persons and 81,534 Chinese-born residents.[336] In 1906, California passed legislation limiting rights to property and public education for Japanese-born American residents.[337] American health officials feared that Japanese and Chinese immigrants carried diseases, particularly bubonic plague, an illness more common in Asia than in the West.[338] Congress reported that Japanese immigrants were heavily involved in trafficking prostitutes.[339] In 1907, a writer for the *Duluth Daily Star* advocated excluding all Asians from the United States on an unapologetically racial basis, admitting his dislike of the Japanese was entirely racial and quoting Rudyard Kipling's assertion that East and West must never meet.[340]

Theodore Roosevelt, president and judo student, interceded and urged restraint. He worried that anti–Japanese laws would sour relations between the United States and Japan.[341] Roosevelt explained that Japan's military power meant that Americans had to treat immigrants from that nation more respectfully than those from nations, such as China, which had no capacity to threaten American security.[342] Roosevelt's comments indicate one reason that the racial gulf was somewhat different for Japanese and Chinese immigrants. The Immigration Act of 1907 provided a compromise between the anti–Japanese factions and those that sought to avoid upsetting the Japanese government.[343] The 1907 Gentleman's Agreement between the United States and Japan eliminated school segregation for Japanese students in California, but allowed the president to stop any immigration he determined was likely to cause labor problems.[344] Roosevelt worked out an agreement with Japan's government to restrict, but not eliminate, Japanese migration to the United States.[345] The decreased migration widened the racial gulf between Asian and European Americans, but did not eliminate interactions between fighters from East and West.

Fans of Western-style martial arts turned their eyes to the ring for evidence that they had nothing to fear from the immigrants they hated. Ad Santel became a famed representative of America and Western-style wrestling in his bouts against Japanese fighters.[346] Santel, like many American wrestlers such as William Muldoon and Duncan Ross, fought challenge matches against

III. Asian Martial Arts Come to the United States, 1850–1941   131

Japanese experts. In 1915 and 1916, Santel defeated Senyrken Noguchi and Tokugoro Ito, two of the most famous Japanese fighters in the United States.[347] These fights were about more than single individuals. After agreeing to fight Tarro Miyake, a jujitsu expert, Santel expressed confidence that he could defeat any jujitsu fighter because such fighters did not practice pinning their opponents and, therefore, could secure victory only by using painful submission holds.[348] This observation is consistent with the general stylistic differences in emphasis between jujitsu and Western wrestling noted by others.[349] In the run-up to a fight between Santel and Miyake, a journalist noted the Japanese had often argued that their fighting arts were superior, but then went on to observe that Santel humiliated them when he repeatedly defeated top-ranked Japanese fighters.[350] The Japanese community in California took issue with the perception, claiming that their art was still superior and that Santel's victories over Ito and Noguchi demonstrated the personal failings of inferior fighters, not those of their art.[351] To redeem the Japanese fight sports, Tarro Miyake came to America for a fight with Santel. Unlike previous style-on-style match-ups that were fought with a mix of rules, Miyake and Santel agreed to a unique arrangement in which the fight would continue until one competitor surrendered, which would ensure an indisputable conclusion.[352] This was consistent with the Japanese preferences and at odds with the Western approach. On October 20, 1917, in an arena packed with recent Japanese immigrants, Miyake conceded defeat at the hands of the American.[353] Santel spent the next decade traveling across the United States and Japan, fighting challenge matches and almost always winning.[354] Somewhere along the line, he began calling himself the world champion of judo, a move that infuriated the Japanese.[355] Upsetting as many Japanese found Santel's victories, his success increased their interest in Western styles of wrestling and laid the groundwork for the birth of American-style wrestling in Japan years later.[356]

Santel's victories attracted only peripheral attention from an America intensely focused on a war that raged across Europe and veered into American shipping lanes. World War I initially damaged the American sporting scene before American involvement in the conflict gave athletics a boost. The International Olympic Committee canceled the 1916 Olympic Games scheduled for Berlin. The American Olympic Committee pointed to its nation's neutral status and offered to host the games in San Francisco, but European officials rejected the idea and resumed the games only after the armistice was implemented.[357] The war impacted Americans more directly when Germany announced a new policy of unrestricted submarine warfare that convinced Congress and President Woodrow Wilson to declare war on Germany on April 2, 1917.[358] American troops encamped along the Mexican border received new orders sending them to Europe. The president called for military volunteers and Congress authorized a draft.[359] The American army rapidly grew from fewer than 250,000 troops to nearly 4 million.[360] Many of these men had never engaged in any form of organized athletics.[361] A writer for the *New York Times* suggested that America's entry into the war provided the "supreme test of manhood."[362] The conflict tested not only millions of American men's strength on the battlefield, but also their ability to resist boredom, disease, insubordination, and depression in camp.

Japanese forms of unarmed combat found new students among American servicemen.[363] Jujitsu practitioners explained the losses experienced by Japanese experts at the hands of American wrestlers by stating that their deadly techniques were forbidden by Western rules and that their art was better suited to life-and-death struggles than sporting events.[364] This concept made jujitsu an obvious place to look for deadly hand-to-hand combat techniques. An American observer took note when the British army adopted jujitsu and reported it made soldiers more successful on the battlefield.[365] Many men who taught Japanese arts to Americans were Europeans, Canadians, and Americans who learned the techniques while living in Japan.[366] The U.S. Army does not appear to have hired any Japanese experts.[367] Allan Smith became the chief American jujitsu instructor.[368] His long resume included a pioneering role as only the fourth foreigner to obtain a black belt in jujitsu, a recognition earned after a decade of training while he was in Tokyo working for the American Trading Company.[369] With the outbreak of war, Smith accepted a captain's commission in the U.S. Army and began teaching jujitsu to American soldiers.[370] He claimed that jujitsu was far superior to boxing, and suggested that his instructor in Japan could have easily defeated Jack Johnson.[371] After winning acclaim from his peers and students, Smith wrote the first jujitsu manual for the American military.[372] He sold his book to civilians with the claim that the art provided small men, women, and children with the skills needed to defend themselves against much larger and stronger aggressors, once again reinforcing the connections between weak bodies and the deadly secrets of Asian martial arts.[373]

While Smith gave aid to the small, large men faced deadly opponents in Chinatowns. In Chinatowns across the nation, American policemen engaged in violent confrontations with dangerous Chinese American gangsters in the first decade of the 20th century. In one fairly typical encounter, police officers, hearing gunshots, discovered a fight between Chinese American and European American men described by a journalist as gangsters in a New York poolroom. The officers sent for reinforcement and broke up the fight only after 30 officers arrived on the scene and waded into the fight.[374]

III. Asian Martial Arts Come to the United States, 1850–1941   133

In another encounter, Sergeant George Willett, a large and powerful member of the Los Angeles Chinatown police squad, attempted to break up a fight between two immigrants. The crowd turned on him, and he fought his way out with skills learned in the boxing ring.[375] Detective Robert Beck of the Harlem police was less fortunate. When he attempted to rescue a laundryman from an assault by three other Chinese immigrants, the trio turned on him, beating him until other officers arrived to rescue him.[376] Not every policeman received help in time. A journalist reported that New York police officers would not enter Chinatown alone because Chinese gangsters frequently killed policemen and left their dead bodies in the streets.[377] While this report seems exaggerated, it speaks to the area's reputation for danger.

A few scattered bits of evidence suggest that some Americans might have realized that Chinese fighters brought something unique into these violent encounters. Chinese martial artists typically kept their knowledge a closely guarded secret, but a few outsiders caught glimpses of their skills. When lawyer Frank Moss attempted to study New York's Chinatown, he sought out a local resident to guide and protect him. He hired Dong Fong, a veteran enforcer for the Tongs who was famous for his bone-shattering punches. Moss revealed that he always felt safe when Fong stood at his side.[378] Leong Yen Gun came to the attention of Chinatown police after murdering a rival, and police records noted that he was a particularly skilled fighter.[379] Sung Chi Liang was a Chinese immigrant living in San Francisco's Chinatown who made his living selling herbal medicines. His special ointment, known as tit daa yeuk jau, became a highly sought-after cure for bruises and sprains.[380] When business was slow, Liang attracted customers with displays of strength and martial arts skill performed with knives. These exhibitions earned Liang the nickname "The Peking Two-Knife Man" and made him famous as a martial artist.[381] Lian might have disappeared into the past without a trace, but he was immortalized in a photograph taken by the famed photographer and ethnographer Arnold Genthe.[382]

The 1920s witnessed a wave of violence and crime in America that spread into Chinatown. Crime in Chinatown presented police with unique challenges. For decades, police officials lamented that their officers were outsiders in the Chinese community, unable to read or speak Chinese and completely unaware of the residents' customs.[383] The police attempted to make up for the imbalance by recruiting officers from among the Chinese immigrants. Rikki K'un, a son of Chinese immigrants with expertise in Kung Fu, agreed to join the force after Tongs beat his parents to death for refusing to pay protection money.[384]

At least one white policeman refused to remain an outsider in Chinatown and broke down cultural barriers. In 1921, Chief of the San Francisco Police Dan O'Brien assigned his childhood friend Inspector Jack Manion, who had experience prosecuting the Italian mafia, to head the department's Chinatown squad.[385] Manion became a member of the Chinatown community, attempted to understand their culture, and became an ally to the law-abiding Chinese.[386] He was less welcoming to the area's gangsters, to whom he offered only bullets, bare fists, and prison terms.[387] In an effort to build cultural understanding across the racial divide and sharpen his skills in unarmed combat, the inspector took Kung Fu lessons.[388] While Chinese immigrants typically displayed a willingness to share knowledge of food, art, and medicine with whites, Chinese masters considered Kung Fu a secret art and often refused to teach it to non–Chinese students for fear their secrets would be used against them. Manion somehow convinced the famed Chai Lee, who also trained Tong enforcers, to make an exception just for him. The burly policemen became an excellent student, hardening his muscles, improving his technique, and making friends with other students. He put his techniques to good use in challenge matches with rivals in the outlaw community and during street fights.[389] The Chinese American community came to love Manion, calling him *Min Bok* (Old Uncle) and making him a guest of honor at numerous social events.[390] Manion's techniques were highly successful. Within three years, he and the Chinese who partnered with him had transformed the San Francisco Chinatown from the scene of gang wars to a peaceful neighborhood where murder was a distant memory.[391] They worked together to transform the racialized understanding of the Chinese residents from pimps and sellers of opium to purveyors of wholesomely exotic foods and musical performances.[392] While some reports of Manion's exploits might be exaggerated, he clearly worked to lessen the racial divide between whites and Chinese city dwellers. Manion's career roughly coincided with the proliferation of inexpensive magazines and paperback books, many devoted to detective stories.[393] In the next few decades, Manion became a model for some of the detectives of popular culture.[394]

Asian tough guys and skilled fighters became fixtures of American popular culture decades before Bruce Lee stole the show. Noting the success of detective novel series such as *Secret Service* and *The New York Detective Library*, publisher Frank Tousey developed his own series.[395] Tousey quickly noticed that the novels which sold best incorporated detective heroes who, like Manion, were physically tough as well as intelligent.[396] As the personification of this ideal, Tousey created James "Old King" Brady, a middle-aged police detective of Irish ancestry.[397] King Brady was often accompanied by his partner and kinsman Harry Brady, a skilled boxer and wrestler who frequently exchanged punches with criminal opponents. Many of Brady's adventures took place in Chinatown and involved Chinese Americans as villains, bystanders, and allies. While the white detectives typically stood as the heroes in these stories, the tales often featured skilled Asian martial artists. Harry Brady once rescued a lady in distress by winning a challenge match against Wo John, a Tong wrestling champion.[398] On another occasion, the Bradys helped save a man nearly dead from kicks inflicted by Chinese American assailants.[399] Other works placed the Asian even closer to the center of the story. Pulp fiction detective Nick Carter worked with the aid of Ten Ichi, a Japanese assistant and bodyguard.[400] The Nick Carter novels made use of the American tendency to associate martial arts with Asians even at this early stage, noting that since Ten Ichi was Japanese, he was, of course, an expert in jujitsu.[401] Growing out of his interest in Japanese martial arts, Harrie Irving Hancock wrote a series of detective stories in which an American detective battled crime with the aid of Imo Sato, a Japanese jujitsu master.[402]

Asian fighters did not just appear in pulp fiction. In 1933, Pearl S. Buck published *All Men Are Brothers*, her translation of the Chinese novel *The Water Margin*.[403] The novel focused on the lives and adventures of a group of martial arts experts in 16th-century China.[404] It enjoyed influence far in excess of its sales, receiving critical praise and encouraging additional interest in Asian characters.[405]

In the first decades of the 20th century, new media provided additional outlets for portrayals of Asian masculinity. Shortly after the end of the Boxer Rebellion, the short film *Chinese Massacring Christians* presented Chinese men as dangerous killers.[406] In 1919, Haworth Pictures released *The Tong Man*, a popular film about crime in San Francisco's Chinatown. The movie's lead character, Ming Tai, a hatchet man whom the Tong orders to kill the father of the woman he loves, wins over the audience with his heroic defiance of the criminal overlords.[407] Following on his success of the *Lone Ranger* radio series, George W. Trendle created the *Green Hornet* radio program in 1936. The show featured a crime-fighting duo led by a white intellectual and his faithful Japanese servant, a martial arts expert.[408] When heightened international tensions made many Americans uncomfortable with a Japanese hero, the producers abruptly transformed Kato into a Filipino.[409] These portrayals were overtly masculine, but the most popular Asians in American popular culture were more ambiguous.

The two most popular portrayals of Asian men in early 20th-century American popular culture were a criminal overlord and a master detective who presented complicated racialized visions of manhood. Fu Manchu began life as a villain in British author Sax Rohmer's 1913 novel *The Insidious Dr.*

Fu Manchu.[410] Ten years later, Fu Manchu made it onto movie screens with the English serial film, *The Mystery of Dr. Fu Manchu*.[411] The character Fu Manchu was a diabolical villain, sinister and criminal. He was both violent and brilliant, attributes often associated with masculinity. Unlike the white men who always defeated him, however, his masculinity was also rooted in evil behavior and ambiguous sexuality.[412] Detective Charlie Chan provided a heroic counterpoint to the evil Fu Manchu. Novelist Earl Derr Biggers first brought Chan to life as a literary character in 1926.[413] Biggers based the fictional Charlie Chan on the real-life Honolulu detective Chang Apana.[414] Although Apana was widely respected as a dangerous brawler, Biggers presented Chan as a softer figure, an effeminate and sexually ambiguous hero.[415] Critics suggest that racist concerns might have motivated Biggers' work, convincing him to undercut his portrayal of Asian masculinity.[416] Chan first made it into the movies in the 1926, less than a year after the release of the first novel, with the film *The House Without a Key*.[417] He was and remains an enormously controversial figure, with some Asian Americans calling him racist stereotype, an Asian version of Uncle Tom.[418] Other critics are more forgiving, suggesting that Charlie Chan was a complicated character, neither stereotype nor ideal.[419] In contrast to the evil Fu Manchu and the hatchet men of pulp fiction, Chan was something more subtle, a charming crime fighter dispensing fortune cookie wisdom.[420] Neither Fu Manchu nor Charlie Chan were portrayed as a martial artist, even though Chan was based on an authentic brawler, but both characters provided Americans with visions of Asian masculinity that were neither cowardly nor servile.

The increasing presence of Asians in fiction took place at the same time as a renewed backlash against actual Asians. By 1920, the 81,502 Japanese-born American residents outnumbered Chinese Americans, who accounted for only 43,560 residents, for the first time.[421] This was a product of an immigration process that was somewhat less restrictive for the Japanese than the Chinese.[422] In the 1920s, pressure against Japanese immigrants continued to build. The Quota Act of 1921 set severe restrictions on immigration from Asia and lesser limits on migration from Europe.[423] In 1922, the U.S. Supreme Court decided that Japanese immigrants were prohibited from becoming citizens of the United States.[424] The Immigration Act of 1924 tightened earlier restrictions and attempted to ensure that new immigrants into the United States came from northwest Europe.[425] Among the act's many features, it excluded immigration of all persons not eligible for citizenship, which since 1922 had included the Japanese.[426] Senator Shortbridge from California argued that Asians were undesirable and unwelcome.[427] The Immigration Act of 1924 passed over the objections of American statesmen, including Secretary of State Hughes, who warned it would enrage the Japanese people and threaten American security. He suggested giving the Japanese the same immigration status as Europeans, a move he felt would satisfy the Japanese government, but Congress rejected his plan.[428] In response to the bill, the Japanese government denounced the American government and declared a trade war.[429] The Japanese community in the United States felt under siege from the increasingly discriminatory legislation and popular sentiment. In response, many immigrants retreated into their own community, cutting off contact with European Americans and withdrawing from many of the Japanese associations that once provided points of cultural interaction between European and Japanese Americans.[430] Observers in the period also noted the increased tendency of the Japanese in America to segregate themselves in response to heightened racial tensions.[431] In turn, the Japanese faced similar problems and responded with similar attempts to isolate themselves in Brazil.[432] The opportunities for interaction between fighters from Japan and the United States dwindled and the racialized gap was widened.

Against a backdrop of increasing immigration restrictions, Americans continued to describe Asian men as more feminine than their white counterparts. An American educator in Shanghai lamented the effeminate habits of young Chinese young men, which included their love of carefully braided hair styles.[433] The educators noted the problems they encountered trying to convince Chinese male students to exercise, describing China as follows:

[In] a country where the people as a whole [are] adverse to physical exercise and where the upper class regards physical training not only as inconsistent with, but derogatory from, the dignity and honor of a gentleman, one endeavoring to introduce physical cultivation has to prepare to meet numerous difficulties.[434]

In 1920, an American physician argued that Japanese men's faces were feminine.[435] An encyclopedia from 1922 claimed Japanese men's bodies were like the bodies of young children or women.[436] A writer for *Popular Science* suggested that Indian men's turbans looked like something only a woman should wear.[437]

In the lead-up to the attack on Pearl Harbor, a few people of the East and West continued attempts to reach out to each other. In 1930, the University of Chicago baseball team toured Asia, playing local teams and complimenting the skills of Asian players.[438] The next year, American flying enthusiasts lined up to meet Japanese pilot Zensaku Azuma on a tour of California after he made the first solo flight from Europe to Japan.[439] The Japanese national equestrian team trained in California in 1932, and their team captain reported that Americans welcomed them everywhere they went.[440] American missionaries continued their efforts to convert Asians to Christianity, even as the expanding conflict on the continent placed their lives in peril.[441]

The martial arts also provided a few positive cultural interactions before war shook up racialized hierarchies and led to shifts in American perceptions of the world. Japanese martial arts continued to grow in America, fighting a rising tide of intolerance toward Asians. The founder of judo, Jigoro Kano, accepted the invitation of a growing judo community in California and visited the United States in the 1930s, giving popular lectures at the University of Southern California.[442] Teams of Japanese judo players toured California, attracting widespread interest from American audiences.[443] Under the guidance of Mutsu Zuiho and Kamesuke Higaonna, the first karate club on American territory to accept white members opened in the basement of Honolulu's First Methodist Church in 1933.[444] Japanese sailors visiting New York fought members of the local judo club in bouts that impressed observers.[445] American fighters formed four new judo associations with American leaders, after obtaining Kano's blessing.[446] In 1940, the first intercollegiate judo competition took place between San Jose State and the University of California at Berkeley.[447] These interactions provided a final moment of friendship between the soon-to-be-warring nations, and represented the last time Asians stood as the primary leaders in the American martial arts community.

The Western martial artists who took control of the American community after the Japanese empire collapsed were already beginning to occupy increasingly important positions of leadership in the years before World War II. In 1933, the University of California at Berkeley played host to American jujitsu experts who worked with members of the California National Guard to demonstrate unarmed combat techniques.[448] Jujitsu experts in the New York Police Department continued training their new recruits in the unarmed combat techniques of jujitsu honed by experiences on American streets.[449] American police officers began using jujitsu as a method to reach out to troubled youth, offering very popular martial arts classes to boys and helping the young men focus their attention on sport rather than crime.[450] In 1939, Jack Sergel, a Los Angeles police officer of Swedish ancestry, won the city's jujitsu championship and earned promotion from patrolman to instructor at the city's police training center.[451] American women increasingly practiced jujitsu, and American experts assured them that the art's emphasis on technique over strength would allow them to defend themselves from male assailants while maintaining feminine bodies.[452] U.S. fighters formed new American-led judo associations, a move Kano accepted.[453] William Fairbairn, a British soldier and police officer who studied Asian martial arts while serving in China and Japan, incorporated Japanese jujitsu and Chinese boxing into his system of

III. Asian Martial Arts Come to the United States, 1850-1941   139

unarmed combat. He disseminated these Asian arts to the United States by publishing books and providing American soldiers with personal lessons.[454] The increasingly prominent role taken by Western martial artists before Pearl Harbor demonstrated the tendency of these Westerners to take ownership of their unique blends of Asian martial arts.

On the eve of the most destructive conflict in history, men from East and West enjoyed partnerships born in the ring, before the violence of war swept away the friendship of the arena and led the way for a new and very different martial arts community to rise from the ashes of atomic fire. Robert Trias's post–World War II karate school was not a first; it was simply another important step in the racial transition of martial arts in America from the property of Asians to Westerners.

IV

"We Live in Our Heroes"

Boxing Reigns Supreme in the United States, 1915–1941

There was considerable personal acrimony and personal elation in the mad noise that went rolling up to the black summer sky when the fight was ended.... The spectacle of Jack Sharkey powdering his nose in the rosin was one of the most satisfactory spectacles in the ring, for he is given to sneering and giving people hard looks, and I do not like sneers or hard looks, as they intimidate me. It is true that Mr. Sharkey did not honor me with a personal sneer or a personal hard look, but we live in our heroes.
—Westbrook Pegler reports on Jack Dempsey's defeat of Jack Sharkey, 1927[1]

They came briskly to the middle of the ring. Louis led with two jolting lefts to the head. Schmeling retreated, but caught a left to the face. Louis fired left hooks and short rights to the head. Louis stepped back and Schmeling glanced a hard right off his jaw. They clinched. Louis scored with hard lefts and rights to the head, draping Schmeling helpless on the ropes with his right arm over the uppermost strand. A left hook pitched Schmeling head foremost to the canvas for a four count. He came up staggering, and dazed. Louis swarmed in with a left and a right, dropping Schmeling to his knees for a one count. Louis measured him. A right landed flush on Schmeling's jaw and the German collapsed. His seconds threw in the towel at the count of four and Referee Arthur Donovan lugged the beaten challenger to his corner. It was a technical knockout. The time was two minutes and four seconds.
—Joe Louis defeats Max Schmeling, 1938[2]

While much of the world focused on the Great War in Europe, Americans turned their attention to a more immediate threat. On March 9, 1916,

IV. Boxing Reigns Supreme in the United States, 1915–1941

the people of Columbus, New Mexico, awoke to the sounds of battle. Mexican guerrillas under Francisco "Pancho" Villa had attacked the town. Although surprised, the town's garrison of American cavalrymen fought back valiantly. Bullets streaked through the air, and buildings went up in flames as the sun rose. After killing 18 Americans and burning much of the town, the Mexicans retreated south in the face of superior American firepower. They left behind a hundred of their dead comrades. It was not an isolated incident, but rather the latest and most serious event in a time of violence and upheaval along the Mexican–American border.

The attack enraged the nation. Newspapers printed calls for vengeance. Congressmen demanded that the army protect the border. U.S. President Woodrow Wilson ordered the Secretary of War to begin planning a campaign into Mexico. Within weeks, an American expedition under the command of John "Black Jack" Pershing entered Mexico in an attempt to apprehend the men responsible for the attack and ensure the safety of the border.[3] Pershing's command initially consisted of an agile column of professional soldiers, hardened by years of active service against Native Americans and outlaws. The active campaign lasted barely a month, as diplomatic wrangling forced the army into a defensive posture. Professionals soon found themselves outnumbered by part-time reservists, called up to defend the border.

In an effort to keep his men in line, the army turned to the saving power of muscular Christian masculinity. General Pershing loathed idleness and feared that excessive free time for his largely unprofessional force would lead to breakdowns in discipline and morale.[4] He began by putting his soldiers through an exhaustive training regimen. In spite of Pershing's best hopes, drilling did not keep soldiers out of trouble, and reports of skyrocketing rates of venereal disease and alcohol abuse reached President Wilson. The administration created the Commission on Training Camp Activities to investigate solutions. The investigators, led by Raymond Fosdick, a corporate executive and minor player in the Democratic Party, concluded that it was not enough to keep men busy and punish rule breakers. They urged the military to build partnerships with civic organizations such as the YMCA and the Knights of Columbus to provide alternative, wholesome, muscular Christian entertainments to compete with the illicit.[5] Many of these organizations—the YMCA, in particular—boasted a long history of working with the military to provide services for military members, and these recommendations built on that history.[6] The administration accepted these recommendations and soon civilian organizations flooded the border camps with reading materials, religious instruction, gramophones, and live entertainment.[7] The YMCA also provided sports diversions, organizing wrestling, boxing, and bayonet fencing tournaments. A spokesman for the Wilson administration acknowledged the rough nature of some of these amusements, but refused to apologize, arguing American soldiers were red-blooded fellows and that only exciting amusements would deter them from seeking out alcohol and prostitutes.[8]

On the border, soldiers embraced fight sports as sources of both recreation and practical skill. Shortly after entering federal service, members of the Washington National Guard began daily training in calisthenics, boxing, and wrestling matches.[9] Cavalrymen built an amphitheater in preparation for weekly boxing and wrestling bouts between soldiers.[10] An officer returning home from the front to train cadets reassured the people of Salt Lake City that their men on the border were in good spirits and excellent physical condition due to a program of long marches, baseball games, wrestling, and boxing.[11] Lieutenant Shannon used his knowledge of the fistic art to subdue two unruly Apache scouts under his command.[12] On the Mexican border, the African American fighter Rufus Williams achieved national fame with his victory over the white pugilist Whitey Burns, winning the regular army's middleweight boxing championship.[13] Williams mentored a younger soldier, Thomas "Speedball" Hayden, who bested his teacher and took the army's middleweight crown before leaving the army and becoming a respected professional pugilist.[14] At the expedition's headquarters in Mexico, 1,500 cheering soldiers enjoyed a boxing tournament provided by regimental champions.[15]

Although he certainly did not intend it, Villa, long a boxing fan and promoter, indirectly contributed to the popularization of boxing in the United States.[16] The program of army athletics provided an enormous success that impressed the nation's civilian and military leadership.[17] The army was not the only promoter of fight sports at this time, however.

World War I initially damaged the American sporting scene before American involvement in the conflict gave athletics a boost. The International Olympic Committee canceled the 1916 Olympic Games scheduled for Berlin. The American Olympic Committee pointed to its nation's neutral status and offered to host the games in San Francisco, but European officials rejected the idea and resumed the games only after the armistice was signed. European boxers left the ring for the battlefield, canceling scheduled bouts with American fighters and disappointing fans.[18] The war impacted Americans more directly when Germany announced a new policy of unrestricted submarine warfare that convinced Congress and President Wilson to declare war on Germany on April 2, 1917. The American troops encamped along the Mexican border received new orders sending them to Europe. The president called for volunteers to fight and Congress authorized a draft. The American army rapidly grew from less than 250,000 troops to nearly 4 million.[19] Many of these men had never before participated any form of organized athletics.[20] A writer for the *New York Times* suggested that America's entry into the war provided the "the supreme test of manhood."[21] The conflict tested millions of American men's strength on the battlefield, as well as their ability to resist boredom, disease, insubordination, and depression in camp.

Building on their success on the Mexican border, an alliance of soldiers, bureaucrats, and civilian volunteers worked together in hopes that the sports they encouraged would benefit American men in uniform. All of the military's sporting programs, like their predecessors on the Mexican border, built on the premise that sports could prepare men for battle and keep them free from temptation in camp.[22] Raymond Fosdick continued his work with the Commission on Training Camp Activities and worked as the civilian aide to the commander of the American expeditionary forces in Europe, General Pershing.[23] Fosdick convinced the New York Athletic Club to donate sporting equipment to the army and navy.[24] The Knights of Columbus raised $3 million for the creation of army recreation centers.[25] Leaders of the Kansas City Athletic Club organized a meet between civilian and military athletes.[26] The YMCA expanded its work with the military, recruited thousands of volunteers, and expressed a particular need for capable athletic directors willing to work with army members.[27] When universities considered suspending their athletic programs to focus on the war, the *New York Times* urged them to reconsider and to realize that sports were a patriotic duty with the power to transform students into citizens and soldiers.[28] The War Department assigned a director of athletics to every army and navy camp.[29] Muscular Christianity was alive and well in the camps, as the faithful promoted sports as one method for building a complete man, one who was strong in body and in spirit.[30] Pershing considered the sport programs an overwhelming success.[31] Popular sports in the camps included baseball, tennis, swimming, running, and, of course, various forms of fight sports.

Wrestling had provided a key component of American military training dating back to the colonial period, and World War I continued this trend. Wrestling possessed long-standing historical and theological connections that no other fight sport could boast. Observers attributed Germany's battlefield successes, in part, to the country's embrace of a scholastic wrestling program that emulated those of ancient Greece and Rome.[32] Ministers working with the YMCA in American army camps urged soldiers and sailors to wrestle as Jacob wrestled.[33] American soldiers practiced wrestling techniques as a form of hand-to-hand combat training.[34] For their part, police volunteers worked with military and civilian wrestling experts to learn techniques that would allow them to maintain order on the home front.[35] Many members of the Students' Army Training Corps at Penn State fulfilled their physical training requirement by taking wrestling classes.[36] Wrestling also provided entertainment for athletes and competitors: the army sponsored such bouts as it had on the Mexican border, in hopes of providing an alternative to the joys of alcohol and prostitutes that often appealed to soldiers.[37] Like their civilian counterparts, the wrestling contests held to benefit the troops failed to attract large audiences and often ended indecisively.[38]

The American government spread the love of pugilism to many men in uniform. The former heavyweight champion, Jim Corbett, headed a War Department committee dedicated to teaching soldiers to box.[39] The War Department attempted to teach the sweet science to every soldier. It nearly succeeded: at war's end, the department reported that in the 19 short months of American involvement, it had taught the manly art to more than 3 million men.[40] Eighteen camps boasted their own professional boxing instructors, and hundreds of amateur boxing coaches helped the professionals teach enormously popular boxing classes.[41] In one afternoon at a single camp, more than 20,000 soldiers took part in boxing bouts.[42] Canadian college professor William J. Jacomb argued that reports from the front demonstrated that skilled boxers were better equipped to kill on the battlefield with fists and bayonets, and published a manual to help soldiers perfect their skills.[43] Henry Ford investigated how the YMCA was spending his donations and concluded that their programs, including their boxing classes, were a wholesome and vital resource for soldiers. Ford especially praised the work of the Reverend "Fighting Parson" Wedge at Camp Grant, who boxed every day before teaching Bible classes in his workout clothes.[44] Veterans returning from the front argued that boxing training, particularly sparring, made men superior fighters.[45] The world lightweight champion, Benny Leonard, took more pride in his work as an army instructor than in his victories in the ring. He expressed his awe at the young men who took to pugilism with enormous enthusiasm, improving at an amazing pace and convincing him that the next generation of boxing champions would come from the ranks of army veterans.[46]

The military also promoted boxing as a spectator sport. Navy recruiters sponsored boxing exhibitions on naval vessels, which attracted huge numbers of young men, many of whom subsequently enlisted.[47] Professional boxers routinely put on shows for large crowds of military men, and even met the services' best fighters in the ring.[48] The fight promoter Jack Herman received approval to show a fight film, in spite of a widespread ban, which contained the patriotic scene of young army officers training as boxers.[49] The first legal professional boxing match in the District of Columbia took place when the

This photograph claims to display the world's largest boxing class. The First, Second, and Third Battalions of 337th Infantry Brigade learn boxing under the direction of their instructor, Billy Armstrong, on June 27, 1918 (Library of Congress Prints and Photographs Division).

War Department invited Benny Leonard to fight in the shadow of the Washington monument.[50]

The celebrated author and coach Sol Metzger argued that World War I killed the nation's prewar sporting culture. He claimed that the conflict would give rise to a new American attitude toward sport, just as the Civil War had done in the previous century. Metzger predicted that millions of men would learn to love the fistic arts while in the service, and that after the war, those men would propel boxing to a position of unprecedented cultural dominance.[51]

Military support for sports continued after the guns fell silent, as athletic directors turned their attention from training men for the current war and toward returning them to civilian lives and keeping them entertained while on garrison duty. At the suggestion of YMCA physical director Elwood S. Brown, the American Expeditionary Forces hosted an Olympic-style set of games that included competitors from 29 nations, who performed for the delight of 875,000 paying spectators in an American-built stadium in France.[52] Within weeks of the armistice, American, British, and Canadian boxers competed in an inter–Allied boxing tournament, which was won by the British army team.[53] The YMCA continued sponsoring very popular boxing matches across Europe during the first half of 1919.[54] The Eastern Department of the U.S. Army began experiments to make boxing training a permanent part of peacetime military service.[55] General Pershing and Vice President Marshall gave elite approval to pugilism when they attended the 1920 army boxing championship.[56] American and French soldiers assigned to occupation duties held a boxing tournament with the assistance of Georges Carpentier, the European heavyweight champion, in 1921.[57] Events verified that Metzger's predictions were accurate, as men who learned to love athletics while in uniform maintained that interest when they returned to civilian life and contributed to the increasing popularity of baseball, golf, and boxing.[58]

American men who were exposed to a muscular Christian vision of masculinity while in uniform spread their knowledge when they returned to

William R. Whipp, boxing instructor at the Racquet Club in Washington, D.C., demonstrating the art of self-defense to a room full of young pupils. Published in 1924 by Harris and Ewing (Library of Congress Prints and Photographs Division).

civilian life. A writer for the New York Times claimed that boxing had become such an important military sport that there was a movement to legalize the sport throughout the nation.[59] He noted that boxing had provided valuable skills on the battlefield and taught men to be confident and decisive in every aspect of their lives.[60] Popular magazines began advertising self-defense manuals that contained techniques taught by army instructors.[61] Competing courses drew most of their material from boxing as taught at the New York Athletic Club, but included special bonus information on wrestling holds and deadly tricks from jujitsu.[62] The Child Conservation League of America recommended that schools and civic clubs teach boys to box as a method of self-defense.[63] A journalist who compared the self-defense systems of boxing and wrestling concluded that boxing was far superior, since it did not teach fighters to entangle themselves with an opponent, but rather kept them free to engage multiple assailants in rapid succession.[64]

Men who learned to love pugilism while in the military became some

IV. Boxing Reigns Supreme in the United States, 1915–1941 147

of the sport's strongest supporters. Veterans clubs organized boxing matches for the delight of spectators.[65] Hundreds of veterans provided security for prizefights in the Bronx.[66] Men returning from service with the army and navy helped revive collegiate boxing programs.[67] Within months of the war's end, General Leonard Wood took charge of the new Army, Navy, and Civilian Board of Boxing Control, a group that worked to elevate and regulate boxing in the American military and civilian worlds.[68] The group quickly expanded to include governors, high-ranking military officers, and influential citizens.[69] When the Federated Churches of Ohio expressed their disapproval of an upcoming championship bout in Toledo, the Army, Navy, and Civilian Board of Boxing Control publicly rebuked the organization, arguing that it was 50 years behind the times, that boxing was a wholesome pastime, and that the churches opposed to pugilism served only to discredit religion.[70]

In spite of condemnations from church leaders, Jess Willard fought Jack Dempsey for the championship in Toledo, Ohio, on July 4, 1919.[71] Willard, one of the largest men to ever wear the heavyweight crown, was an aging 38-year-old veteran, best known as the Great White Hope who defeated Jack Johnson in 1915.[72] Jack "The Manassa Mauler" Dempsey was the audacious challenger, a man born into poverty in Manassa, Colorado, who worked in the mines and picked fruit before his boxing career took off. He entered the arena in Toledo 14 years younger, 58 pounds lighter, and 6 inches shorter than the champion.[73] Jack Johnson once declared that Willard was too large and too strong to ever suffer a knockout, but Dempsey intended to prove him wrong. Roughly 45,000 fans, including 500 women, crowded the arena, braving the nearly 100-degree heat.[74] Willard entered the arena and offered his hand to the challenger. Dempsey shook gloved hands with the giant, but it was the last time Willard felt comfort from the gloves that became vehicles of pain when the bell rang moments later. Dempsey immediately revealed his answer to the riddle of Willard's size and strength. Instead of trying to overpower the giant like his predecessors, the challenger fought evasively, using his superior speed and agility to remain clear of the big man's strikes. The mauler refused to move in straight lines, throwing neither jabs nor over-hand rights. Every punch flew through an unpredictable curving trajectory as Dempsey provided his elder with a lesson in the geometry of suffering.[75] He punished Willard with flurries of twisting, curving blows that seemed impossible to avoid or block.[76] When the bell rang to begin the fourth round, the bloodied Willard refused to resume, and the referee declared Dempsey the winner by technical knockout. Boxing experts expressed their admiration for Dempsey's performance and congratulated him on his success.[77] The new heavyweight king became one of the most famous men in America. Although no one seemed to realize it at the time, years later it became clear that Dempsey's knockout of Willard initiated boxing's golden era.[78]

The new pugilistic king reigned over an America rapidly evolving into a boxer's paradise. Boxing always was, and remains forever, a sport of the city.[79] It contrast to the large spaces needed for baseball games and the expensive equipment required by golfers, aspiring boxers needed nothing more than their fists, or perhaps a cheap pair of gloves, and just enough space to swing their fists. These distinctions made pugilism an amusement of the most crowded and poorest urban neighborhoods. Boxing thrived in urban spaces, and as they expanded, so did pugilism. The U.S. census reported in 1920 that a majority of Americans lived in urban areas for the first time in the nation's history.[80] Americans continued to move West, and by 1920 the final agricultural frontiers closed as farming replaced ranching in many of the remote grasslands. Western cities continued to grow: by 1920, Los Angeles was the largest city in the West, with a population of 577,000 residents.[81] Boxing's embrace of the timed round, its rapid pace, and its highly visible action made it ideally suited to fighters from industrialized workplaces and to large crowds of spectators.[82] Workers continued to migrate from farm to nonfarm occupations, and by 1920 both the percentage and the raw numbers of farm workers decreased for the first time.[83] The millions of veterans who learned to box while in the service provided ready-made audiences for boxing matches and as the years wore on, they began to support pugilism with their political as well as their demographic strength.

In 1920, New York State Senator James Walker introduced a bill to legalize professional boxing in the state that permanently changed American boxing history.[84] Walker's legislation proposed to license everyone associated with boxing, including managers, fighters, and referees. A board of three commissioners would carefully supervise every aspect of the sport, revoking licenses and leveling criminal sanctions to enforce regulations.[85] Walker acted at the suggestion of the Army, Navy, and Civilian Board of Boxing Control.[86] The Board of Trustees of the United American War Veterans sent the state legislature a letter supporting the bill and arguing that well-regulated boxing must become an American institution.[87] Many veterans, including army chaplains, supported the bill.[88] A coalition of women, clergymen, and reformers opposed the legislation and boxing in general.[89] At a public hearing to discuss the bill, the conversation became heated as Senator Walker addressed his critics, whom he accused of lacking a manly spirit of sporting blood. As he explained, he had no time for anyone who disliked boxing.[90] On May 25, 1920, Governor Alfred E. Smith demonstrated that he, too, did not care for the bill's opponents as he signed Walker's proposal into law. The Walker Law

Jack Dempsey (right) punches Jess Willard (left) in Toledo, Ohio, on July 4, 1919, and wins the world heavyweight boxing championship. Published in 1919 by Pulitzer Publishing Company (Library of Congress Prints and Photographs Division).

was an enormously influential piece of legislation that inspired other states and remains in effect in New York today, albeit in amended form.[91]

Other states followed New York's lead, passing legislation modeled on the Walker Law. As in New York, veterans organizations supported these bills. The new boxing commissions faced a daunting task—the quest to rescue pugilism from its long association with the worst aspects of humanity and elevate it into a sweet and virtuous science. As part of this effort, newly formed state boxing commissions banded together into the National Boxing Association to establish a uniform system of organization and rankings.[92]

The governor of New York knew just the man to head his state's commission—William Muldoon, the famed solid man of sport and an iconic leader in the muscular Christianity movement. In 1921, he stood as an elder statesman of fight sports, respected by reformers for his embrace of clean living and admired by fight fans as a skilled boxer, wrestler, and dear friend of His Fistic Highness, John L. Sullivan.[93] Muldoon was a consummate insider, a veteran of six decades in the fight world, who understood the ring as well as the world of politics and economics that surrounded it.[94] In his new role, Muldoon presided over the first modern athletic commission in American history. The New York governor made it clear that if the new commission did not succeed in cleaning up boxing, he would push for a repeal of the Walker Law.[95]

Muldoon and his commission succeeded beyond anyone's expectations. They played a vital role in bringing light into the dark world of pugilism. Muldoon took a hands-on approach, visiting fighters in their training camps and denouncing unsafe working conditions.[96] He declared war on gamblers, and built a coalition of promoters, managers, and club owners to fight them. The commission revoked the licenses of referees and judges found guilty of associating with known gamblers.[97] The commissioner used his personal influence to convince fighters to fight for charity fund raisers, which helped win over boxing critics. Under Muldoon's leadership, the commission publicly denounced fighters, even those outside their jurisdiction, who engaged in shady business practices.[98] It even pushed for a ban on smoking at boxing matches.[99] Muldoon never hesitated to promote the sport, praising the fighters he licensed as the most talented and entertaining in history. Jack Dempsey argued that Muldoon was the father of American boxing who saved the sport from destruction and forever earned a place in the heart of every fighter and fight fan.[100]

Muldoon's work on the boxing commission witnessed controversies as well as triumphs. When Floyd Johnson signed to fight Fred Fulton, Muldoon attempted to block the bout, demanding that Johnson first fight in a charitable show sponsored by Muldoon.[101] In 1923, the African American fighter Harry Wills challenged Jack Dempsey for the heavyweight championship. Dempsey accepted the challenge, but Muldoon refused to authorize the bout. In a highly controversial decision, he argued that he was not motivated by racial concerns, but instead worried that the fight would damage the sport by attracting

IV. Boxing Reigns Supreme in the United States, 1915–1941

very large sums of money that would lead to a corrupting, commercializing effect on boxing. He flatly stated that the bout would not take place as long as he remained chairman of the commission.[102] State Senator Walker, author of the Walker Law and a man never at a loss for words, tore into Muldoon and threatened to push for an end to legal boxing if the commission blocked the bout due to racism or absurd objections regarding the commercialization of a sport long awash in cash.[103] Muldoon then decided he was so worried about commercialization that he banned all title bouts until further notice, a move he argued the fans would support.[104] A journalist who interviewed fight fans in Chicago discovered that some agreed with Muldoon's actions.[105] Less than a week after Muldoon refused to license the Wills fight, the other commissioners removed Muldoon from his post as chairman, a move that surprised and angered him.[106] Muldoon remained an associate commissioner and continued to work with the commission and promote boxing.[107] The reorganized commission agreed to license a fight between Dempsey and Wills, at which point Dempsey refused. The New York commission stripped Dempsey of his license, forbidding him to box in the state, and the two men never met in the ring.[108]

While Muldoon and his associates tried to keep boxing clean, gangsters solidified their power around the edges. Flush with money from illegal booze, organized crime began bankrolling fighters and accelerating the process of commercializing sport that Muldoon protested so vigorously.[109]

If the 19th century was the era of the sporting press, then the 20th century was the age of sporting broadcasts. In the first decades of the century, American radio and American boxing grew up together, building on their mutual successes. In 1916, an amateur radio station in High Bridge, New York, began providing news reports. The first commercial broadcasts in the United States began with KDKA Pittsburgh's coverage of the 1920 presidential election. On April 21, 1921, Johnny Ray and Johnny Dundee fought in the first boxing match broadcast over radio.[110] Stations experimented with broadcasts of sporting events including golf, boat racing, and tennis. Soon, coverage emphasized a triumvirate of baseball, college football, and boxing.[111] America found its first broadcast media star in the smiling visage of the Manassa Mauler when Jack Dempsey knocked out French challenger Georges Carpentier in the fourth round of an exciting championship fight.[112] The 80,000 fans who viewed the fight in person were dwarfed by the 300,000 who listened in over the radio.[113] The first photograph ever transmitted over the radio was an image of the bout sent to France for publication in a Paris newspaper.[114] A journalist examining the rise of the radio telephone in 1922 argued that the fight provided the most important demonstration of the radio's potential.[115] In 1923, journalists began broadcasting reports from boxers' training camps in the lead-up to big fights. In the same year, 2 million fans across the nation listened to live coverage of Willard's fight with Firpo.[116] Indeed, the desire to listen to boxing convinced many Americans to buy radios. A single New York department store estimated that it sold more than $90,000 worth of radios to fans determined to hear Tunney fight Dempsey for the heavyweight championship in 1927.[117] The rise of boxing on the radio mirrored a broader embrace of the technology. In 1922, only one out of every 400 households contained a radio; by 1930, that number had increased to one in three.[118]

Radio did not offer the same support for wrestling. By the second decade of the 20th century, wrestling was pushed onto the periphery of American life because it was no longer consistent with the dominant vision of American masculinity.[119] Wrestling suffered from a decline for many years. The sport struggled with an historical public perception that authentic wrestling contests were uninteresting.[120] By the first decade of the new century, experts estimated that 90 percent of wrestling matches concluded with prearranged outcomes, and the remaining 10 percent made for painfully boring shows.[121] Wrestling was an agrarian sport, closely connected to farming communities.

Heavyweight boxing champion Jack Dempsey entertains an audience as he pretends to punch the famous magician Harry Houdini while the lightweight boxing champion Benny Leonard restrains Houdini. Published by the Bain News Service, probably in the early 1920s (Library of Congress Prints and Photographs Division).

IV. Boxing Reigns Supreme in the United States, 1915–1941   153

By 1920, however, the majority of the Americans lived in cities.[122] Boxing, with its emphasis on excitement and urban life, was far more consistent with the vision of urban, spectacle-centered, passionate manhood that increasingly dominated the lives and ideals of American men by the early 20th century.[123]

Wrestling's problems were hardly limited to the United States. Foreign visitors noted a similar change in Europe.[124] Military athletic directors who promoted wrestling matches during the Great War reported mediocre attendance figures.[125] After the war, interest in serious professional wrestling took another nosedive. The sporting press noted public disinterest and stopped covering wrestling at the same time that boxing coverage skyrocketed, which further accelerated grappling's decline.[126] Wrestling did not perform well on the new medium of radio. Unlike fast-paced sports such as baseball and boxing, which provided commentators with action they could readily describe verbally, wrestling bouts tended to move much more slowly and subtly, which did not make for exciting or popular broadcasts.[127] A journalist observed that thrilling radio broadcasts of boxing bouts convinced many members of the younger generation across the globe to abandon wrestling in favor of boxing.[128] Wrestling remained an important participatory sport in schools and gyms, but its days as a spectator sport were over. As wrestlers slipped into the shadows, boxers, in turn, moved into the spotlight.

In an age dominated by popular athletes, no star shone brighter than that of Jack Dempsey. His victory over Jess Willard in 1919 catapulted him into stardom. His numerous title defenses—particularly those over French champion Georges Carpientier and Argentine Luis Firpo—cemented his reputation as one of the finest boxers of all time.[129] Following his 1923 victory over Firpo, Dempsey spent nearly three years away from the ring and focused on acting.[130] He underwent plastic surgery to improve his appearance in hopes he would get more acting jobs.[131] Like his predecessor John L. Sullivan, Dempsey found acting and public appearances provided far easier paychecks than fighting for a living. The Universal Picture Corporation signed Dempsey to a 10-movie deal for the huge sum of $1 million.[132] He moved to Los Angeles and made friends with the biggest names in Hollywood. While in Hollywood, he enjoyed romances with several leading ladies before marrying in Estelle Taylor in 1925. The only real blemish on his public image was the reoccurring accusations that Dempsey dodged the draft in World War I. These rumors continued to reappear periodically even after a court found him not guilty of the charge, and an American Legion post made him an honorary commandant.[133]

After taking an extended break from the ring, Dempsey returned to face the greatest challenges of his career. On September 23, 1926, he fought challenger Gene "The Fighting Marine" Tunney in defense of his title. Tunney was a lifelong New Yorker, born of recent Irish immigrants. Unlike the supposedly draft-dodging Dempsey, Tunney interrupted his boxing career to volunteer for service with the Marines in World War I, during which he honed his fighting skills, winning the light heavyweight championship of the American Expeditionary Forces.[134] To prepare for the fight, he watched film of Dempsey's previous fights, replaying them over and over again while looking for weaknesses. The 133,732 fans who packed Sesquicentennial Stadium in Philadelphia represented the largest crowd ever assembled for a boxing match to that date.[135] The nearly $2 million they paid to attend set another boxing record.[136] Another 39 million fans listened to the fight over the radio, 100 of whom died while listening to the broadcast.[137] Dempsey entered the ring a heavy favorite, but spent all 10 rounds just barely surviving Tunney's onslaught.[138] The champion avoided a knockout, but the judges gave the victory to the challenger on points. Dempsey left the arena to the sounds of fans cheering for the vanquished brawler who had fought on against overwhelming force.[139]

In the fight's aftermath, Dempsey received almost as much praise from the fans as Tunney, because he embodied masculine virtues. A sportswriter speculated that while Tunney appeared to provide everything the fans admired—military service, personal virtue, and a respectful demeanor—Dempsey won the fans over with his manly charm.[140] He displayed heart in the ring, refusing to quit even when the struggle was clearly hopeless, and demonstrated good humor in defeat, explaining his battered face to his startled wife, by joking that he forgot to duck.[141] Jimmy Powers, writing for the *Evening News*, concluded that Dempsey received cheers because he was the best kind of man.[142]

Dempsey briefly considered retirement, but decided to give the ring another try. After several months of intensive training, the former champion fought Jack Sharkey in New York on July 21, 1927, and increased his stature as an icon of American masculinity. The good-natured veteran was a sentimental favorite over the sneering, bragging Sharkey.[143] A flash of the old Mauler stepped into the ring, as he knocked out the younger fighter in the seventh round with a flurry of punches so rapid that fans argued endlessly if it was a right or a left that actually put Sharkey on the ground.[144] Once again, it was as much Dempsey's ability to connect with the crowd as his fighting skills that made him a fan favorite. An experienced telegraph operator covering the fight called out for Dempsey to kill his younger opponent, encouraging the pugilist that "There's life in us old fellows yet."[145] This comment indicates how age provides another point of connection between fighters and

IV. Boxing Reigns Supreme in the United States, 1915–1941   155

their fans. Westbrook Pegler, an observer on the scene, confessed that he took offense when Sharkey glared at Dempsey and gained deep satisfaction when Dempsey knocked Sharkey to the mat. Pegler admitted that his emotions were a bit irrational since he was just a witness to the struggle rather than a participant in it, but he considered his feelings understandable since "we live in our heroes."[146]

With Dempsey's demonstration that he could still deliver knockout blows and his popularity higher than ever, he began to prepare for a rematch with Tunney. On September 22, 1927, 150,000 fans packed the stands of Chicago's Soldier Field to see Dempsey fight Tunney once again.[147] The $2,658,660 gate stood as the all-time highest-earning fight until Ali fought Spinks more than half a century later.[148] More than 70 radio stations broadcast the fight to an estimated worldwide audience of 50 million listeners.[149] Gamblers gave a slight edge to Dempsey in highly volatile betting. The fighters stood in stark contrast as the opponents shook hands: Dempsey's face was covered in several days' worth of scraggily beard, and Tunney's was groomed to perfection.[150] The fight began with good exchanges from both fighters. In the seventh round, Dempsey's former glory returned for a moment as he knocked Tunney to the ground with a perfect left hook.[151] According to new Illinois Boxing Commission rules, which were explained to both men in advance of the bout, a fighter knocking down his opponent should go to the neutral corner while the referee counted. This practice was intended to prevent a fighter from crowding over his opponent and knocking him back down as soon as he reached his feet, but before he was fully recovered. When Dempsey failed to immediately go to the neutral corner, the referee Dave Barry stopped counting while he waited for Dempsey to go to the corner. This penalized Dempsey and gave Tunney vital seconds to recover.[152] Tunney spent the rest of the fight avoiding Dempsey's onslaught before winning by a judges' decision, just as he had won the first encounter.[153]

Allegations of fraud and misconduct swirled throughout the fight world in the bout's aftermath. Both Tunney and Dempsey received support from members of organized crime, and Dave Barry owned a speakeasy with mob connections.[154] The fight went down in history as "the long count fight," and remains one of the most controversial contests in boxing history.[155] The judges declared Dempsey a loser, but the fans proclaimed him a winner. They admired his aggression, and many felt the referee cheated him by holding up the letter rather than the spirit of the rules.[156] Dempsey accepted defeat graciously, defending Tunney's role in the affair and attributing the loss to his own failure to quickly return to the neutral corner.[157]

Dempsey retired after the fight and lived out a long life. When he lost his fortune in the stock market crash of 1929, he fought enough exhibition bouts to get back on his feet, but he never again boxed seriously. He opened a restaurant where he spent his time sitting in a corner booth, signing autographs, and enjoying the affections of an endless stream of fans who came by to share a smile and a handshake with their hero.[158] When America went to war once again in 1941, Dempsey volunteered for the Coast Guard in spite of his advanced age and finally killed the rumors that he was a draft dodger.[159] Dempsey, perhaps in a way no other champion before or since achieved, lived out a long and dignified retirement. He expressed his undying appreciation for his fans and was never too busy or too important for them. He died quietly on May 31, 1983, at the advanced age of 87.[160] Perhaps no one better understood or summarized the allure of Jack Dempsey than his biographer and friend Roger Kahn, who praised the champion more as a heroic man than as a great fighter.

> What I can say with certainty is that across the years of encounters with Dempsey, I came away with a strong feeling for the man. As these pages testify, I liked what I found—the candor, the quiet pride, the kindness, the wit, the fists like boulders, and the rousing horseplay, as when he insisted that I spar with him. Gentle he was, but he never let you quite forget that he was Jack Dempsey, who in his prime could lick any son of a bitch in the world.
> He is a rare thing: close up, as from afar, he was a hero.[161]

Asian fighters continued to make their mark on the periphery of American life as Dempsey passed from pugilist to retiree. Unlike the jujitsu-exporting Japanese, Asian Americans from areas outside Japan tended to adopt Western arts rather than promote their own. David Kui Kong Young, a very successful boxer of Chinese ancestry, became a source of tremendous pride for the Asian American community in the 1930s.[162] Walter Cho, the son of Korean immigrants, boxed professionally in the bantamweight division during the 1930s.[163] The Filipino Francisco Guilledo, who fought under the nickname Pancho Villa, became the flyweight boxing champion of the world and one of the most popular pugilists of the era. He died unexpectedly in 1925 from an infected tooth at the height of his fame, a tragedy that saddened fight fans around the world.[164] Asian Americans often entered the boxing ring for the same reason that appealed to members of every other persecuted and marginalized group: boxing paid far better than unskilled labor.[165] In the 1930s, no group was more persecuted or marginalized in the United States than African Americans, and it was from their ranks that America's greatest champion in a generation emerged.

Joe Louis, like so many of the great pugilists, traveled from poverty to wealth on the strength of his fists and his manly bearing. He was born in

IV. Boxing Reigns Supreme in the United States, 1915–1941   157

1914, near Lafayette, Alabama, and named Joseph Louis Barrow. He was the son of dirt-poor tenant farmers and the grandson of slaves.[166] While he was still a young boy, his family moved to Detroit, Michigan.[167] His mother gave Louis money for violin lessons, but he spent it on boxing lessons at the Brewster Recreation Center instead.[168] While only 19 years old, Louis earned national fame when he won the Golden Gloves championship for amateur boxers in 1934.[169] The victory brought Louis to the attention of the African American gangster John Roxborough, who became Louis's manager and patron.[170]

In Louis's professional boxing debut, he faced the Norwegian American Jack Kracken. In the first round, Louis punched his opponent so hard that the hapless pugilist fell out of the ring and into the lap of the Illinois athletic commissioner.[171] Louis pummeled his way to victory over some of the finest boxers in the world, including Max Baer and Primo Carnera.[172] Jack Dempsey publicly praised the rising star, referring to him as a fine fighter with excellent technique and the leading contender for the championship.[173] By January 1936, Louis was well on his way to the heavyweight crown with a record that included 27 victories, 23 by knockout, and not a single defeat.[174] The press

Flyweight boxing champion Pancho Villa poses with rival pugilist, Elino Flores. This image might be a promotional photograph for an event held at Ebbets Field, Brooklyn, on September 14, 1922, which starred both fighters and several others. Photograph is part of the Frank and Frances Carpenter Collection (Library of Congress Prints and Photographs Division).

poked racist fun at Louis on occasion, laughing at his supposed lack of intellect, but generally respected his widespread popularity born of morality, toughness, and modesty.[175] Louis was a particular favorite of the African American community and his one-man victories in the ring gave hope to millions fighting their own battles, often with far less success.[176]

Only one man stood between Louis and the title shot he craved. Before he could fight for the championship, he had to face the former world champion from Germany, Max Schmeling. Louis and Schmeling agreed to face each other in New York in a fight that captivated audiences on both sides of the Atlantic.[177]

In preparation for the fight, Louis relaxed, but Schmeling worked.[178] Louis selected the resort town of Lakewood, New Jersey, for his training camp. He relaxed and played golf. His trainer Jack Blackburn worried aloud that Louis was not prepared, but expressed confidence that Louis would buckle down and improve in time for the bout.[179] The German Schmeling trained at Napanoch, New York, high in the mountains, where he hoped the thin air would help him build his cardiovascular strength.[180] In contrast to Louis's love for the golf course, Schmeling preferred a steady diet of sparring, calisthenics, and shadow boxing. Visitors to his camp expressed awe for the German's work ethic and skills.[181] They noted that in spite of Louis's impressive performance in previous fights, Schmeling was undoubtedly the best-prepared and highly tuned combatant who ever agreed to step into the ring with Louis.[182] Days before the fight, both pugilists put on sparring exhibitions in their camps for visitors. Both fighters impressed their guests in spite of their very distinct approaches to training, stimulating interest in the coming bout.[183] Schmeling told reporters that he had discovered Louis's weakness after many hours of watching fight films. His manager predicted that Louis was about to experience the first loss of his career.[184] Gamblers did not listen: going into the fight, they favored Louis by a six to one margin.[185]

On the evening of June 19, 1936, Schmeling and Louis stepped into a ring constructed in Yankee Stadium. Only 39,878 fans watched in person. Many choose not to brave the pouring rain that delayed the fight. Others stayed away because they were convinced Louis would quickly destroy the German in a straightforward and not terribly entertaining fashion.[186] The men entered the arena looking remarkably similar in spite of the racial divide between the grandson of slaves and the man from the Third Reich. Their skin tones were only a minor shade apart, both wore their dark hair short with completely shaven faces, and they clothed themselves in dark-colored trunks and shoes of almost identical cut. For two rounds, the fighters sparred cautiously, with Louis appearing to have a slight advantage. In the third round, Louis got aggressive and began to damage his opponent, but Schmeling stayed

IV. Boxing Reigns Supreme in the United States, 1915–1941 159

alive. The tide shifted in the fourth round. Schmeling delivered a vicious right knocking Louis to the mat. For seven more rounds, Schmeling kept up a tireless offensive, battering the crowd favorite and delivering blows Louis could not return.[187] Both fighters staggered, exhausted by the struggle.[188] In the 12th round, Schmeling dug deep for a final assault. He charged Louis, landing a series of blows that knocked the American to the canvas in defeat.[189]

The startling upset propelled the fight into a place of symbolic importance that few had anticipated. Schmeling received enormous praise from the German press, which had largely ignored him going into the fight. Adolf Hitler sent personal congratulations to the victorious boxer and flowers to the pugilist's wife. The Reich's marshal of propaganda, Joseph Goebbels, called the bout a victory for all of Germany and Schmeling a national representative.[190] Sportswriters noted the fickle attentions of the German leadership, who paid no attention to Schmeling before the fight, but suddenly treated him like an old friend after he bested Louis.[191] A newspaper produced by the German Nazi Party bestowed the event with an even larger significance, arguing that Schmeling fought not for nation but for white supremacy, and on that basis deserved praise from Americans as well as Germans.[192] Some white Americans agreed. A white bartender in a Manhattan hotel cheered when he heard of Louis's fall and shouted racial slurs.[193] A writer for the *United Press* dismissed Louis in the most derogatory terms, insulting his race, manhood, and physical appearance.[194]

Louis, long a hero to the black community lay vanquished, and many blacks shared his grief. Across the nation, black men and women wept openly at the defeat of their champion.[195] In Harlem, some African Americans rioted, assaulting whites and destroying property.[196] Most sportswriters, even those who criticized Louis's overconfidence and failure to prepare for the fight, still defended him as a man. They rejected allegations of a rigged fight, arguing that Louis was a deeply moral man whose honor was simply not for sale.[197] By any reasonable standard, Schelling's victory entitled him to a title shot, but boxing was now enmeshed in global politics to an unprecedented degree. Many of the most influential voices in the sport did not trust Germany, hated its racial policies, and feared that if Schmeling got the heavyweight belt, Hitler would ensure that it forever remained German property. American boxing officials proceeded to use lies, fraud, and backroom deals to ensure that Schmeling did not get a title shot.[198]

Louis returned to the gym, trained, and rebuilt his reputation. When fans suggested that a doctor might have doped him, Louis and his camp denied the allegations, and made no excuses for a defeat they attributed to Louis's overconfidence.[199] Louis learned from his mistakes.[200] Within weeks

American heavyweight boxing champion Joe Louis (left) prepares to attack the German pugilist Max Schmeling (right) on June 20, 1936. The fight between two men served as a preview of the conflict awaiting their respective nations in World War II. Published in 1936 by the *New York World-Telegram* and the *Sun* newspaper (Library of Congress Prints and Photographs Division).

of losing to Schmeling, Louis reentered the ring against Jack Sharkey, winning with a knockout in the third round. In December, he needed just one punch and 26 seconds to knock out Eddie Simms and earn his 27th knockout victory.[201] He followed up with three more wins in 1937.[202] The string of victories put him in line for a title shot. On June 22, 1937, the reigning world heavyweight champion, James "Cinderella Man" Braddock, a New Yorker of Irish descent, faced Louis at Comiskey Park in Chicago for the title.[203] Experts estimated that the bout brought $5 million and 50,000 fans into the Depression-wracked city.[204] For seven rounds, the fighters engaged briskly, each demonstrating the skills and courage that made him worthy of his place at the center of the boxing world. In the eighth round, Louis threw a picture-perfect right that put Braddock to sleep and made Louis the new champion.[205] For the first time since Jack Johnson, the heavyweight championship of the world belonged to a black man.

Louis's victory presented the boxing world with a conundrum that could only find resolution in the ring. Journalists pointed out that while Louis wore the title, he did so only because of political concerns that treated an American man—even one whose ancestors came from Africa—more favorably than a German.[206] Schmeling deserved the title shot after he beat Louis, and no one seemed inclined to pretend otherwise as they bent every rule, perhaps wisely, to keep the belt away from the Nazis.[207] Schmeling's victory over Louis gave credence to the critics who argued that the heavyweight crown belonged on the white head of Max Schmeling. Racist journalists pointed gleefully to the apparent absurdity of Louis's crown as they leveled racial slurs at the new champion.[208] In the end, Louis and Schmeling agreed to fight once more and determine definitively the rightful owner of the heavyweight belt.[209]

The first encounter between Louis and Schmeling became larger than the competitors only after it ended, but the rematch took on a broader significance before the fighters ever agreed to meet. It provided enormous symbolism as a showdown between the greatest champions of two powerful nations rapidly moving toward war.[210] By June 1938, German–American relations were badly deteriorating. The Nazis were on the move, rebuilding their military, and President Franklin D. Roosevelt denounced Nazi aggression in Europe. Schmeling's reputation in America was diminished because of his connection to the Nazis.[211] This condemnation came in spite of the fighter's tendency to stand up to the Fuehrer, his rejection of Nazi awards, and his refusal to fire his Jewish American manager, Joe Jacobs.[212] In a bizarre twist of events, the same German Nazi newspaper that had proclaimed Schmeling's first victory a international triumph for the white race and a victory for all Germany denounced American journalists on the eve of the second bout for turning the fight into a racial and political issue.[213] Louis's star rose as Schmeling's fell. American sportswriters displayed open hostility toward Schmeling and encouraged Louis to use any dirty trick at his disposal to keep the title in American hands.[214] Weeks before the fight, Louis visited the president at the White House. Roosevelt asked Louis if he could feel the pugilist's muscles; once he was satisfied that Louis was a strong as he looked, he told the boxer that the nation needed those muscles to defeat Germany.[215] Louis, in fact, saw himself as a representative of his nation and felt the awesome responsibility to not let the country down.[216]

On June 22, 1938, Louis and Schmeling entered an arena in the center of Yankee Stadium, looking almost identical to the men who had met two years earlier. Eighty thousand fans packed the stands, fidgeting and chattering, charged with nervous energy they could not hope to contain.[217] Cynical journalists noted that regardless of which fighter won, the event was already a

Senator F. Ryan Duffy of Wisconsin (left) engages in a playful sparring match with Senator Allen Ellender of Louisiana as their colleagues debate the conference report on the $375 million flood control bill on June 15, 1938. A smiling photographer looks on in the background. Published in 1938 as part of the Harris & Ewing Inc. Photography Collection (Library of Congress Prints and Photographs Division).

victory for the city of New York, which was awash in 30,000 visitors who injected $3 million into the local economy.[218]

The fight was quicker and more decisive than anyone dared hope or fear. In the first and only round, the action began quickly as Louis landed a series of lefts and rights that stunned the German.[219] When Schmeling attempted to retreat, Louis followed, beating him without mercy.[220] Schmeling fought on gamely as he staggered uncertainly. The German's coach realized that his fighter was hopelessly outmatched and threw in the towel, ending both the fight and the beating. The two minutes and four seconds of flying leather went down in the record books as the shortest championship bout in the sport's history.[221] The crowd went completely insane. Incoherent screams poured from reddened faces surrounded by wildly flailing appendages.[222] Even the dignitaries in the crowd expressed their tremendous joy. The gov-

Two young boys box while their peers look on in one of the nation's numerous rough Depression-era boxing gyms. The photograph was taken in 1941 in Washington, D.C., and is included in the Harris & Ewing Collection (Library of Congress Prints and Photographs Division).

ernor of Michigan was one of the first visitors in the champion's dressing room. He fumbled with words as he attempted to explain his heartfelt gratitude to Louis. A journalist considered the scene in which a powerful politician expressed personal thanks to the grandson of a slave as evidence that America, for all its problems, might just have a chance at a long and noble future.[223] Schmeling's dressing room was a bit lonelier.

Schmeling's loss was an eventful moment in the history of German fight sports. German radio broadcasts cut the transmission short as soon as Schmeling got into trouble.[224] The Nazi Party announced its discovery that Schmeling was only 11/12 Aryan. Hitler banned movies of the fight, at least until the ministry of propaganda edited it with scenes from the first bout.[225] The German news service denied altering the films, claiming they were unable to show the films because they arrived late.[226] The Fuehrer declared boxing a stupid sport and made its practice illegal in Germany. While the Nazis were at it, they recalled their ambassador from Washington just hours after Schmeling hit the canvas.[227] Since professional boxer was no longer a viable occupation in the Reich, Schmeling became eligible for the draft. He eventually enlisted in the paratroopers, got wounded while fighting British soldiers on the island of Crete, and ended up as a prisoner of war.[228]

After the fight, Joe Louis entered the pantheon of American sporting heroes. Jack Dempsey, the most respected former fighter still alive, had predicted Schmeling would beat Louis for a second time, but he apologized for his doubts and praised the champion's performance.[229] Across the nation, African Americans celebrated.[230] Many members of the community saw Louis as their champion, as evidence that a black person could win over the forces of racial injustice. Martin Luther King, Jr., often told the story of a young black man suffering execution in the gas chamber who called out for Joe Louis and begged the champion to save him. King saw the story as evidence of what Louis meant to the black community. The young convict believed that Louis would care because they shared a race, and believed Louis alone possessed the capacity to save him because he was the world's finest fighter.[231] Although Louis did not save the young man, he gave hope to many Americans of every race. His fame spread to white Americans who cheered for a black man to whip a white one and celebrated his win as a victory for democracy.[232] Louis's fists gave Americans a boost of confidence in dark days. He told Americans that they could triumph over Germany just as he had prevailed over Schmeling, and they believed.[233]

On the eve of America's entry into World War II, the expansion of television and movies helped popularize American fight sports. The showing and especially the transportation across state lines of filmed boxing matches were controversial and largely illegal by the second decade of the 20th century.[234] Authorities occasionally made exceptions. In 1917, the fight promoter Jack Herman obtained approval to show a fight film that contained the patriotic scene of young army officers training as boxers.[235] In 1935, Senator Warren Barbour, a former boxer and enthusiastic fight fan, tried to repeal federal laws against fight films but failed.[236] With unconcealed hypocrisy, the state of Virginia allowed theaters to show films of Louis's defeat by Schmeling, but retained the ban on fights Louis won.[237] In 1939, boxing appeared on American television for the first time when the experimental New York television station broadcast a bout between heavyweights Lou Nova and Max Baer.[238] Also in 1939, the journalist Shirley Povich predicted that boxing on television would soon make fight films irrelevant as the airwaves carried scenes of pugilistic glory.[239] Barbour resumed his work to legalize fight films in the same year. He argued that the law was unpopular and widely ignored, that boxing was a very popular sport, that the fears of racial unrest that motivated the ban were no longer a concern, and that the appearance of boxing on television made the law anachronistic.[240] Expert witnesses such as Jack Dempsey testified that the ban deprived fighters of needed income and boxing coaches of an important instructional aide.[241] Congress and the president agreed with Barbour's conclusions and ended the federal ban on fight films in 1940.[242] The sweet science enjoyed unprecedented popularity in the United States. Across the nation, virtually every man possessed some knowledge of the fistic arts, from the halls of Congress to threadbare gymnasiums. Boxing stood at the pinnacle of life, but it would not last at this lofty perch for long. When America was drawn into World War II, much of the nation's attention and many of its young men were drawn to Asia, the scene of new challenges for America and America's fight sports.

V

"Everybody Was Kung Fu Fighting"

Asian Martial Arts Gain Unprecedented Popularity in the United States, 1941–1981

> While Haines—the crowd favorite—took a very traditional, wide and deep stance as if to invite his challenger into his powerful domain, Lewis darted in and out on the balls of his feet. Every master of the day knew that it was a wide stance such as Baines displayed which permitted a karate stylist to project the kind of power that could break bricks and cement blocks. Yet in spite of popular belief, Lewis seemed to have no problem scoring points against the stationary Baines. Each time Baines would attempt a kick; Lewis would intercept it by jamming Baines' kicking leg, and would then counter with a left hook or a double-punch combination. When Baines attempted a karate punch, Lewis would trap the striking hand and counter with a strike of his own.
> —Karate expert Greg Baines fights kickboxer Joe Lewis, 1970[1]

In 1941, the United States stood at the gates of one of its greatest national challenge since the Civil War. The Second World War, like the first, raged for several years before the United States became a combatant. America's relations with the Axis powers of Germany, Italy, and Japan deteriorated over numerous economic, political, and strategic conflicts. On December 7, 1941, Japan launched a surprise attack on American forces at Pearl Harbor, Hawaii. America declared war on Japan in response; the remaining Axis powers supported their ally, declaring war on the United States.[2] America faced the prospect of global war for a second time in barely two decades. Angered by the surprise

V. Asian Martial Arts Gains Popularity in the U.S., 1941–1981   167

attack, hardened by years of economic hardship, and led by an inspiring chief executive, America entered the conflict unified in ways unimaginable in the years before Japanese bombs destroyed American ships and sailors.[3] Seemingly, overnight, almost every aspect of American life became subordinate to the war effort. Japanese Americans and their loved ones were forced into internment camps, men left civilian jobs for military service, factories turned plowshares into swords, women left households for factories, and pugilists left the ring for the battlefield.

American fighters joined their fans in line at the recruiting stations. Jack Dempsey had faced criticism during his boxing career because he did not serve in the military during World War I, but he refused to make the same mistake twice. Within days of the attack on Pearl Harbor, Dempsey attempted

Even in the harsh conditions of a Japanese internment camp, people found time for a saving touch of barbarism. A watchful instructor looks on during a judo class held in the Rohwer Relocation Center, McGehee, Arkansas, where lessons were held every afternoon and evening. Photograph taken on November 25, 1942 (National Archives at College Park—Still Pictures [RD-DC-S], Record Group 210: Records of the War Relocation Authority, 1941–1989).

to volunteer as a private in the army. Although he passed all of the physical tests, the army rejected the 46-year-old retiree as too old. The Coast Guard offered to make an exception for the aging pugilist. Dempsey eventually rose to the rank of commander, directed physical fitness and hand-to-hand combat training programs, made numerous public appearances, and participated in the invasion of Okinawa.[4] Inaccurate rumors briefly circulated that he died in the assault.[5] Gene Tunney, a Marine in World War I and the heavyweight boxing champion more recently, became the navy's athletic director during the war; like his former opponent, he earned the rank of commander.[6] These were just two of the numerous boxing champions and former champions who served in the armed forces. Others included James "Cinderella Man" Braddock, Benny Leonard, and Max Baer. More than 4,000 boxers eventually served during World War II and more than 50 became casualties.[7]

The most famous boxer in uniform was undoubtedly the reigning heavyweight champion and icon of black manhood, Joe Louis, who did his part to ensure victory over the Axis and further blur the racial lines of American masculine identity. The Brown Bomber rushed to the recruiting office after the attack on Pearl Harbor and proclaimed his willingness to take on the Japanese with his fists.[8] He worked in cooperation with other boxers and fitness experts in uniform, directing athletics and performing in morale-building boxing exhibitions.[9] In an effort to differentiate itself from racist Nazi Germany, the American government held up Private Joe Louis as a symbol of masculinity for American men of every race.[10] Propaganda featuring Louis aided in blurring the racial boundaries of American masculine identities. Building on Louis's ability to reach out the African American community, the American government appropriated John Henry's legendary status as a strong black man in propaganda that used Henry as symbol of a strong, multiracial United States.[11]

The civilian boxing circuit effectively evaporated overnight. Half of all boxing clubs went out of business within a year of the Pearl Harbor attack, as a direct result of the international conflict.[12] Eleven states witnessed a complete shutdown of boxing.[13] The National Boxing Association declared a freeze on the titles held by fighters in active service, a move the association acknowledged was good for the nation, but bad for the sport.[14] The nation's leading boxing analysts noted the problems and predicted a greatly diminished sport, at least for the moment. Boxing experts named welterweight Barney Ross the most valuable man in pugilism based not on his performance in the ring, but on his heroism while fighting on Guadalcanal.[15] During the war, almost all the boxing shows that took place were between servicemen on leave or at military-sponsored exhibition bouts held to maintain morale and encourage the sale of war bonds.[16]

V. Asian Martial Arts Gains Popularity in the U.S., 1941–1981

The military reused many of its World War I–era training programs, offering up fight sports both as a virtuous masculine alternative to vice and as preparation for the battlefield. As in the previous conflict, the military assigned an athletic director to each camp who directed sporting activities.[17] Civic organizations sponsored boxing and wrestling matches to promote the sale of war bonds. The civilian New York City Defense Recreation Committee, working in coordination with religious organizations, provided free admission to movies, baseball games, and boxing matches for members of the armed forces.[18] Civilian experts traveled to distant military bases, teaching sports, including boxing, to men on active duty. A partnership of civilian boxing officials and military officers developed a boxing-based physical training program for 17-year-old boys to prepare them for military service.[19] Military camps formed rival boxing teams that competed for both bragging rights and the entertainment of comrades in the stands.

Boxing, while still popular, soon faced a new challenger for soldierly attention and official praise. Football—which had emerged as an increasingly popular sport among civilians between the world wars—became a favorite in the military camps. Military officers praised the team spirit of football as more conducive to the mindset they wanted to build in the ranks than the more individualistic pursuits of boxing and wrestling.[20] Journalists suggested that football's emphasis on violence, fitness, and cooperation made it the best sport for military training.[21] However, unlike football, boxing offered the chance to train men to kill with their bare hands, a useful battlefield skill, and the sweet science continued to provide a component of military hand-to-hand combat training.[22] Here, too, boxing faced a new challenger.

American men engaged in the deadliest war in history sought out the deadliest approaches to unarmed combat, further complicating the racial component of American masculinity. Asian martial artists had long claimed that their techniques failed in the ring because their best tactics were too deadly for a sporting competition.[23] With the outbreak of war, Americans suddenly decided that deadly techniques sounded just about right. William Fairbairn, a British soldier and police officer who studied Asian martial arts while serving in China and Japan, was one of the first men to produce a hybrid style that included techniques from Asian fighting systems, which he called "defendu." By 1926, Fairbairn had begun spreading his ideas to United States by publishing books and instructing American Marines serving in Asia.[24] The British government loaned Fairbairn to the U.S. military during the war, as an instructor of unarmed combat.[25] A 1943 unarmed combat manual written by Major Rex Applegate, an American intelligence operative who worked with the British commandos, argued that the Queensbury Rules were dead, and that only an embrace of every possible technique could provide an effective system of unarmed combat.[26] Journalists encouraged fighting men to embrace the historic art of gouging, using every tool and dirty trick at their disposal to defeat their enemies.[27] Ironically, American soldiers had given up gouging a century before under a combination of religious and legal prohibitions. Building on these older ideas, by 1944 the Marines had devel-

Marine Corporal Arvin Lou Ghazlo demonstrates a judo-inspired technique on Marine Private Ernest C. Jones. Before the war, Ghazlo served as martial arts instructor to the Georgia State Police. The photograph was created in April 1943 by the Department of Defense (National Archives at College Park—Still Pictures [RD-DC-S], Record Group 127: Records of the U.S. Marine Corps, 1775–1999).

oped a unique hybrid style of unarmed combat, which blended techniques from jujitsu, wrestling, savate (French kickboxing), Chinese martial arts, and boxing into a single art. They called this practice judo for lack of a better term, although it bore scant resemblance to traditional judo.[28] Like scientists of mayhem, the Marines experimented with a variety of fighting styles, occasionally pitting men against each other in fights completely without rules to determine the ideal formula.[29] It was not that American servicemen embraced Eastern arts to the exclusion of Western methods, but rather that they were willing to learn from Asian men to create hybrid systems. Some soldiers clung to the old ways. They made a racialized association between boxing and whiteness as opposed to Asian arts and being like Asians.[30] Men like pugilist-turned-naval-commander Gene Tunney argued that boxing provided a superior means of unarmed combat.[31] Over time, a chorus that embraced a synthesis of styles from the East and West drowned out these conservative voices.

After years of struggle, the most destructive conflict in human history ended in 1945. On April 30, 1945, Adolf Hitler committed suicide in his bunker beneath Berlin. On May 7, Germany formally surrendered to the Allied forces.[32] Japan held out a little longer. On August 6, 1945, the United States detonated an atomic bomb over the Japanese city of Hiroshima. When Japan did not immediately surrender, Nagasaki became the second city, and so far the last, destroyed by an atomic blast.[33] The Soviet Union declared war on Japan the same day. On August 15, 1945, Japan surrendered.[34] World War II was over, but a new conflict was just beginning. Soldiers shifted from active combat in a major war to Cold War garrison duty. Hundreds of thousands of American soldiers, sailors, airmen, Marines, and civilians served in Asia with the allied occupation forces after the war.[35] Men on garrison duty attempted to transform much of Asia into a bulwark against communism, influenced its culture, and learned from locals. Many of the martial arts they learned while in Asia were nothing new in the United States. However, most of these sports were limited to grappling techniques, made little headway, or were hybrid styles.[36]

Masculine need rather than economics drove the initial spread of Asian striking arts in the United States after World War II. While grappling arts such as jiujutsu were reasonably well established on the periphery of American life before the attack on Pearl Harbor, striking arts—including karate and taekwondo—were largely unknown in the United States before American veterans, trained in Asia, brought them home after the war. Robert Trias led the charge as the first documented instructor of an Asian striking art in the continental United States. While serving in the navy in the south Pacific, he spent his leisure hours training for the navy middleweight boxing championship. Tung Ge Hsing, a Chinese missionary and an expert in karate, approached Trias, flattering the sailor and asking for a fight.[37] Trias agreed. With a crowd of American servicemen looking on, the tiny Chinese fighter then provided Trias with the worst beating of his life, emasculating him in front of his comrades.[38] Looking up at his conqueror from the ground, the vanquished American immediately asked Hsing for lessons.[39] The monk gladly provided those lessons, and transformed Trias from defeated opponent into an eager disciple. Trias's reasons for abandoning boxing for karate were clearly cultural rather than economic. Boxing held out the promise of wealth to men capable of proving themselves in the ring, but karate offered only the possibility of becoming a better fighter who would never again face defeat and emasculation.

When Trias returned home to the United States, he began to spread the message about karate. In 1946, Trias returned home to Phoenix, Arizona, and began offering some of the first karate lessons on the American mainland.[40] He joined the Arizona Highway Patrol, indicating that karate was more hobby than profession for the ex-sailor.[41] He later expanded his school, offered lessons to the cream of Phoenix society, and built a relationship with the Japanese Karate Association.[42] Trias was not alone in this venture: other American veterans opened similar schools in the years following Japan's surrender.[43] Trias built relationships with other karate instructors and created nationwide standards for professional conduct and athletic competitions. In 1948, he founded the United States Karate Association, the first organization of its kind in America.[44] Early competitions stressed stylistic purity and artistic movement, while rejecting the brutality of "anything goes" fights, even though it was an "anything goes" fight that convinced Trias of karate's value.[45] Trias, however, soon faced competition from a former enemy with a very different approach.

American karate received another boost when Mas Oyama, a famed fighter and believer in the saving power of fight sports from Asia, came to the United States. Born in Korea in 1923, Oyama served as a mechanic in the Japanese air force during World War II.[46] After the conflict, he turned his attention to the martial arts. He identified with the Japanese people even though he was Korean, indicating another strangely shaped identity that did not follow national contours. Oyama, in a move similar to Duffield Osborne's call for a saving touch of barbarism, believed that Japan could find redemption in karate as the country's people embraced a renewed warrior code, rooted in their warrior past.[47] In contrast to the strict restraint of contests sponsored by Trias, Oyama encouraged his students to perfect their techniques in a process of full-contact fights unhindered by weight classes or protective

V. Asian Martial Arts Gains Popularity in the U.S., 1941-1981

padding, and restrained only by a philosophical commitment to the ideals of the warrior's code and a desire to demonstrate ideal form.[48] In 1952, the Wrestling Association of Chicago heard of Oyama's crowd-pleasing "anything goes" tournaments and invited him to put on demonstrations in the United States. Oyama toured the United States later that year. When he demonstrated kata—choreographed solo routines of techniques—American audiences expressed indifference.[49] However, when he fought challenge matches against boxers and wrestlers, crowds rewarded him with cheers.[50] They expressed awe when he broke boards and bricks with his bare hands. These breaking demonstrations gave rise to the popular perception of karate as a mystical art that granted superhuman powers.[51]

Karate built an important beachhead in the 1940s, but the bright lights still focused on the sweet science. Boxing resumed a place of cultural dominance after the guns of war fell silent, propelled forward by its starring role on television. Going into the 1946 championship fight between Joe Louis and Billy Conn, television executives predicted that the big prizefight would finally demonstrate the possibilities of the new technology.[52] Boxing was ideally suited to early television technology. Pugilism, unlike rival sports such as football or baseball, took place in a very small, confined, and well-lit space. This made it easy for a single camera to capture every moment of action without moving, an approach impossible with stadium sports such as baseball or football.[53] The Louis versus Conn fight went out over the airwaves to fans in seven states and the District of Columbia.[54] The National Broadcasting Company sponsored an exclusive party to show the fight at the Hotel Statler for members of Congress, Supreme Court justices, and high-ranking military officers.[55] Sportswriters supported the new medium, admitting that it was not quite the same as seeing the fight in person, but it was still pretty good and far better than paying the $100 it cost for the best seats at the event.[56]

Louis's fight with Conn initiated a new era for television and for boxing. Boxing became a mainstay of early television programming. In 1950, roughly 25 million television viewers witnessed Joe Louis lose his crown to Ezzard Charles. The fight's huge and very satisfied viewership demonstrated the viability of TV to the few remaining doubters.[57] Boxing and television soon cemented a mutually beneficial partnership. On October 26, 1951, television viewers witnessed Louis's last professional fight as he fell to the canvas before the onslaught of Rocky Marciano, a young soldier turned heavyweight crown contender. In tribute to the fallen hero, stations concluded their broadcast by playing footage of Louis's 1938 victory over Max Schmeling, leaving viewers with a parting image of Louis as national hero, rather than defeated pugilist.[58]

Rocky "The Blockbuster" Marciano defeated Louis as a step on his path to boxing's pantheon. Marciano was, in the opinion of *New York Times* reporter Robert Lipsyte, the ultimate example of American manhood.[59] He was born in 1923 into a family of working-class Italian immigrants in Brockton, Massachusetts. Marciano dropped out of school at age 14 to go to work as an unskilled laborer. He joined the army in World War II and began boxing when he discovered that the officers allowed members of the boxing team to skip kitchen duty.[60] He quickly displayed a talent for pugilism, rising through the ranks of the military boxing circuit. Marciano found tougher challenges among civilian competitors. In one of his first amateur bouts, an exhausted and struggling Marciano kicked his opponent in the testicles and lost the bout by disqualification.[61] He returned to the gym and soon seemed unstoppable, winning every fight, most of them by knockouts. He developed a unique style, destroying his opponents with barrages of heavy-handed punches while simply ignoring whatever damage his adversaries delivered. By fall of 1952, Marciano boasted an amazing record of 43 wins, almost all by knockout, and no losses.[62] He never limited himself to American competitors, defeating Canadians like Eddie Ross; the former champion of Italy, Gino Buonvino; and Harry Haft, an Austrian Jew who learned to box when SS guards forced him to fight for their amusement while he was imprisoned at Auschwitz.[63] In 1952, Marciano became the world heavyweight championship with a knockout victory over Jersey Joe Walcott.[64] After suffering a knockout blow at Marciano's hands, top-ranked contender Archie Moore said that getting in the ring with the Blockbuster was like trying to fight an airplane propeller, a never-tiring, unfeeling, forever-advancing, steel-bladed, pain machine.[65]

Marciano became "a mythic archetype" of American ethnic manhood, further complicating combinations of ethnicity and masculinity.[66] While Italian Americans never faced the same discrimination faced by African Americans or other nonwhite groups, ethnic whites often suffered from mistreatment in mid–20th-century America. Famed sportswriter Shirley Povich observed that Marciano managed to combine toughness and kindness in an oddly lovable package that most of the public found irresistible, although Marciano was sometimes ridiculed for his Italian heritage.[67] The smiling man from Brockton was a hero to the nation's ethnic working-class men, an example (whom many hoped to emulate) of a fighter who traveled from anonymity to stardom. Marciano became a folk hero to Italian Americans, who were all too happy to see one of their own as champion. Many immigrants with roots far from Italy also admired the son of immigrants and looked to him as proof that recent arrivals, or at least their children, could succeed in the United States.[68]

Marciano's reign did not last long. In 1955, after defending his title six

V. Asian Martial Arts Gains Popularity in the U.S., 1941–1981 175

times, he retired.[69] Officially, he retired because his family asked him to, saddened by his frequent absences and worried about the damage he suffered in the ring. Behind closed doors, the corruption of boxing disgusted and angered Marciano, who was willing to give up prize money to wash his hands of a culture that he found increasingly revolting.[70] He left behind a record of 49 professional wins and no losses, a feat never equaled.[71] Although the *Rocky* films starring Sylvester Stallone were not based on Marciano's life, he did inspire certain aspects of Stallone's blue-collar, Italian boxing champion.[72]

The same year that Marciano left boxing, disgusted by its corruption, a bright-eyed former pugilist opened a school with an infectious sense of optimism. Edmund Kealoha Parker came to mainland America to serve his God and stayed to become a patriarch of recreational violence. Parker was born near Honolulu in 1931, to a family that once sat on the Hawaiian throne.[73] As a young man, he studied judo and boxing, before becoming the student of William Kwai Sun Chow and his Chinese-based martial arts at the Honolulu YMCA.[74] Parker was only one of many students in Chow's very popular classes. While focusing on Chow's instruction, Parker continued to study other arts and incorporate techniques from karate, Kung Fu, judo, and boxing into a personal blend that he eventually called American Kenpo Karate.[75] During the Korean conflict, he served in the Coast Guard, and by a lucky twist of fate (or his family's influence) received a posting in Hawaii, which allowed him to continue his studies under Chow.[76]

A devout Mormon, Parker traveled to Utah's Brigham Young University, after concluding his military service in 1954, to resume his education. While still a student in 1954, he began teaching karate at a local health club, and shortly thereafter joined the university faculty, becoming the first karate instructor in American history to teach a martial arts course for college credit.[77] In 1955, Parker opened his first karate school. The following year he graduated with a degree in psychology and moved to Pasadena, California, where he opened a karate studio, a term he chose to emphasize the artistic nature of his work.[78]

Parker's embrace of techniques regardless of their origin occasionally put him into conflict with more traditional martial artists. Parker responded unapologetically, explaining that stylistic purity was an absurd myth.[79] He argued that every martial art grew from interactions with even its harshest critics, and stood on the shoulders of travelers and experimenters. When pressed to consider purity, the irreverent Parker mocked the concept and famously argued, "When pure knuckles meet pure flesh, you can't get any purer than that."[80] As Parker hung up the sign for his Pasadena studio, a visitor from Korea began to complicate the purity of martial arts even further.

The Korean War (which began in 1950 and still technically continues, although combat largely ceased in 1953) and the resulting interactions of nations brought Americans and Koreans into unprecedented contact. In 1956, Jhoon Ree, a Korean army officer, came to Texas as part of a program to build relationships between the militaries of Korea and America.[81] Rhee was an expert in the Korean martial art of taekwondo, a style of fighting with roots in Korea's distant past, but peppered with Chinese and Japanese influences brought to the peninsula by soldiers returning from service in World War II.[82] The art of taekwondo differed from its Chinese and Japanese counterparts primarily in its emphasis on high kicks, which experts claimed were more useful in combat because of their longer reach than punches.[83] At the suggestion of the Reverend Frosty Rich, advisor to the Christian student organization at Southwest Texas State College, Rhee began offering martial arts classes to students.[84] When Rhee finished his commitment to the Korean military in 1957, he returned to the United States for good with Rich's help, setting up martial arts programs at Texas colleges and military bases. Since "karate" was a common term by 1957 but "taekwondo" was unknown, he referred to his art as Korean karate.[85] Rhee trained a cadre of students who became instructors and spread taekwondo across America. His classes attracted former boxers, who were convinced that Rhee's focus on flexibility and high kicks provided an excellent and unique workout.[86]

Proponents of Asian martial arts made inroads with the American public, but boxing remained at center stage. In 1960, the world boxing community focused on the Olympic stage in Rome. The 1960 Summer Olympics transformed Cassius Clay into a national celebrity and provided him with another step on his path to legend. Clay was born into a working-class home in Louisville, Kentucky, on January 17, 1942. When thieves stole the 11-year-old Clay's bike, he reported it to the police. At the police station, he saw officers boxing, became captivated, and quickly began training with the police.[87] By 1960, the confident 18-year-old boxer boasted an impressive record of 121 wins and only 7 losses, fighting as both a light heavyweight and a heavyweight.[88] His record included two Golden Gloves championships and two Amateur Athletic Union titles.[89] That May, he earned a place on the Olympic squad with a third-round knockout at the tryouts.[90] The national press took note of the young fighter, complimenting his impressive physique and sharp technique, and predicting that he would offer the United States its best shot at a gold medal in boxing.[91]

In Rome, the talkative and outgoing Clay quickly became the most popular star of the games.[92] Clay made good on his admirer's hopes, chewing through the best fighters in the world on his way to the finals. In the gold medal bout, he destroyed his Polish opponent Zbigniew Pietrzykowski, a European champion and returning Olympic medalist, in a ferocious display that left the Pole battered and dripping blood.[93] The impressive victories on the world stage made Clay the hottest boxing prospect in the world. In October, he signed a contract to fight professionally.[94]

As Clay entered the professional ranks, Congress took aim at the sport, concerned about the corruption that had alienated Marciano years before. Congressional investigations into boxing helped undermine popular perceptions that the sport was a virtuous expression of vigorous masculinity. Senator Estes Kefauver from Tennessee began an investigation into boxing in March 1960. This investigation grew out of hearings Kefauver held dealing with organized crime starting in 1950. Information uncovered in those hearings indicated that the mafia was involved in boxing corruption, and Kefauver was determined to uncover the truth.[95] In June, former middleweight boxing champion Jake LaMotta confessed before Congress that he threw fights as part of an illicit deal to get a title shot.[96] Top-ranked heavyweight contender Sonny Liston denied any personal connections to the mafia, but acknowledged the presence of underworld figures in boxing.[97] Former boxing promoter James D. Norris painted a far bleaker picture. He testified that organized crime thoroughly corrupted boxing. He claimed boxing commissioners, fighters, and promoters all worked in partnership with gangsters. He concluded that only the federal government had the authority and resources needed to purge the sport.[98] An editorial in *Sports Illustrated* acknowledged that rumors of corruption had plagued boxing for many years, but argued that the public trust in the sport sat at an all-time low in 1960.[99]

The Tennessee senator attempted to solve the problems with boxing that his investigation uncovered. After hearing from 36 witnesses and producing nearly 2,000 pages of documents, the investigation convinced Kefauver and many other leaders that Norris was correct when he asserted that only federal intervention could save boxing.[100] Kefauver proposed the creation of a federal boxing commission to clean up the sport. U.S. Attorney General Robert Kennedy and other leaders gave the idea half-hearted support.[101]

Deaths in the ring did additional damage to boxing. In the 1960s, a long line of collegiate boxing fatalities culminated in the death of Charlie Mohr, a widely acclaimed boxer at the University of Wisconsin.[102] His tragic demise pushed boxing off almost every college campus, depriving it of recruits and status.[103] In 1962, television cameras broadcast the bout in which Benny "Kid" Paret suffered a fatal punch, setting off worldwide protests against boxing and reinvigorating Kefauver's demands for reform.[104]

The deaths, combined with Kefauver's hearings, convinced many sponsors to withdraw their sponsorship of boxing, and the sport's alliance with the television networks began to unravel as the sweet science lost its dominant space on the airwaves.[105] The bill authorizing a federal boxing commission languished in Congress before finally failing in 1963, the same year Kefauver died.[106] The federal boxing commission remained an unrealized dream, but in 1964 Congress passed an alternative bill that made any attempts to influence a boxing match a federal offense.[107] Kefauver's work gave boxing a savage series of body blows by providing conclusive evidence of boxing's corruption and highlighting deaths in the ring, even as lawmakers failed to pass legislation that might have cleaned up the sport. Boxers continued to fight as they navigated the violence of the ring and the corruption that surrounded it.

As Cassius Clay's pugilistic star rose, he adopted an over-the-top masculine persona borrowed from a professional wrestler. Clay took inspiration from the professional wrestler Gorgeous George and projected an arrogant demeanor that proclaimed his greatness while mercilessly insulting his opponents.[108] In rhyming verses, the challenger declared that he was unbeatable and heaped scorn on his opponents. He argued that his gold medal proved his status as the greatest fighter in the world, and his title fight against reigning champion Sonny Liston was nothing more than a formality.[109] At the prefight weigh-in, Clay taunted and insulted an impassive Liston with his trademark rhymes, convincing the attending physician that Clay might be insane and motivating the local boxing commission to consider fining the challenger for inappropriate behavior.[110] An observer, noting the looming draft, suggested that shortly after the fateful fight Clay would enter the army as the richest private and worst poet in the service.[111] As part of his persona, Clay often called himself "the prettiest"—a claim only the heavyweight champion of the world could make without undermining public perceptions of his masculinity.[112]

While gamblers put their money on Liston, promoters put it on the sport itself. Vince McMahon, who became wealthy from promoting professional wrestling, arranged to show the fight at several of the nation's largest theaters.[113] McMahon and other investors hoped the title fight between Ali and Liston could help boxing's profitability rebound from the setbacks created by Paret's death and Kefauver's hearings.[114] The business of fight promotion, however, was caught up in the racial conflict sweeping the nation. When it appeared that some movie theater owners might segregate audiences in violation of their contract with broadcasters, the fight promoters decided to accept a loss and canceled the showing in those venues.[115] In spite of the racial problems, the promoters did well, drawing an audience of more than 500,000 fans to theaters across the nation and selling more than $3 million in tickets.[116]

On February 25, 1964, Clay and Liston met in Miami to determine the heavyweight championship. The fighters entered the ring in front of a live audience of 8,297 fans, a tiny audience in comparison to previous title fights.[117] Once again, Clay demonstrated his antagonistic persona. As referee Barney Felix instructed the fighters, Clay launched a verbal tirade of threats and abuse that struck Liston harder than any punch.[118] The bell rang and the fighters began their pugilistic work. It was a classic boxing match-up.[119] The older, heavier Liston threw heavy-handed punches with slow deliberation. The taller, younger, and more energetic Clay playfully danced and jabbed with lightning speed. After six rounds of vigorous boxing, Liston sat exhausted in his corner. He informed the referee that he was in pain from a shoulder injury, caused by throwing punches too hard, and refused to continue.[120] When the referee announced Liston's defeat, Clay reacted with characteristic emotion. He jumped, danced, and insulted the sportswriters who picked Liston to win.[121] Some reporters acknowledged their miscalculation by pointing to Liston's impressive record; others responded to Clay's insults with a few of their own.[122]

The fight's aftermath witnessed more conflict than the fight itself. In spite of journalistic predictions that the army would soon force Clay into uniform, he dodged the bullet, flunking the induction tests and enduring accusations that he intentionally failed them so as to avoid service.[123] Within days of the fight, the chairman of the Senate's Antitrust and Monopoly Subcommittee suspected a corrupt bargain and demanded an inquiry.[124] Sportswriters outlined the various backroom deals that preceded the bout, which made the fighters look bad, if not exactly criminal.[125] After a month-long investigation, the Florida State Attorney General declared that the fight was authentic, while admitting that several incidents surrounding the fight (such as Liston's association with known gamblers) gave observers cause to demand an investigation.[126] While the continued allegations of corruption bothered a swath of America, Clay's next move was as unprecedented as it was infuriating to many Americans.

With the heavyweight crown on his head, Ali decided to carry his loud, unapologetic, and unconventional persona out of the ring and into his daily life, becoming the first openly political heavyweight champion and further complicating American masculine identities.[127] In 1964, Clay announced his conversion to Islam, a faith he said gave him a sense of peace and enabled his victory over Liston.[128] He changed his name to Muhammad Ali, a moniker suggested by Elijah Muhammad, leader of the Nation of Islam and an advocate of racial separation.[129] The press responded with varying degrees of anger and laughter.[130] Ali took a side in a great struggle raging within the African

American community during the 1960s. Moderates like Martin Luther King, Jr., a student of Mahatma Ghandi's techniques of nonviolent resistance, advocated peaceful opposition to injustice. Other African Americans, such as Malcolm X and Stokely Carmichael, were unwilling to compromise. They saw no virtue in moderation and criticized King's rejection of armed self-defense. In 1964, Ali made a conscious choice to take part in the struggle and to ally himself with the uncompromising and unapologetic voices in the struggle. He became friends with Malcolm X and Elijah Muhammad.[131] This decision made him an enemy to many Americans who opposed the struggle in general or simply Ali's approach to it. King was one of Clay's most outspoken critics and condemned him for allying himself with advocates of racial separation.[132] Whatever Ali's conversion might have meant for the soul of the pugilist or the racial struggles of the nation, the fans and the critics of the sweet science agreed that Ali's latest revelation was bad for boxing.[133] Ali cast himself in the masculine mold of Jack Johnson, openly cultivating and enjoying confrontations with whites.[134]

While Ali's popularity plummeted with many Americans, a new hero emerged on the West Coast. After years of building a U.S. community of Asian-influenced martial artists, Ed Parker and his associates were ready to show the world what America's best could do in a highly publicized tournament. In 1964, Parker held the first Long Beach International Karate Championship. The event featured sparring matches, but consistent with many martial arts practitioners' distaste for brutal "anything goes" fights, competitors pulled their strikes, turning their bouts into games of ferocious-looking tag.[135] Some fighters wanted nothing to do with games of tag, but were still happy to participate in the event.[136] Stars of American martial arts including Jhoon Rhee, Takayuki Kubota, Anthony Mirarian, and Tstomu Oshhima gave demonstrations for large crowds.[137]

Bruce Lee, a global man and relative newcomer to American martial arts, stole the show from more established experts. Lee was born in San Francisco in 1940, but lived most of his life in Hong Kong. As a young man, he studied Chinese martial arts under the legendary master Yip Man and won championships in Western-style boxing and Cha-Cha dancing.[138] In 1959, he moved to the United States, fleeing a string of arrests for petty crimes and hoping to take advantage of his American birth and make a new start as a citizen of the United States.[139] He gave popular martial arts demonstrations in Seattle in 1961.[140] When a Japanese karate student, Uechi, took issue with Lee's remarks about karate, they agreed to settle the issue with a full-contact fight. On the handball court of the nearby YMCA, Lee and Uechi agreed on rules, selected a referee, and attracted a small crowd of spectators. Uechi kicked Lee in the stomach. Lee knocked Uechi to the ground with a flurry of rapid punches, kicked the downed karate practitioner in the face, and ended his assault only when the referee intervened and declared Lee the winner.[141]

In 1963, Lee opened his first martial arts school, authored his first manual, and became friends with Ed Parker.[142] Lee's most impressive feat was a technique he called the one-inch punch. He stood facing another martial artist, placed his fist one inch from the volunteer's chest, and then launched his punch and sent the other man flying to the ground.[143] Lee intended his displays not as cheap parlor tricks, but as inspiration for fighters to reconsider the limits of their arts and their bodies.[144] Ed Parker filmed Lee's performance and showed it to television producer William Dozier, who was in the market for an Asian sidekick in an upcoming series. The producer was impressed and, in 1966, cast Bruce Lee as Kato in the television series *The Green Hornet*. The series transformed Lee from a martial arts instructor into an international celebrity.[145] It also brought him unwanted attention from Chinese-born martial artists.

Lee's determination to build partnerships with men of every race and nation placed him in danger. A coalition of Chinese instructors sent their best fighter, Wong Jack Man, to challenge Lee to a fight. If Man won, Lee would have to stop teaching whites.[146] The ultimatum enraged Lee, who demanded the fight take place instantly. The Chinese delegation recoiled in shock, surprised that their threat had not intimidated Lee. After a moment of confusion, Man suggested rules. Lee refused, insisting on an "anything goes" encounter. Man reluctantly agreed.[147] Lee launched into Man with a furious combination of punches. Man absorbed punishment for a few seconds before running away. Lee followed him, knocking him to the ground and punching his downed opponent in the face until Man begged for mercy, at which point Lee finally relented.[148] The Chinese experts left defeated, never again demanded that Lee stopped teaching Caucasians, and settled for denouncing him behind his back.[149] Meanwhile, as Lee explored martial arts as performance and conflict resolution techniques, others developed them as a sport.

The next several years found the American martial arts community wracked by controversy as it tried to find its identity. In 1965, Jhoon Rhee collaborated with civic groups and retired Admiral Arleigh Burke to hold a karate championship in Washington, D.C. NBC Sports broadcast the event.[150] Unlike the games of tag at Parker's event, the 1965 tournament witnessed vigorous fights, even though competitors were supposed to limit themselves to light contact. After showing only a few moments of a bloody fight between fierce rivals Mike Stone and Walt Worthy, shocked television producers cut the broadcast.[151] Many members of the martial arts community were no more impressed with the action in Rhee's subsequent tournaments. Female fighters engaged in bouts that included hair-pulling, scratching, and face slapping. Judges refused to penalize the women for these rule violations, shrugging their shoulders and claiming that women were capable of little else. Rhee joked about the brutality of the fairer sex, while making no efforts to resolve the issue, and a female fighter demanded women boycott karate tournaments until officials held women to the same standards of conduct as men.[152] In 1967, the Chicago-based World Karate Federation announced a tournament to finally settle the question of the nation's greatest fighter in which all pretense of restraint was dropped and fighters were allowed to use practically any technique as long as they wore boxing gloves and groin protectors.[153] Organizers offered a prize of $10,000 to the winner.[154]

Many of America's most prominent martial arts experts expressed outrage at the "anything goes" event. Robert Trias argued it was a fiasco with the power to kill karate.[155] Jhoon Ree agreed, forbidding any of his students from attending.[156] Tsutomu Oshima, a leader in the Southern California Karate Association, argued that karate was and should remain an art, not a sport.[157] Roger Price, writing for *Sports Illustrated*, agreed that karate was not a sport. He acknowledged that the Asian martial arts provided elite soldiers with deadly skills, but ridiculed the average karate practitioner as an idiotic child with bloodlust in his heart, gleefully trading his pennies for an ineffective at-home course in felonious assault.[158] Algene Caraulia, Illinois Director of the U.S. Karate Association, made an argument rooted in history. He claimed that boxing prospered because it progressed from a brawl to a sport. Caraulia saw the upcoming Chicago tournament as a backward step that would take karate from a refined sport to a display of mindless brutality.[159]

In spite of Caraulia's rosy picture of the sweet science, that sport was actually wrestling with challenges every bit as problematic as, if in no way similar to, those faced by karate. During the 1950s and 1960s, karate made only meager progress toward overtaking boxing as mass entertainment, but football increasingly became the most popular test of American manhood.[160] Although boxing and football were very different sports, both attracted fans primarily with their violence.[161] As with boxing, television helped make football more popular. Better television technologies, including superior cameras, microphones, and slow-motion instant replays, facilitated coverage of football.[162] Football executives changed their sport to make it more suitable to television, incorporating larger numbers on players' jerseys to make individual players easier to distinguish on television screens and changing the use of time-outs to better facilitate commercial breaks.[163] By 1963, football was beginning to challenge boxing for the attention of television audiences. In 1967, professional football held its first Super Bowl, which quickly exceeded everyone's expectations and became the highest-rated program on television each year.[164] In 1968, the first athletes inducted into the new Alabama Sports Hall of fame included seven football players, and a single boxer, former heavyweight champion Joe Louis.[165] Later the same year, famed sportswriter Sid Ziff explained to readers that he loved football more than boxing because the gridiron's combination of teamwork, emphasis on controlling territory, and violence made it the most military sport.[166]

Football made its gains against a boxing world suffering from a heavyweight champion whose outside-the-ring politics damaged his sport's popularity with many Americans. Ali's adoption of Black Power politics, conversion to Islam, and refusal to serve in the military made him a controversial figure with many Americans. In 1966, the U.S. government lowered its draft standards, making Ali and many other previously ineligible men subject to the draft.[167] The conflict in Vietnam, and the draft that supplied many of its soldiers, divided the nation and the African American community.[168] When the draft board attempted to induct Ali in 1967, he refused, proclaiming himself a Muslim minister and a conscientious objector—a highly controversial move that earned the champion both praise and condemnation.[169] It was also a rather odd claim from a man who made a living punching people in the face. In addition to his religious claims, Ali proclaimed, "I ain't got no quarrel wit them Viet Cong," and further explained, "No Viet Cong ever called me nigger."[170]

Several American boxing commissions stripped Ali of his heavyweight crown, but foreign boxing officials ignored the move and continued to list Ali as the world champion, demonstrating that the oddly shaped communities of global sports such as boxing often ignored nations.[171] A court convicted Ali of draft evasion, fined him $10,000, and sentenced him to five years in prison.[172] Ali told reporters that the sanctions only made him a better man. No longer content to call himself "the greatest," Ali proclaimed himself a hero to the black community.[173] The revocation of Ali's crown angered many blacks, who spoke out on behalf of the champion and picketed fights in protest.[174] In contrast, a sportswriter argued that Ali's obnoxious personality and politics made it nearly impossible to enjoy his tremendous athletic performances.[175]

America's highest court eventually sided with Ali. In 1971, the U.S. Supreme Court overturned his conviction for draft evasion by a vote of eight to zero. In a controversial decision, the justices ruled that the prosecutor failed to prove the legality of the draft board's rejection of Ali's claim for conscientious objector status.[176]

Scholars often focus on Ali's popularity, but Ali's celebrity existed primarily within certain demographics that rarely supported boxing.[177] Throughout his career, foreigners loved him more than Americans did.[178] This once again highlights the oddly shaped identities of fight fans, who paid little attention to national boundaries. Promoters recognized the problem faced by Ali in the United States and staged many of his fights abroad.[179] Many veterans and working-class whites—two of the groups that had most strongly supported boxing in times past—resented Ali and his acquittal for draft evasion, even as the pugilist's stature grew among opponents of the war.[180]

Ali's embrace of Black Power and opposition to the conflict in Vietnam made him a leader in the revolt of the black athlete.[181] This revolt consisted of a pattern of often-controversial opposition to racial oppression within the larger struggles for racial equality in the 1960s.[182] It began with African American athletes who protested segregationist policies in cities where they played, and quickly expanded into a broader movement including support for Black Power and opposition to the conflict in Vietnam.[183] The grassroots movement received intellectual recognition and guidance from star athlete turned college professor Harry Edwards.[184] The revolt peaked at the 1968 Mexico City Olympic Games, where African American athletes used their positions on the world stage to protest mistreatment of blacks in America and around the world.[185] When Tommie Smith and John Carlos received gold and bronze medals for the 200-meter race, they gave the clenched-fist Black Power salute, creating both enormous controversy and one of the truly iconic images in Olympic history.[186]

Heavyweight boxing champion Muhammad Ali, photographed in 1967 by Ira Rosenberg. This was the year after the champion refused to serve in the military and proclaimed, "I ain't got no quarrel with them Vietcong" (Library of Congress Prints and Photographs Division).

Arthur Ashe, the tennis great and another member of the revolt, argued that Ali inspired a generation of black athletes to speak out and made gestures like those of Smith and Carlos possible.[187]

Occasionally, a fight becomes a symbolic combat between two models of masculinity and pierces the boundaries of fight sports. When John L. Sullivan and Jim Corbett fought, they represented their social classes, with Sullivan the unapologetically hedonistic working-class hero and Corbett wrapping himself in a cloak of middle-class moderation. Jim Jefferies fought Jack Johnson as a representative of white American manhood against his dark-skinned rival. Joe Louis represented democracy's American manhood against Max Schmeling from Nazi Germany. Ali's 1971 fight with interim champion "Smokin'" Joe Frazier fell into this pattern, providing a symbolic battle between different African American masculinities.[188] In the days before the fight, Ali denounced Frazier as an "Uncle Tom" who turned his back on his race.[189] If Ali's bravado and open defiance of the established order made him a fighter in the mold of Jack Johnson, then his opponent's attempts to improve his race's position while working within the established order made him more reminiscent of Joe Louis. For a moment, the United States became a nation of boxing fans, with many Americans hopping for Ali's greatest triumph and many others wishing for his demise.[190] Some of those spectators were unwilling to limit the violence to the ring, sending death threats to Frazier and calling in bomb scares to his hotel.[191]

Frazier's masculine identity differed from Ali primarily in his response to the great social questions of the 1960s. Like Ali, Frazier displayed enormous talent as an amateur pugilist, won a gold medal in the Olympics, and became a professional boxer.[192] Frazier and Ali's lives diverged during their professional careers. Frazier volunteered for service in Vietnam but, like Ali, flunked the entrance examination.[193] When the draft board lowered the standards, he obtained an exemption based on his patriarchal role as sole support for his wife and young children.[194] Frazier felt no more sympathy for Ali's political causes than for the whites who looked to him as a fist of vengeance to silence the controversial pugilist. Frazier expressed no desire to be anyone's hero; he wanted only to live in seclusion, supporting his family, boxing, and riding motorcycles in his free time. Frazier encouraged people to work within the system, rather than oppose it.[195] He gave to charity quietly, expressing no desire to draw attention to himself or his good deeds.[196] Many conservative blacks and whites respected the simple family man with little to say about matters that took place outside the ring.[197] When Ali insulted Frazier, Frazier responded by calling his opponent a mouthy braggart who talked about Black Power while refusing to open his wallet or actually help anyone.[198]

The fight between Frazier and Ali drew huge audiences for a contest of fighters and masculinities. The two champions met on March 8, 1971, at Madison Square Garden in New York City.[199] The stands groaned under the weight of 20,455 fans.[200] Observers noted visual clues to the audience members' loyalties, with Ali's fans choosing exotic fashions and Frazier's preferring conservative attire.[201] Their counterparts watching on movie screens across the world outnumbered the observers in the arena. When theaters in San Francisco sold out, angry fans tried to shove their way in.[202] In Los Angeles, fans who did get seats agreed the color picture provided the best image they had ever seen.[203] The broadcast crossed the Atlantic, attracting one of the largest television audiences in British history.[204] It also crossed the continental divide into South America, where the Brazilian sports magazine *Placar* put Ali's image on the cover and devoted extensive attention to the fight.[205]

The bout was a classic stylistic match-up between two fighters who were undefeated in professional competition. Ali relied on quickness and agility, Frazier on aggression and punches that landed with the force of sledgehammers.[206] The quiet man pushed the action from its first moments, relentless in his advance. Ali slipped and dodged, but rarely countered with any effect.[207] It was not a close fight, but it was an exciting one, filled with quick movements and heavy punches, even if Ali provided most of the movement and Frazier the majority of the punches.[208] By the 15th round, Frazier's superiority was obvious, and the judges awarded the bout to Frazier by unanimous decision.

Many Americans viewed the result as more cultural than athletic.[209] One reader expressed anger that *Life* magazine's coverage of the bout failed to provide an image of Frazier's fist crushing Ali's mouth, an image he longed to see.[210] Some sportswriters criticized Ali's performance as a pathetic effort that revealed neither the speed nor the violence of his previous work.[211] *Sports Illustrated* declared the fight the death of Ali's legend and provided the world with an iconic image of a retreating Ali falling backward in the face of an advancing Frazier.[212] The only camera allowed in Ali's dressing room lay in the hands of one of the champion's dearest old friends. He refused to snap even a single image, deciding that in that moment he was more friend than journalist, and that no friend would allow the world to see the man who proclaimed himself "the greatest" lying sad and helpless, wrecked more by inner pain than exterior injuries.[213] Norman Mailer acknowledged that Ali lost, but argued that by standing up to a full 15 rounds of punishment and never giving up in spite of the pain, he finally demonstrated that he was a man.[214] Not everyone agreed that Frazier bested Ali. *Ebony* printed several letters to the editor that claimed Ali was the better fighter in the ring and attributed the loss to racist judges. Others denounced journalists for displaying similar racism in their coverage of the event.[215]

Ali recovered quickly, and took up karate to improve his punching power in preparation for a rematch with Frazier.²¹⁶ As Ali added karate techniques to his boxing, other fighters added a sense of old-fashioned boxing to their karate.

In spite of the controversies within the martial arts community, some fighters continued to explore the martial arts as sports. Joe Lewis grew up in North Carolina, reading bodybuilding magazines, lifting weights, and dreaming of someday becoming a professional wrestler.²¹⁷ While serving with the Marines in the 1960s, he encountered judo, but thought little of the art since wrestlers occasionally joined the classes and easily dominated the judo students. He thought little more of karate since karate men only punched the air and never actually fought anyone. While stationed on Okinawa, Lewis met Marines with black belts in karate who applied Marine toughness and athleticism to the Eastern techniques. Infatuated with this mode of fighting, he began studying karate.²¹⁸ Lewis, like many karate practitioners in the military, thought little of the kata and point karate competitions of most martial arts tournaments. To test their skills, the Marines strapped on the padded gloves, chest protectors, and helmets of kendo (Japanese-style fencing) and fought with few rules.²¹⁹ The emphasis on full-power strikes and wrestling techniques with few restrictions made the bouts more like 19th-century boxing than contemporary karate.

When Lewis's service ended, he returned to the United States, began training with Bruce Lee, and adopted his philosophy of embracing techniques from every art.²²⁰ Lewis proved his skills in karate tournaments around the nation, even as he chaffed under their restrictions.²²¹ As Lewis and Lee built a multiracial coalition of fighters, other enthusiasts organized a new fight sport.

A fusion of ideas from East and West led to the establishment of American kickboxing. Lee Faulkner, movie stunt man and sports fan, began work as a fight promoter in the 1970s.²²² Faulkner found American karate tournaments boring, but was intrigued by the kickboxing matches he witnessed while working in Asia.²²³ Unlike competitors in American martial arts tournaments, Asian kickboxers made no pretense of restraint. They went after each other with few rules and arsenals of bone crushing techniques including punches, kicks, elbow blows, knee strikes, and wrestling holds. By the mid–1960s, the sport was very popular across much Japan, Thailand, Korea, and the Philippines. Fighters wore the lightly padded gloves used in the Thai sport of muay thai, a full-contact fight sport very similar to the new sport of kickboxing.²²⁴ Faulkner envisioned an Americanized version of the sport in which fighters fought like American boxers and wore regulation boxing gloves, but incorporated techniques from Asian martial arts.²²⁵

In 1970, Faulkner's plans became reality when he sponsored a kickboxing match between two fighters who championed very different masculinities. Joe Lewis was the traditional white American hero with rippled muscles, blond hair, and blue eyes, who entered the arena clothed in blue sweatpants, with boxing shoes on his feet—clothing typical for a Western athlete.[226] He was still fresh from his service with the Marines and at that point more Western athlete than Asian artist. His opponent, Greg Baines, was a Black Muslim in the model of Muhammad Ali.[227] He fought bare footed and clothed in the pants from his karate uniform.[228] Baines was a more traditional martial artist, steeped in the culture and philosophy of karate, as seen through the prism of Black Power.[229] After several rounds of intense action, Lewis knocked Baines out cold with a right cross to the chin, in the first bout of American kickboxing.[230] A ringside announcer referred to the fight as kickboxing, and the sport of American kickboxing drew its first breath, with Lewis as its first superstar.[231] *Sports Illustrated* observed that Lewis's technique was almost indistinguishable from that of a boxer: he threw a few kicks, but did almost all of his damage with conventional boxing-style punches. Lewis admitted as much, but rejected suggestions he enter boxing since he attributed his success to his ability outbox karate fighters, a strategy that would not work against experienced pugilists.[232]

American television coverage of Asian style kickboxing began in the same year of 1970.[233] Also in that crucial year of 1970, sportswriters introduced their readers to kickboxing, explaining—consistent with Faulkner's vision—that the sport was boxing with the additional inclusion of kicks, karate chops, and punches with gloved hands.[234]

Like boxing in the previous century, kickboxing encountered legal problems along with enthusiastic fans. The California Athletic Commission ruled that kickboxing was not permitted in that state because the laws prohibited all fight sports with the exception of wrestling and boxing; since kickboxing was a unique sport, distinct from both boxing and wrestling, it was therefore illegal.[235] Fight promoter Aaron Banks staged kickboxing matches in New York in 1971 without contacting the New York Athletic Commission, but acknowledged he could not fly under the radar for long.[236] In that same year, the Nevada Athletic Commission, eager to maintain its position at the center of American fight sports, took the initiative in its territory by becoming the first state to offer licenses to kickboxing promoters.[237]

Unlike Banks, businessman Sam Allred decided he could avoid trouble by initiating a conversation with local regulators in New Mexico. After considerable persuasion, the government granted Allred a license to promote kickboxing in Albuquerque as long as he abided by most of the same regulations faced by boxing promoters, including buying insurance and hiring referees.[238] He then staged kickboxing bouts for large audiences of enthusiastic fans.[239] The martial artist Joe Lewis became the first champion of a new, and increasingly legal, sport at just about the same time that his instructor became the star of a new genre of entertainment.

After Bruce Lee's successful demonstration at the Long Beach Karate Championships, he pursued a dual career as actor and martial artist. He expanded his martial arts schools and attracted additional students. The *Green Hornet* television series lasted only a single season, but made a tremendous impression on entertainment executives and inspired martial artists around the world.[240] After the series ended, Lee played a series of minor roles in movies and on television. Producers passed him over for the lead in the series *Kung-Fu* in 1971, based on their fears that American audiences would not accept an Asian leading man, suggesting that the racial boundaries of American masculinity were still present, if greatly weakened.[241] Rejected by American executives, Lee returned to Hong Kong in 1971 and starred in the movie *Fists of Fury*, which broke box office records in Hong Kong. Later the same year, he stared in another hit Hong Kong-based film, *The Chinese Connection*. Finally convinced of Lee's ability to draw an audience, Warner Brothers partnered with Hong Kong moviemakers to create *Enter the Dragon*, with Lee as the leading actor and screenwriter.[242] Bruce died at the age of 32 under mysterious circumstances (probably due to an allergic reaction to a medication) after completing filming, but before the movie hit theaters.[243] His Hong Kong funeral attracted 25,000 mourners and his family buried him in the same costume he wore in *Enter the Dragon*.[244] The film grossed more than $200 million globally, which made it an enormous commercial success.[245] It played particularly well in Asia and with nonwhite, urban, young people in America.[246] In death, Lee became an anti-imperialist hero to the disaffected. The film became the most influential martial arts movie in history and cemented Lee's status as a martial artist and movie star shortly after he died.[247]

Bruce Lee promoted fight sports primarily by providing fighters of many backgrounds with an example, rather than by actually fighting. Millions of American began training in the martial arts after receiving inspiration from Lee's movies.[248] He was particularly popular with African Americans, who admired him as one of the few nonwhite leading men.[249] The sport of kickboxing, which arose in the 1970s, highlighted the obvious influence of Lee, his students, and his philosophy of combing aspects of every martial art.[250] Lee brought Eastern and Western cultures together, teaching Chinese arts to Caucasians, even when he faced opposition from other Chinese, and giving many Westerners a glimpse of Western-influenced Asian arts in action.[251]

Lee's costar in *Enter the Dragon*, Jim Kelley, incorporated some of Lee's techniques into his own arsenal.[252] Olympic and professional boxing champion Sugar Ray Leonard admired Lee's movements and attempted to emulate some of his techniques in the boxing ring.[253] Professional boxer, kickboxer, and martial artist Maurice Smith admitted that he was unsure if Lee could actually fight since Smith saw only the scripted routines of his movies, but, real or illusionary, Smith derived inspiration from Lee's performances.[254] Lee's work even inspired musical appreciation. After seeing *Enter the Dragon* in 1974, Jamaican-born disco singer Carl Douglas wrote a song titled "Kung Fu Fighting" that sold 9 million copies worldwide and topped the charts in the United States, Great Britain, and several other countries.[255] The chorus stated in part, "Everybody was Kung Fu fighting." While not everybody in America was Kung Fu fighting, many were—and the Asian-style arts gained unprecedented popularity.

In the 1960s and 1970s, an increasingly large and influential American martial arts community made inroads with elite and ordinary men who were eager to prove their manhood. Ed Parker, who helped Lee get his first big break, courted entertainment royalty from his West Coast schools. Elvis Presley studied under Parker after picking up some karate while serving with the army in Germany and later incorporated karate movements into his dance routines.[256] Parker's other students included Frank Sinatra, Warren Beatty, and Robert Wagner.[257] Parker used his connections with Hollywood to promote martial arts and increase their presence in movie fight scenes, which inspired growing numbers of ordinary Americans to take up the arts. In New York City, the Chinese instructor Master Chin took advantage of the popularity of the television series *Kung-Fu* and filled his classes with assorted urban toughs and former boxers.[258] Based in Texas, Skipper Mullins became a celebrated karate instructor to Marines and FBI agents eager to ensure that they never faced the emasculation of losing a fight.[259] Jhoon Rhee opened a school in Washington, D.C., and sent letters of to many members of Congress offering his services. Many senators and representatives, including some former boxers, were intrigued by the possibility of an innovative workout and became Rhee's enthusiastic students.[260] Washington elites became active members of the martial arts community as well as students. Senator Milton Young served as president of the United States Tae Kwon Do Association and retired Admiral Arleigh Burke provided sponsorship for Rhee's karate tournaments.[261] When Senator Young's opponents argued he was too old for reelection to another term, the 75-year-old taekwondo student broadcast a political commercial in which he broke boards with his bare hands, using his martial skill as proof of his manhood and vitality.[262] The ad worked: Young told the press that martial arts made his reelection possible.[263]

V. Asian Martial Arts Gains Popularity in the U.S., 1941–1981   191

Against a backdrop of increasing popularity and acceptance for Asian martial arts, the king of American boxing made a fool of himself in one of the most absurd farces in the history of fight sports. Ali, never at a loss for insults or boasting, inadvertently set the entire fiasco in motion.[264] After his 1971 loss to Joe Frazier, Ali staged a comeback, eventually regaining the heavyweight crown in 1974 with an eight-round knockout of George Foreman.[265] The old Ali seemed back from the dead. He bragged endlessly, but backed up his mouth with a series of impressive title defenses. Ali rode a wave of acclaim. A survey of American sportswriters named the controversial pugilist the best fighter of all time.[266] He continued using his fame to advance his political causes. His ghost-written 1975 autobiography claimed that he threw away his Olympic gold medal after suffering racist harassment at the hands of a white biker gang. However, in an interview Ali denied the story, admitting that he actually lost the medal and never even read the book.[267] In 1975, when he met Ichiro Yada, a Japanese wrestling promoter working in America, Ali asked Yada if Asia contained any fighter willing to face the champion. He offered to pay $1 million to any Asian fighter who could best him.[268] The boast made headline news in Japan.[269] The story caught the eye of Japanese professional wrestler Antonio Inoki. At a press conference in Tokyo on Ali's way to a fight in Malaysia, a spokesman for Inoki delivered a letter containing a formal challenge for Ali to fight Inoki. The heavyweight champion eagerly accepted, threatening to knock out the wrestler in five minutes, and punctuating his threat by punching a photo of Inoki included in the letter.[270] The opportunity appealed to Ali's enormous ego, and he believed it provided him with a chance to prove that he was the greatest fighter in the world, not just the greatest boxer.[271] Ali backed off his offer to pay $1 million, but instead agreed to fight for a fee of $6 million, the biggest payday of his life.[272] Inoki would receive all of the proceeds from the live ticket sales and $2 million from the television rights.[273] Promoters advertised the fight as the World Martial Arts Championship.[274]

For all Ali's bravado, Inoki was unlike any man the champion had ever faced. Inoki was a global champion. Born in Japan, he was a star athlete during his high school years spent in Brazil, and was a student of Western-style wrestling, karate, and judo.[275] He trained under the legendary Belgian wrestler Karl Gotch and closely emulated Gotch's aggressive style.[276] For most of Inoki's career, he performed in Western-style professional wrestling matches with prearranged outcomes.[277] In the early 1970s, Inoki began promoting a more realistic style of wrestling, distinct from the very acrobatic and flashy techniques used by many other professional wrestlers.[278] Inoki's fights became a mainstay of Japanese television; by 1975, he was as famous in Japan as Ali was in the United States.[279] Inoki's style walked the line between the real and the scripted as he helped develop a variety of Asian-influenced, Western-style professional wrestling that became more like the serious fighting style it originated as before economics pushed it into farce.[280] He fought in the United States, but Americans showed little interest and attendance at his events was poor.[281] The Japanese fighter could fight as well as anyone in the world, even if he spent most of his career throwing matches. Before taking on Ali, he bested the Olympic gold medalist in judo, Wilhelm Ruska. Many observers suspected it was a scripted fight, but both Inoki and Ruska assured journalists that it was authentic.[282] Inoki and his students later became pioneers of genuine style-on-style match-ups that demonstrated the value of their approach to martial arts both as mass entertainment and as legitimate fighting styles.[283] If things had gone differently, the Ali–Inoki might have accelerated the process of blending the various fighting styles, but the absurdity that actually ensued probably delayed those developments.

The press devoted considerable attention to Ali's thoughts on the upcoming bout. At a press conference, a journalist suggested to Ali that the upcoming fight was ridiculous. Ali angrily dismissed the idea, arguing that the fans wanted to see what happened when the world boxing champion fought a wrestler.[284] Another reporter pressed a similar question a moment later, asking if Ali would agree that the event was a degrading spectacle for the world's boxing champion.[285] This time Ali contradicted his earlier comment, arguing that the fight was ridiculous, but insisting that he so dominated boxing that he had to seek out new and absurd challenges.[286] While discussing finances with reporters, he mentioned buying a house for his wife even though he planned to file for divorce. When reached for comment, Khalilah Ali admitted she was surprised to hear of the looming divorce, but said she was happy to wash her hands of her husband.[287] The challenge-seeking pugilist ranted, raved, insulted, and threatened his Japanese counterpart.[288]

In contrast to the animated and outrageous boxer, Inoki's calm, humble, and deadly serious masculine demeanor impressed American journalists.[289] He responded to Ali's insults with mischievous smiles and humorous remarks delivered through his translators. The wrestler told Ali he enjoyed their conversations, even though the boxer was very silly. In response to Ali's threats, Inoki laughed and told his opponent to take care and not damage his fists when delivering his terrible punches.[290] In a later press conference, he seemed more focused. He explained that he possessed a violent arsenal adopted from judo, karate, and wrestling. Inoki promised the fans that he would prove Ali was not the greatest fighter in the world.[291]

Observers questioned the authenticity of the bout in spite of the seem-

V. Asian Martial Arts Gains Popularity in the U.S., 1941–1981   193

ingly sincere comments from the fighters. John Hall of the *LA Times* argued that every fighter knew that even the world's greatest boxer stood no chance against a skilled wrestler; he therefore concluded that the whole encounter was a farce since Ali was far too smart to risk his neck and his career in a real fight with Inoki.[292] Fight fans agreed and saw the event as a huge defeat for the sweet science before it even began. Wrestlers were generally seen as better fighters than boxers in "anything goes" matches, even if pure wrestling was boring, so either Ali would suffer a humiliating defeat to a foreign rival or he would win and demonstrate that the world's champ was willing to star in a fixed fight.[293] Nobody accurately predicted the fiasco, although many understood the forces that made it possible.

Rules for the fight provided a very contentious issue in contract negotiations and remain shrouded in controversy today. When asked in a press conference, Ali claimed that he had no idea what the rules were.[294] The *Chicago Tribune* reported a straightforward set of regulations in which either fighter could win by knockout or wrestling-style pin.[295] The reality was far different. As Hall correctly deduced, Ali was not about to risk his neck in an authentic match with Inoki.[296] The plan was for Ali to beat up Inoki for several rounds; Inoki would fight on gamely until the noble Ali begged the referee to end the bloodshed. While Ali played humanitarian, Inoki would sneak up behind the boxer and pin him, winning the fight. Ali would appear noble, and Inoki would claim a victory, of sorts.[297] After arriving in Tokyo, Ali saw Inoki train and got worried that the wrestler might not remain on script.[298] He nearly backed out before agreeing to fight on the condition that Inoki accept a new set of rules, under which Inoki could not tackle, throw, or kick Ali unless one knee was on the ground at the time. The rules were to remain a secret. Inoki reluctantly agreed.[299]

On June 26, 1976, fans enjoyed a preliminary fight before Ali and Inoki entered the arena. In Shea Stadium, before showing the main event on large movie screens, professional wrestler Andre the Giant fought the pugilist Chuck Wepner.[300] Wepner was better known for his recent loss in a boxing match with Ali.[301] The aptly named giant dwarfed his heavyweight opponent, weighing in at 440 pounds, exactly double Wepner's 220 pounds.[302] Wepner displayed aggression, peppering the Giant with punches that landed, although they did little real damage.[303] In the third round, Wepner belted his opponent with the fight's harshest blow.[304] The enraged wrestler grabbed Wepner and threw him out of the ring and into the stands.[305] The pugilist failed to return to the ring within the agreed 20-second limit and the referee declared Andre the Giant victorious.[306] A cynic among the press corps doubted the authenticity of the contest, noting that the savage-looking techniques left the fighters unmarked.[307] In spite of the doubts, the fight was at least entertaining.[308] It increased Andre the Giant's fame and did no damage to Wepner's.[309] The victorious Andre argued that the bout demonstrated once again that in fight with no rules, a boxer had no chance against a skilled grappler. He might land a few stinging blows as the wrestler closed the distance, but once locked in a violent embrace, the pugilist always lost.[310]

With the preliminaries over, Ali and Inoki entered a ring in Tokyo's Budokan Martial Arts Hall for the main event. Since the new secret rules prevented Inoki from using any wrestling moves or kicks from the standing position, Inoki's only options were to box Ali, which would have ended with a knockout by Ali in moments, or to engage in some kind of bizarre kicking with one leg while the other remained on the ground. Inoki opted for the kicks.[311] All 15 rounds proceeded in remarkably similar fashion. Inoki lay on the ground and kicked Ali in the legs, and Ali insulted Inoki's manhood in broken Japanese.[312] When Inoki managed to entangle the boxer's legs and trip him, the referee intervened and put Ali back on his feet.[313] Inoki briefly trapped Ali against in the corner, leading the world heavyweight-boxing champion to climb backward onto the ropes with a look on his face that was equal measures surprise, fear, and outrage.[314] Halfway through the fight Ali wanted to give up and go home, but his entourage reminded him that he was the world boxing champion and convinced him to stay.[315] Ali threw five total punches, only one of which connected.[316] After 15 rounds of nonsense, the referee declared it a draw.[317] The live crowd threw garbage, vandalized the arena, and began chanting for a refund.[318] An observer declared it the worst fight he had ever witnessed.[319]

In spite of the relative success of Andre's fight with Wepner, the main event was a disaster for Ali and boxing, just as many observers predicted. When reporters pointed out that fans, many of whom spent $1,000 for their seats, felt disappointed, Ali shrugged and pointed out that he just made $6 million.[320] Ali's smugness was short lived. He limped out of the ring with his legs badly bruised and filled with potentially lethal blood clots. Within days, his doctor hospitalized him.[321] His finances fared no better. Japanese promoters refused to pay Ali due to their unhappiness with his performance.[322] Former boxing champions denounced Ali as undignified and American sportswriters urged the authorities to lock Ali and Inoki in jail for fraud.[323] Famed boxing commentator Bert Sugar poured contempt on Ali, describing the bout as little more than a carnival exhibition of a dancing bear.[324] *Jet* magazine directed most of its venom toward Inoki, criticizing his refusal to stand up and box Ali, but still saved plenty for the boxing champion who chose to taunt rather than attack his opponent.[325] An observer compared boxing to professional wrestling and argued pugilism was suffering from its death throes.[326] Ali's ringside physician, Ferdie Pacheco, agreed, referring to Ali's decision to fight Inoki as a stupid move that traded immediate cash for long-term damage to his career, dignity, and health. Pacheco later concluded that Ali never fully recovered from the injuries Inoki inflicted on his legs, which forever robbed him of his trademark speed and agility.[327] Ali continued to fight for several more years, but consistent with Pacheco's analysis, he never again knocked out an opponent.[328] America's champion—the man sports-writers proclaimed the greatest pugilist of all time—lay in a hospital bed forever debilitated by a smiling Asian face whose body and reputation suffered little in the exchange.

Although Inoki was somewhat humiliated by the bout initially, he quickly rebuilt his reputation. His fans concluded that he outwitted the clumsy American.[329] Inoki apologized to the fans for his lack of aggression and promised never to disappoint them again.[330] The fight increased Inoki's international notoriety and he rode his newfound fame into a worldwide tour.[331] He sued Ali for $700,000 but agreed to drop the suit in exchange for a rematch under simple boxing versus wrestling rules.[332] Ali declined the call for a rematch. Inoki used his fame as a path into politics. He served in the Japanese parliament and as a diplomat.[333]

Ali was hardly the only American suffering from defeat in the 1970s, a time when many American men experienced devastating setbacks. The term "crisis of masculinity" is often overused. Either manhood exists only in a state of perpetual crisis or, more likely, writers overuse the term. Contrary to what some writers seem to think, there is no evidence that American men perpetually descend into crisis at every momentary setback.

However, if American masculinity ever suffered a crisis (a debatable assertion), it was almost certainly in the late 1970s. American manhood often took strength from victorious armies and took a hit with the American retreat from Vietnam in 1973 and another with the fall of Saigon in 1975.[334] Like Ali, American soldiers nursed their wounds after returning home from a defeat at the hands of a smiling Asian enemy who refused to fight by Western standards. The decade also witnessed a serious recession and shift to a postindustrial society that destroyed many men's identities rooted on the shop floor and in the role of breadwinner.[335] The Black Power movement grew, in part, out of an effort by African American men to reclaim their manhood in the 1960s.[336] By the late 1970s, it lay dead, drowned in the blood of murdered black leaders, recession, and right-wing politics.[337] The decade also witnessed the growth of the women's liberation movement, much of which treated men as enemies and challenged male dominance.[338] Iran's seizure of American hostages in 1979 and the Jimmy Carter administration's inability to rescue them incinerated whatever martial pride American men might have retained after Vietnam.[339]

Even the traditionally male domain of sports failed to provide men with a place of refuge. American women made impressive athletic gains during the 1970s. In 1972, Congress passed the Title IX legislation, forbidding any school receiving federal funding from discriminating based on gender. The bill's authors aimed it primarily at law and medical schools that limited female enrollments, but the legislation most radically altered athletic programs. Schools withdrew some funding from male sports, disbanded hundreds of male teams, poured money into female athletics, and made collegiate athletics less overwhelmingly male.[340] The following year, male tennis player Bobby Riggs challenged the outstanding female player Billie Jean King to a highly publicized battle of the sexes. King won, demonstrating that women had the capacity to best men in the athletic arena. Women even entered fight sports. In 1974, the University of California at Berkeley opened its wrestling program to women.[341] In 1975, Jackie Tonawanda, a boxer marketed as the female Ali, knocked out male kickboxer Larry Rodania as part of the All Martial Arts Tournament broadcast on ABC's *Wide World of Sports*.[342] Ignoring the objections of male fighters, in 1978 the New York State Athletic Commission granted professional boxing licenses to women for the first time. Tonawanda was one of the first to proudly display her new license to enter the male-dominated world of pugilism.[343] Nearly a century before her achievement, Duffield Ossborne had urged men to embrace boxing as "a saving touch of barbarism" to ensure that they remained masculine.[344] In the 1970s, women entered the male sanctuary, proving with savage punches to male bodies that they, too, could embrace a little barbarism. Consider it a crisis of masculinity or just a series of steel-toed kicks to the testicles, but the 1970s were a rough time to be a guy in America.

Ali's troubles did not end with the close of the terrible decade. He retired briefly in 1979 after losing the heavyweight boxing title to Leon Spinks.[345] In 1980, he attempted an ill-advised comeback. On October 2, he faced a younger, stronger, and far tougher Larry Holmes at Caesar's Palace in Las Vegas, Nevada.[346] Before the fight, Holmes told reporters that he had enormous respect for Ali, regarding him as one of the all-time greats, but he urged the 38-year-old veteran to cancel the fight and walk away from the ring without doing any further damage to his body and his reputation.[347] Ali responded with his characteristic insults.[348] Whatever might have remained of Ali's legend died in the ring that day. Holmes destroyed the aging veteran, demolishing the once-great champion.[349] The younger fighter seemed to feel pity for his opponent, occasionally ignoring opportunities to punish Ali and intentionally missing with punches to avoid causing any more damage than a win required.[350] One fan left after the second round, unwilling to see Ali absorb any more punishment.[351] A ringside reporter abandoned his journalistic impartiality and screamed at the referee, demanding that he end the fight while Ali was still breathing.[352] After 10 rounds, Ali's trainer stepped in, throwing in the towel and putting an end to the fight.[353] Sportswriters denounced Ali for disappointing the fans.[354] After the bout, the defeated Ali tested positive for prescription painkillers and faced possible revocation of his Nevada boxing license as a result.[355]

Ali still refused to quit. He agreed to face Jamaican fighter Trevor Berbick in 1981. For once, Ali expressed respect and admiration for an opponent. Heaping praise on Berbick and arguing that his adversary was a highly skilled pugilist and a gentleman, Ali told reporters that if he could best the Jamaican, he could once again make a run at the title.[356] The result surprised almost nobody other than Ali. The former champion suffered a humiliating defeat in which Ali ran from Berbick's relentless assaults. Dave Anderson, writing for the *New York Times*, argued that Ali "was running from himself really, running from what he had once been and from what he had hoped to be again."[357] Anderson observed sadness in the champion's eyes as he rested after the ninth round: "That's when he knew he was 39 year old, that's when he knew he would never enter a ring again."[358] Ali left the ring defeated.

Ali's life symbolized everything America was and had hoped to be. Born during World War II, he grew up in a triumphant America. In 1960, Ali, like his nation, stood proudly victorious on the global stage. Both Ali and America then suffered setbacks as the decades rolled on. The country fought against itself, torn by struggles over civil rights at home and defeated on distant battlefields. By the end of the 1970s, Ali and America both laid defeated, tired, and humiliated, damaged by an Asian enemy who refused to play by the rules, and surpassed on the international stage by opponents from nations that most Americans could not find on a map. The pugilist and his nation limped into the new decade on battered legs propelled by a mind clouded with worry. Perhaps nobody summarized Ali and American fight sports in this era better than the legendary writer Hunter S. Thompson:

> That was always the difference between Muhammad Ali and the rest of us. He came, he saw, and if he didn't entirely conquer—he came as close as anybody we are likely to see in the lifetime of this doomed generation.[359]

VI
"We Shall Not Stand by Helplessly"
The Birth of Mixed Martial Arts, 1981 to the Present

We shall not stand by helplessly and allow a great American institution to be so threatened by the cottage-cheese mentality pervasive in society. Is Donahuemanology rampant in the land? Is nothing sacred? Let the bleeding hearts trash all the arms sales and rock 'n' roll lyrics they want, but, hey, stay away from violence in sports.... Let's be serious and admit it. We're looking for the wheels to go over the wall. We're waiting for the Blackhawks and the Bruins to take off the gloves and begin socking the "eh's" out of each other. Preferably wade into the stands and molest a few cops, too. We're desperately hoping that the next time John McEnroe and Ivan Lendl scream at each other, they won't meekly appeal to the chair but instead say something like ... "You want some of me?" ... and start duking it out right on Centre Court. We're just praying we're not dealing bridge at the country club the night Mike Tyson rearranges one of his no-talent palooka dance partners into a vegetable. What a guy, Tyson! Once raised pigeons. Now reduces people to pulp. The American Dream....
So raise your hands and be counted. Don't fade into the woodwork.[1]

Randy comes out throwing strikes and Chuck looks to counter punch. Randy lands an overhand right followed by a cross and he clinches with Chuck. Before Randy can start the dirty boxing, Liddell breaks free. McCarthy calls time as Couture looks like his eye was poked. The doctors check it out as you can imagine how Dana White was panicking. The doctor tells Big John that Randy is fine and able to continue. Fight RESUMES.... Chuck lands a left that stuns Couture, who charges at Chuck. Randy throws but lands noth-

ing while Liddell lands a right and another right and RANDY COUTURE IS DOWN. Chuck pounces on him with a few more strikes as Big John McCarthy steps in and stops the fight. Liddell is pumped up and is one happy man. They cut to the crowd and Forrest Griffin looks stunned.
Your winner and NEW UFC Light Heavyweight Champion is Chuck "The Iceman" Liddell via KO at 2:06 of the first round.[2]

In 1979, Ronald Reagan announced his candidacy for president of the United States. His campaign emphasized simple themes of Reagan as a vigorous father figure, with the power to lead America back to the greatness it once enjoyed. The message resonated with the many Americans who bought into the idea of a cowboy-in-chief, electing Reagan to the presidency in a landslide.[3] Reagan-era American masculinity was often the arrogant strut of a chest-thumping bully who wore power ties and subjugated small nations. However, some American men responded to the malaise and despair of the 1970s by seeking out new and dangerous challenges. For a view of the authentic manhood, we must turn our attention away from the boardrooms filled with power-lunching yuppies and the halls of the Pentagon where old men in starched uniforms bullied weak neighbors. We must shift our focus to the ring, to the scene of that saving touch of barbarism, where American men struggled valiantly to regain their manhood or die trying.

During the 1980s, boxing suffered from internal disarray and allegations of external corruption, making the ring a more complicated, though still likely, place to prove manliness. In 1963, Congress had voted down Senator Kefauver's proposal for a federal boxing commission.[4] This rejection made American boxing different from its great pugilistic rival of the United Kingdom, which enjoyed the benefits of a national organization under the British Boxing Board of Control beginning in 1929.[5] American pugilism remained a deeply divided sport, with no unified structure or regulations. Every state operated under its own commission or simply ignored the sport completely. Nongovernmental organizations attempted to fill the organizational void in America and bridge international divides. By the 1980s, 10 separate boxing organizations competed for attention. The most important of these in the United States were the World Boxing Council, the World Boxing Association, and the International Boxing Federation. Each produced its own regulations and crowned its own champions, artificially transforming one of the simplest sports into one of the most perplexing. This proliferation also made boxing more confusing than other American sports such as basketball, football, and baseball, all of which boasted largely unified organizations by the Reagan era. Journalists continued to reveal connections between organized crime

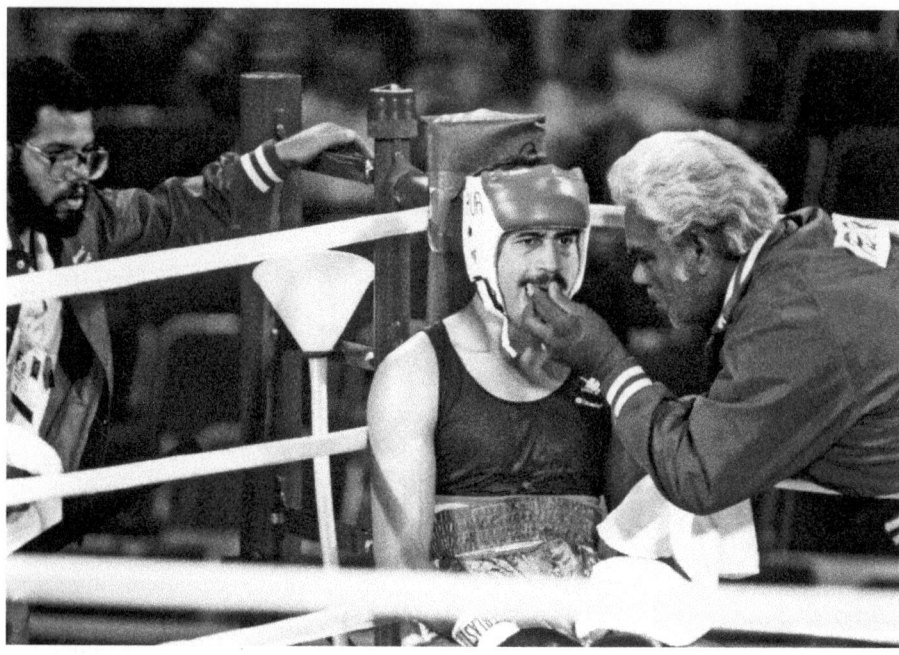

American soldier Aristides Gonzalez from Fort Bragg, North Carolina, receives advice from his coach during a boxing match with Paulo Tuvale of Samoa at the 1984 Summer Olympics in Los Angeles. Gonzalez won the bronze medal. Photograph taken by Ken Hackman (National Archives at College Park—Still Pictures [RD-DC-S], Record Group 330: Records of the Office of the Secretary of Defense, 1921–2008).

and boxing, but in a new twist the gangsters were sometimes Japanese, rather than Italian or Irish as in previous decades.[6] In 1980, in one of the most controversial fights in pugilistic history, Roberto Duran surrendered his title while suffering not from the Bruce Lee–inspired punches of his opponent Sugar Ray Leonard, but instead from a stomach ache in a bout that left Duran's fans feeling betrayed after a fight few observers took seriously.[7] As damaging as connections to organized crime and disappointing fights were to the sweet science, they provided only headaches for a sport that increasingly appeared little more than a fast route to suicide.

As medical science improved, knowledge of the damage boxing did to human bodies became clearer. The sport's death toll also continued to rise during the 1980s. Welsh boxer Johnny Owen died after getting knocked out during a bout in Los Angeles, sparking controversy and an official investigation.[8] In 1982, Ray "Boom Boom" Mancini killed his opponent Duk Koo Kim in a widely publicized Las Vegas bout.[9] Doctors had long suspected that boxing caused long-term damage, but by the early 1980s they had conclusive evidence from a series of studies. In 1982, citing recent studies, the British Medical Association condemned the sport and pushed for an international ban.[10] The next year, the American Medical Association followed suit, expressing concern for the long-term injuries suffered by boxers and pushing for a ban on the sport in America.[11] Muhammad Ali became the decade's most high-profile victim when doctors diagnosed him with Parkinson's disease, possibly caused by head trauma suffered in the ring.[12] These developments once again highlighted the supreme sacrifice that the ring often demanded and led fans to wonder if the price was too high.

In the previous century, boxing earned cultural dominance and legal recognition in large measure because its advocates made a convincing argument that the new scientific pugilism was distinct from the bare-knuckle hooliganism detested by decent people.[13] Millions of Americans, particularly from the upper and middle classes, accepted the proponents' claims that whatever physical damage men might endure in the arena was more than offset by the benefits boxing bestowed on their manhood and their souls by training them in the manly art.[14] Fighters encased their hands in padded gloves, convinced that horsehair could shield them from harm. As the 1980s wore on, observers began to question this approach and to suspect that scientific pugilism offered little more than corruption, confusion, injury, and death.[15] If gloves offered insufficient protection, then why wear them? If boxing organizations only complicated the sport, then why submit to their demands? American fight fans were disillusioned with boxing, but still felt the needs that had brought them to pugilism's door so many years before. Like a middle-aged husband bored with a sagging wife, America began looking for new thrills.

Some Americans found those thrills in the arms of a lover named "tough man." In 1979, Michigan businessman Art Dore held the first of the tough man contests.[16] The events caught on as the new decade of the 1980s began, providing many men with just the excitement they wanted. The new sport provided a test of old-fashioned toughness, not scientific pugilism. Dore limited the events to only the most amateur of pugilists, forbidding professionals and experienced amateurs from entering, and attracting a diverse range of self-proclaimed tough guys including farmers, bartenders, ministers, construction workers, and policemen. Proving that some females of the 1980s found prize money and local celebrity just as alluring as their male counterparts, women also entered tough man contests, fighting other women and facing the same dangers.[17] Tough man's rules were based on those for mainstream boxing, but the participants attempted to get as close to old-fashioned brawling as the law allowed by exploiting the patchwork of regulations and legal loopholes.[18] Some fighters wanted to fight bare-knuckle, and the promoters were inclined to allow them, until they discovered that doing so might result in arrests.[19] Some areas did not regulate any fight that offered small enough prizes; in those places, the organizers simply reduced the awards to a level that put them outside the bounds of regulation.[20] This flexibility indicates once again that cultural need trumped economic determinism.

The duration and numbers of rounds varied from event to event, but tough man competitions typically lasted for only three or four rounds of a single minute in duration. This format that tended to produce very intense fights, as opposed to the more leisurely pace of conventional boxing bouts that consisted of 10 to 12 rounds of two to three minutes each.[21] Tough man competitors fought in only two weight classes or none at all, in contrast to the eight weight classes commonly recognized in modern boxing. The laxer regulations often resulted in mismatches between fighters of vastly different sizes, but even these minimal regulations meant little to promoters willing to ignore their own rules. Organizers required physical exams to ensure competitors were healthy enough to fight but, as with weight classes, often looked the other way, allowing pugilists with serious health issues into the ring. The bouts became slaughterhouses where big fighters pummeled small ones and the out-of-shape fell prey to the physically fit.[22] In these poorly regulated combats, David often died at the hands of Goliath. Throughout the decade, the events killed numerous men and women, outraging observers and motivating politicians to ban the sport.[23]

For all the controversies and problems it engendered, tough man filled a need. Men and women flocked to the events, filling the stands and lining up for their turn in the ring.[24] Tough man competitions may have competed with mainstream boxing for attention, but still scientific pugilists did not give up on the masses. In the middle of the decade, many fans turned their attention to the East in hopes that a falsetto-voiced savior might redeem their sport.

In the first two decades of Mike "Kid Dynamite" Tyson's life, he traveled a meteoric course from petty criminal to failed pugilistic messiah for a troubled sport. Tyson was born in Brooklyn, New York, on June 30, 1966. His construction-worker father never married his mother, Lorna Tyson, and left the family behind when Mike was only two. Lorna Tyson turned to welfare to survive, but she bore little resemblance to the mythical welfare queen of Reagan's rhetoric.[25] There were no Cadillac sedans or crystal chandeliers in Mike Tyson's world, only government cheese in his belly and hours consumed with play on the city's dangerous streets. Like many young men in those circumstances, he drifted into trouble and became a guest of a various juvenile detention centers.²⁶ While he was at one such correctional facility, the boxing manager and trainer Cus D'Amato caught sight of Tyson and decided the young man had pugilistic potential. Boxing fans had long defended their sport as a rare path out of poverty for men in desperate circumstances. Tyson lived that dream, at least for a few years. He proved D'Amato's suspicions correct, compiling an impressive amateur record and turning pro while still a teenager.²⁷ He won his first 19 professional fights, all by knockout.²⁸ Less than two years after beginning his professional career, he faced Trevor Berbick for the World Boxing Council (WBC) heavyweight crown, the same Jamaican-born Canadian who had ended Ali's career several years before.²⁹

> Ten seconds into the second round, a right dropped Berbick; he jumped up immediately and unwisely. Still he refused to run. "I made a silly mistake," he said later. "I tried to prove my manhood." Near the end of the second round, that mistake got him knocked silly. Tyson ripped Berbick with a right hand to the kidney, missed a right uppercut, and then slammed a left hook to Berbick's temple. For a moment, Berbick hung there; then, like a puppet that had just had his strings snipped, he collapsed onto his back. At the count of three, he struggled up but lurched into the ropes. At six, he was up, only to tumble over onto his right shoulder. At nine, he stayed up, swaying like a reed in an every-which-way wind.³⁰

The fight ended quickly and decisively. Berbick later recalled that in the second round he made a dumb mistake when he charged toward his young opponent in an effort to "prove my manhood."³¹ As the previous description reveals, Tyson responded with a devastating series of punches to Berbick's kidneys and temple that left the older man lying helpless on the ground. The referee intervened, ending the bout and making the 20-year-old the youngest heavyweight champion in the sport's history and the new holder of the WBC belt.³²

If Tyson's victory was not national redemption, then at least it was step in that direction. Other fighters still held the rival championship titles bestowed by the World Boxing Association and the International Boxing Federation, but the public and press made little note of the incomplete victory. Dave Anderson, in the *New York Times*, proclaimed the birth of a Tyson era and celebrated him as the rebirth of Ali.³³ Tyson humanized many of boxing's best attributes: he was born into poverty, abandoned by his father, and was a petty criminal in his childhood who turned it all around under the watchful eye of a paternal boxing coach who guided him into manhood, where the young pugilist earned fame and fortune pummeling foreigners for the delight of millions. At the end of 1986, Tyson stood as the king of all creation, enjoying a moment that could not last.

During the same era, Americans also sought redemption in simulated violence. Martial arts movies first came to America in the 1960s and 1970s with badly dubbed Asian films.[34] Bruce Lee, standing at the intersection of East and West, helped catapult them forward with his enormously successful 1973 movie *Enter the Dragon*.[35] Lee shared the screen with many costars, including the African American karate champion Jim Kelly, the Italian American actor turned martial artist John Saxon, and Chuck Norris, a red-haired newcomer to movies.[36] In a story similar to that of many of his predecessors, including Robert Trias and Joe Lewis, Norris picked up the Korean martial art of Tang So Do while serving with the U.S. Air Force in Korea.[37] After completing his service, Norris began teaching his new craft and climbing the ranks in point karate tournaments. He found minor celebrity in both pursuits, became a friend and teacher to Steve McQueen, and took a series of minor acting jobs. Bruce Lee's death provided a vacuum in the martial arts world, and Chuck Norris worked to fill the gap. He was the ideal movie star for the Reagan era, with his military record, conservative politics, athletic accomplishments, and a preference for simple stories in which down-on-their-luck Americans defeated foreigners, communists, and drug dealers, as part of a larger trend of reinvigorated American action heroes that also included Sylvester Stallone and Arnold Schwarzenegger.[38] Similar to Norris, Jean Claude Van Damme, a Belgian actor who typically played American characters, starred in several very popular films, such as *Bloodsport* and *Kickboxer*, that portrayed Americans using martial arts to defeat evil foreigners.[39] These movies, and many more like them, helped reassure Americans that their nation remained strong.

Martial arts movies also branched out into children's entertainment. In 1984, Columbia Pictures released *The Karate Kid*, starring Ralph Macchio and Pat Morita. Directed by John Avildsen, who also made *Rocky*, the film was a retelling of the classic boxer's tale for the karate generation, with an emphasis on fighting as a rite of passage.[40] The film earned high praise from critics and the love of huge American audiences.[41] The Teenage Mutant Ninja Turtles, a group of martial arts–practicing turtles, made the leap from comic books and Saturday-morning cartoons into the movies in a 1990 feature film that quickly grossed more than $100 million.[42] Even Chuck Norris got in on the act with his 1992 movie *Sidekicks*, in which he played himself and fulfilled the dreams of a boy who wanted to compete in a karate tournament as a partner to the famed martial artist.[43] These movies increased the popularity of martial arts and brought waves of children into karate schools across America. Karate instructors took advantage of the trend, changing the names of their schools and their arts to ones popularized by movies. David Deaton, owner of a karate school in Tennessee, took marketing further than most, giving karate demonstrations in movie theaters and taking his students to watch *The Teenage Mutant Ninja Turtles* movie after class.[44] Many martial arts movies did well in theaters, but did even better in the home video market.

The 1980s and 1990s were an era of technological as well as cultural changes. It was possible to use even the earliest movie projectors at home, provided the viewer could afford the enormous expense and had enough room to set up the cumbersome equipment, which very few Americans did. The Japanese led the way with systems more suited to the home in the 1960s, although they made more impact with schools and small businesses than individual consumers.[45] The first practical models of home video players did not appear in the United States until the late 1970s. While they were still expensive and imperfect technologies, they were good enough to attract some sales. Early advertising campaigns marketed the systems primarily as a way to avoid missing favorite programs since for the first time a person could record a TV program and watch it later.[46] As the new players caught on, they began to facilitate other uses. Businesses sprung up to rent and sell movies for consumers to watch at home and major Hollywood studios got on board, offering videocassette versions of their products. Video recording technologies such as camcorders designed to work with the new players also became popular, allowing people to produce their own content in addition to watching commercially produced materials. In 1982, only 4 percent of American households own a VCR; two years later, that share had jumped to 19 percent; and before the decade ended, more than 60 percent of American households enjoyed the benefits of a home video player.[47] This change is often called the video revolution in recognition of how it forever changed the relationship between the creators and the consumers of entertainment.[48] It also led to a revolution in the world of fight sports.

Fight sports often spring from migrations. In the 19th century, collar and elbow wrestling caught on in Vermont because large numbers of Irish immigrants brought it with them across the Atlantic. Boxing took root in urban cities when they filled with immigrants from the British Isles. This urban sport became a dominant American activity only when the center of national culture moved along with large numbers of former farmers from the backcountry to the emerging cities. Asian martial arts finally set down substantial roots, in spite many years of failed efforts by missionaries of violence, only when large numbers of American men brought them home after years spent in Asia during military tours of duty. Each time a new fight sport attracted a large portion of the American public's loyalty, it did so only after a major movement of human bodies brought young men into personal contact with new methods of mayhem. Ideas changed when men cracked strangers' skulls, demonstrating the superiority of new ideas with the most intimidating of personal interactions. The history of these sports is more than a simple chart of migrations, but the movement of people always provides a crucial component to the story. This nearly universal rule held constant for centuries, but it changed in the 1990s. Home video changed how Americans were entertained.[49] The humble video player also did something more: it changed how men fought. It allowed a handful of fighters to reach beyond the personal, giving strangers a glimpse of new methods of unarmed combat, and it transformed viewers into disciples.

Home videos made an enormous impact in the martial arts world during the 1980s. American martial artists originally became aware of the powers of video during the 1960s, when Japanese judo, karate, and sumo schools began recording bouts to improve judging of hotly contested fights.[50] American fighters recognized that the new technology was already changing the world of fight sports. With the popularization of home video players in America during the early 1980s, martial arts experts began selling instructional videos directly to consumers. Men whose fathers learned martial arts from picture books or personal interactions got many of their own lessons via videocassette.[51] Many of these courses were in familiar arts such as karate and judo, but others were in the esoteric techniques of arnis, akido, and Brazilian jujitsu, a recent arrival in America with deep roots in Latin America.[52]

At the turn of the 20th century, Japanese judo experts fanned out across the globe bringing knowledge of their nation and their art to the world. Koizami Gunji traveled across Europe, initiating a judo craze across the continent, particularly in France and Great Britain.[53] Yoshiaki Yamashita came to America, befriended President Theodore Roosevelt, and taught judo at Harvard, Annapolis, and West Point.[54]

Ground fighting expert Mitsuyo Maeda spread the good word to several nations, including the United States, before settling in Brazil.[55] In the moist, warm atmosphere of Rio de Janeiro, Maeda tapped into the Brazilian tradition of vale tudo ("anything goes") fights, won a series of thrilling matches, and became a celebrity.[56] His fame facilitated a friendship with the Gracie clan, a politically connected family of Scottish ancestry. The Gracies helped Japanese immigrants get settled into new homes in Latin America. In appreciation, Maeda taught the Gracies his personal blend of judo he still called by the older name of jujitsu. Maeda owed much of his success to his emphasis on ground fighting. His strategy was typically simple: rush the opponent, get the foe to the ground, and pull, twist, and gouge until bones snapped and blood flowed. This approach worked particularly well in the Western hemisphere, where most of his opponents were either boxers with no experience in ground fighting or Western-style wrestlers with little knowledge of Japanese submission holds.[57]

The Gracies and other Brazilians became enamored with the new ideas, adopted Maeda's approach, enshrined the Japanese immigrant as their patriarch of mayhem, and continued to refine his techniques.[58] They adapted Maeda's ideas into a new art they called Brazilian jujitsu. Throughout the 20th century, the Gracies fanned out into the streets, fighting anyone who dared face them in vale tudo matches, and leaving a trail of shattered bodies and larger-than-life legends in their wake.[59] When Carlos Gracie opened his first martial arts school, he placed a provocative ad in Brazil's leading newspaper, *O Globo*, stating simply, "If you want to get your face beaten and smashed, your butt kicked, and your arms broken, contact Carlos Gracie."[60] Although brash, it was hardly an idle boast. The Gracies did not always win, but they won often enough to enshrine themselves as national celebrities. The Gracies counted both presidents and vice presidents of Brazil among their numerous students, and tens of thousands of fans filled stadiums to watch Gracies take on foreign foes for national glory.[61] Getúlio Vargas, Brazil's dictator at the time, was one of the family's greatest admirers and granted Helio Grace a pardon when he was sent to prison for assaulting a gymnastics instructor.[62] The Gracies briefly made it onto Brazilian television in 1959 with a program titled *Herois do Ringue* ("Heroes of the Ring"), which featured vale tudo matches between fighters from different styles.[63] The network canceled the show when a Brazilian jujitsu expert and friend to the Gracies, Alberto Barretto, snapped his opponent's arm and exposed a compound fracture to the viewers—a bit graphic even for the fight-loving Brazilians.[64] Despite this setback, vale tudo competitions and the Brazilian jujitsu experts who often won them continued to attract students and fans.[65]

Having largely captured the Brazilian imagination, the Gracies came to America. In 1978, Rorion Gracie moved to America and founded the first Brazilian jujitsu school in America.[66] He set up operations in California and tried to worm his way into the movies by working as a stuntman, fight choreographer, and movie extra. He made connections in Hollywood with business people who helped him grow his school. Following the formula that worked so well in Brazil, Rorion fought anyone willing to enter the ring with him.[67] He took advantage of the new trend in video and began selling homemade tapes through *Black Belt* magazine. His tapes came with the ringing endorsement of Rorion's new friend and training partner, Chuck Norris.[68] Unlike many of the formally instructive videos on the market, the works titled "Gracie Jiu Jitsu in Action" or "Gracies in Action" were little more than camcorder-captured examples of Gracies doing what they always did, breaking the bones of anyone foolish enough to accept their challenge.[69] In 1989, Steve Barnes reviewed the videos for *Black Belt* and urged readers to purchase them by using language that suggested Rorion Gracie was the second coming the martial messiah, Bruce Lee.[70] Many readers took Barnes' advice, and the videos made a huge splash with many fighters. The Gracie brand got another boost later in 1989, when *Playboy* ran an interview with Rorion, detailing his street fights and proclaiming him "the toughest man in the west."[71]

Rorion Gracie took advantage of the new technology of the home video player to spread word of his style-on-style match-ups at about the same time another new technology allowed spectators to test their reflexes in simulated combat. Specifically, video games provided another method of spreading ideas about fight sports. Physicist Willy Higginbotham invented the first video game in 1958 while working for the Brookhaven National Laboratory because he wanted something interesting to show his lab's visitors. His simple tennis simulator was very primitive, but popular around the lab.[72] With improved technology, video games eventually moved out of the laboratories and into arcades and living rooms in the 1970s, thanks to classics like *Pong*, *Space Invaders*, and *Breakout*. Fighting games quickly entered the market. The first in this genre was the 1976 arcade game *Heavyweight Champ*, which provided a crude boxing simulation that players directed with unusual controllers shaped like boxing gloves.[73] The 1984 game *Karate Champ* was more successful as well as more typical of later games with its joystick-style controls. It sought to re-create the experience of karate tournaments with one-on-one combat between pajama-clad fighters and bonus rounds of board breaking.[74] These games made it possible for people (particularly children) who were unable to participate in fight sports because of isolation, physical limitations, or parental prohibitions to make some small connection to the world of boxing championships and karate tournaments.

A new era of fighting took off at the end of the 1980s with increasing penetration of home video game systems and the creation of two iconic game series. Beginning in the late 1980s, the *Street Fighter* series of games took over the market; even today, it remains the standard by which all other fighting games are judged.[75] The game's Japanese designers at Capcom clearly took inspiration from Bruce Lee's *Enter the Dragon*, with game play being constructed around an international fighting tournament. Each cartoon-style character boasted a unique combination of ethnicity, nationality, and fighting style, including a heavily muscled wrestler, from Russia; a boxer bearing a striking resemblance to Mike Tyson, from the United States; a bizarre green-skinned wild man, from Brazil; a painfully thin yoga guru, from India; a

V. The Birth of Mixed Martial Arts, 1981 to the Present 209

female Kung Fu practitioner, from China; as well as almost identical karate experts from Japan and the United States.[76] Fighters traveled around the world as they played the game, fighting for fans on each fighter's home turf. The game eventually expanded into the movies with a screen adaptation starring Jean Claude Van Damme.[77]

Inspired by *Street Fighter*'s success, developers at rival company Midway released *Mortal Kombat* in 1992.[78] It offered realistic characters in place of the cartoonish figures in *Streetfighter*, and substituted streams of blood for animated stars to indicate a fighter was in trouble. Nevertheless, the basic premise of an "anything goes" tournament with a diverse array of characters remained intact, even though the emphasis was a little more Asian than global.[79] Characters included the Bruce Lee clone Liu Kang, an American movie star named Johnny Cage, a ninja named Sub Zero, and an American female spy Sonya Blade.[80] Like *Street Fighter*, the new game became the basis for a major movie. In an innovative effort at promotion, the moviemakers created an Internet website for the game and film.[81]

These fighting games—*Mortal Kombat* especially—concerned many Americans. Parents worried about how the violent games might affect their children.[82] Observers argued that violent video games, particularly *Mortal Kombat*, increased violent behavior among children.[83] In spite of these concerns, or perhaps because of them, children fell in love with fighting games. Capcom sold roughly 60,000 *Street Fighter II* arcade machines, and their popularity rescued many arcades from bankruptcy.[84] *Mortal Kombat* became the most popular video game released up to that time.[85] Playing the two games became a rite of passage for many young boys.[86] The games were a tool of conflict resolution for opponents who decided to let fictional characters absorb the pain of disagreements.[87] Over time, the virtual affected perceptions of the actual, leading journalists in the next decade to describe the new fight sport of mixed martial arts as a video game played in real life.[88] As virtual fight sports won over fans, however, actual fight sports encountered difficulties.

American kickboxing made some limited gains in popularity during the 1980s and 1990s. It attracted competitors from the ranks of low-ranking boxers, who were convinced that if they learned a few kicks they could win the glory denied them in their preferred sport. Other fighters came into the sport from a multitude of Asian-inspired martial arts. The fighters received help from Judy and Don Quine, a married couple with ties to American movie studios. The Quines attended their first karate tournament at the insistence of their son, who expressed an interest in self-defense classes. The couple enjoyed the exhibition, but became convinced that if the sport emphasized the entertainment of spectators rather than the personal enjoyment of the participants, karate might provide a financially viable mass entertainment. When executives from ABC heard about the Quines' interest, they asked the couple for advice about upcoming karate broadcasts, and the Quines became important promoters of American karate competitions.[89] They urged reforms such as moves toward standardized rules, competition in boxing rings rather than on karate mats, and requirements that competitors fight bare chested so that viewers could enjoy a view of their toned male physiques.[90] The Quines, and the events they sponsored, specifically rejected the rougher muay thai techniques of grappling, kneeing, and head butting, which Judy Quine deemed inconsistent with gentlemen.[91] Some fighters accepted the suggestions, which were somewhat successful in the 1980s, with kickboxing events attracting increasing attention from live and television audiences.[92] The sport also attracted greater cultural prominence when John Cusack proclaimed kickboxing the sport of the future in the 1989 movie *Say Anything*.[93]

In spite of some suggestions by sportswriters and the Quines that the American martial arts community coalesced around the new sport, the activity itself and its specific parameters remained controversial among martial artists. The debates were nothing new. Years ago, many of the most important figures in American martial arts, such as Robert Trias and Jhoon Rhee, had expressed grave misgivings about full-contact karate fights, and others, such as Tsutomu Oshima, had completely rejected the concept of karate as sport.[94] Some members of the martial arts community came to the Asian-style arts primarily because they sought spirituality, cultural insights, and esoteric knowledge.[95] Other martial artists treated the arts as an innovative and fun exercise program. The fitness karate crowd grew with the advent of hybrid arts such as Tae Bo and cardio kickboxing, which stood somewhere between traditional karate and jazzercise aerobics.[96] Members of all of these groups found kickboxing's exclusive emphasis on sport troubling, and they expressed little interest in wearing boxing gloves.[97] Many martial artists continued to repeat Ohsima's argument that karate was, and must remain, an art rather than a sport. Martial arts competitions were perfectly acceptable to these enthusiasts as long as judges evaluated competitors artistically and did not encourage full-power strikes with no concern for technique or discipline.

The controversies affected the sport's popular appeal. A 1992 event that promoters predicted would finally bring kickboxing into the mainstream by displaying a night of fights involving some of the best kickboxers in the world provided mostly disappointment to the 14,000 spectators crowded into a Las Vegas arena.[98] Rules provided a point of major disagreement going into the event, and the resulting odd patchwork of compromises and agreements ensured confusion among fighters, fans, and even the referee.[99] Kickboxing struggled to bring fighters and fans together under a single umbrella, but the controversies over rules and approach paled in comparison to the scandal that wrecked boxing in this period.

In spite of high hopes by many fans and sportswriters, the last years of the 1980s were a tough time for Mike Tyson. He continued to amass victories, following up on his capture of the World Boxing Council crown and becoming the undisputed world heavyweight boxing champion of the world in 1987 after besting James Smith for the World Boxing Association title and Tony Tucker for the International Boxing Federation belt.[100] Tyson won, but his mediocre performances seemed lackluster in comparison to the awe-inspiring dominance that he had demonstrated in earlier fights.[101] The next year he married the aspiring actress Robin Givens in a move that surprised his manager, who expressed hope that married life would help the champion settle down.[102] The nuptials appeared to do just the opposite, leading to a short-lived and turbulent marriage. When it ended just months after it began, neither party came out looking very good. Givens became the most hated woman in America, widely viewed as a glamorous and manipulative gold digger who married the champion only for his millions.[103] Tyson came off even worse, as a physically abusive and foolish bully who, journalists argued, led a personal life that made him unworthy of respect or admiration.[104] Instead of a boxing messiah, Tyson began to look like a talented but imperfect pugilist with little character or intellect.

Any hopes boxing fans might have had for Tyson make progress in the early 1990s were dashed within weeks of the New Year. In 1990, Tyson faced Buster Douglas, a challenger so little regarded that bookies refused to take bets on the fight.[105] Douglas did little to inspire confidence, expressing little optimism at the press conferences, revealing a plan to hit Tyson, while acknowledging that this particular strategy seemed unlikely to work.[106] But in one of the biggest boxing upsets in history, Douglas sent Tyson to the mat with a flurry of punches in the 10th round.[107] In spite of the referee's declaration of a knockout and what looked like a straightforward defeat to most fans, Tyson continued calling himself the champion, arguing that the referee threw the fight for Douglas by giving the challenger extra seconds to recover after an eighth-round knockdown, a claim the referee angrily denied.[108] Previous ring champions such as Muhammad Ali and Jack Dempsey had won praise from observers when they responded to defeat with stoic charm, but sportswriters had nothing positive to say about Tyson's reaction to his first professional defeat, referring to the dethroned king as a "crybaby."[109] Then the sport's various governing bodies got in on the act, squabbling among themselves about who won and what it meant for the rankings and various titles. The entire event turned the stomachs of many fans, who were upset by Tyson's poor performance in the ring and by the corruption, confusion, and poor sportsmanship displayed by many parties in the fight's aftermath.[110] Tyson was sinking, but he was still far from the bottom.

In 1991, Tyson's troubled personal life once again overshadowed his pugilistic accomplishments. In September 1991, an Indiana grand jury indicted Tyson on a charge that he raped Desiree Washington, a teenaged contestant in the Miss Black America Beauty Pageant.[111] Both Tyson and Washington agreed that they met during the pageant and later had sex in Tyson's hotel room, but Tyson claimed that their actions were consensual rather than criminal.[112] Steve Wulf, writing for *Sports Illustrated*, noted that the grand jury testimony revealed numerous incidents of Tyson acting in a sexually aggressive manner toward women, convincing Wulf that even if Tyson was not a rapist, he was at the very least a menace to society and an embarrassment to boxing.[113] Gamblers gave five to one odds in favor of an acquittal for Tyson.[114] The jury found Washington's account more persuasive than Tyson's, declaring him guilty on all charges. It was another tragedy for boxing, a further tarnish on a once-noble sport. It was also far more than that. The guilty verdict came as a shock to many women who had witnessed Clarence Thomas's confirmation to the Supreme Court in spite of Anita Hill's allegations of sexual harassment just weeks before and expected a similar outcome in this case. The scholar and author Joyce Carol Oates argued in a contemporary article that Tyson's conviction represented a victory for women, as the legal system, for once, refused to blame a victim and punished a celebrity for his crimes against a woman.[115] Tyson eventually served three years in prison because of the conviction.[116] His incarceration took him out of the boxing scene, sending the sweet science's biggest celebrity and greatest embarrassment to prison at about the same time some of the nation's lesser-known and less-felonious fighters traveled to Japan.

Inoki's fiasco with Ali in 1976 might have delayed Japanese acceptance of style-on-style match-ups, but it did not eliminate them forever. Japanese mixed martial arts grew out of professional wrestling, with events gradually shifting from scripted routines to authentic competitions in the 1980s.[117] Japanese fighters mixed karate and boxing into their unique take on Western-style wrestling, creating a hybrid art they called shoot fighting.[118] The art took its name from the aggressive charge or "shoot" wrestlers employed to close the distance and take down their opponents.[119] Proponents of the new sport founded the Shooto organization in 1986 to begin promoting these fights, not as an occasional exhibition, but as a separate sporting league; Shooto began hosting fights later in the year, with the first professional event occurring in 1989.[120] Initially, no foreigners appeared in these events, though it is unclear if this was by contrivance or by convenience.[121] American fighters noted the new Japanese sport with interest and by 1991, some American fighters had begun training in the art.[122] The owner of seven karate schools and national kickboxing champion of Ecuador, Bart Cavvavale, began offering classes from his Miami school in the new art and selling training videos to distant students at about the same time.[123] Within a few years, Americans began competing in Japanese events. Erik Paulson, a Minnesota native with a background in judo, taekwondo, and boxing became the first American to win a shoot fighting title in Japan.[124] The Shooto organization soon faced competition from rival promotions in Japan such as Pancrase.[125] One such promotion eventually provided at least one destitute young man with international glory.

Ken Shamrock's early life bore distinct similarities to Mike Tyson's. Shamrock was born Kenneth Kilpatrick into a poverty-stricken, fatherless home, which he fled when he was only 10.[126] At the age of 14, he owned little except a record of petty crimes that brought him to the Shamrock Boy's Ranch in California, a place of salvation for some and another step on the path to prison for many others. Ken made an instant connection with the kindly patriarch Bob Shamrock, who eventually adopted Ken and became his father in all but blood. Bob and his wife Dee Dee believed in the saving power of sport, emphasizing athletic competition and encouraging boys with disagreements to settle matters in carefully refereed backyard boxing matches. Ken Shamrock embraced the family ethos, becoming a star football player and victor in three tough man boxing tournaments.[127] He briefly played college football before leaving school with poor grades.

With no education and few talents, Shamrock's future appeared bleak. He worked as a bouncer in several rough bars, but made little money in a job that offered no hope of advancement. Shamrock tried life on the professional wrestling circuit, but the fixed routines turned off the young man who considered himself a serious athlete and thought theatrics beneath him. He heard that a promoter was holding auditions in Tampa, Florida, looking for Americans willing to compete in a Japanese fighting circuit more interested in athleticism than acting and offering good wages for anyone who could make the cut. Shamrock decided to try it. After a grueling tryout, which included 500 squats and wrestling bouts with several opponents in quick succession, the scout told Shamrock to pack his bags.[128]

In Japan, Shamrock quickly became a star, fighting in Japanese professional wrestling matches and in authentic style-on-style match-ups. When he faced professional kickboxer Don Nielsen in 1992, he needed only 45 seconds to shoot in, take Nielsen to the mat, and twist the kickboxer's leg until he conceded defeat.[129] The victory caught the eye of promoters for the Pancrase organization, an emerging promotion that sponsored authentic fights based on the rules of Japanese professional wrestling. Pancrase fighters did not wear gloves and could win by knockout or submission. Competitors were allowed to wrestle, kick, and deliver open-handed strikes to the head and close-fisted blows to the body.[130] Shamrock did well in the new promotion, attracting attention from Asian fans and American promoters planning a similar event in the United States.

The story of mixed martial arts in America is largely the story of confluent evolution. By 1993, the efforts of several men, including Shamrock, coming from very different directions collided in the creation of America's first mixed martial arts promotion, the Ultimate Fighting Championship.

The Gracies in California continued building their reputation in the early 1990s with the help of an American businessman. While serving with the U.S. Marines during the conflict in Vietnam, Art Davie witnessed an "anything goes" fight between a kickboxer and a wrestler in Thailand, which he found fascinating and never forgot. By the early 1990s, his fatigues collected dust as he enjoyed a career as a prominent advertising executive in California, but the long-remembered scene made him susceptible to the Gracie spell.[131] Davie enjoyed the Gracies in Action videos and became a disciple of the Brazilian clan, but suggested a new marketing approach. With Rorion Gracie's hesitant permission, he began a direct mailing campaign to sell the videos, a clever move that spread the family's glory and netted a tidy profit of $100,000.[132] Davie's successful marketing grabbed the Gracies' attention and convinced them to take his ideas very seriously. Davie suggested the time was right for the next step, a live tournament in the model of the bout he witnessed many years ago in Thailand.[133] The concept bore a striking similarity to *Herois do Ringue*, the series booted off Brazilian television decades ago, and was entirely consistent with the Gracie approach to fighting. The Gracies quickly agreed, convinced that Brazilian jujitsu was the ultimate fighting art and that the tournament, much like the Gracies in Action videos, would demonstrate their superiority.[134]

In agreement on the basic concept, Davie and the Gracies began making serious plans. They convinced another Gracie student, John Milius—a Hollywood insider and larger-than-life character who provided the inspiration for John Goodman's character Walter Sobachak in *The Big Lebowski* and is best known for his work on *Conan the Barbarian*—to help with production.[135] The team quickly agreed on an "anything goes" single-elimination tournament, but they disagreed on the arena. Davie wanted a boxing ring surrounded by a moat filled with alligators. Milius, inspired by the pankrationists of ancient Greece, suggested the competitors fight in a pit. Davie later revealed in an interview that other ideas included a Plexiglas-enclosed ring, which was rejected since it would reflect light and make it difficult to film, and a ring surrounded by various combinations of moats, sharks, alligators, and electric fences. They even pondered the feasibility of a Mad Max–style "thunder dome" suspended from the ceiling. Finally, Rorion and Milius agreed on an eight-sided mat surrounded by a five-foot-tall chain-link fence, which was both practical and distinctive; they called their invention the octagon.[136] Officially, there were no rules. Rorion Gracie later revealed that only two techniques were even discouraged. The organizers informed fighters that if they bit or gouged an opponent, they would have to pay their victim $1,000, but the fight would continue.[137] The promoters did not require the padded gloves that had long distinguished scientific exhibitions from brawls. The group sold the idea to Robert Meyorwitz, a Manhattan-based pioneer in the emerging pay-per-view television market. Davie, Meyorwitz, and Rorion Gracie formed the Semaphore Entertainment Group (SEG) to run the event. They called the event "The War of the Worlds," but later changed it to "The Ultimate Fighting Championship." The organizers understood that their event sat somewhere between sport and felony, so they decided to host the event in Colorado, which had no boxing commission and therefore lacked at least one level of bureaucracy that might interfere with their plans.[138] SEG hired Alberto Barretto, the Brazilian jujitsu fighter who became famous in 1959 when he broke his opponent's arm on television, to referee the event.[139] They also contracted with a team of analysts and announcers, which included Bill Wallace, a retired kickboxing champion; Kathy Long, an active kickboxing champion; and Jim Brown, a retired football player.[140]

Now the conspirators just needed fighters. Rickson Gracie wanted to represent his family. Hardened by years of vale tudo fights in Brazil and a lifetime of training, he was probably the most dangerous Gracie, but Rorion chose Rickson's much smaller and much younger brother Royce. In an interview Rorion revealed that he chose Royce because he was small and youthful, which made him look unintimidating—a fact that would make his victory an even greater triumph for the family and their system.[141] The promotion signed on seven other fighters culled from their extensive contacts within the global fighting scene, including Gerard Gordeau, a savate fighter (a style of kickboxing popular primarily in France) who traveled from his home in Holland for the event; Kevin Rosier, a three-time World Karate Association champion; and Zane Grey, a kenpo karate fighter. Art Jimmerson, the International Boxing Federation's North American champion in the cruiserweight division, represented the sweet science. Patrick Smith, a two-time winner of the bare-knuckle karate Sabaki challenge, brought a very different approach to punches. Teli Tuli, a professional sumo wrestler on the Japanese circuit and former boxer, brought a unique combination of skills to Denver. Ken Shamrock, regarded with good reason by observers as Gracie's most dangerous opponent, rounded out the tournament.[142] The promoters also signed on two alternate fighters—Jason Delucia, a Kung Fu expert who had lost a challenge fight to Rickson Gracie the previous year, and Trent Jenkins, a kenpo karate stylist—in case anyone dropped out of the tournament.[143]

On November 12, 1993, the event began. Meyorwitz sat in nervous anticipation. No one had ever put on an event quite like this in America, and he pondered all the ways it could go horribly wrong.[144] In the first fight of the evening, the savate champion Gerard Gordeau faced professional sumo wrestler Telia Tuli. The wrestler danced into the ring wearing nothing but a floral Hawaiian skirt. He danced playfully, waiting for the pale-skinned, tattooed, shaved-head Gordeau to enter. When the bell sounded and the fight began, the combatants briefly circled before Tulia charged and attempted to tackle his adversary. Gordeau sidestepped the assault and kicked Tulia in the face, sending a tooth flying into the crowd. The referee stepped in and stopped the fight. From the sidelines, Rorion Gracie screamed with rage at the referee. There were no rules and certainly no provision for a referee stoppage. Rorion yelled for Gordeau to keep kicking Tulia in the face.[145] In spite of pleas from the sidelines, Baretto ended the fight, making up his own rules and declaring Gordeau the winner.[146] At the commentator's table, Bill Wallace joked to Kathy Long that he was going to go find the tooth and sell it to the tooth fairy.[147]

In spite of the humor and rule confusion, the show continued. Consistent with the Rorion's expectations, Royce defeated all three of his opponents with relative ease. He distracted Jimmerson with leg kicks before shooting in and taking the boxer to the mat, where the pugilist promptly surrendered.[148] Shamrock fared somewhat better, briefly putting Gracie in a difficult position, before the Brazilian took Shamrock's back and choked him into submission.[149] In the tournament's final and championship bout, Gracie easily defeated Gordeau, choking him out and forcing his surrender. The broadcast ended with a triumphant Royce Gracie wearing a championship medal as Bill Wallace thanked the audience for watching.[150]

The first UFC event proved an important success for the emerging mixed martial arts community in America. It drew 86,895 pay-per-view buys—an impressive figure that demonstrated the popular appeal and financial viability

V. The Birth of Mixed Martial Arts, 1981 to the Present   217

Royce Gracie, the first winner of the Ultimate Fighting Championship, demonstrates a choke hold on a student while other pupils look on. Photograph produced on August 21, 2010. Courtesy of Peter Gordon and Wikimedia Commons. Published under a Creative Commons License.

of mixed martial arts in the United States.[151] Going into the event, many observers suspected that the UFC was nothing more than professional wrestling with amateur actors and fixed fights.[152] That suspicion died as Tuli's tooth flew into the stands.[153] Bill Wallace suggested that Royce benefited from his family's role in creating the event, which included padded mats and mostly lackluster grapplers. These elements, he said, helped Royce win, and ensured the promotion served as an advertisement for the Gracies.[154] Even as he criticized the event, Wallace confirmed that the fights were authentic and that Gracie possessed enormous talent.[155] Whatever else the event might have been, it was clearly real, even if, as Wallace suggested, the tournament was somewhat contrived. Perhaps no voice better summarized the evening's lesson than ringside commentator Jim Brown, who observed, "What we have learned here is that fighting is not what we thought it was."[156]

The events of November 12, 1993, accelerated a process that was changing how Americans thought about fights. It convinced many observers that boxing champions and karate black belts stood no chance against a skilled grappler, a fact that had been noted by many experts at least since Ali agreed to face Inoki in 1976.¹⁵⁷ It fueled a global revolution in fight sports, spawning imitators around the world.¹⁵⁸ Boxing, though diminished, remained America's favorite fight sport and its biggest star in decades attempted a comeback in 1995.

Mike Tyson attempted to change his life while in prison. He was raised Catholic, but became a Baptist in a widely publicized 1988 ceremony conducted by Jesse Jackson. Tyson later confessed in an interview that the conversion was nothing more than a publicity stunt orchestrated by his promoter, Don King.¹⁵⁹ While in prison for rape, the former champion encountered a new religion. From 1942 to 1946, Elijah Muhammad had served a sentence for draft evasion and took the opportunity to spread his faith among his fellow prisoners.¹⁶⁰ Many black prisoners found the Nation of Islam's vocal opposition to racism in America very appealing.¹⁶¹ Malcolm X became one of the most famous converts of the Islamic presence in American prisons, and subsequently became an outspoken critic of white power.¹⁶² Tyson, who maintained his innocence and attributed his conviction to a racist legal system, may have found the Nation of Islam's opposition to white racism attractive.¹⁶³ While in prison, he began taking classes in the faith and converted before his release. Tyson told interviewers that he converted to Islam because he sought redemption, admitting that he was no angel, but professing a desire to become a better man.¹⁶⁴

When women's groups opposed plans to welcome Tyson back to Harlem, the Reverend Al Sharpton denounced them as not speaking for the black community.¹⁶⁵ A black female writer for the *Village Voice* shot back at Sharpton, arguing that his support of Tyson was proof that many black men were happy to sacrifice women if they could preserve a male hero in the bargain.¹⁶⁶ In an effort to demonstrate the sincerity of his conversion, the former prisoner gave hundreds of thousands of dollars to children's charities, and the public largely accepted his dedication to a new life at face value.¹⁶⁷ When Muhammad Ali, the last great boxing champion, announced his support for and conversion to Islam, he encountered resentment from many Americans.¹⁶⁸ Tyson received no such condemnations. Critics hated him because they saw him a dangerous rapist, not because of his religion.¹⁶⁹

The very different responses to Tyson's and Ali's conversions indicated how much America and boxing had changed in just a few years. Ali converted at a time of extraordinary conflict in the United States. These conflicts included the revolt of the black athlete, the conflict in Vietnam, struggles over civil rights, and the Cold War.¹⁷⁰ Many Americans took Ali very seriously not just as a fighter, but as an iconic masculine role model; at the time, the heavyweight boxing champion was still considered the Emperor of Masculin-

V. The Birth of Mixed Martial Arts, 1981 to the Present   219

ity.[171] When Tyson converted, there was no comparable revolt of black athletes to lead and no hugely unpopular war to oppose. While the civil rights movement continued to grind forward, it was increasingly pushed to the periphery of American life. Partly as a result of these broader shifts that meant Tyson could not readily identify himself with larger movements, he was never an iconic figure outside of the boxing world like Ali. Tyson considered himself a masculine icon in the model of Ali, but most Americans never accepted the idea.[172] Even men who admired Tyson's skills in the ring often ridiculed his love of pigeons, falsetto voice, inability to accept defeat gracefully, and troubled relationships with women.[173] Tyson was many things in the eyes of American men, but he was certainly not the Emperor of Masculinity.

The differences in the public reactions to the conversion experiences to Ali and Tyson also provide an example of the greater, although certainly imperfect, American tendency toward religious toleration of Muslims in the 1980s and 1990s. During this period, the Nation of Islam continued to suggest black nationalist solutions to America's problems, but its pleas became less urgent, less confrontational, and therefore less divisive in an America less willing to accept racial discrimination against racial minorities.[174] Tyson also benefited from a demographic shift. The Muslim population in the United States increased significantly from 1960 to 1990.[175] By 1990, more than half a million Americans considered themselves Muslims, making them the third-largest faith in America, outnumbered only by Jews and Christians.[176] New immigrants and American-born Muslims built hundreds of schools and expanded outreach programs during the decade.[177] Muslims also gained unprecedented official acceptance during the 1990s. In 1991, the African American Muslim leader Siraj Wahhaj became the first Muslim to lead a prayer to begin a session of the U.S. House of Representatives.[178] The shift toward greater toleration was hardly limited to Muslims. A combination of the civil rights movement, Supreme Court decisions, legislative acts, and demographic shifts made America a scene of unprecedented religious toleration by the 1990s.[179]

Richard Hoffer, writing for *Sports Illustrated*, argued that Tyson's fall and possible redemption made him a more interesting fighter. He was no longer a simple man with extraordinary talents; he was a complicated, troubled, great athlete struggling somewhere between occasional flashes of superhuman power that propelled him into the stratosphere and failings that pulled him back to the dirt.[180] Hoffer, like many other Americans, was unsure what might happen when Tyson returned to the ring, but no one wanted to miss the show.[181] Ali had claimed that the religion of peace empowered him in the ring.[182] Tyson converted to the same religion at a time when that community boasted unprecedented numbers and acceptance in America. Only time would tell if Tyson would obtain the same benefits as Ali from his newfound faith and find pugilistic redemption to go along with his spiritual rejuvenation.

Once a free man, Tyson began his quest to regain his championship. He first agreed to take on Peter McNeely, a Boston journeyman boxer. Experts argued that McNeely stood absolutely no chance against Tyson, even going so far as to suggest the bout was nothing more than fraud.[183] Others argued that the fight would not be fixed in the conventional sense of paying a fighter to throw the bout, because boxing promoters had long ago progressed beyond such simple methods and learned instead to ensure an outcome by placing ferocious-looking incompetents into fights against highly skilled competitors.[184] In spite of the lackluster predictions, the fans were interested. Almost 17,000 fans packed into the MGM Grand in Las Vegas and viewers at home paid $90 million to see it on pay per view, a record-breaking total.[185] Truth proved stranger than prediction. Tyson battered and beat McNeely for 89 seconds before McNeely's manager Vinny Vecchione mysteriously wandered into the ring; the referee responded by disqualifying McNeely.[186] The posh, celebrity-studded crowd booed and shouted, hissing their disapproval.[187] Numerous sportswriters called the whole thing a farce, comparing it to professional wrestling, and suggesting Tyson's great comeback bout was another tragedy for boxing.[188]

The former champion next fought Buster Mathis, Jr., a match-up that generated more scorn. Once again, the experts agreed that Tyson was fighting an opponent with no chance at victory.[189] One sportswriter, noting that Mathis weighed in at 224 pounds, declared it a good weight for a human sacrifice.[190] Tyson knocked out Mathias in the third round, in a bout one journalist summarized as a comical mismatch between a convicted rapist and an overweight amateur, promoted by con artists.[191]

Tyson, having padded his record with two disappointing wins, then began his title shots. Fans and sportswriters gave him somewhat higher marks for his March 1996 knockout victory over the British fighter Frank Bruno, which earned Tyson the World Boxing Council heavyweight title.[192] Although Tyson was a champion once again, his victory led to a defeat outside the ring. Tyson chose to fight Bruce Seldon, holder of the World Boxing Association title, rather than the leading WBC contender, Lennox Lewis. This move angered WBC officials as well as Lewis, and the entire sordid mess ended up in court, where a judge demanded Tyson fight Lewis. Tyson then tried to buy his way out of the conflict with a payment to Lewis.[193] Negotiations fell apart and Tyson went ahead with his fight against Seldon, losing his WBC title outside of the ring, in exchange for a chance to win the WBA title inside the arena.[194] Fans and sportswriters once again expressed disgust at the backroom politics that had come to characterize the not-so-sweet science.[195] Tyson defeated Seldon with a first-round knockout, winning the WBA title, but the fans were unimpressed. The crowd booed, hissed, and then joined together for a rousing chant that the fight was fixed.[196] Journalists and fans offered up Tyson and his comeback tour as another example of the corruption and fraud inexorably tied up in boxing.[197] Even as many Americans rejected boxing when they saw through its deceptions, however, they condemned a new sport because they accepted the sport's illusions.

The owners of the Ultimate Fighting Championship intentionally promoted the sport as a dangerous activity, hoping to attract fans with the promise of greater and more authentic violence. UFC executives joked about the possibility of death in the ring to reporters.[198] Promoters billed the UFC as a blood sport and bragged about the injuries combatants suffered in the cage.[199] Promoters sold videos with the tagline "There Are No Rules."[200] A press release for the second UFC event informed the public that fights would end only by surrender, doctor's intervention, knockout, or death.[201] The back cover of the home video version of the second UFC event held in 1994 described the new sport as an authentic fight for survival in which anything was possible. During a fight in Detroit, a UFC ringside commentator told viewers that a fighter's chokehold could rip his opponent's head from his shoulders.[202] Fighters also helped perpetuate the popular perception of the UFC as a life-or-death struggle. Early UFC champion Royce Gracie acknowledged that mixed martial arts fans often tuned in hoping to see the promised carnage.[203] The danger and mayhem, however, were largely an illusion.

The UFC initially differentiated itself from other fight sports by loudly proclaiming its embrace of unrestrained violence and no-rules fights, but violence in the Ultimate Fighting Championship always existed with boundaries. In the UFC's very first fight, the referee stopped the bout after a competitor lost a tooth and received minor cuts to his face.[204] The rules did not allow the referee to end the fight, but he did anyway, thereby ensuring that the unfortunate sumo wrestler escaped the octagon with only minor injuries. Bill Wallace, an early UFC commentator and famed kickboxer, understood the informal nature of the UFC's rules and exposed them to the readers of *Black Belt* magazine. He pointed out that while not considered a rule, the fights all took place within a carefully designed arena, which included a padded floor. The padded surface favored grapplers, like the Gracies, over kickboxers like him, and made ferocious-looking takedowns far less damaging.[205]

On at least one occasion, fighters limited the violence with a mutual agreement. At the fourth UFC event, jujitsu expert Jason Fairn and the kickboxer Guy Mezger agreed to refrain from hair pulling, elbow strikes, and head butts—an agreement they abided by in their bout.[206] A *Black Belt* reader from California made similar observations, noting that fights were limited to one-on-one battles and that competitors came into the octagon with a personal honor code that prevented them from resorting to nastier tactics such as punches to the throat and grabbing the testicles, which were perfectly legal under the early UFC's rules.[207] The acclaimed wrestler Dan Severn pinned Royce Gracie to the floor of the octagon in a bout, but then refrained from unleashing the full range of violence available within the UFC's rules. He later explained that he struggled more with his own conscience than with Gracie.[208] Severn was a lifelong athlete, a product of the top-ranked wrestling program at Arizona State University. He could not bring himself to break out of his own internal understanding of a fight and punch Gracie in the throat—a technique legal in the octagon, but repellent to his personal morality.[209] Severn's experience demonstrates that informal rules often limited the sport's violence.

The Ultimate Fighting Championship fit within a broader pattern of shifts in the popular culture during the 1990s. In 1988, the Writers Guild went on strike, which threw television networks into a mad scramble and led to greater reliance on reality shows, such as *Cops*, which substituted contrived reality for crafted scripts and high production values.[210] Audiences found reality shows appealing primarily because they provided authenticity and information.[211] The UFC likewise promised its fans authenticity and knowledge, the same mix that attracted fans to MTV's *The Real World* and *Cops*. Some early promoters of mixed martial arts preferred the terms "reality combat" and "reality fighting" as names for the new sport.[212] Perhaps not surprisingly, then, one journalist attributed the UFC's early success to the realism craze of the 1990s.[213]

Perhaps nothing better demonstrated the desire of many American men for realism than a work of popular fiction. *Fight Club* was an award-winning novel published in 1996 by Chuck Palahniuk. Following the book's success, 20th Century–Fox created a movie adaptation starring Edward Norton and Brad Pitt, which quickly became a hugely popular cult classic. The work focuses on an unnamed narrator who becomes dissatisfied with his life as a white-collar corporate worker, concluding that the consumer goods he had long sought to own simply ended up owning him. He eventually finds spiritual redemption in bare-knuckle, "anything goes" fights, explaining, "I don't want to die without a few scars."[214] The author's attempt to save his soul with violence is consistent with the path traveled by many men, dating back to prehistory. Film critic Roger Ebert astutely noted that the movie was a scornful rejection of violence, but he also observed that viewers typically enjoyed the action and failed to grasp the lesson. He predicted that far more men would leave the movie and get into fights than would discuss the underlying philosophy.[215] Observers and fans often connected the new sport of mixed martial arts and *Fight Club*. An article on mixed martial arts published by *Slate* was titled "Fight Clubbed" and argued that the new sport was essentially a real-life version of the film.[216]

The mix of violence and reality was mostly a marketing gimmick, yet a fairly successful one for the Ultimate Fighting Championship. At the first UFC event, commentator Jim Brown concluded that mixed martial arts demonstrated that real fights were often surprising, and one of the greatest surprises was the dullness of many encounters.[217] A journalist who attended an early event told his readers that while the idea of no-holds-barred fights seemed thrilling, the reality was often quite boring.[218]

The fights were mostly bare knuckle, which gave the appearance of greater danger, but bare fists were actually far less likely to cause the serious head injuries that often killed boxers, a fact well understood by the UFC's organizers.[219] No fighter lost his life or even suffered a serious injury in the octagon. A few bouts ended in impressive-looking knockouts and others concluded when the referee stepped in, but most went to the ground, where they eventually ended when a combatant surrendered to a painful, but never lethal submission hold.[220] Ken Shamrock and rival wrestler turned mixed martial artist Dan Severn grappled inconclusively in Detroit, where the crowd booed the fighters.[221] When fans failed to pack the seats at a UFC event, promoters hired actors to protest the violence and drum up crowds.[222] The UFC's chief medical advisor, former boxing physician Dr. Richard Istrico, revealed that mixed martial artists suffered far less brain damage than boxers did.[223] These facts put UFC executives in the awkwardly contradictory position of selling their product with slogans of unrestrained violence and then defending themselves by pointing out that it was all a show. When pressed for details, SEG executive Meyrowitz confirmed Istrico's analysis that the danger was mostly a marketing gimmick and that the sport was actually quite safe.[224]

When the UFC failed to deliver on its promises of bloody mayhem, some fans got bored, resulting in mediocre attendance at some events.[225] Other fans saw through the illusions, realizing that the UFC was not exactly what the promoters promised, but deciding it still made for a good show. The UFC's popularity rose dramatically, with viewership increasing by more than 350 percent during the promotion's first two years.[226] The new sport provided authentic fights as an appealing alternative to the corruption of boxing and the over-the-top theatrics of professional wrestling.[227]

Ironically, while the early UFC promoters played up the violence in an effort to attract fans who often saw through their marketing, politicians were far more gullible, or at least more inclined to play dumb. Official condemnation of the burgeoning sport began before organizers even bolted the octagon together. American politicians were taking aim at violent media as the 1990s began. In the first year of the decade, Congress passed the Television Violence Act, which aimed to limit the violent content on television that some studies had indicated damaged children.[228] Congress followed up this legislation with threats to regulate violent video games, like *Mortal Kombat*, in 1993.[229] Politicians soon expanded their crusade against an event that proudly promised to stream unrestrained violence directly into American living rooms.[230] When the mayor of Denver saw a video of UFC bouts, he found the show repulsive and began working to ensure the sport never again came to his city.[231]

At the federal level, U.S. Senators Ben Nighthorse Campbell, Roy Romer, Nolbert Chavez, and John McCain all became vocal opponents of the new sport they claimed was a street fight.[232] When Larry King interviewed McCain, the senator enumerated his objections, which all essentially came down to the new sport's rejection of traditional boundaries of violence. These UFC elements included the use of knee and elbow strikes; use of over-the-top language, such as the reference to lethal punches; the lack of governmental regulation; the use of bare-knuckle punches; and the personal revulsion professional boxers and members of the general public felt when they viewed video clips of the events.[233] When a reporter for *Slate* pressed the senator to explain why he seemed to persecute mixed martial artists with an almost religious vigor, he exploded with rage, arguing that if the reporter did not share his visceral revulsion, they had nothing more to discuss.[234] McCain became the UFC's most powerful opponent, sending personal letters to the governor of every state urging these leaders to take whatever steps they could to ensure mixed martial arts events did not take place in their states.[235] His efforts helped convince lawmakers in several states to ban mixed martial arts.[236] Quickly running out of possible scenes for a fight, the UFC fled to areas with few regulations and more welcoming attitudes, such as Alabama.[237]

Elliot Gorn used his position as the highly regarded author of *The Manly Art* to condemn mixed martial arts and its esthetic of violence, falling for the same marketing gimmicks that fooled many politicians.[238] The danger of the octagon that he cited was an illusion, but one that attracted persecution and condemnation. By comparison, far nastier and far more real things took place in the boxing ring.

Death in the arena was a marketing ploy for mixed martial artists, but a tragic reality for boxing. During the 1990s, 11 fighters died in boxing rings across the world, including six in the United States.[239] When the promising featherweight Jimmy Garcia died as a result of the injuries he suffered fighting at Caesar's Place, *Sports Illustrated* memorialized the loss, referred to boxing as a cruel sport, and argued that everyone who enjoyed boxing should stand at the foot of Garcia's hospital bed and view the awful cost.[240] Fifteen days after an Atlantic City bout, Stephan Johnson, who repeatedly ignored his mother's pleas to end his boxing career, died because of his injuries.[241] Dylan Baker, a 19-year-old amateur pugilist, died the day after he was knocked unconscious in a Golden Gloves tournament in spite of the fact that he was wearing protective head gear.[242] The deaths, corruption, and brutality of the ring led calls to outlaw boxing.

Boxing deaths may have made the papers, but Mike Tyson's special blend of brutality shocked even the most callous observers. Tyson did not keep the WBA crown for long. On November 11, 1997, he lost the title to Evander Holyfield in an 11-round slugfest that ended with Tyson beaten and battered.[243] Tyson complained that Holyfield delivered illegal head butts, but the referee ruled it accidental contact.[244] They met for a rematch on June 28, 1997. Holyfield began the fight by once again demonstrating his superiority to Tyson. Then things got interesting. Tyson "chomped down on Holyfield's right ear, taking off about a one-inch chunk, and spit it onto the canvas."[245] After getting approval from the ringside physician, the referee allowed the bout to continue, but warned Tyson to behave. Tyson promptly bit Holyfield's left ear, angering the referee, who promptly disqualified Tyson.[246] The ruling angered Tyson, who charged Holyfield until police officers entered the ring and restrained him. The amputated portion of Holyfield's ear was eventually located. The Nevada State Athletic Commission revoked Tyson's license and fined him $3 million, a penalty many fans considered far too lenient.[247] Journalists argued that Tyson's bite provided another black eye for boxing. Critics listed it as just one more example of the brutality that characterized boxing and proved it should be outlawed.[248]

In spite of the fact that the UFC's violence was largely an illusion and boxing's was all too real, mixed martial arts received far greater criticism from powerful enemies. Indeed, by the end of the 1990s, the UFC was in serious trouble. Many fans loved mixed martial arts, but powerful enemies, primarily Senator John McCain, worked to outlaw the new sport. In 1997, McCain became chairman of the Senate's Commerce Committee, which, among other things, regulated cable television. He immediately used his influence to pressure cable providers to stop carrying UFC broadcasts.[249] Fans of the UFC argued that McCain was a corrupt politician who served boxing promoters rather than his constituents.[250] Most of the programmers bowed to the pressure, and the number of American homes with access to UFC live broadcasts dropped from roughly 24 million to fewer than 12 million.[251] The assault resulted in greatly diminished pay-per-view sales, which dropped from highs of around 300,000 buys per show to barely 15,000 per show.[252] The UFC also encountered problems in finding locations willing to host live shows. New York, long a home of boxing, outlawed mixed martial arts events in the state in 1997.[253] In 1998, the Ontario Athletic Commission rejected the UFC's attempts to hold an event in the province.[254]

With so many doors slamming in their faces, the UFC promoters looked for windows. They began offering access to their shows over the Internet to bypass the cable companies.[255] The outlaw sport also began reaching out to regulators and getting the approval of some athletic commissions to hold events.[256] The California Athletic Commission drew up regulations to license mixed martial arts in the state, including a set of rules that eventually became the unified standards for the sport, but the state legislature rejected the commission's work and refused to authorize any mixed martial arts events.[257] SEG's campaign to win over politicians nearly bankrupted the company but led to only limited recognition of the sport.[258]

Politicians assaulted UFC from the top, while at the same time potential fighters and fans flourished from below. All popular sports require a large pool of amateur players and enthusiasts to provide fans and participants. When wrestling at militia musters and county fairs provided a rite of passage for farmers, wrestling dominated the American sporting scene. As the nation urbanized and millions of men became pugilists during World War I, boxing began to dominate. Their sons and grandsons took up Asian-style arts and ended scholastic boxing programs out of fear of corruption and death in the ring. Diminishing numbers of boxers set off a domino effect that resulted in fewer men choosing to become boxing coaches, which in turn made it more difficult for aspiring pugilists to find help in becoming a good boxer.[259] Collegiate wrestling programs faced very different challenges. In the 1990s, because of gender discrimination lawsuits, colleges began eliminating less popular men's teams, such as wrestling, and reallocating funds to women's sports.[260] Some wrestling coaches wisely responded by welcoming women onto their teams, and the infusion of female participation saved programs while providing women with their own touch of that saving barbarism.[261] Wrestlers entered mixed martial arts for many reasons, including a desire to demonstrate the effectiveness of their art.[262] As boxing programs diminished and wrestling programs faced new challenges, Asian-style martial arts became more common.

V. The Birth of Mixed Martial Arts, 1981 to the Present

By the dawn of the 21st century, only 4,084,000 Americans participated in boxing, but 6,161,000 engaged in martial arts. By 2007, the gulf had widened even further, with only 2,279,000 Americans boxing, 6,885,000 engaging in martial arts, and 3,313,000 wrestling.[263] Boxing drew mostly from boxing programs, but mixed martial arts welcomed fans, fighters, and promoters from every category. The new sport's talent pool expanded further with the American military's endorsement. In 1997, U.S. Army Ranger Lieutenant Colonel Mike Ferriter became hooked on the new sport and pioneered the creation of a new hand-to-hand combat program that incorporated lessons learned in mixed martial arts competition.[264] The large pool of possibilities gave birth to some very important actualities for the new sport.

Dana White ranks as one of the most crucial figures in the history of mixed martial arts, as a figure halfway between P.T. Barnum and His Fistic Highness John L. Sullivan. He was born in 1969 to a single mother who moved the family from Massachusetts to Las Vegas when White was still a child. His mother encouraged her son to do well in school, but he demonstrated interest

Two U.S. Army soldiers compete in a combatives tournament while spectators cheer them on at Aberdeen Proving Grounds, Maryland, on February 3, 2007. U.S. Army Photograph by Pvt. 1st Class Tiffany Dusterhoft produced February 3, 2007 (National Archives at College Park—Still Pictures [RD-DC-S], Record Group 330: Records of the Office of the Secretary of Defense, 1921–2008).

in little except mouthing off to his teachers and boxing.²⁶⁵ After a childhood split between his grandparent's home in Maine and his mother's residence in Las Vegas, White grew into a promising amateur boxer, fight promoter, and fitness club owner.²⁶⁶ The UFC caught White's eye not long after it held its first event. He enrolled in Brazilian jujitsu classes in Las Vegas and became an avid student. In jujitsu class, White met several up-and-coming UFC fighters, including Chuck Liddell and Tito Ortiz, and he became their manager.²⁶⁷

Now an established member of the American mixed martial arts community, White heard that the UFC might be up for sale. He quickly took the news to the Fertitta brothers, billionaires with strong ties to the city's gaming industry whom he knew from the city's boxing and jujitsu scenes, and made a bold offer. If they bought the UFC, White would get 10 percent of the company and run the daily operations as the company's president.²⁶⁸ The Fertittas agreed, bought out SEG for $3 million, and founded a new company, called Zuffa (*Zuffa* is an Italian word meaning "fight"), to run the UFC.²⁶⁹ Consistent with the new company's origins on the jujitsu mats, the brothers agreed that if they could not come to an agreement by any other means, the decision would go to the winner of a Brazilian jujitsu bout.²⁷⁰

Zuffa, with White at the lead, quickly implemented an aggressive strategy to save the UFC. White's primary goals were to expand the UFC's television presence and to acquire official approval from athletic commissions, particularly in Nevada. Regulators in New Jersey, already beginning to look into the possibility of regulating mixed martial arts before Zuffa took over, began sanctioning mixed martial arts events in 2001.²⁷¹ New Jersey welcomed the UFC at least in part in an effort to replace the decreased state income that had resulted from a decline in revenue-generating boxing events.²⁷² Lorenzo Fertitta, a former member

Dana White, the president of the Ultimate Fighting Championship. Photographed on February 8, 2008 (courtesy of Justin Moore and Wikimedia Commons. Published under a Creative Commons License).

of the Nevada Athletic Commission, used his personal friendships to convince the commission to license the UFC in Nevada.[273] White negotiated deals with Fox Television, convincing the network to broadcast hour-long UFC highlight reels and begin coverage of the sport.[274] The new management also got UFC back onto all of the major pay-per-view networks, leading to an impressive 150,000 buys for UFC 40, a 2002 event held in the MGM Grand casino in Las Vegas.[275] The event also broke ground as the first UFC event broadcast live in Australia.[276]

White also changed the UFC's marketing approach. The executives at SEG had sold the sport with slogans such as "There Are no Rules," which emphasized danger, lack of rules, and possible death. This put them in the awkward position of contradicting their own marketing campaigns to defend their enterprise. Zuffa approached things very differently and marketed the UFC as a serious sport, with authentic action conducted by world-class athletes, under the new slogan "As Real as It Gets."[277] White and the Fertittas often get credit for this turnaround, transforming a failing outlaw spectacle into a serious sport.[278] However, the reality is somewhat more subtle. The UFC was already attempting to obtain official acceptance, regulation, and mainstream appeal under SEG's ownership.[279] Zuffa was far more successful at this strategy, but White, for all his efforts, did not invent the idea.

Having succeeded in their plan, the new owners expected huge profits to start rolling in.[280] The Fertittas and White were disappointed when their business plan did not deliver success as quickly as they had hoped. In 2004, Zuffa reported that it had lost $34 million since buying the UFC.[281] Because the initial plan failed to bring in profits, White got desperate and tried something unprecedented in the history of mixed martial arts.

The Ultimate Fighting Championship always fit within the genre of reality television owing to its promises of knowledge and authenticity, but it took a more obvious move into the medium to ensure profitability for the UFC. Fight sports, and mixed martial arts in particular, always struggled with how to connect fighters and audiences. Early in the UFC's history, promotional materials, such as posters, identified fighters as practitioners of competing arts, promising bouts between styles, with little indication of race, nationality, or even actual people. Broadcasts paid considerable attention to the competitors' rival disciplines, providing short documentaries on the history and philosophy of the various martial arts represented in the event.[282] At the second UFC, ringside announcer Brian Kilmeade explained to viewers that these fighters represented not only themselves, but also their rival arts.[283]

The UFC owners decided to employ a new strategy: they would attempt to present fighters as individuals, not as faceless representatives of competing arts. White and the Fertitta brothers decided to make their own reality show based around two teams of fighters living in a house and training together. Each team would consist of a group of promising young fighters led by an experienced veteran, and the season would culminate with one fight between the two coaches, and another bout between the best fighters from each of the opposing teams.[284] The winning contender would earn a contract to fight in the UFC.[285] Zuffa picked crowd favorites, and friendly rivals, Chuck Liddell and Randy Couture to lead the rival teams in the crucial first season of the program they titled *The Ultimate Fighter*.[286] The executives reached out to experienced fighters, incorporating their ideas into the program's design. The show, they recognized, would provide a soap opera for the unapologetically masculine. Since none of the networks were interested in producing the show, the UFC organization produced it on its own and then attempted to sell it to anyone willing to air it.[287] It soon found a partner with Spike, a new cable channel that called itself "the first network for men."[288]

It was a brilliant idea, but once again Zuffa encountered problems. When the first teams of martial artists moved into the house to begin filming, a rival—and very similar—show based around boxing, *The Contender*, had already began broadcasting episodes.[289] When the contestants on *The Ultimate Fighter* discovered that Zuffa expected them to fight without additional compensation, while their rivals on *The Contender* received $25,000 for each bout, *The Ultimate Fighter* contestants began to grumble about refusing to fight unless they receive a comparable deal.[290] The Fertittas got wind of the trouble and demanded White fix the problem. The angered president ran down to the set, determined that the show must go on. He gathered the fighters and gave a speech that has provided the mixed martial arts community with an endlessly quoted summation of the sport's values.[291]

> Hey, boys. Gather around, guys. Get closer over here. To be honest with you, I didn't want to do this on camera but I am not happy right now. I haven't been happy all day. I have the feeling that some guys here don't want to fight. I don't know if that's true or not true or whatever, but I don't know what the fuck everybody thought they were coming here for. Does anybody here not want to fight? Did anybody come here thinking that they would not fight? No? Speak up. Anybody who came here thinking they weren't going to fight, speak up. Let me hear it.... Do you want to be a fucking fighter? ... That is my question and only you know that.... Anybody who says they don't—I don't fucking want you here and I'll throw you the fuck out of this gym so fucking fast your head'll spin. You'll be sitting over at the other fucking house playing checkers. It's up to you. I don't care. Cool? I love you all. That's why you're here. Every guy that's in this room right now, your coaches dig. They believe in you. I just want to make sure you all want to be fucking fighters. That's it. That's all I want to know. Cool?"[292]

V. The Birth of Mixed Martial Arts, 1981 to the Present   231

The brief monologue highlights the sport's core identity as an authentic contest between fighters. White demands to know, "Does anyone here not want to fight?" He asks the group, "Did anybody come here thinking that they would not fight?" White repeatedly asks them, "Do you want to be a fucking fighter?," claiming "That is my question" and "All I want to know," suggesting that nothing matters except a genuine desire to be a fighter. He urges the men to engage in personal reflection since "only you know" if "you want to be a fucking fighter." He explains that being a fighter is not about "cutting weight," "living in a fucking house," "fucking girls," or "signing autographs." He explains, "It is hard work" and "a job." He reassures them, "Every guy that's in this room right now, your coaches dig" and "They believe in you," in what appears to be an attempt to reassure the men that they are personally liked by their esteemed coaches. Finally he holds out the sport's rewards by claiming, "You have the opportunity to fucking make money, be famous, and do something for the sport here." Cynics might suggest that White was simply conning his employees into dropping their demands for higher wages, but the day after giving his speech, White announced bonuses for competitors who fought on camera, thereby ending any possibility of a fighter deserting the program over compensation.[293] The incident provides evidence of the sport's unique place as a product of twin desires for authenticity and profit. White was happy to pay fighters, as long as they were willing to fight for free.

The Ultimate Fighter provided Zuffa with a major financial and cultural success. It scored particularly well with males aged 18 to 34. Roughly 407,000 viewers in that demographic alone tuned in for the show, a figure only a few thousand viewers below ESPN's NFL pregame show.[294] It soundly defeated the rival boxing program *The Contender*, which suffered from low ratings, cancellation, allegations of corruption, and the tragic death of a contestant.[295] The much anticipated series finale drew a huge audience of 2.6 million viewers.[296] The executives at Spike were very happy with the success and signed contracts for additional seasons of the program and the creation of more UFC-based programming. These programs, in turn, exposed more Americans to mixed martial arts and promoted UFC pay-per-view fights.[297] No event benefited more from the publicity than UFC 52, the long-awaited event featuring a bout between the rival coaches on *The Ultimate Fighter*, Randy Couture and Chuck Liddell.

On April 16, 2005, fans assembled in the MGM Grand as well as around television and computer screens to witness the two rivals fight for the UFC's light heavyweight belt.[298] They made for a study in subtle contrasts. Randy Couture was the aging veteran with a lifetime of training in Greco-Roman wrestling perfected during his military service, in collegiate wrestling championships, and at Olympic training camps.[299] Liddell, Couture's junior by six years, was a more diverse mixed martial artist with collegiate wrestling experience, a black belt in karate, and numerous wins on the professional kickboxing circuit.[300] Couture's receding hairline contrasted sharply with Liddell's Mohawk and Asian-inspired tattoos. In the stands, 14,274 fans looked on, joined remotely by fans enjoying roughly 300,000 pay-per-view buys.[301] These impressive figures gave UFC 52 the largest live and remote audience in the UFC's history to date.[302] The media lavished unprecedented attention on the event, and on the rival combatants.[303] The fighters touched gloves and the fight began.

> Randy comes out throwing strikes and Chuck looks to counter punch. Randy lands an overhand right followed by a cross and he clinches with Chuck. Before Randy can start the dirty boxing, Liddell breaks free. McCarthy calls time as Couture looks like his eye was poked. The doctors check it out as you can imagine how Dana White was panicking. The doctor tells Big John that Randy is fine and able to continue. Fight RESUMES.... Chuck lands a left that stuns Couture, who charges at Chuck. Randy throws but lands nothing while Liddell lands a right and another right and RANDY COUTURE IS DOWN. Chuck pounces on him with a few more strikes as Big John McCarthy steps in and stops the fight. Liddell is pumped up and is one happy man. They cut to the crowd and Forrest Griffin looks stunned.
> Your winner and NEW UFC Light Heavyweight Champion is Chuck "The Iceman" Liddell via KO at 2:06 of the first round.[304]

The undercard also featured a classic welterweight bout between Matt Hughes and Frank Trigg, which many fans consider one of the greatest fights in the history of mixed martial arts.[305] A new generation of fans, lured in by the reality series, tuned in for UFC 52, loved what they saw, and became loyal fans.[306]

The events of April 16 provided a watershed moment in the history of mixed martial arts. The event ensured that the UFC did not die and provided a major step on the path to mainstream acceptance.[307] Zuffa is a private company that rarely discloses its financial data, but evidence indicates that this was the moment when American mixed martial arts became a profitable enterprise for the first time. The partnership of cable television, particularly Spike, and pay per view greatly improved the UFC's cash flow.[308] Rumors indicate that 2005 was the first year Zuffa stopped losing money.[309]

Johns Hopkins Medical center provided additional fuel for claims that mixed martial arts were safe in the first ever study comparing injury rates between the rival fight sports. In 2006, the researchers concluded that mixed martial artists experienced injury rates similar to those in other fight sports, with boxers and kickboxers experiencing far higher rates of knockouts and corresponding brain injuries.[310] Even John McCain eventually came around, admitting that while he was not a fan of mixed martial arts, he recognized that the sport had turned a corner, making significant progress; McCain then ended his crusade against the UFC.[311] Less than a year after the UFC 52 event, the *Wall Street Journal* declared the end of an era and the birth of a new one.

> For decades, Las Vegas was the biggest venue for boxing's prizefights, featuring ring stars like Evander Holyfield, Mike Tyson, Riddick Bowe, and Lennox Lewis. But with few new marquee names and younger spectators craving harder, faster action, heavyweight boxing's golden era has faded. The Ultimate Fighting Championship is muscling in with corporate sponsors, pay-per-view specials and star-flecked audiences.[312]

A recent scholarly study of the sport's audience provided an even more definitive conclusion.

> Mixed martial arts is an extremely popular combat sport, especially among young men, and appears to have eclipsed boxing and wrestling as the favored combat sport among this demographic.[313]

With American males aged 18 to 34 firmly in the new sport's embrace, the UFC began to expand. Dana White discussed his plans to extend the sport's reach with Pramit Mohapatra of the *Baltimore Sun*. White expressed his desire to continue making gains among older men, particularly boxing fans. White also explained his plans to expand the UFC into Europe, Canada, and Mexico with a series of events in those areas. When the interviewer asked him about the possibility of women fighting in the UFC, which he once claimed would never happen, White backed off his previous comments somewhat.[314] He explained that the sport encountered enough resistance eliminating the cultural bias against men engaging in mixed martial arts, and expressed hesitation in taking on the inevitable backlash against women engaging in the same sport. White admitted that he was not personally a fan of women fighting, but acknowledged that some female fighters were amazingly talented. The interviewer accepted that women would not enter the octagon anytime soon, but pressed White for a long-term prediction, and White admitted that women might become stars of the UFC at some point in the future.[315]

Other promoters gladly took up the opportunity White passed over. Strikeforce, a rival to the UFC, promoted mixed martial bouts between female competitors. In 2009, Christine Cyborg Santos defeated Gina Carano in a fast-paced brawl broadcast by Showtime that entertained a live audience of more than 13,000 and received approving commentary from *Sports*

Illustrated.[316] Eventually, even the UFC relented, and on February 23, 2013, former Marine Liz Carmouche was defeated by Rhonda Rousey, an Olympic medalist in judo, in the organization's first fight between women.[317]

Mixed martial arts enjoy a place at the table, but the debate is hardly resolved. Dana White continues to promote his sport with a constant stream of Twitter messages, interviews, and appearances on nationally broadcast news programs. A 2007 exchange on National Public Radio between the journalist Robert Siegel and White regarding the sport of mixed martial arts helps to illustrate the debate that still rages.

> SIEGEL: I've watched a video online of a bout, which ends with one fighter delivering, I think, eight or nine consecutive blows in the face to his opponent who is down on his back at that moment. And there's something about it—it doesn't say just a game. There's something about it that says come here for blood and for brutality.
> MR. WHITE: Well, that's how some people see it. The reality is, the reason you think that way is because we grew up with, you know, the John Wayne culture. Never hit a man when he's down. You know, in the John Wayne movies, he'd knock a guy down and instead of jumping on him and hitting him, he'd stand and back up and punch him again.
> SIEGEL: Yeah.
> MR. WHITE: You know, that's the society we come from. Most of these other countries out there, martial arts has been a part of their culture forever. And the reality is, you hit a man standing up with a lot more force than you can when the man is on the ground. We could sit here all day and debate on how safe this is or how unsafe that is; there really aren't very many sports out there that there aren't any deaths in. There's never been a death in the UFC. Polo can't say that there's never been death. You'd be surprised to hear how many kids die every year playing high school football.[318]

Siegel and White highlight the conflict at the heart of this book. These men are very similar individuals with a very different view of this fight sport. Both Siegel and White are middle-aged, English-speaking, white males born within a few miles of each other in New England. They share a culture. White refers to John Wayne as an icon of masculinity "we grew up with." In spite of their similarities, these men look at the same sport of mixed martial arts and see something very different. Robert Siegel looks at mixed martial arts and sees brutality; White looks at the same events and sees a sport. Both men came from the same culture, but White alone seems to embrace values from outside his childhood experiences. White compares the culture he shares with Siegel to the values of "these other countries," countries that White sees as worthy of imitation, but that Siegel does not wish to emulate. Siegel and White provide an example of a much larger debate playing out in sports bars,

V. The Birth of Mixed Martial Arts, 1981 to the Present

Edward Gonzalez, of Fight Club 29, delivers a powerful blow to Ed West during a mixed martial arts tournament held at Santa Ana High School in Orange County, California, July 26, 2008. Notice that Gonzalez is striking West even though West is on the ground. Striking a downed opponent is forbidden in boxing and many other fight sports, but is perfectly acceptable in mixed martial arts. Many Americans who are more familiar with the rules of boxing find this technique repulsive. This photograph was taken by Cpl. Nicole A. LaVine (courtesy of the United States Marine Corps).

living rooms, and gyms across the nation. In these debates, increasing numbers of Americans are taking White's side in the argument. Mixed martial arts events routinely attract more viewers than boxing and dominate the younger demographics, with very few viewers under 35 preferring boxing to mixed martial arts.[319]

This battle in the war for cultural dominance between boxing and mixed martial arts is only the most recent in a series of conflicts between fight sports. Nearly 130 years ago, Duffield Osborne urged men to seek "a saving touch of barbarism" in the ring, and many American men eagerly embraced a salvation found there. That search continues. A hundred years after Osborne spoke of violent salvation, Curry Kirkpatrick issued his own call, urging American men to embrace an unashamedly violent masculinity. The scene of that search has changed from grassy field to canvas ring to octagonal cage. Its spectator and participant populations expand, drawing in races and occasionally a gender previously excluded from American fight sports. The techniques change, incorporating methods from distant shores. The ring evolves, but it never dies. The ring can never die.

In 1910, Theodore Roosevelt gave a speech at the Sorbonne in Paris that serves as fitting end to this book. He told the assembled crowd, "It is not the critic who counts," but instead "the credit belongs to the man who is actually in the arena," the man who "at the best knows in the end triumph of high achievement, and who at the worst, if he fails at least fails while daring greatly." If this book has done anything worthwhile, it has paid homage to the men and women who enter the arena. It has traced the outline of that place, documenting its shifts and providing insights into how and why it changed over four centuries of American history. Fight sports have changed and will undoubtedly continue to evolve, but the fighters in the arena remain at the center. I hope I have given them the credit they so richly deserve.

Chapter Notes

Preface

1. Duffield Ossborne, "A Defense of Pugilism," *North American Review* 146, no. 377 (April 1888): 430–435, p. 435.
2. Ibid.
3. Curry Kirkpatrick, "Good Old Violence: It's as American as Apple Pie, the Flag and Jack Tatum," *Sports Illustrated* (January 5, 1987): 66.
4. Ibid.
5. Nancy Cheever, "The Uses and Gratifications of Viewing Mixed Martial Arts," *Journal of Sports Media* 4, no. 1 (Spring 2009): 25–53, p. 50.
6. "Advertisements," *North Carolina Gazette*, March 24, 1775; Thomas L. Altherr, Larry K. Menna, George B. Kirsch, Gerald R. Gems, Steven A. Riess, and Douglas Owen Baldwin. "A Kentucky Fight," *Origins of Modern Sports*, Vol. 2 of *Sports in North America: A Documentary History* (Gulf Breeze, FL: Academic International Press, 1992), 174.
7. Robert Walsh, *An Appeal from the Judgments of Great Britain Respecting the United States of America, Part First* (Philadelphia: Mitchell, Ames, and White, 1819), 469; "Barbarism no. II" *Religious Remembrancer* (June 21, 1817).
8. Fredrick Palmer, "Jujitsu and Damurizu," *Munsey's Magazine* 27, no. 4 (July 1902): 584–587, p. 586.
9. Elliott J. Gorn, *The Manly Art: Bare-Knuckle Prize Fighting in America* (Ithaca, NY: Cornell University Press, 2010), 66.
10. Jeffrey T. Sammons, *Beyond the Ring: The Role of Boxing in American Society* (Urbana: University of Illinois Press, 1988), 236.
11. Geoffrey C. Ward, *Unforgivable Blackness: The Rise and Fall of Jack Johnson* (New York: A. A. Knopf, 2004), 131.
12. Michael T. Isenberg, *John L. Sullivan and His America* (Urbana: University of Illinois Press, 1988), 10.
13. Scott Beekman, *Ringside: A History of Professional Wrestling in America* (Westport, CT: Praeger, 2006), 18.
14. Gerald W. Morton and George M. O'Brien, *Wrestling to Rasslin: Ancient Sport to American Spectacle* (Bowling Green, OH: Bowling Green State University Popular Press, 1985), 2.
15. Gorn, *The Manly Art,* 37.
16. Sammons, 4.
17. Beekman, 48.
18. Micol Seigel, *Uneven Encounters: Making Race and Nation in Brazil and the United States* (Durham, NC: Duke University Press, 2009), xii.
19. Robin D. G. Kelley, "But a Local Phase of a World Problem: Black History's Global Vision, 1883–1950," *Journal of American History* 86 no. 3 (December 1999): 1045–1077, p. 1077.
20. Michael Poliakoff, *Combat Sports in the Ancient World: Competition, Violence, and Culture* (New Haven: Yale University Press, 1987): 7.
21. Donald G. Kyle, *Sport and Spectacle in the Ancient World* (Malden, MA: Blackwell, 2007), 23.
22. Thomas Desch-Obi, *Fighting for Honor: The History of African Martial Art Traditions in the Atlantic World* (Columbia: University of South Carolina Press, 2008), 192.
23. Joanna Bourke, *An Intimate History of Killing: Face-to-Face Killing in Twentieth-Century Warfare* (New York: Basic Books, 1999), 1, 55.
24. Ibid., 2.
25. Dave Grossman, *On Killing: The Psychological Cost of Learning to Kill in War and Society* (Boston: Little, Brown, 1996), 136.
26. Ibid., 236.
27. Ibid., 75.
28. Andrea Smalley, "I Just Like to Kill Things: Women, Men and the Gender of Sport Hunting in the United States, 1940–1973," *Gender & History* 17 (2005): 183–209, p. 183.

29. John Lawrence Sullivan and Dudley Allen Sargent, *Life and Reminiscences of a Nineteenth Century Gladiator* (London: Routledge, 1892), 115.
30. Ibid., 242.
31. Ibid., 269, 103.
32. Joyce Carol Oates, *On Boxing* (Garden City, NY: Dolphin/Doubleday, 1987), 255.
33. Sullivan and Sargent, 269, 234.
34. Chuck Liddell and Chad Millman. *Iceman: My Fighting Life* (New York: Dutton, 2008), 133.
35. Genesis 3: 26-28, Bible: Contemporary English Version.
36. A. Black, G. Cunningham, E. Fluckiger-Hawker, E. Robson, and G. Zólyomi, *The Electronic Text Corpus of Sumerian Literature* (Oxford: 1998), http://www-etcsl.orient.ox.ac.uk/.
37. Kisari Mohan Ganguli Vyasa, Protap Chandra Roy, and Sundarī Bāla Roy, *The Mahabharata of Krishna—Dwaipayana Vyasa* (Calcutta: Bharata Press, 1889), 27–28.
38. Eric Foner, *Tom Paine and Revolutionary America* (New York: Oxford University Press, 1976), 48.
39. John Harriott, *Struggles Through Life, Exemplified in the Various Travels and Adventures in Europe, Asia, Africa, and America, of Lieut. John Harriott* (London: Printed for the author by J. Skirven; Longman, Hurst, Rees & Orme, 1808), 108; Henry Bibb and Lucius C. Matlack, *Narrative of the Life and Adventures of an American Slave* (New York: Author, 1849), 23, http://galenet.galegroup.com/servlet/Sabin?af=RN&ae=CY105731948&srchtp=a&ste=14>.
40. Frances Manwaring Caulkins, *History of Norwich, Connecticut: From Its Possession by the Indians, to the Year 1866* (Hartford, CT: Author, 1866), 214, 331.
41. Elliot Gorn, "'Gouge and Bite, Pull Hair and Scratch': The Social Significance of Fighting in the Southern Backcountry," *American Historical Review* 90, no. 1 (February 1985), 20.
42. State of North Carolina, Samuel Swann, and Edward Moseley, *A Collection of All the Public Acts of Assembly, of the Province of North Carolina: Now in Force and Use. [1715-1752] Together with the Titles of All Such Laws as Are Obsolete, Expir'd, or Repeal'd. And Also, an Exact Table of the Titles of the Acts in Force. Revised by Commissioners Appointed by an Act of the General Assembly of the Said Province, for That Purpose; and Examined with the Records, and Confirmed in Full Assembly*, (New Bern, NC: James Davis, 1752), 320.
43. "Advertisements." *North Carolina Gazette* (March 24, 1775).
44. Ibid.
45. Eric Foner, *Tom Paine and Revolutionary America* (New York: Oxford University Press, 1976), 66.
46. Gorn, "Gouge and Bite, Pull Hair and Scratch," 20.
47. Henry Knox, "Henry Knox Militia Plan of 1786," *Papers of the War Department*, http://wardepartmentpapers.org/docimage.php?id=806&docColID=46550&page=16.
48. Beekman, 54.
49. See, for example, Robert Griswold, "American Manhood," *Contemporary Sociology* 23, no. 1 (January 1994): 104; and Clyde Griffen, "American Manhood," *American Historical Review* 99, no. 3 (June 1994), 960.
50. Anthony E. Rotundo, *American Manhood: Transformations in Masculinity from the Revolution to the Modern Era* (New York: Basic Books, 1993), 222.
51. Allen Guttmann and Lee Thompson, *Japanese Sports: A History* (Honolulu: University of Hawai'i Press, 2001), 68.
52. Brian Watson, *Judo Memoirs of Jigoro Kano: Early History of Judo* (Victoria, BC: Trafford, 2008), 15.
53. Joseph R. Svinth, "Professor Yamashita Goes to Washington," *Journal of Combative Sport* (October 2000), http://ejmas.com/jcs/jcsart_svinth1_1000.htm.
54. "News from Jap Wrestler," *Washington Post* (November 26, 1906).
55. Morton and O'Brien, 73.
56. "The Wrestlers," *Chicago Daily Tribune* (July 27, 1884).
57. "Celebrated Mr. Santel to Wrestle Jap Expert," *LA Times* (March 31, 1916).
58. Teiichi Yamagata, "Jiu-Jitsu, The Art of Self-Defense," *Leslie's Monthly Magazine* LIX, no. 1 (November 1904): 91–100, p. 92.
59. Gorn, *The Manly Art*, 224; Robert Edgren, "The Fearful Art of Jiu Jitsu," *Outing Magazine* XLVII, no. 3 (December 1905): 322–328, p. 323.
60. "Here's Detail of Shortest Title Fight on Record," *Chicago Daily Tribune* (June 23, 1938).
61. Sergio Ortiz, "Robert Trias: Pioneer of U.S. Karate," *Black Belt* (April 1976): 36–39, p. 38.
62. Ronald Yates, "Inoki Issues Warning for Ali," *Chicago Tribune* (May 16, 1976); Keith Elliot Greenberg, *Pro Wrestling: From Carnivals to Cable TV* (Minneapolis, MN: Lerner Sports, 2000), 73.
63. Robert Lipsyte, "Clay Is Exultant," *New York Times* (February 26, 1964); Poshek Fu and David Desser, *The Cinema of Hong Kong: History, Arts, Identity* (Cambridge: Cambridge University Press, 2000), 33.
64. Lindy Lindell, *Metro Detroit Boxing* (Chicago: Arcadia, 2001), 97.
65. "Macho Mayhem," *New York Times* (December 26, 1980).
66. Lindy Lindell, *Metro Detroit Boxing* (Chicago: Arcadia, 2001), 97.

67. Bob Ottum, "Not Just a Lot of Kicks," *Sports Illustrated* (January 24, 1983): 36–39, 77–79, p. 39.
68. See, for example, Jordan Breen, "A Blood Called Shooto," *Sherdog* (May 8, 2009), http://www.sherdog.com/news/articles/1/A-Blood-Called-Shooto-17377.
69. Danny Plyler and Chad Seibert, *The Ultimate Mixed Martial Arts Training Guide: Techniques for Fitness, Self-Defense and Competition* (Cincinnati: Betterway Sports, 2009), 22.
70. Seigel, xii.
71. Jonathan Snowden and Kendall Shields. *The MMA Encyclopedia* (Toronto: ECW Press, 2010), 69.
72. Tani E. Barlow, Madeleine Yue Dong, Uta G. Poiger, Priti Ramamurthy, Lynn M. Thomas, and Alys Eve Weinbaum, "The Modern Girl around the World: A Research Agenda and Preliminary Findings," *Gender & History* 17, no. 2 (August 2005): 245–294, p. 288; Helen Lovatt, *Statius and Epic Games: Sport, Politics, and Poetics in the Thebaid* (Cambridge: Cambridge University Press, 2005), 16.

Introduction

1. Desch-Obi, 62.
2. Pindar, "For Diagoras of Rhodes Boxing: Match 464 BCE," http://www.perseus.tufts.edu/hopper/text?doc=Perseus%253Atext%253A1999.01.0162%253Abook%253DO.%253Apoem%253D7.
3. Genesis 3: 26–28, Bible: Contemporary English Version.
4. Dennis D. Hudson and Margaret H. Case, *The Body of God: An Emperor's Palace for Krishna in Eighth-Century Kanchipuram* (Oxford: Oxford University Press, 2008), 141.
5. Thomas Green, *Martial Arts of the World: An Encyclopedia* (Santa Barbara, CA: ABC-CLIO, 2002), 705.
6. Morton and O'Brien, 7.
7. Black, et al.
8. John Harris, *The Epic of Gilgamesh: A Prose Rendition Based upon the Original Akkadian, Babylonian, Hittite and Sumerian Tablets* (Lincoln, NE: Writers Club Press, 2001), 11.
9. Andrew George, *The Epic of Gilgamesh: The Babylonian Epic Poem and Other Texts in Akkadian and Sumerian* (London: Penguin, 2003), 17.
10. Andrew George, *The Epic of Gilgamesh: The Babylonian Epic Poem and Other Texts in Akkadian and Sumerian* (London: Penguin, 2003), 63.
11. Green, *Martial Arts of the World*, 338.
12. Ibid., 787.
13. Poliakoff, 27; Morton and O'Brien, 7.
14. Nigel B. Crowther, *Sport in Ancient Times* (Westport, CT: Praeger, 2007), 22; Mark Golden, *Sport and Society in Ancient Greece* (Cambridge: Cambridge University Press, 1998), 31.
15. Kyle, 30.
16. Green, *Martial Arts of the World*, 26.
17. Steve Craig, *Sports and Games of the Ancients* (Westport, CT: Greenwood Press, 2002), 50.
18. Green, *Martial Arts of the World*, 26.
19. Vyasa, et al., 27–28.
20. For a detailed examination of deaths in modern boxing, see Joseph R. Svinth, "Death Under the Spotlight: The Manuel Velazquez Boxing Fatality Collection," *Journal of Combative Sport* (November 2007), http://ejmas.com/jcs/jcsart_svinth_a_0700.htm.
21. Kyle, 52.
22. Craig, 80.
23. Poliakoff, 104.
24. Jim Parry, *Sport and Spirituality: An Introduction* (New York: Routledge, 2007), 19.
25. Morton and O'Brien, 8.
26. Kyle, 54.
27. For more information on this concept, see Poliakoff, "Appendix: Combat Sport, Funeral Cult, and Human Sacrifice," 149–157. Polikoff does not believe that fight sports grew from human sacrifice, but he notes that other scholars disagree with his conclusion.
28. Kyle, 36.
29. Plato, John M. Cooper, and D. S. Hutchinson, *Complete Works* (Indianapolis, IN: Hackett, 1997), 1481.
30. Gloria G. Brame, William D. Brame, and Jon Jacobs, *Different Loving: The World of Sexual Dominance and Submission* (London: Century, 1997), 463.
31. Allen Guttmann, *Women's Sports: A History* (New York: Columbia University Press, 1991), 25.
32. William H. Freeman, *Physical Education, Exercise, and Sport Science in a Changing Society* (Sudbury, MA: Jones and Bartlett, 2012), 78.
33. Euripides, Peter Burian, and Alan Shapiro, *The Complete Euripides* (Oxford: Oxford University Press, 2009), 35.
34. Margaret D. Costa and Sharon Ruth Guthrie, *Women and Sport: Interdisciplinary Perspectives* (Champaign, IL: Human Kinetics, 1994), 20.
35. Poliakoff, 113.
36. Homer, *The Iliad; and, the Odyssey* (Radford, VA: Wilder Publications, 2007), 230.
37. Poliakoff, 114.
38. *Barea athela* translates to "the heavy events." This reflects the tendency of large fighters to dominate these sports in which there were no weight classes (Kyle, 124). The Greeks' grouping of these sports into a separate category indicates their view that while these were distinct events, they were interrelated and separate from other sports.

39. Poliakoff, 23.
40. Ibid.
41. Kyle, 125.
42. For the most detailed examination of boxing gloves in the ancient past written to date, see Steven Ross Murray, "Boxing Gloves of the Ancient World," *Journal of Combative Sport* (July 2010), http://ejmas.com/jcs/2010jcs/jcsart_murray_1007.html.
43. Poliakoff, 54. The term *pankration* means "complete victory," which accurately describes what its champions achieved.
44. Morton and O'Brien, 10.
45. Green, *Martial Arts of the World*, 411.
46. Ibid.
47. Stephen Gaylord Miller, *Arête: Greek Sports from Ancient Sources* (Berkeley: University of California Press, 1991), 90.
48. Jason Koing, *Athletics and Literature in the Roman Empire* (Cambridge: Cambridge University Press, 2005), 216.
49. Lovatt, 157.
50. Ibid., 142.
51. Marcus Junkleman, "Greek Athletics in Rome: Boxing, Wrestling, and the Pancreation," in Eckhard Kohne, Cornelia Ewigleben, and Ralph Jackson, *Gladiators and Caesars: The Power of Spectacle in Ancient Rome* (Berkeley: University of California Press, 2000), 75–76.
52. Lovatt, 16.
53. Sarah B. Pomeroy, *Spartan Women* (Oxford: Oxford University Press, 2002), 28.
54. Ibid.
55. Lovatt, 185.
56. Sextus Propertius and Lawrence Richardson, *Elegies I–IV* (Norman: University of Oklahoma Press, 1976), 380.
57. Joyce E. Salisbury, *Encyclopedia of Women in the Ancient World* (Santa Barbara, CA: ABC-CLIO, 2001), 258.
58. Green, *Martial Arts of the World*, 706.
59. Sally Wilkins, *Sports and Games of Medieval Cultures* (Westport, CT: Greenwood Press, 2002), 95–96. While the stories of Bodhidarma as the founder of Kung Fu appear frequently, some scholars take issue with the idea and claim that Bodhidarma was "a fictional creation of historians writing many centuries later" (Craig, 50).
60. Wilkins, 82.
61. Guttmann and Thompson, 14.
62. Ibid.
63. Ibid., 15.
64. Desch-Obi, 11.
65. Mungo Park, *The Life and Travels of Mungo Park* (Edinburgh: Nimmo, Hay & Mitchell, 1838), 14.
66. Chinua Achebe, *Things Fall Apart* (New York: Anchor Books, 1994), 30.
67. Maya Talmon-Chvaicer, *The Hidden History of Capoeira: A Collision of Cultures in the Brazilian Battle Dance* (Austin: University of Texas Press, 2008), 135.
68. Park, 14.
69. Murray.
70. Thomas Green, "Dambe: Traditional Nigerian Boxing," *Journal of Combative Sport* (September 2005), http://ejmas.com/jalt/2005jalt/jcsart_Green_0905.html.
71. Jeanmarie Fenrich, Paolo Galizzi, and Tracy Higgins, *The Future of African Customary Law* (Cambridge: Cambridge University Press, 2011), 501; Ifi Amadiume, *Re-inventing Africa: Matriarchy, Religion, and Culture* (London: Zed Books, 1997), 147.
72. Desch-Obi, 59.
73. Ibid., 65.
74. Ibid.
75. Green, 133.
76. Tertullian, "Spectacles," http://www.pseudepigrapha.com/LostBooks/tertullian_spectacles.htm.
77. Tony Perrottet, *The Naked Olympics: The True Story of the Ancient Games* (New York: Random House, 2004), 190.
78. Anil Taneja, *World of Sports Indoor* (Delhi: Gyan Publishing, 2009), 61. Jeffrey Hull disagrees with this often-repeated story, arguing that the official prohibition of boxing was a myth and that boxing died away with the fall of Rome for reasons that are simply unclear. Jeffrey Hull, "Getting Punchy: Fight-Fighting, Wrestling and Fight Books," 4, http://www.thehaca.com/essays/Getting-Punchy.pdf.
79. Jack Anderson, *The Legality of Boxing: A Punch Drunk Love?* (Abingdon, UK: Birkbeck Law Press, 2007), 8.
80. Diane Morgan, *Essential Islam: A Comprehensive Guide to Belief and Practice* (Santa Barbara, CA: Praeger, 2010), 167.
81. Richard A. Gabriel, *Muhammad: Islam's First Great General* (Norman: University of Oklahoma Press, 2007), 49.
82. Ibn Kathīr, Ismāīl ibn Umar, and Trevor Le Gassick, *The Life of the Prophet Muhammad: A Translation of Al-Sīra Al-Nabawiyya* (Reading, UK: Center for Muslim Contribution to Civilization, 1998), 54.
83. John Renard, *Friends of God: Islamic Images of Piety, Commitment, and Servanthood* (Berkeley: University of California Press, 2008), 95.
84. Green, *Martial Arts of the World*, 706.
85. James Riordan and Robin Jones, *Sport and Physical Education in China* (London: E & FN Spon, 1999), 54.
86. Chris Crudelli, *The Way of the Warrior* (London: Dorling Kindersley, 2008), 159.
87. Eric Dunning and Dominic Malcolm, *Sport* (London: Routledge, 2003), 185.
88. Ibid., 192, 193.
89. Crudelli, 173.

90. Ibid., 335.
91. Pat McCarthy and Mike Lee, *Classical Kata of Okinawan Karate* (Burbank, CA: Ohara, 1987), 16.
92. Patricia Ann Lynch, *Native American Mythology A to Z* (New York: Facts on File, 2004), 57.
93. Thomas L. Altherr, Larry K. Menna, George B. Kirsch, Gerald R. Gems, Steven A. Riess, and Douglas Owen Baldwin, "Boxing," *Sports in the Colonial Era*, Vol. I of *Sports in North America: A Documentary History* (Gulf Breeze, FL: Academic International Press, 1992), 102.
94. Craig, 131.
95. *Columbus and Columbia: A Pictorial History of the Man and the Nation* (St. Louis, Mo: Riverside, 1892), 132.
96. Craig, 176.
97. Mounir A. Farah and Andrea Berens Karls, *World History: The Human Experience* (Columbus, OH: Glencoe/McGraw-Hill, 2001), 185.
98. See, for example, Alexander Pope, *The Iliad of Homer* (London: H. G. Bohn, 1852), 436.
99. Beekman, 5.
100. Morton and O'Brien, 16.
101. William J. Baker, *Playing with God: Religion and Modern Sport* (Cambridge, MA: Harvard University Press, 2007), 15.
102. Beekman, 4.
103. Baldassarre Castiglione and Leonard Eckstein Opdycke, *The Book of the Courtier* (New York: Scribner's, 1903), 179.
104. Alison Weir, *Henry VIII: The King and His Court* (New York: Ballantine Books, 2001), 105.
105. Morton and O'Brien, 17.
106. Francis Rouse, *Archaeologiae Atticae Libri Septem: Seven Books of the Attick Antiquities* (Oxford, UK: Leonard Lichfield, 1649), 205.
107. John McClelland, *Body and Mind: Sport in Europe from the Roman Empire to the Renaissance* (London: Routledge, 2006), 57.
108. Chauncey Brewster Tinker, *Beowulf* (New York: Newson, 1902), 43; George Stevens and William Shakespeare, *The Plays of William Shakespeare* (London: Baldwin, 1811), 119.
109. For an example of a sermon referring to this passage, see "Of Satan's Temptations" in Thomas Froysell and Richard Steele, *Sermons Concerning Grace and Temptations* (London: T. Parkhurst, 1678), 179. For the original account, see American Bible Society, *The Holy Bible Containing the Old and New Testaments: King James Version* (New York: Bartleby.com, 2000), 32:22–26, http://bartleby.com/108/.
110. Beekman, 4–5.
111. Jeffrey L. Forgeng, *Daily Life in Elizabethan England* (Westport, CT: Greenwood Press, 1995), 199.
112. Victoria E. Burke and Jonathan Gibson, *Early Modern Women's Manuscript Writing: Selected Papers from the Trinity/Trent Colloquium* (Aldershot, UK: Ashgate, 2004), 99.
113. Betty Travitsky and Anne Lake Prescott, *Female and Male Voices in Early Modern England: An Anthology of Renaissance Writing* (New York: Columbia University Press, 2000), 6.
114. Altherr, et al., Vol. I, 1.
115. Allen Guttmann, "Puritans at Play? Accusations and Replies," in David Kenneth Wiggins, *Sport in America: From Wicked Amusement to National Obsession* (Champaign, IL: Human Kinetics, 1995), 5.
116. Altherr, et al., Vol. I, 3.
117. Guttmann, "Puritans at Play?" 6.
118. T. H. Breen, "English Origins and New World Development: The Case of the Covenanted Militia in Seventeenth-Century Massachusetts," *Past & Present* 57 (November 1972): 80.
119. John William Allen, *English Political Thought 1603–1660 1* (London: Methuen, 1938), 281.
120. Bruce Colin Daniels, *Puritans at Play: Leisure and Recreation in Colonial New England* (New York: St. Martin's Press, 1995), 168, 207.
121. Altherr et al., Vol. I, 3.

Chapter I

1. State of North Carolina, et al., 320.
2. Tim McNeese. *Myths of Native America* (New York: Four Walls Eight Windows, 2003).
3. Altherr et al., Vol. II, 174.
4. The Society of Friends (Quakers) actually took a far dimmer view of sports than their Puritan neighbors, condemning them as "needless and vain" (Altherr et al., Vol. I, 16).
5. Altherr, et al., Vol. I, 5.
6. William Bradford and Charles Deane, *History of Plymouth Plantation: Reprinted from the Massachusetts Historical Collection, Edited with Notes* (Boston: Author, 1856), 112.
7. Nancy Struna, "Puritans and Sport: The Irretrievable Tide of Change," in Steven A. Riess, *The American Sporting Experience: A Historical Anthology of Sport in America* (New York: Leisure Press, 1984), 17.
8. Altherr, et al., Vol. I, 118; Daniels, 164.
9. Baker, *Playing with God*, 19.
10. Craig, 176.
11. See, for example, William Wood, *Wood's New England's Prospect*, Publications of the Prince Society (Boston: Author, 1865), 97; Thomas Osborne, *A Collection of Voyages and Travels, Consisting of Authentic Writers in Our Own Tongue, Which Have Not Before Been Collected in English, or Have Only Been Abridged in Other Collections. Compiled from the Curious*

and Valuable Library of the Late Earl of Oxford (London: Thomas Osborne, 1745), 893; "Peroufe's Voyage Round the World," *Scots Magazine* (March 1799), 162.

12. See, for example, Bryan Edwards, *The History, Civil and Commercial, of the British Colonies in the West Indies in Two Volumes. By Bryan Edwards* (London: John Stockdale, 1793), Vol. I, 67.

13. "Nova Francia: or the Description of that Part of New France, Which Is One Continent with Virginia," in Osborne, 893.

14. Harriott, 108.

15. Wood, 97.

16. William Crow, *The Indian: A Poem in Six Cantos* (London: Lackington, Allen, 1806), 38, 529.

17. Guttmann, "Puritans at Play?" 9.

18. Baker, *Playing with God*, 19.

19. James Charles, "Gymnastic," in *A New and Enlarged Military Dictionary, in French and English; in Which Are Explained the Principal Terms ... of All the Sciences That Are ... Necessary for an Officer and Engineer* (London: T. Edgerton, 1810), 255; T. H. Breen, "English Origins and New World Development: The Case of the Covenanted Militia in Seventeenth-Century Massachusetts," *Past & Present* 57 (November 1972), 80.

20. *A Collection of State Tracts, Published on Occasion of the Late Revolution in 1688, and during the Reign of King William III* (London, 1705), 601.

21. Richard P. Gildrie, "Defiance, Diversion, and the Exercise of Arms: The Several Meanings of Colonial Training Days in Colonial Massachusetts," *Military Affairs* 52, no. 2 (April 1988), 54.

22. John, Winthrop and James Kendall Hosmer, *Winthrop's Journal "History of New England" 1630–1649. Edited by J. K. Hosmer ... with Maps and Facsimiles* (New York: Scribner's, 1908), 42.

23. Baker, *Playing with God*, 19.

24. Beekman, 7.

25. Nancy L. Struna, *People of Prowess: Sport, Leisure, and Labor in Early Anglo-America. Sport and Society* (Urbana: University of Illinois Press, 1996), 79.

26. Daniels, 98.

27. Margaret E. Backus, "Gala Days in Old New England," *Connecticut Magazine* 10 (1906): 485; Sandra L. Oliver, *Saltwater Foodways: New Englanders and Their Food, at Sea and Ashore* (Mystic, CT: Mystic Seaport Museum, 1995), 22.

28. Sarah Knight, *The Private Journal of a Journey from Boston to New York, in the Year 1704, Kept by Madam Knight* (Albany, NY: Frank H. Little, 1865), 53.

29. David W. Conroy, *In Public Houses: Drink and the Revolution of Authority in Colonial Massachusetts* (Chapel Hill, NC: Published for the Institute of Early American History and Culture [Williamsburg, VA] by University of North Carolina Press, 1995), 82; W. J. Rorabaugh, *The Alcoholic Republic: An American Tradition* (New York: Oxford University Press, 1979), 19–20.

30. Altherr, et al., Vol. I, 100.

31. Henry Tufts, *The Autobiography of a Criminal* (Port Townsend, WA: Loompanics, 1993), 103.

32. Altherr, et al., "Wriestling," Vol. I, 102.

33. Baker, *Playing with God*, 19.

34. Daniels, 211, 217.

35. Ibid., 186.

36. Richard Clive Simmons, *The American Colonies from Settlement to Independence* (New York: W. W. Norton, 1981), 100.

37. Thomas L. Purvis, *Colonial America to 1763* (New York: Facts on File, 1999), 17.

38. Steven A. Riess, *City Games: The Evolution of American Urban Society and the Rise of Sports* (Urbana: University of Illinois Press, 1989), 1.

39. Struna, *People of Prowess*, 198.

40. Elizabeth H. Pleck, *Domestic Tyranny: The Making of American Social Policy against Family Violence from Colonial Times to the Present* (Urbana: University of Illinois Press, 2004), 29.

41. Bruce Colin Daniels, *Puritans at Play*, 197.

42. Struna, *People of Prowess*, 145.

43. Daniels, 168.

44. See, for example, "Of Satan's Temptations," 179.

45. Duane Hamilton Hurd, *History of Essex County, Massachusetts: With Biographical Sketches of Many of Its Pioneers and Prominent Men*, Vol. 2, Part 1 (Philadelphia: J. W. Lewis, 1888), 1163.

46. Anil Taneja, *World of Sports Indoor* (Delhi: 2009), 61.

47. Daniels, 168.

48. For a particularly insightful examination of the legacy of anti–Sabbath restrictions on sport in America, see Kristen M. Anderson and Christopher W. Kimball, "The Saints on Sunday: Ballparks and Sabatariansim in St. Paul," *Nine* 17, no. 1 (2008).

49. Kevin Schultz, *America Unbound: A U.S. History Primer* (Boston: Cengage Learning, 2009), 65.

50. John Hammond, "Advice to Immigrants to Maryland, 1655," in Ernest Ludlow Bogart and Charles Manfred Thompson, *Readings in the Economic History of the United States* (New York: Longmans, Green, 1916), 14.

51. Struna, *People of Prowess*, 79–80.

52. Altherr, et al., Vol. I, 92.

53. Ibid., 90.
54. Anderson, 13.
55. Nicholas Hobbes, *Who Would Win a Fight Between Muhammad Ali and Bruce Lee? The Sports Fan's Book of Answers* (London: Atlantic, 2008), 33.
56. Tertullian, "Spectacles."
57. For example, see Martin Luther's advocacy of wrestling in Baker, *Playing with God*, 15.
58. John Peter Sugden, *Boxing and Society: An International Analysis* (Manchester, UK: Manchester University Press, 1996), 11.
59. Ibid., 11.
60. Kasia Boddy, *Boxing: A Cultural History* (London: Reaktion, 2008), 28.
61. Egan, *Or, Sketches of Ancient and Modern Pugilism* (London: Sherwood, Jones, 1823), 21.
62. David Marley, *Wars of the Americas: A Chronology of Armed Conflict in the New World, 1492 to the Present* (Santa Barbara, CA: ABC-CLIO, 1998), 100, 134, 143.
63. John Locke and Robert Hebert Quick, *Some Thoughts Concerning Education* (Cambridge: Cambridge University Press, 1895), 176.
64. Thomas Salmon, *Modern History of the Present State of All Nations*, 3rd ed., Vol. 3 (London: T. Longman, T. Osborne, J. Shuckburgh, C. Hitch, S. Austen, and J. Rivington), 450.
65. William Byrd, Louis B. Wright, and Marion Tinling, *The Secret Diary of William Byrd of Westover, 1709-1712* (Richmond, VA: Dietz Press, 1941), 405.
66. Rorabaugh, 26.
67. Altherr, et al., Vol. I, 8-11.
68. Gerald Lee Gutek and Patricia Gutek, *Plantations and Outdoor Museums in America's Historic South* (Columbia: University of South Carolina Press, 1996), 83.
69. Byrd, et al., 415; John Fiske, *Old Virginia and Her Neighbors Volume 2* (London: Gardners Books, 2007), 281.
70. Morton and O'Brien, 19.
71. Altherr, et al., Vol. I, 233.
72. Thomas J. Sharf, *History of Baltimore City and County; From the Earliest Period to the Present Day, Including Biographical Sketches of Their Representative Men. Illustrated* (Philadelphia: Louis H. Everts, 1881), 844.
73. Fredrick Douglass, *Narrative of the Life of Fredrick Douglass, an American Slave* (London: H. G. Collins, 1851), 69.
74. Bibb and Matlack, 23.
75. John C. Rodriguez, *Reconstruction in the Cane Fields: From Slavery to Free Labor in Louisiana's Sugar Parishes, 1862-1880* (Baton Rouge: Louisiana State University Press, 2001), 25.
76. James Riordan and Arnd Krüger, *The International Politics of Sport in the Twentieth Century* (London: E & F N Spon, 1999), 151.
77. Bibb and Matlack, 23.
78. Douglass, 69.
79. Boddy, 44.
80. Desch-Obi, 77, 83, 99.
81. Ibid., 77, 83.
82. Gorn, "Gouge and Bite, Pull Hair and Scratch," 20.
83. See, for example, Thomas Anburey, *Travels through the Interior Parts of America in a Series of Letters by an Officer* (London: Lane, 1789), 349; "American Annals; or a Chronological History of America, from Its Discovery," *Select Reviews, and Spirit of the Foreign Magazines* (April 1810).
84. Gorn, "Gouge and Bite, Pull Hair and Scratch," 42.
85. State of Delaware and James Booth, *Laws of the State of Delaware: From the Fourteenth Day of October, One Thousand Seven Hundred, to the Eighteenth Day of August, One Thousand Seven Hundred and Ninety-Seven, in Two Volumes* (New-Castle: Samuel and John Adams, 1797), 68.
86. *A New Voyage to Georgia by a Young Gentleman: Giving an Account of His Travels to South Carolina, and Part of North Carolina. To Which Is Added, a Curious Account of the Indians. By an Honourable Person. And a Poem to James Oglethorpe* (London: J. Wilford, 1735), 24.
87. State of North Carolina, et al., 320.
88. Altherr, et al., "Laws against Maiming," Vol. I, 98.
89. State of North Carolina, "Minutes of the Upper House of the North Carolina General Assembly North Carolina. General Assembly March 31, 1752–April 15, 1752," Vol. 4 (New Bern, NC: James Davis, 1752), 1318.
90. State of Virginia and William Waller Hening, *The Statutes at Large. Being a Collection of All the Laws of Virginia, from the First Session of the Legislature, in the Year 1619: Published Pursuant to an Act of the General Assembly of Virginia, Passed on the Fifth Day of February, One Thousand Eight Hundred and Eight: Volume I* (Richmond: Samuel Pleasants, Jr., 1809), 520.
91. Philip Vickers Fithian and Hunter Dickinson Farish, *Journal and Letters of Philip Vickers Fithian, 1773-1774: A Plantation Tutor of the Old Dominion* (Williamsburg, VA: Colonial Williamsburg, 1943), 63.
92. "Advertisements," *North Carolina Gazette* (March 24, 1775).
93. See, for example, John Potter, *Archæologia Græca, or, the Antiquities of Greece. The Fourth Edition, Etc.* (London: F. Knapton, 1722), 317; John Potter, *Archæologia Græca: The Military Affairs of the Grecians: Some of Their Miscellany Customs* (London: G. Strahan, 1751), 317.
94. Locke and Quick, 176.
95. "On the Resemblance Between the Welsch and Grecian Customs," *Gentleman's Magazine* 28 (1758): 484.

96. Charles Rollin, *Histoire ancienne des Egyptiens, des Carthaginois, des Assyriens, des Babyloniens, des Medes et des Perses, des Macedoniens, des Grecs. 2* (Amsterdam: Compagnie, 1733): Charles Rollin, *The Ancient History of the Egyptians Carthaginians, Assyrians, Babylonians, Medes and Persians, Macedonians, and Grecians. By Mr. Rollin, Translated from the French,* Vol. 4 (London: Printed for J. and F. Rivington, R. Baldwin, Hawes, Clarke and Collins, R. Horsfield, W. Johnston, and nine others in London, 1774), 88.

97. Helvétius, *De L'esprit: Or, Essays on the Mind, and Its Several Faculties. Written by Helvetius. Translated from the Edition Printed under the Author's Inspection* (London: Printed for the translator; sold by Mr. Dodsley and Co.; Mess. Millar, Nourse, and Tonson; Mess. Hitch and Hawes; Mr. Fletcher, Oxford; Mr. Merril, Cambridge; and J. Coote, 1759), 327.

98. For example, see Jacob Christoph Beck and August Johann Buxtorf, *Supplement zu dem Baselischen allgemeinen historischen Lexicon* (Basel: Bey Johannes Brandmüller Aelter seel. Erben und gedruckt bey Johannes Christ, 1742), 316.

99. Benjamin Franklin, "Proposals Relating to the Education of Youth in Pennsylvania," http://www.franklinpapers.org/franklin/framedVolumes.jsp.

100. John Adams diary 6, December 2, 1760–March 3, 1761 [electronic edition], *Adams Family Papers: An Electronic Archive* (Massachusetts Historical Society), http://www.Masshist.org/digitaladams/.

101. Colonial Society of Massachusetts, *Transactions* (Boston: Colonial Society of Massachusetts, 1895), 271.

102. Baker, *Playing with God,* 20.

103. Daniels, 207.

104. "Journal of the Meetings of the President and Masters of William and Mary College," *William and Mary Quarterly* 2, no. 2 (October 1893), 124.

105. Charles Jeffery Smith, "Plan for an Academy at Providence, in New Kent," *William and Mary Quarterly* 3, no. 1 (January 1923), 101.

106. Bonnie S. Ledbetter, "Sports and Games of the American Revolution," *Journal of Sport History* 6, no. 3 (Winter 1979), 29.

107. Altherr, et al., "Wrestling," Vol. I, 103.

108. Kendall F. Haven, *Voices of the American Revolution: Stories of Men, Women, and Children Who Forged Our Nation* (Englewood, CO: Libraries Unlimited, 2000), 305.

109. Morton and O'Brien, 20.

110. Joseph Plumb Martin, James Kirby Martin, and Joseph Plumb Martin, *Ordinary Courage: The Revolutionary War Adventures of Joseph Plumb Martin* (Malden, MA: Blackwell, 2008), 96.

111. Altherr, et al., "Boxing," Vol. I, 94.

112. Pierce Eagan and George Cruikshank, *Boxiana, or, Sketches of Ancient and Modern Pugilism: From the Days of the Renowned Broughton and Slack to the Heroes of the Present Milling Era!* (London: G. Smeeton, 1818), 444: Simon Schama, *Rough Crossings: Britain, the Slaves, and the American Revolution* (New York: Ecco, 2006), 112.

113. Francois Jean Chastellux, George Grieve, and George Washington, *Travels in North-America, in the Years 1780–81–82* (New York: White, Gallaher, & White, 1827), 292.

114. William Winterbotham, *An Historical, Geographical, Commercial, and Philosophical View of the American United States, and of the European Settlements in America and the West-Indies, Volume 3* (Newark: J. Ridgway, York Street; H. D. Symonds, Paternoster Row; and D. Holt, 1795), 212.

115. Anburey, 349.

116. Ibid., 375.

117. Ibid., 347.

118. Ibid., 348.

119. Ibid., 349.

120. Ibid., 350.

121. Henry Knox, "Henry Knox Militia Plan of 1786," *Papers of the War Department,* http://wardepartmentpapers.org/docimage.php?id=806&docColID=46550&page=16.

122. See, for example, "Games and Combats Practiced in Greece," *The Evangelical Intelligencer* (October 1808).

123. John Adams diary 6, .

124. John Adams, *A Defense of the Constitutions of Government of the United States of America ... By John Adams,* Vol. I (London: John Stockdale, 1794), 259.

125. "The Effayift. no. VII. Apology for Wrestling," *The Massachusetts Magazine; or Monthly Museum* (September 1793), 548.

126. "On the Practice of Gouging," *The American Museum; or, Repository of Ancient and Modern Fugitive Pieces* (May 1787).

127. "Intelligence," *The Weekly Magazine of Original Essays* (April 13, 1799).

128. "American Annals; or a Chronological History of America, from Its Discovery," *Select Reviews, and Spirit of the Foreign Magazines* (April 1810).

129. Charles William Janson, "Janson's Stranger in America," *The Eclectic Review* III, Part I (January–June 1807): 474.

130. Altherr, et al., "Laws against Maiming," Vol. II, 143.

131. Ibid., 143.

132. Ibid., 144.

133. Ibid., 144.

134. Martin F. Schmidt, *Kentucky Illustrated: The First Hundred Years* (Lexington: University Press of Kentucky, 1992), 196.

135. Altherr, et al., "Laws against Maiming," Vol. II, 144–146.
136. See, for example, *Respublica v. Joseph Langcake and John Hook*, 1 Yeats 415, 175 WL 708 (Pa. 1795): *State v. Chandler*, 9 N.C. 439, 1823 N.C. LEXIS 33, 2 Hawks 439 (Nc. 1823); *The State v. Neil Crawford*, 13 N.C. 425, 1830 N.C. LEXIS 79 (Nc. 1830).
137. John K. Mahon, *History of the Militia and the National Guard, The Macmillan Wars of the United States* (New York: Macmillan, 1983), 19.
138. Isaac Weld, *Travels through the States of North America and the Provinces of Upper and Lower Canada, during the Years 1765, 1796, and 1797* (London: J. Stockdale, 1799), 193.
139. Fortescue Curning, *Sketches of a Tour to the Western Country, 1807–1809* (Cleveland: A. H. Clark, 1904), 237.
140. Thomas Ashe, *Travels in America Performed in 1806: For the Purpose of Exploring the Rivers, Alleghany, Monongahela, Ohio, and Mississippi, and Ascertaining the Produce and Condition of Their Banks and Vicinity* (London: Printed Newburyport, MA; reprinted for W. Sawyer & Co. by E. M. Blunt, 1808), 86.
141. Ibid., 87.
142. Elijah Parrish, *A New System of Modern Geography, or, A General Description of All the Considerable Countries in the World: Compiled from the Latest European and American Geographies, Voyages and Travels : Designed for Schools and Academies* (Newburyport, MA: Thomas and Whipple, 1810), 109.
143. Guion Griffis Johnson, *Ante-bellum North Carolina: A Social History* (Chapel Hill: Academic Affairs Library, University of North Carolina at Chapel Hill), 2002, http://docsouth.unc.edu/nc/johnson/menu.html.
144. Inchiquin, the Jesuit, pseud. [Charles Jared Ingersoll], *Remarks on the Review of Inchiquin's Letters Published in the Quarterly Review; Addressed to the Right Honourable George Canning. By an Inhabitant of New-England*, 1815.
145. Altherr, et al., "Laws against Maiming," Vol. II, 146.
146. See, for example, S. A. Ferrell, *A Ramble of Six Thousand Miles through the United States of America* (London: E. Wilson, Royal Exchange, 1832), 71: W. H. Woodson, *History of Clay County, Missouri* (Topeka, KS: Historical Pub., 1920), 40.
147. This view of a largely irreligious 18th-century South is consistent with the historiography of religion in the South. See, for example, Christine Leigh Heyerman, *Southern Cross: The Beginnings of the Bible Belt* (New York: A. A. Knopf, 1997), 5, 8.
148. "Miscellanies," *Antijacobin Review and Magazine* (September–December 1807): 111.
149. Heyerman, 8.

150. William Gilmore Simms, *Border Beagles: A Tale of Mississippi, Vol. 1* (Philadelphia: Carey & Hart, 1840), 279.
151. Tertullian, "Spectacles."
152. "Confessions of a Rambler," *Repository of Arts, Literature, Fashions, Manufactures, & C.* III, no. XV (March 1, 1824): 225–229, p. 229.
153. "Toughtale's Travels in America," *New York Review* (June 1825): 57–71, in *New York Review and Antheneum Magazine* I (May–November 1825) (New York: E. Bliss & White, 1825), 67.
154. John Bull, *John Bull in America; or, the New Munchausen* (New York: Charles Wiley, 1825), 159.
155. John E. Findling and Frank W. Thackeray, *What Happened? An Encyclopedia of Events That Changed America Forever* (Santa Barbara, CA: ABC-CLIO, 2011), 1.
156. Daniel Walker Howe, *The Political Culture of the American Whigs* (Chicago: University of Chicago Press, 1979), 127.
157. "Volume VII, Part I," *The Panoplist, and Missionary Magazine* (April 1809): 515.
158. James E. Wise, *Durham: A Bull City Story* (Charleston, SC: Arcadia, 2002), 36.
159. Christopher J. Olsen, *Political Culture and Secession in Mississippi: Masculinity, Honor, and the Antiparty Tradition, 1830–1860* (Oxford: Oxford University Press, 2000), 52.
160. Gary Laderman and Luis D. León, *Religion and American Cultures: An Encyclopedia of Traditions, Diversity, and Popular Expressions, Volume One* (Santa Barbara, CA: ABC-CLIO, 2003), 315.
161. Laura Edwards, *The People and Their Peace: Legal Culture and the Transformation of Inequality in the Post-Revolutionary South* (Chapel Hill: University of North Carolina Press, 2009), 8.
162. Altherr, et al., "Laws Against Maiming," Vol. II, 143–146.
163. See. for example, *Respublica v. Joseph Langcake and John Hook*, 1 Yeats 415, 175 WL 708 (Pa. 1795): *State v. Chandler*, 9 N.C. 439, 1823 N.C. LEXIS 33, 2 Hawks 439 (Nc. 1823); *The State v. Neil Crawford*, 13 N.C. 425, 1830 N.C. LEXIS 79 (Nc. 1830).
164. Johnson, *Ante-bellum North Carolina*, 2002.
165. Morton and O'Brien, 21: Beekman, 9.
166. Beekman, 5.
167. George B. Kirsch, Othello Harris, and Claire Elaine Nolte, *Encyclopedia of Ethnicity and Sports in the United States* (Westport, CT: Greenwood Press, 2000), 142.
168. Tony Collins, John Martin, and Wray Vamplew, *Encyclopedia of Traditional British Rural Sports* (London: Routledge, 2005), 218.
169. Dale A. Somers, *The Rise of Sports in New Orleans; 1850–1900* (Baton Rouge: Louisiana State University Press, 1972), 53.

Chapter II

1. Pierce Egan, *Boxiana, or, Sketches of Ancient and Modern Pugilism: Comprising the Only Original and Complete Lives of the Boxers* (London: Printed for the booksellers, 1830), 494–495.
2. Ossborne, 435.
3. Egan, 362–363.
4. Harry S. Laver, *Citizens More Than Soldiers: The Kentucky Militia and Society in the Early Republic* (Lincoln: University of Nebraska Press, 2007), 3.
5. H. Knox, "Washington's Plan," *Niles Weekly Register* (January 7, 1815).
6. Theodore Roosevelt, *Louisiana and the Northwest: 1791–1807* (New York: Putnam, 1896), 245.
7. "The Militia," *Examiner* 1, no. 3 (November 22, 1813): 33–41, p. 41.
8. "On Turning Militia Men into Soldiers," *Examiner* 1, no. 3 (November 22, 1813): 41.
9. Carl Edward Skeen, *Citizen Soldiers in the War of 1812* (Lexington: University Press of Kentucky, 1999), 56.
10. James B. Roberts and Alexander G. Skutt, *The Boxing Register: International Boxing Hall of Fame Official Record Book* (Ithaca, NY: McBooks Press, 2006), 37.
11. Paul Magriel, "Tom Molineaux," *Phylon* 12, no. 4 (1951): 329–336, p. 329.
12. Boddy, 44; Roberts and Skutt, 37.
13. Roberts and Skutt, 37.
14. Boddy, 44.
15. Roberts and Skutt, 37.
16. Egan, 363.
17. Magriel, 331.
18. Ibid.
19. Roberts and Skutt, 37.
20. Paul Magriel, "Tom Molineaux," 331.
21. Boddy, 44.
22. Ibid.
23. Roberts and Skutt, 37.
24. Magriel, 335.
25. Ibid.
26. Roberts and Skutt, 37; Magriel, 336.
27. Bertram Wyatt-Brown, *Honor and Violence in the Old South* (New York: Oxford University Press, 1986), 356.
28. "Bradford Powell," *Vermont Historical Gazetteer* 2 (1871): 286–287, p. 286.
29. David Block, *Baseball Before We Knew It: A Search for the Roots of the Game* (Lincoln: University of Nebraska Press, 2005), 247.
30. Eron Rowland, *Mississippi Territory in the War of 1812, Vol. 4* (Baltimore: General. Pub., 1968), 87.
31. Bill Richmond and Tom Molineaux, both men of African ancestry, were the first two American-born fighters to compete as boxers in Europe. For more information on these two fighters, see Gorn, *The Manly Art*, 19–22, 24.
32. Desch-Obi, 203.
33. Ibid., 204.
34. Jeffrey W. Bolster, *Black Jacks: African American Seamen in the Age of Sail* (Cambridge, MA: Harvard University Press, 1997), 118.
35. Desch-Obi, 203.
36. Ibid.
37. Rodriguez, *Reconstruction in the Cane Fields*, 25.
38. Adrian Harvey, *The Beginnings of a Commercial Sporting Culture in Britain, 1793–1850* (Aldershot, UK: Ashgate, 2004), 45.
39. "CANT," *New Monthly Magazine and Monthly Journal*, American ed. (January 1, 1821).
40. Stephen Vaughn, *Encyclopedia of American Journalism* (New York: Routledge, 2008), 61.
41. Rodriguez, *Reconstruction in the Cane Fields*, 25.
42. Gorn, *The Manly Art*, 38; Vaughn, 61.
43. Timony, 29; Gorn, *The Manly Art*, 38.
44. Altherr, et al., Vol. I, 132.
45. Boddy, 27.
46. Robert Walsh, *An Appeal from the Judgments of Great Britain Respecting the United States of America, Part First* (Philadelphia: Mitchell, Ames, and White, 1819), 469.
47. "Art: On Training," *Analectic Magazine* (November 1817).
48. Altherr, et al., "Boxing," Vol. I, 133.
49. Gorn, *The Manly Art*, 38; Vaughn, 69.
50. "Barbarism no. II," *Religious Remembrancer* (June 21, 1817).
51. John Bristed, *America and Her Resources; Or, A View of the Agricultural, Commercial, Manufacturing, Financial, Political, Literary, Moral and Religious Capacity and Character of the American People* (New York: James Eastburn, 1818), 450.
52. A. F. M. Willich and Thomas Cooper. *The Domestic Encyclopedia, or, A Dictionary of Facts and Useful Knowledge, Chiefly Applicable to Rural & Domestic Economy: With an Appendix, Containing Additions in Domestic Medicine, and the Veterinary and Culinary Arts* (Philadelphia: Abraham Small, 1821), 291.
53. David Dudley Field, *A Statistical Account of the County of Middlesex, in Connecticut* (Middletown, CT: Clark & Lyman, 1819), 30–31.
54. D. B. Warden, *A Statistical, Political, and Historical Account of the United States of North America; From the Period of Their First Colonization to the Present Day, Vol. II* (London: Longman, Hurst, Rees, Orme, and Brown, and Hurst, Robinson, 1819), 373.
55. Henry Potter, *The Office and Duty of a Justice of the Peace: And a Guide to Sheriffs, Coroners, Clerks, Constables, and Other Civil Officers. According to the Laws of North-Carolina, with an Appendix Containing the Declaration of Rights and Constitution of This State, the Con-*

stitution of the United States, with the Amendments, Thereto; and a Collection of the Most Approved Forms (Raleigh, NC: J. Gales & Son, 1816), 148.

56. "Foreign Articles," *Niles Weekly Register* 12 (July 12, 1817): 318.

57. William Tell Harris, *Remarks Made During a Tour through the United States of America, in the Years 1817, 1818, and 1819* (London: Sherwood, Neely, & Jones, 1821), 110.

58. Willich and Cooper, 294.

59. John Palmer, "Athletic Sports and Spectacles in America," *Sporting Magazine: Or a Monthly Calendar of the Transactions of the Turf, the Chase and Every Other Diversion Interesting to the Man of Pleasure, Enterprise, and Spirit* 3 (1819): 165–168, p. 166.

60. Boddy, 76.

61. Gorn, *The Manly Art*, 31.

62. Boddy, 77.

63. Noah Norcester, "Review of Boxing," in *The Friend of Peace, Vol. II* (Cambridge: Hilliard and Metcalf, 1821), 4–6.

64. Willich and Cooper, 292.

65. Boddy, 76.

66. Gorn, *The Manly Art*, 32.

67. Barratt O'Hara, *From Figg to Johnson; A Complete History of the Heavyweight Championship, Containing Dates and Accurate Descriptions of Every Contest for the World's Boxing Title from the Time of the First Champion Down to the Present Day* (Chicago: Blossom Book Bourse, 1909), 117.

68. Boddy, 77.

69. Gorn, *The Manly Art*, 42.

70. Ira Rosenwaike, *Population History of New York City* (Syracuse, NY: Syracuse University Press, 1972), 36.

71. Jack Tager, *Boston Riots: Three Centuries of Social Violence* (Boston: Northeastern University Press, 2001), 107.

72. Richard Briggs Stott, *Jolly Fellows: Male Milieus in Nineteenth-Century America* (Baltimore: Johns Hopkins University Press, 2009), 110.

73. Guy Reel, *The National Police Gazette and the Making of the Modern American Man, 1879–1906* (New York: Palgrave Macmillan, 2006), 113.

74. Egan, 300.

75. Boddy, 37.

76. Dawne Y. Curry, Eric D. Duke, and Marshanda A. Smith, *Extending the Diaspora: New Histories of Black People* (Urbana: University of Illinois Press, 2009), 208.

77. Thomas Tracy, *Irishness and Womanhood in Nineteenth-Century British Writing* (Farnham, UK: Ashgate, 2009), 71.

78. Egan, 495.

79. Ibid., 496.

80. Roberts and Skutt, 19.

81. Nat Fleischer, Sam Andre, and Don Rafael, *An Illustrated History of Boxing* (New York: Citadel Press/Kensington, 2001), 34.

82. Roberts and Skutt, 19.

83. Henry Downes Miles, *Pugilistica: The History of British Boxing Containing Lives of the Most Celebrated Pugilists; Full Reports of Their Battles from Contemporary Newspapers, with Authentic Portraits, Personal Anecdotes, and Sketches of the Principal Patrons of the Prize Ring, Forming a Complete History of the Ring from Fig and Broughton, 1719-40, to the Last Championship Battle between King and Heenan, in December 1863* (Edinburgh: J. Grant, 1906), 127.

84. Francis Dowling, *Fistiana; Or, The Oracle of the Ring* (London: Clement, 1841), 58.

85. Dowling, 30; Fleischer et al., 34.

86. Dowling, 30.

87. O'Hara, 119.

88. Dowling, 30.

89. "The Championship of England," *Spirit of the Times* (October 11, 1845).

90. Julian Norridge, *Can We Have Our Balls Back, Please? How the British Invented Sport* (London: Allen Lane, 2008), 26.

91. Roberts and Skutt, 19.

92. Barry D. Jordan and Joseph E. Herrera, *Medical Aspects of Boxing* (London: Springer Verlag, 2008), 5.

93. Rodriguez, *Reconstruction in the Cane Fields*, 25.

94. Jordan and Herrera, 5.

95. "The Late Fight between Nick Wark and Deaf Burke," *Spirit of the Times* (October 31, 1840); A. Winch, *Life and Battles of Yankee Sullivan, Embracing Full and Accurate Reports of His Fights with Hammer Lane, Tom Secor, Harry Bell, Bob Caunt, Tom Hyer, John Morrisey* (Philadelphia: A. Winch, 1854), 22; James M. Rose and Alice Eichholz, *Black Genesis* (Detroit: Gale Research, 1978), 131.

96. Rodriguez, *Reconstruction in the Cane Fields*, 28.

97. Riess, *City Games*, 16; Beekman, 10.

98. Gorn, *The Manly Art*, 131.

99. Stott, 2.

100. I-hwa Yi, *Korea's Pastimes and Customs: A Social History* (Paramus, NJ: Homa Sekey Books, 2006), 111.

101. Beekman, 54.

102. See, for example, Hurd, 1163.

103. Numerous previous scholars have promoted the view of wrestling as an agrarian sport. See, for example, Richard Sisson, Christian K. Zacher, and Andrew R. L. Cayton, *The American Midwest: An Interpretive Encyclopedia* (Bloomington: Indiana University Press, 2007), 889; Nolan Zavoral, *A Season on the Mat: Dan Gable and the Pursuit of Perfection* (New York: Simon & Schuster, 1998), 36.

104. See, for example, "Choice of a Profession," *New England Farmer* 18, no. 28 (January 15, 1840): 240; Abel Brewster, *Free Man's Companion* (Hartford, CT: Canfield Printer, 1827), 114; Maria L. Sanford, "The Labor Question," *Pennsylvania School Journal* 27 no. 3 (September 1878): 81–85, p. 82.
105. See, for example, Thomas Jefferson, *Notes on the State of Virginia* (Boston: Lilly and Wait, 1832); Thomas Jefferson, *Notes on the State of Virginia* (Philadelphia: Sherman & Co. Printers, 1885).
106. State of Michigan, *Transactions of the State Agricultural Society* (Lansing: R. W. Ingals State Printer), 95.
107. See, for example, "Wrestling Society" *Famer's Magazine* 1, no. 1 (May 1834): 12–13, p. 12; "The Check-Rein," *Southern Cultivator* 13 no. 11 (November 1854): 340; Ettrick Shepherd, "On the Changes in the Habits, Amusements, and Condition of the Scottish Peasantry," *Journal of Agriculture* (1832): 256–263, p. 262.
108. Justo L. Gonzalez, *The Reformation to the Present Day* (San Francisco: Harper & Row, 1984), 326.
109. Barry Hankins, *American Evangelicals: A Contemporary History of a Mainstream Religious Movement* (Lanham, MD: Rowman & Littlefield, 2008), 15.
110. Ted Ownby, *Subduing Satan: Religion, Recreation, and Manhood in the Rural South, 1865–1920* (Chapel Hill: University of North Carolina Press, 1993), ix.
111. Ibid.
112. Christopher J. Olsen, *Political Culture and Secession in Mississippi: Masculinity, Honor, and the Antiparty Tradition, 1830–1860* (Oxford: Oxford University Press, 2000), 52.
113. Beekman, 10.
114. "The Gathering: Toronto to Athletic Games," *Spirit of the Times* (November 2, 1839).
115. "American Indians," *Religious Remembrancer* (July 6, 1822).
116. "The Frazer River Indians," *Ballou's Pictoral Drawing-Room Companion* (August 21, 1858).
117. See, for example, M. L. Weems, *The Life of George Washington: With Curious Anecdotes, Equally Honourable to Himself, and Exemplary to His Young Countrymen* (Philadelphia: Joseph Allen, 1833), 26.
118. "Life of Lincoln," *White Cloud Kansas* (September 6, 1860).
119. "On Dits in Sporting Circles," *Spirit of the Times* (November 29, 1845).
120. "Effects of Training," *Journal of Health* (June 13, 1832).
121. Riess, *City Games*, 19.
122. Ibid.
123. "The Championship of England," *Spirit of the Times* (October 11, 1845).
124. Riess, *City Games*, 20.
125. "Suicide of Johnny Broome," *Spirit of the Times* (June 30, 1855).
126. Arthur Ashe, *A Hard Road to Glory. Boxing: The African-American Athlete in Boxing* (New York: Amistad, 1993), 5.
127. Desch-Obi, 100.
128. "Life on the Gulf of Mexico," *The Rover* (July 26, 1843).
129. Winch, 22; Rose and Eichholz, 131.
130. "Vanderlyn," *American Monthly Magazine* 3 (May 1837): 490.
131. Rose and Eichholz, 131.
132. "The Great International Fight," *Spirit of the Times* (May 5, 1860).
133. Winch, 9; Stott, 110.
134. Stott, 110.
135. Timony, 25.
136. Isenberg, 61.
137. Winch, 35.
138. Guy Reel, *The National Police Gazette and the Making of the Modern American Man, 1879–1906* (New York: Palgrave Macmillan, 2006), 117.
139. Winch, 35.
140. Arne K. Lang, *Prizefighting: An American History* (Jefferson, NC: McFarland, 2008), 17.
141. "Newport, The Outsider," *Spirit of the Times* (November 11, 1848).
142. Stott, 110.
143. Timony, 28.
144. "Trial of Hyer," *Liberator* (March 30, 1849).
145. Timony, 28.
146. Isenberg, 77.
147. "The Great Prize Fight, between Tom Hyer & Yankee Sullivan," *Sprit of the Times* (February 17, 1849).
148. Stott, 110.
149. Tyler Anbinder, *Five Points: The 19th-Century New York City Neighborhood That Invented Tap Dance, Stole Elections, and Became the World's Most Notorious Slum* (New York: Free Press, 2001), 206.
150. Lang, 17.
151. Anbinder, 206.
152. "Article 1,—No Title," *Knickerbocker* (October 1850).
153. Stott, 110.
154. Ibid., 113.
155. "The Battle of Fools," *New York Evangelist* (June 14, 1855).
156. "Hints on Moral Training," *Friend's Review* (November 20, 1847).
157. Helen Rose Fuchs Ebaugh, *Handbook of Religion and Social Institutions* (New York: Springer, 2005), 295.
158. Michael Bellesiles, *1877: America's Year of Living Violently* (New York: New Press, 2010), 276.

159. "Muscular Heathenism," *New York Times* (April 30, 1860).
160. See, for example, "Fugitives Remanded to Slavery," *Liberator* (May 4, 1860).
161. Shirley Samuels, *Facing America: Iconography and the Civil War* (New York: Oxford University Press, 2004), 7.
162. Beekman, 10.
163. Gerald R. Gems, Linda J. Borish, and Gertrud Pfister, *Sports in American History: From Colonization to Globalization* (Champaign, IL: Human Kinetics, 2008), 135.
164. Dave Zirin, *A People's History of Sports in the United States: 250 Years of Politics, Protest, People, and Play* (New York: New Press, 2008), 40.
165. Beekman, 10.
166. Gary W. Gallagher, *The Wilderness Campaign* (Chapel Hill: University of North Carolina Press, 1997), 202.
167. Jeff Leen, *The Queen of the Ring: Sex, Muscles, Diamonds, and the Making of an American Legend* (New York: Atlantic Monthly Press, 2009), 15.
168. A. F. Hill, *Our Boys: The Personal Experiences of a Soldier in the Army of the Potomac* (Philadelphia: John E. Potter, 1864), 161.
169. Richard E. Matthews, *The 149th Pennsylvania Volunteer Infantry Unit in the Civil War* (Jefferson, NC: McFarland, 2007), 121.
170. George Augustus Sala, *My Diary in America in the Midst of War* (London: Tinsley Bros., 1865), 258.
171. "Sporting," *New York Times* (August 18, 1864).
172. "Later from Europe," *Abingdon Virginian* (January 1, 1864).
173. *The Semi-Weekly Shreveport News* (January 8, 1864; October 14, 1861).
174. "A Pugilistic Novelty," *The Smoky Hill and Republican Union* (April 24, 1862).
175. Stott, 112.
176. "Sports in Camp," *Maine Farmer* (January 16, 1862).
177. "Old Soldiers," *Anderson Intelligencer* (February 21, 1861).
178. Gorn, *The Manly Art*, 160.
179. Gerald R. Gems, Linda J. Borish, and Gertrud Pfister, *Sports in American History: From Colonization to Globalization* (Champaign, IL: Human Kinetics, 2008), 135.
180. Edward L. Molineux, "Physical and Military Exercises in Public Schools: A National Necessity," *American Journal of Education* (June 1862).
181. John Swett, "Thirteenth Annual Report, of the Superintendent of Public Instruction of the State of California for the Year 1863," *Appendix to the Journals of State Assembly of the Fifteenth Session of the Legislature of the State of California, Vol. 1* (Sacramento: O. M. Clayes State Printer, 1864), 112.

182. *Columbia Daily Phoenix* (July 24, 1865).
183. "On the Battlefield," *New York Daily Tribune* (September 20, 1862).
184. "Treatment of Black Soldiers," *Chicago Tribune* (April 9, 1864).
185. Samuel R. Watkins, *Co. Aytch* (Chattanooga, TN: Times Printing, 1900), 10.
186. William H. Freeman, *Physical Education, Exercise, and Sport Science in a Changing Society* (Sudbury, MA: Jones and Bartlett, 2012), 145.
187. Lang, 25.
188. Jordan and Herrera, 5.
189. Ibid.
190. M.P. McCrillis, "Boxing and No-Holds-Barred-Fighting: The Histories of the Two Arts Are Similar," *Black Belt* (October 1999): 64–69, 167, p. 67.
191. Eric Dunning, *Sport Matters: Sociological Studies of Sport, Violence, and Civilization* (London: Routledge, 1999): 59.
192. Ibid.
193. Murray.
194. "Article 2, No Title," *Sprit of the Times* (July 30, 1836); Gorn, *The Manly Art*, 47.
195. Gorn, *The Manly Art*, 20.
196. Green, *Martial Arts of the World*, 466.
197. Leen, 33.
198. Morton and O'Brien, 29.
199. "Sporting," *New York Times* (August 18, 1864); Stott, 237.
200. Stott, 237.
201. Edward Winslow Marin, *The Secrets of the Great City: A Work Descriptive of the Virtues and the Vices. of New York City* (New York: Jones Brother, 1868), 417.
202. Stott, 238.
203. Ibid.
204. Marin, 416–418; Stott, 238.
205. For example, see "A Female Boxing Match," *New York Times* (March 17, 1876); "The Prize Ring," *National Police Gazette* (April 28, 1883).
206. Stott, 238.
207. John J. Jennings, *Theatrical and Circus Life, or, Secrets of the Stage, Green-Room and Sawdust Arena: Embracing a History of the Theatre from Shakespeare's Time to the Present Day* (Mansfield, OH: Mansfield Union, 1883), 393.
208. D. Appleton and Company and Roger S. Baskes Collection (Newberry Library), *Appletons' Dictionary of New York and Vicinity* (New York: D. Appleton, 1883), 14.
209. State of New York, *Testimony Taken before the Senate Committee on Cities Pursuant to Resolution Adopted January 20, 1890* (Albany: J. B. Lyon, 1891), 1203.
210. Samuel Anderson Mackeever, *Glimpses of Gotham; and, City Characters* (New York: National Police Gazette Office, 1880), 59.
211. Ibid.

212. Isenberg, 85.
213. Beekman, 23.
214. "Policemen: On Their Muscle," *Washington Post* (March 16, 1878).
215. Beekman, 23.
216. Morton and O'Brien, 27
217. Keith Elliot Greenberg, *Pro Wrestling: From Carnivals to Cable TV* (Minneapolis, MN: LernerSports, 2000), 14.
218. Beekman, 26.
219. "The Champion Wrestler Thrown," *New York Times* (September 4, 1882).
220. Morton and O'Brien, 27; Beekman, 23.
221. Beekman, 23.
222. Charles Barnard, "The Training Table," *Chautauquan* (September 1892); "Muldoon Curing Gen. Bell," *New York Times* (October 14, 1907).
223. Lang, 22.
224. Beekman, 23.
225. James Henry Potts, *Black and White or the Saloon versus Temperance: The Greatest Problem Confronting Our Nation Today* (Detroit: F. B. Dickerson, 1908), 221.
226. "Bans Dempsey–Wills Bout in This State," *New York Times* (February 3, 1823).
227. Clifford Putney, *Muscular Christianity: Manhood and Sports in Protestant America, 1880-1920* (Cambridge, MA: Harvard University Press, 2001), 15.
228. Beekman, 22.
229. "A Slogging Parson," *National Police Gazette* (September 9, 1882).
230. William Edwards, *Art of Boxing and Science of Self-Defense, Together with a Manual of Training* (New York: Excelsior, 1888), 25.
231. Beekman, 22.
232. R. K. Fox, *Boxing: With Hints on the Art of Attack and Defense and How to Train for the Prize Ring* (New York: R. K. Fox, 1889), 7.
233. "Our Boys and Girls," *LA Times* (September 26, 1897).
234. Erwin Fahlbusch and Geoffrey William Bromiley, *The Encyclopedia of Christianity* (Grand Rapids, MI: Wm. B. Eerdmans, 1999), 179.
235. T. De Witt Talmage, *Sermons* (New York: Harper, 1872), 288.
236. Theodore Roosevelt, *Theodore Roosevelt: An Autobiography* (New York: Scribner's, 1913), 29.
237. "College Athletic Sports," *New York Times* (November 4, 1882).
238. "Fighting with Bare Knuckles, *New York Times* (November 21, 1884).
239. "Fact and Rumor," *Harvard Crimson* (February 12, 1887).
240. "A Professor of Pugilism for Harvard University," *Fibre and Fabric* (December 30, 1893).
241. "Club Chat About Sports," *New York Times* (November 22, 1896).

242. William J. Baker, *Sports in the Western World* (Urbana: University of Illinois Press, 1988), 165.
243. "An Assault at Arms at Booth's," *New York Times* (February 22, 1879).
244. "Police Athletic Club," *New York Times* (June 24, 1877).
245. Baker, *Sports in the Western World*.
246. "To Foster Amateur Athletics," *New York Times* (January 22, 1888).
247. "Amateur Athletic Union Events," *New York Times* (March 14, 1888).
248. "Amateur Athletic Affairs," *New York Times* (November 20, 1890).
249. "Boss M'Laughlin's Slander," *New York Times* (October 4, 1893).
250. David G. McComb, *Sports: An Illustrated History* (New York: Oxford University Press, 1998), 115.
251. Bill Mallon and Ian Buchanan, *Historical Dictionary of the Olympic Movement* (Lanham, MD: Scarecrow Press, 2006), 36.
252. "Riot at a Sparring Match," *Washington Post* (December 16, 1894).
253. Guy Reel, *The National Police Gazette and the Making of the Modern American Man, 1879-1906* (New York: Palgrave Macmillan, 2006), 117.
254. Ibid.
255. Howard P. Chudacoff, *The Age of the Bachelor: Creating an American Subculture* (Princeton, NJ: Princeton University Press, 1999), 187.
256. Reel, 4.
257. Frank L. Mott, *A History of American Magazines. 2. 1850–1865* (Cambridge, MA: Harvard University Press, 1938), 325; Rodriguez, *Reconstruction in the Cane Fields*, 29.
258. Joyce Duncan, *Sport in American Culture: From Ali to X-Games* (Santa Barbara, CA: ABC-CLIO, 2004), 345.
259. Chudacoff, 187.
260. R. K. Fox, *Boxing*; R. K. Fox, *Edward Hanlan, America's Champion Oarsman, with History and Portrait. Also, History and Portrait of Edward A. Trickett, the Great Australian Oarsman* (New York: R. K. Fox, 1880); Richard K. Fox Publishing Co., *The New Book of Rules: Official and Standard; Together with the Rules of the Amateur Athletic Union* (New York: Richard K. Fox, 1913).
261. Lang, 20.
262. Klaus J. Bade and Myron Weiner, *Migration Past, Migration Future: Germany and the United States* (Providence, RI: Berghahn Books, 1997), 45.
263. John Powell, *Encyclopedia of North American Immigration* (New York: Facts on File, 2005), 60.
264. Beekman, 48.
265. Green, *Martial Arts of the World*, 446.

266. Powell, 161.
267. "Japanese Scenes," *Ballou's Pictorial Drawing-Room Companion* (May 10, 1856).
268. Beekman, 20.
269. Ibid.
270. "The 'Police Gazette' Medal for Mixed Wrestling," *National Police Gazette* (June 24, 1882).
271. "Points for Correspondents," *National Police Gazette* (January 27, 1894).
272. "A Tug for the Trophy," *National Police Gazette* (July 21, 1883).
273. "A Coming Prize Fight," *Washington Post* (February 15, 1881).
274. "A Telegraph Compact," *Washington Post* (March 31, 1882).
275. "Bishop Lughlin Dead," *New York Times*) December 30, 1891).
276. Vaughn, 61.
277. Bert Randolph Sugar, *Bert Sugar on Boxing: The Best of the Sport's Most Notable Writer* (Guilford, CT: Lyons Press, 2003), 61.
278. Ibid., 48.
279. Roberts and Skutt, 44.
280. Ibid.
281. Ibid.
282. Brian McKenna, *Early Exits: The Premature Endings of Baseball Careers* (Lanham, MD: Scarecrow Press, 2007), 158.
283. Sullivan and Sargent, 71.
284. Roberts and Skutt, 44–45.
285. William Vincent Shannon, *The American Irish: A Political and Social Portrait* (Amherst: University of Massachusetts Press, 1989), 97.
286. Morton and O'Brien, 27.
287. "Sullivan's Sparing Tour," *New York Times* (February 13, 1882); Sullivan and Sargent, 125.
288. Adam J. Pollack, *John L. Sullivan: The Career of the First Gloved Heavyweight Champion* (Jefferson, NC: McFarland, 2006), 70.
289. Stott, 225.
290. Isenberg, 152.
291. Mark Edward Lender and James Kirby Martin, *Drinking in America: A History* (New York: Free Press, 1982), 109.
292. Stott, 225.
293. "Sullivan Meets a Master," *New York Times* (July 1, 1884).
294. Daniel B. Turney, "Don't Like His Indorser," *Washington Post* (July 18, 1889).
295. Stott, 225.
296. Robert George Rodriguez, *The Regulation of Boxing: A History and Comparative Analysis of Policies among American States* (Jefferson, NC: McFarland, 2009), 29.
297. Pollack, 10.
298. Simon Gardiner, *Sports Law* (London: Cavendish, 2004), 622; Anderson, 51.
299. Pollack, 10.
300. Roberts and Skutt, 45.
301. "Kilrain and Sullivan," *Washington Post* (December 2, 1888).
302. "Sullivan in Fine Shape," *Washington Post* (June 24, 1889).
303. Armond Fields, *James J. Corbett: A Biography of the Heavyweight Boxing Champion and Popular Theater Headliner* (Jefferson, NC: McFarland, 2001), 36.
304. "The Bigger Brute Won," *New York Times* (July 9, 1889).
305. Ibid.
306. Sullivan and Sargent, 217.
307. Anderson, 52.
308. Pollack, 199.
309. Ibid., 65.
310. Sullivan and Sargent, 120.
311. Colleen Aycock and Mark Scott, *The First Black Boxing Champions: Essays on Fighters of the 1800s to the 1920s* (Jefferson, NC: McFarland, 2011), 32.
312. Ibid.
313. Gregory Bond, *Jim Crow at Play: Race, Manliness, and the Color Line in American Sports, 1876–1916* (Ph.D. thesis, University of Wisconsin–Madison, 2008), 149.
314. Ibid.
315. Pollack, 158.
316. Donald L. Deardorff and Robert J. Higgs, *Sports: A Reference Guide and Critical Commentary, 1980–1999* (Westport, CT: Greenwood Press, 2000), 17.
317. Judith E. Harper, *Women during the Civil War: An Encyclopedia* (New York: Routledge, 2004), 456.
318. Theresa Ann Case, *The Great Southwest Railroad Strike and Free Labor* (College Station: Texas A&M University Press, 2010), 18.
319. George Rogers Taylor and Irene D. Neu, *The American Railroad Network, 1861–1890* (Cambridge, MA: Harvard University Press, 1956), 2.
320. Leen, 34.
321. Isenberg, 147.
322. Taylor and Neu, 1.
323. Conrad Taeuber, *People of the United States in the Twentieth Century* (Washington, D.C.: Government Printing Office, 1972), 176.
324. Dennis W. Johnson, *The Laws That Shaped America: Fifteen Acts of Congress and Their Lasting Impact* (New York: Routledge, 2009), 97.
325. Robert D. Mitchell and Paul A. Groves, *North America: The Historical Geography of a Changing Continent* (Totowa, NJ: Rowman & Littlefield, 1987), 285.
326. Riess, *City Games*, 86, 109.
327. Rotundo, 19.
328. Gorn, *The Manly Art*, 141.
329. Rotundo, 222.
330. Ibid., 239.

331. Ibid.
332. George B. Kirsch, Othello Harris, and Claire Elaine Nolte, *Encyclopedia of Ethnicity and Sports in the United States* (Westport, CT: Greenwood Press, 2000), 110.
333. Roberts and Skutt, 44.
334. F. Daniel Somrack, *Boxing in San Francisco* (Charleston, SC: Arcadia, 2005), 11; Roberts and Skutt, 44.
335. Roberts and Skutt, 88.
336. Ibid., 44.
337. "Kilrain Loses," *LA Times* (February 18, 1890).
338. "Sullivan Meets a Master"; Turney.
339. "The Bigger Brute Won."
340. "Corbett Reappointed," *Chicago Daily Tribune* (March 5, 1890).
341. "Have a Care Mr. Corbett!" *Washington Post* (August 25, 1892).
342. "Corbett at Atlanta," *Chicago Daily Tribune* (September 11, 1892).
343. "After the Battle," *Chicago Daily Tribune* (September 9, 1892).
344. "Bets Declared Off," *Washington Post* (May 23, 1891).
345. "Have a Care Mr. Corbett!"
346. "Sullivan's Opinion of Corbett," *Washington Post* (June 30, 1891).
347. Rowland George Allanson-Winn Headley, *Boxing* (London: A. D. Innes, 1897), 182.
348. "Big Ones Compared," *Chicago Daily Tribune* (September 5, 1892).
349. Lang, 31.
350. "Pen Picture of the Olympic Arena," *Chicago Daily Tribune* (September 8, 1892).
351. "Vanquished at Last," *Washington Post* (September 8, 1892).
352. "Return of the Gladiators: Corbett Travels in Triumphal State and Sullivan in a State of Intoxication," *Washington Post* (September 10, 1892).
353. Peter Williams, *The Sports Immortals: Deifying the American Athlete* (Bowling Green, OH: Bowling Green State University Popular Press, 1994), 124.
354. Ibid., 123.
355. Stott, 225.
356. Isenberg, 152.
357. Gorn, *The Manly Art*, 247.
358. "Have a Care Mr. Corbett!"
359. John Peter Sugden, *Boxing and Society: An International Analysis* (Manchester, UK: Manchester University Press, 1996), 29.
360. Roberts and Skutt, 44, 88.
361. "Corbett at Atlanta"; "After the Battle."
362. "Wizard Edison's Wonders," *Washington Post* (May 14, 1891).
363. Dan Streible, *Fight Pictures: A History of Boxing and Early Cinema* (Berkeley: University of California Press, 2008), 58.
364. "The Veriscope," *New York Times* (May 26, 1897).
365. Roberts and Skutt, 686.
366. Robert Niemi, *History in the Media: Film and Television History in the Media* (Santa Barbara, CA: ABC-CLIO, 2006), 191.
367. "Coney Island's Prize Ring," *New York Times* (October 10, 1893).
368. "The Week in Review," *Congregationalist* (June 28, 1894).
369. "Corbett Says Riordan Was Diseased," *Chicago Daily Tribune* (November 18, 1894).
370. "Fight Films," *LA Times*, March 23, 1897.
371. Rodriguez, *The Regulation of Boxing*, 41.
372. Lang, 31.
373. Riess, *City Games*, 174.
374. Sammons, 18.
375. Riess, *City Games*, 174.
376. Sammons, 18.
377. Anderson, 53.
378. Riess, *City Games*, 174.
379. Rodriguez, *The Regulation of Boxing*, 111.
380. Ibid.
381. I. N. Love, "The State of Nevada the Mecca of Pugilists," *Medical Mirror* 8 (1897): 209.
382. State of California, *The Statutes of California and the Amendments to the Codes* (Sacramento: A.J. Johnston, 1899), 153.
383. Sammons, 24.
384. Jordan and Herrera, 713.
385. David Kenneth Wiggins, *Sport in America: From Wicked Amusement to National Obsession* (Champaign, IL: Human Kinetics, 1995), 169.
386. Ibid., 202.
387. Steven W. Pope, *Patriotic Games: Sporting Traditions in the American Imagination, 1876–1926* (New York/Oxford: Oxford University Press, 2005), 142.
388. Alfred A. Woodhull, *Personal Hygiene, Designed for Undergraduates* (New York: J. Wiley & Sons, 1906), 78.
389. Donald J. Mrozek, *Sport and American Mentality, 1880–1910* (Knoxville: University of Tennessee Press, 1983), 56.
390. "The Naval Academy," *New York Times* (April 3, 1892).
391. Stephen E. Ambrose, *Duty, Honor, Country; A History of West Point* (Baltimore: Johns Hopkins University Press, 1966), 246.
392. "Club Chat about Sports."
393. Edward Conradi, "Latin in the High School," *Pedagogical Seminary* (March 1905): 9.
394. "Teaching the Boy to Fight," *Washington Post* (May 31, 1904).
395. See, for example, "New Field for Women," *Washington Post* (October 19, 1911).
396. See, for example, Arthur Dean, "Your Boy and Your Girl," *Washington Post* (October 18, 1927).

397. Beekman, 26; Pollack, 10.
398. Beekman, 26.
399. "How Trick Wrestlers Deceive the Public against Their Own Interests," *National Police Gazette* (February 25, 1905).
400. J. Ed Grillo, "Sporting Comment," *Washington Post* (January 6, 1910).
401. Roberts and Skutt, 53.
402. David G. Schwartz, *Roll the Bones: The History of Gambling* (New York: Gotham Books, 2006), 340.
403. Roberts and Skutt, 124.
404. "Gossip of the Boxing Ring," *Washington Post* (September 14, 1908).
405. Colleen Aycock and Mark Scott, *Joe Gans: A Biography of the First African American World Boxing Champion* (Jefferson, NC: McFarland, 2008), 63.
406. Roberts and Skutt, 147.
407. "Jack Johnson Beats Martin," *LA Times* (February 6, 1903).
408. "Burns Willing to Box Negro," *LA Times* (July 19, 1907); "With the Heavy-Weights," *Washington Post* (December 10, 1906).
409. "Burns Favorite Over Negro Fighter," *New York Times* (December 25, 1908).
410. Robert W. Thurston, *Lynching: American Mob Murder in Global Perspective* (Farnham, UK: Ashgate, 2011), 266.
411. See, for example, "Yesterday at Reno," *Chicago Daily Tribune* (July 5, 1910); John Ridley, "A True Champion vs. the Great White Hope," *National Public Radio* (June 22, 2011); "Jack Johnson Jailed Again," *New York Times* (January 21, 1910).
412. Gail Bederman, *Manliness and Civilization: A Cultural History of Gender and Race in the United States, 1880–1917* (Chicago: University of Chicago Press, 1996), 5.
413. "Jack Johnson Wins," *New York Times* (December 26, 1908).
414. Franklin F. Johnson, "Biennial of Odd Fellows," *Afro-American* (1914).
415. Billy Lewis, "The War Has Broken Up the Fight Game in Europe," *Freeman* (September 12, 1914).
416. Ridley.
417. Roberts and Skutt, 147.
418. "Yesterday at Reno."
419. "Jack Johnson Jailed Again."
420. "Jack Sits with White Women," *LA Times* (May 1, 1910).
421. "Yesterday at Reno."
422. Joe S. Jackson, "Sporting Facts and Fancies," *Washington Post* (February 3, 1911).
423. Grillo.
424. Randy Roberts, *Papa Jack: Jack Johnson and the Era of White Hopes* (New York: Free Press, 1985), 114.
425. Ibid.
426. Bederman, 5.
427. Roberts and Skutt, 686.
428. "Johnson Flees to Canada," *Chicago Daily Tribune* (June 27, 1913).
429. "Detailed Story of the Havana Fight by Rounds," *Chicago Daily Tribune* (April 6, 1915).
430. Rotundo, 257.
431. See, for example, Gorn, *The Manly Art*, 31; "Sullivan Meets a Master"; "President Tries Jiu Jitsu."

Chapter III

1. "All SIN," *Chicago Daily Tribune* (October 23, 1876).
2. "A Brutal Wrestling Match," *New York Times* (January 29, 1886).
3. Alexander DeConde, Richard Dean Burns, and Fredrik Logevall, *Encyclopedia of American Foreign Policy: Vol. 2, E–N* (New York: Scribner's, 2002), 204.
4. Gary Y. Okihiro, *The Columbia Guide to Asian American History* (New York: Columbia University Press, 2001), 69.
5. "Asiatic Slave Trade," *New York Daily Times* (July 22, 1853).
6. June Drenning Holmquist, *They Chose Minnesota: A Survey of the State's Ethnic Groups* (St. Paul: Minnesota Historical Society Press, 1981), 531.
7. Roger Daniels, *Coming to America: A History of Immigration and Ethnicity in American Life* (New York: HarperCollins, 1990), 239.
8. Robert G. Lee, *Orientals: Asian Americans in Popular Culture* (Philadelphia: Temple University Press, 1999), 9.
9. Nicole Constable, *Romance on a Global Stage: Pen Pals, Virtual Ethnography, and "Mail-Order" Marriages* (Berkeley: University of California Press, 2003), 178.
10. Gary Y. Okihiro, *The Columbia Guide to Asian American History* (New York: Columbia University Press, 2001), 141.
11. William Travis Hanes and Frank Sanello. *The Opium Wars: The Addiction of One Empire and the Corruption of Another* (Naperville, IL: Sourcebooks, 2007), 13.
12. "Opium," *Journal of the Philadelphia College of Pharmacy* 1, no. 4 (November 1827): 110.
13. "Opium Trade to China," *Christian Watchman* (September 14, 1938).
14. "The Chinese Trade," *Corsair* (January 4, 1840).
15. "China," *New Yorker* (October 8, 1839).
16. See, for example, "The Chinese War," *Christian Register* (November 27, 1841) and "England and China," *Brother Jonathan* (February 12, 1842).
17. See, for example, "Chinese War Junks,"

Catholic Telegraph (May 23, 1840) and "The Chinese Army," *Family Magazine* (May 1, 1847).
18. "Peace with China," *Albion* (December 24, 1842).
19. "The Opening of China," *Boston Recorder* (February 2, 1842).
20. "China," *American Review* 1, no. 3 (March 1848): 231.
21. "Poor China," *New York State Mechanic: A Journal of the Manual Arts, Trades, and Manufactures* (February 4, 1843).
22. William Gill, "The Chinese Army," *United Service* (November 1880): 614–632, p. 629.
23. Silas Pinckney Holbrook, *Sketches, by a Traveler* (Boston: Carter and Hendee, 1830), 271.
24. "China: Character and Prospects of the Chinese Rebellion," *New York Times* (April 20, 1853).
25. "The Chinese," *Home Magazine* (September 1855).
26. "A Case of Chloroform, and a Mission to China," *Home Journal* (September 2, 1848).
27. Green, *Martial Arts of the World*, 26.
28. Craig, *Sports and Games of the Ancients*, 50.
29. Green, *Martial Arts of the World*, 706.
30. Ibid.
31. Sally Wilkins, *Sports and Games of Medieval Cultures* (Westport, CT: Greenwood Press, 2002), 95–96. While the stories of Bodhidarma as the founder of Kung Fu appear frequently, some scholars take issue with the idea and claim that Bodhidarma was "a fictional creation of historians writing many centuries later" (Craig, *Sports and Games of the Ancients*, 50).
32. Zhongyi Tong and Tim Cartmell. *The Method of Chinese Wrestling* (Berkeley, CA: North Atlantic Books, 2005), 6.
33. Green, *Martial Arts of the World*, 706.
34. James A. Flath and Norman Smith. *Beyond Suffering: Recounting War in Modern China* (Vancouver: UBC Press, 2011), 155.
35. G. T. Brettany, *The People of Asia* (Naga, Delhi: Kalpaz, 2005), 228.
36. Marcus Ackroyd, *Advancing with the Army Medicine, the Professions, and Social Mobility in the British Isles, 1790–1850* (Oxford: Oxford University Press, 2006), 336; Frederick W. Mote, *Imperial China, 900–1800* (Cambridge, MA: Harvard University Press, 1999), 274.
37. Marvin C. Whiting, *Imperial Chinese Military History: 8000BC–1912AD* (Lincoln, NE: iUniverse, 2002), 424.
38. Nicola Di Cosmo, *Military Culture in Imperial China* (Cambridge, MA: Harvard University Press, 2009) 220, 230.
39. Kam Louie, *Theorising Chinese Masculinity: Society and Gender in China* (Cambridge: Cambridge University Press, 2002), 7; Putney, *Muscular Christianity*, 132.

40. Whiting, 424.
41. "Chinese Characteristics," *Albion* (April 15, 1843).
42. "A Chinaman's Ball," *North American Miscellany* (June 1, 1852).
43. "The Chinese in California," *Littell's Living Age* (December 15, 1849).
44. See, for example, "The Chinese in California," *Baltimore American* (December 22, 1849) and "The Chinese in California," *Friends' Weekly Intelligencer* (December 29, 1849).
45. Henry M. Field, "The Chinese in California," *New York Evangelist* (August 14, 1851).
46. Ibid.
47. "Chinese in California," *Maine Farmer* (January 1, 1852).
48. "Linen Washing in California," *Scientific American* (December 27, 1851).
49. David L. Eng, *Racial Castration: Managing Masculinity in Asian America* (Durham, NC: Duke University Press, 2001), 17.
50. Lee, *Orientals*, 9.
51. John Zumerchik and Steven Laurence Danver, *Seas and Waterways of the World* (Santa Barbara, CA: ABC-CLIO, 2010), 241.
52. Stephen R. Turnbull, *The Samurai Swordsman: Master of War* (North Clarendon, VT: Tuttle, 2008), 37.
53. H. Paul Varley, *Japanese Culture* (Honolulu: University of Hawaii Press, 2004), 107.
54. William E. Deal, *Handbook to Life in Medieval and Early Modern Japan* (Paradise, CA: Paw Prints, 2010), 128.
55. Linda K. Menton, *The Rise of Modern Japan* (Honolulu: Curriculum Research & Development Group, University of Hawaii, 2003), 12.
56. Peter Whitfield, *Cities of the World: A History in Maps* (Berkeley: University of California Press, 2005), 129.
57. Oscar Ratti and Adele Westbrook, *Secrets of the Samurai: A Survey of the Martial Arts in Feudal Japan* (Rutland, VT: Tuttle, 1981), 24.
58. "China," *Albion* (August 15, 1840).
59. Guttmann and Thompson, 68.
60. "Japanese Scenes," *Ballou's Pictorial Drawing-Room Companion* (May 10, 1856).
61. "Mr. Harris in Japan," *Circular* (January 27, 1859).
62. "An American's Report of the Japanese," *Friend* (May 18, 1861).
63. "A Glimpse of Japan," *Albion* (August 7, 1869).
64. Eiji Oguma, *A Genealogy of 'Japanese' Self-Images* (Melbourne: Trans Pacific Press, 2002), 11.
65. Thomas J. Rimmer and Van C. Gessel, *The Columbia Anthology of Modern Japanese Literature* (New York: Columbia University Press, 2005), 815.
66. Monica Chiu, *Asian Americans in New*

Notes—Chapter III

England: Culture and Community (Durham, NH: University of New Hampshire Press, 2009), 69.

67. Ellis S. Krauss and Benjamin Nyblade, *First Contacts to the Pacific War* (London: Routledge Curzon, 2004), 2.

68. "Protection to the Japanese," *New York Times* (May 19, 1860).

69. "The Japanese in New York," *Independent* (June 21, 1860).

70. "Wrestling Matches of Girls," *Chicago Tribune* (August 20, 1867).

71. "Peculiarities of the Japanese," *Christian Observer* (August 30, 1860).

72. Chiu, 71.

73. Ibid., 72.

74. "The Japanese Jugglers," *Chicago Tribune* (March 10, 1867).

75. "The Condition of Little All Right," *New York Times* (June 14, 1867).

76. "Interview with the Japanese Troupe," *New York Times* (April 9, 1871).

77. Chiu, 71.

78. "The Japanese in Philadelphia," *New York Times* (June 13, 1860).

79. "The Aborigines of Japan," *Supplement to the Courant* 33, no. 11 (May 30, 1868): 88.

80. "The Japanese," *Albion* (November 16, 1872).

81. Benjamin Smith Lyman, "The Character of the Japanese," *Journal of Speculative Philosophy* 19, no. 2 (April 1885): 133–174, p. 172.

82. "The Condition of Little All Right."

83. "Interview with the Japanese Troupe."

84. "The Literature of the Japanese," *Friend* (March 27, 1852).

85. "Japan," *Democrat's Review* (April 1, 1852).

86. "Japan," *Eclectic* (January 1, 1853).

87. "Shameshima Goi," *New York Times* (December 16, 1870).

88. "The Japanese," *American Phrenological Journal* (February 1868).

89. "Japan," *Merry's Museum and Parley's* (July 1, 1852).

90. "The Japanese and Chinese," *Southern Planter* (November 1860).

91. "Japan, Japanese, and Chinese," *Sprit of the Times* (August 18, 1860).

92. "Japan," *Eclectic*.

93. Martin Marger, *Race and Ethnic Relations: American and Global Perspectives* (Belmont, CA: Wadsworth, 1991), 292.

94. "Interview with the Japanese Troupe."

95. Marc S. Gallicchio, *The African American Encounter with Japan and China: Black Internationalism in Asia, 1895–1945* (Chapel Hill: University of North Carolina Press, 2000), 51.

96. United States Bureau of the Census, "Region and Country or Area of Birth of the Foreign-Born Population, with Geographic Detail Shown in Decennial Census Publications of 1930 or Earlier: 1850 to 1930 and 1960 to 1990," http://www.census.gov/population/www/documentation/twps0029/tab04.html.

97. "Labor Riots," *Chicago Tribune* (March 29, 1867).

98. Phillip H. Round, *The Impossible Land: Story and Place in California's Imperial Valley* (Albuquerque: University of New Mexico Press, 2008), 107.

99. "Japanese Immigrants," *New York Times* (June 5, 1869).

100. Sam Chamberlain, "Silk Culture," *Ohio Farmer* (October 6, 1877).

101. "Social Science Association," *Independent* (February 25, 1869).

102. Ibid.

103. United States Bureau of the Census.

104. Damien Kingsbury and Leena Avonius. *Human Rights in Asia: A Reassessment of the Asian Values Debate* (New York: Palgrave Macmillan, 2008), 196.

105. Richard W. Bulliet, *The Earth and Its Peoples: A Global History* (Boston: Houghton Mifflin, 2007), 802.

106. Examples of this attitude abound in both primary and secondary sources. See, for example, the career of Sorakichi Matsuda as revealed in Joseph R. Svinth, "Japanese Professional Wrestling Pioneer: Sorakichi Matsuda," *In Yo: Journal of Alternative Prospectives* (November 2000; updated January 2005), http://ejmas.com/jalt/jaltart_Svinth1_1100.htm.

107. Mark V. Wiley, *The Secrets of Cabales Serrada Escrima* (Boston: Tuttle, 2001), 60.

108. Thomas A. Green and Joseph R. Svinth, *Martial Arts in the Modern World* (Westport, CT: Praeger, 2003), 114.

109. D. David Dreis, "The Tyrants of the Tongs," *Black Belt* (June 1968): 26–31, p. 28.

110. Green and Svinth, 114.

111. Charlotte Brooks, *Alien Neighbors, Foreign Friends: Asian Americans, Housing, and the Transformation of Urban California* (Chicago: University of Chicago Press, 2009), 15.

112. Wiley, *The Secrets of Cabales Serrada Escrima*, 60.

113. "Labor Riots," *Chicago Tribune* (March 29, 1867).

114. Jonathan H. X. Lee and Kathleen M. Nadeau, *Encyclopedia of Asian American Folklore and Folklife* (Santa Barbara, CA: ABC-CLIO, 2011), 236.

115. Huping Ling, *Chinese St. Louis: From Enclave to Cultural Community* (Philadelphia: Temple University Press, 2004), 9.

116. See, for example, "This and That," *Flag of Our Union* (December 11, 1869).

117. "A Glimpse of San Francisco," *Lippincott* (June 1, 1870).

118. Cesare Lombroso, Mary Gibson, and Nicole Hahn Rafter, *Criminal Man* (Durham, NC: Duke University Press, 2006), 322.

119. Gary Y. Okihioro, *The Columbia Guide to Asian American History* (New York: Columbia University Press, 2001), 141.
120. Paul Chan Pang Siu and John Kuo Wei Tchen, *The Chinese Laundryman* (New York: New York University Press, 1987), xvii.
121. For more information on the Chinese bachelor subculture, see the definitive work on the subject, Paul Chan Pang Siu and John Kuo Wei Tchen's *The Chinese Laundryman*.
122. Stott, 241.
123. Timothy J. Gilfoyle, *City of Eros: New York City, Prostitution, and the Commercialization of Sex, 1820–1920* (New York: W. W. Norton, 1992), 18.
124. Ibid., 218, 219.
125. Carol Green Wilson, *Chinatown Quest: The Life Adventures of Donaldina Cameron* (Stanford, CA: Stanford University Press, 1931), vii; John D'Emilio and Estelle B. Freedman, *Intimate Matters: A History of Sexuality in America* (New York: Harper & Row, 1988), 135; Brian Donovan, *White Slave Crusades: Race, Gender, and Anti-Vice Activism, 1887–1917* (Urbana: University of Illinois Press, 2006), 112.
126. Yong Chen, *Chinese San Francisco, 1850–1943* (Stanford, CA: Stanford University Press, 2002), 88.
127. Stott, 17.
128. Marlon K. Hom, *Songs of Gold Mountain: Cantonese Rhymes from San Francisco Chinatown* (Berkeley: University of California Press, 1987), 26.
129. Frank E. Hagan, *Introduction to Criminology: Theories, Methods, and Criminal Behavior* (London: Sage, 2010), 410.
130. Friederike Assandri and Dora Martins. *From Early Tang Court Debates to China's Peaceful Rise* (Amsterdam: Amsterdam University Press, 2009), 61.
131. W. M. Shattuck, *Annual Report of Health Officer of the City of Sacramento* (Sacramento: James Anthony Printers, 1863), 6, 11.
132. Annie Morris, "A Glimpse of San Francisco," *American and Continental Monthly* I, no. 6 (September 1870): 548–555, p. 548.
133. Ibid.
134. "A Glimpse of San Francisco," *Lippincott* (June 1, 1870).
135. Auber Forestier, "More about California," *Saturday Evening Post* (March 19, 1870).
136. "This and That," *Flag of Our Union* (December 11, 1869).
137. Todd Vogel, *Rewriting White: Race, Class, and Cultural Capital in Nineteenth-Century America* (New Brunswick, NJ: Rutgers University Press, 2004), 123.
138. Kevin Starr, *Americans and the California Dream, 1850–1915* (New York: Oxford University Press, 1993), 132.
139. Charles J. McClain, *Chinese Immigrants and American Law* (New York: Garland, 1994), 96.
140. Ibid.
141. "Chinese versus Irish," *Maine Farmer* (July 30, 1870).
142. "Particulars of the Los Angelos Tragedy," *New York Evangelist* (November 16, 1871).
143. Sue Fawn Chung, *In Pursuit of Gold: Chinese American Miners and Merchants in the American West* (Urbana: University of Illinois Press, 2011), 43.
144. "Rioting in San Francisco," *New York Times* (July 25, 1877).
145. Alexander Saxton, *The Indispensable Enemy: Labor and the Anti-Chinese Movement in California* (Berkeley: University of California Press, 1995), ix.
146. Charles J. McClain, *Chinese Immigrants and American Law* (New York: Garland, 1994), 96.
147. Rosanne Currarino, *The Labor Question in America: Economic Democracy in the Gilded Age* (Urbana: University of Illinois Press, 2011), 11.
148. Bruce Nissen, *Unions in a Globalized Environment: Changing Borders, Organizational Boundaries, and Social Roles* (Armonk, NY: M. E. Sharpe, 2002), 132.
149. "The Labor Question," *New York Times* (August 18, 1870).
150. Sue Fawn Chung, *In Pursuit of Gold: Chinese American Miners and Merchants in the American West* (Urbana: University of Illinois Press, 2011), 42.
151. "San Francisco Difficulty," *New England Farmer* (March 6, 1880).
152. "Editorial," *Chicago Daily Tribune* (February 22, 1880).
153. Susie Lan Cassel, *The Chinese in America: A History from Gold Mountain to the New Millennium* (Walnut Creek, CA: AltaMira Press, 2002), 128.
154. John Joseph Jennings, *Theatrical and Circus Life* (Cincinnati: Forshee & McMakin, 1882), 343.
155. Roger Daniels and Otis L. Graham. *Debating American Immigration, 1882–Present* (Lanham, MD: Rowman & Littlefield, 2001), 8.
156. Ibid.
157. "The Chinese in California," *New York Times* (July 31, 1873).
158. "Hatchet Men," *LA Times* (January 28, 1882).
159. Richard H. Dillon, *The Hatchet Men: The Story of the Tong Wars in San Francisco's Chinatown* (New York: Coward-McCann, 1962), 100.
160. "All SIN."
161. "The English Mail," *Te Aroha News* (January 9, 1889).
162. "Wild Cats of California," *LA Times* (September 20, 1896).

Notes—Chapter III

163. Fredric J. Masters, "Highbinders," *Chautauquan* 14, no. 5 (February 1892): 554–558, p. 556.
164. "A Fiendish Fight," *National Police Gazette* (February 28, 1885).
165. Green, *Martial Arts of the World*, 446.
166. "Fierce Fight between Two Chinamen," *New York Times* (June 15, 1872).
167. Ibid.
168. "The Prize Ring," *National Police Gazette* (March 10, 1883).
169. "A Chinese Wrestling Match," *National Police Gazette* (September 10, 1887).
170. John Powell, *Encyclopedia of North American Immigration* (New York: Facts on File, 2005), 161.
171. United States Bureau of the Census.
172. Ibid.
173. Ronald T. Takaki, *Strangers from a Different Shore: A History of Asian Americans* (Boston: Little, Brown, 1989), 29.
174. Linda Eisenmann, *Historical Dictionary of Women's Education in the United States* (Westport, CT: Greenwood Press, 1998), 23.
175. Richard D. Alba, Albert J. Raboteau, and Josh DeWind, *Immigration and Religion in America: Comparative and Historical Perspectives* (New York: New York University Press, 2009), 107.
176. Beekman, 20.
177. Green and Svinth, 63.
178. "Two Famous Wrestlers," *Washington Post* (May 2, 1884).
179. Maarten van Bottenburg, *Global Games* (Urbana: University of Illinois Press, 2001), 97.
180. Alex Butcher, *Judo: The Essential Guide to Mastering the Art* (London: New Holland, 2001), 10.
181. Allen Guttmann, *Games and Empires: Modern Sports and Cultural Imperialism* (New York: Columbia University Press, 1994), 138.
182. Brian Watson, *Judo Memoirs of Jigoro Kano: Early History of Judo* (Victoria, BC: Trafford, 2008), 69.
183. Green, *Martial Arts of the World*, 213.
184. Watson, 15.
185. Joseph R. Svinth, "Professor Yamashita Goes to Washington," *Journal of Combative Sport* (October 2000), http://ejmas.com/jcs/jcsart_svinth1_1000.htm.
186. Guttmann and Thompson, 103.
187. Ramin Kordi, *Combat Sports Medicine* (London: Springer, 2009), 324.
188. H. Irving Hancock, *Jiu-Jitsu Combat Tricks; Japanese Feats of Attack and Defense in Personal Encounter* (New York: G. P. Putnam's Sons, 1904), 146.
189. Perry Peake, "A Woman's Self Defense for Women," *Health and Vim* (May 1912), http://martialhistory.com/2008/02/a-womans-self-defence-for-women/.
190. "Suffragists Form Volunteer Police Force," *Evening News* (October 13, 1914).
191. "Jiu—Jitsu for Militants," *New York Times* (August 20, 1913).
192. "Washing Makes Suffragist," *New York Times* (April 11, 1909).
193. Hancock, 146.
194. Laura Spielvogel, *Working out in Japan: Shaping the Female Body in Tokyo Fitness Clubs* (Durham, NC: Duke University Press, 2003), 217.
195. Franklin H. Brown, "Physical Work in Japan," *Physical Training* 18, no. 7 (May 1921): 312–315, p. 312.
196. Arthur Rugh, "Flashes from Associations Outposts," *Young Men* 39, no. 10 (July 1914): 534.
197. Beekman, 22.
198. "The Wrestlers," *Chicago Daily Tribune* (July 27, 1884).
199. Michael A. Bellesiles, *1877: America's Year of Living Violently* (New York: New Press, 2010), 276.
200. Svinth, "Japanese Professional Wrestling Pioneer: Sorakichi Matsuda."
201. "A Well-Known Wrestler Dead," *New York Times* (August 17, 1891).
202. Green, *Martial Arts*, 446.
203. "A Well-Known Wrestler Dead."
204. "Two Famous Wrestlers," *Washington Post* (May 2, 1884).
205. "The Wrestlers," *Chicago Daily Tribune* (July 27, 1884).
206. Svinth, "Japanese Professional Wrestling Pioneer: Sorakichi Matsuda."
207. "A Well-Known Wrestler Dead."
208. Svinth, "Japanese Professional Wrestling Pioneer: Sorakichi Matsuda."
209. "A Well-Known Wrestler Dead."
210. "Two Famous Wrestlers."
211. Spencer Tucker, *The Encyclopedia of the Spanish-American and Philippine-American Wars: A Political, Social, and Military History* (Santa Barbara, CA: ABC-CLIO, 2009), 66.
212. Victor Purcell, *The Boxer Uprising: A Background Study* (Cambridge: Cambridge University Press, 1963), 121.
213. Sen Hu and Jielin Dong. *The Rocky Road to Liberty: A Documented History of Chinese Immigration and Exclusion* (Saratoga, CA: Javvin Press, 2010), 39.
214. Craig L. Symonds, *The Naval Institute Historical Atlas of the U.S. Navy* (Annapolis, MD: Naval Institute Press, 1995), 116.
215. Andrew Anthony Buffalo, *Hard Corps: Legends of the Corps* (New York: S&B Publishing, 2004), 9.
216. John Foxe, *Voices of the Martyrs* (Orlando, FL: Bridge-Logos, 2007), 213.
217. Paul S. Reinsch, "China against the World," *Forum* (September 1900): 67–75, p. 70.

218. "Fanatics of China," *Nashua Daily Telegraph* (July 12, 1900).
219. "Dark for Foreigners," *Washington Post* (June 25, 1900).
220. "Among the New Books," *Chicago Daily Tribune* (May 9, 1901).
221. "Secular News," *Christian Observer* (August 29, 1900).
222. "Lee Toy Talks of Boxers," *Philadelphia Record* (June 25, 1900).
223. Tucker, 68.
224. Michael Nylan and Thomas A. Wilson, *Lives of Confucius: Civilization's Greatest Sage through the Ages* (New York: Doubleday, 2010).
225. Bruce A. Elleman, *Modern Chinese Warfare, 1795–1989* (London: Routledge, 2001), 116.
226. Jachinson Chan, *Chinese American Masculinities: From Fu Manchu to Bruce Lee* (New York: Garland, 2001), 38.
227. Hsing-han Liu and John Bracy, *Ba Gua: Hidden Knowledge in the Taoist Internal Martial Art* (Berkeley, CA: North Atlantic Books, 1998), 18.
228. Tucker, 476.
229. Ibid., 476.
230. John Durand, *The Boys: 1st North Dakota Volunteers in the Philippines* (Elkhorn, WI: Puzzlebox Press, 2010), 184.
231. Bruce A. Haines, *Karate's History and Traditions* (Rutland, VT: Charles E. Tuttle, 1968), 72.
232. Mark V. Wiley, *Filipino Martial Arts: Cabales Serrada Escrima* (Rutland, VT: C. E. Tuttle, 1994), 17.
233. Ibid., 21.
234. "Spain Made Them Vicious," *Baltimore American* (March 12, 1899).
235. "Topics of the Times," *New York Times* (December 10, 1903).
236. "More Troops Needed in the Philippines," *New York Times* (July 16, 1900).
237. "Conditions in Mindanao," *New York Times* (August 13, 1900).
238. Jeff Kinard, *Pistols: An Illustrated History of Their Impact* (Santa Barbara, CA: ABC-CLIO, 2003), 162.
239. Michael Lee Lanning, *The African-American Soldier: From Crispus Attucks to Colin Powell* (Secaucus, NJ: Carol, 1997), 97.
240. Edward M. Coffman, *The Regulars: The American Army, 1898–1941* (Cambridge, MA: Belknap Press of Harvard University Press, 2004), 48.
241. Howard Zinn, *The Twentieth Century: A People's History* (New York: Harper & Row, 1984), 29.
242. Wiley, *Filipino Martial Arts*, 17.
243. Barbara Mercedes Posadas, *The Filipino Americans* (Westport, CT: Greenwood Press, 1999), 75.
244. "The Soldiers' Testimony," *Clinton Morning Age* (October 8, 1899).
245. "Brave Little Quezon," *Lewiston Morning Tribune* (August 3, 1944).
246. Wiley, *The Secrets of Cabales Serrada Escrima*, 60.
247. "Personal," *Japan and America* II, no. 8 (August 1902): 14–16, p. 15.
248. "Jiu-Jitsu," *New York Times* (September 2, 1905).
249. Arthur Rugh, "Flashes from Associations Outposts," *Young Men* 39, no. 10 (July 1914): 534.
250. "Notes and Comments," *The Oriental Economic Review* (January 10, 1911).
251. "Japan to Produce Next Jim Jeffries," *Reading Eagle* (January 19, 1908).
252. Ibid.
253. H. Irving Hancock, *Japanese Physical Training: The System of Exercise, Diet, and General Mode of Living That Has Made the Mikado's People the Healthiest, Strongest, and Happiest Men and Women in the World* (New York: G. P. Putnam's Sons, 1903), 7.
254. "Jiu Jitsu the Feature of Chase's Bill of Vaudeville Novelties," *Washington Post* (April 23, 1905).
255. Svinth, "Professor Yamashita Goes to Washington."
256. Dakin Burdick, *The American Way of Fighting: Unarmed Defense in the United States, 1845–1945* (Ph.D. thesis, Indiana University, 1999), 144.
257. "About Japanese Who Live in New York," *New York Times* (July 24, 1904).
258. Hamilton Raymond, "Mysterious Judo Comes to America," *Atlanta Constitution* (September 12, 1920).
259. "A Chinese Slogger," *National Police Gazette* (August 12, 1882).
260. "Icelander Downs JiuJitsu Wrestler," *New York Times* (March 31, 1913).
261. H. F. Leonard and K. Higashi, "American Wrestling vs. Jujitsu," *Cosmopolitan* XXXIX, no. 1 (May 1905): 33–42, p. 42.
262. "Summer Theatricals," *Washington Post* (June 25, 1905).
263. Svinth, "Professor Yamashita Goes to Washington."
264. "Summer Theatricals."
265. Ibid.
266. "President Tries Jiu Jitsu," *New York Times* (December 31, 1904).
267. "News from Jap Wrestler," *Washington Post* (November 26, 1906).
268. Nori Bunasawa and John Murray, *The Toughest Man Who Ever Lived* (Las Vegas: Innovations), 43.
269. Svinth, "Professor Yamashita Goes to Washington."
270. "Cadets Down the Jap," *New York Times* (February 21, 1905).

Notes—Chapter III

271. Green and Svinth, *Martial Arts*, 65.
272. "The Police Athletic Club," *New York Times* (May 10, 1877).
273. Linda España-Maram, *Creating Masculinity in Los Angeles's Little Manila: Working-Class Filipinos and Popular Culture, 1920s–1950s* (New York: Columbia University Press, 2006), 90.
274. Beekman, 42.
275. "Jiu Jitsu Too Much for M'adoo's Athletes," *New York Times* (December 23, 1904).
276. Ibid.
277. "Beware of Jiu-Jitsu," *Meriden Daily Journal* (May 16, 1905).
278. "Jiu Jitsu Subdued Him," *New York Times* (January 31, 1911).
279. "Policewomen to Wrestle," *New York Times* (March 8, 1914).
280. "Police Carnival Today," *New York Times* (July 27, 1918).
281. Ibid.
282. James A. Tyner, *Oriental Bodies: Discourse and Discipline in U.S. Immigration Policy, 1875–1942* (Lanham, MD: Lexington Books, 2006), 11.
283. J.H. Kellogg, "Degeneracy of Mankind," *Battle Creek Idea* 4, no. 47 (October 27, 1911): 1–2, p. 2.
284. "Jiu-Jitsu and the Police," *New York Times* (December 24, 1904).
285. "Jiu-Jitsu to Be Avoided," *Hudson Independent* (May 19, 1905).
286. "Jiu Jitsu Too Much for M'adoo's Athletes."
287. "London Policewomen Use Jiu Jitsu in Capturing a Crook," *Milwaukee Sentinel* (December 25, 1914).
288. "How the Japs Strike a Blow," *National Police Gazette* (August 13, 1904).
289. "Police Show by Citizens," *New York Times* (August 12, 1916).
290. Marilynn S. Johnson, *Street Justice: A History of Police Violence in New York City* (Boston: Beacon Press, 2003), 87.
291. "Policeman Beat Jiu-Jitsu," *New York Times* (January 21, 1905).
292. Harrie Irving Hancock, *Physical Training for Children by Japanese Methods; A Manual for Use in Schools and at Home* (New York: Putnam, 1904), x.
293. H. Irving Hancock, *Jiu-Jitsu Combat Tricks; Japanese Feats of Attack and Defense in Personal Encounter* (New York: G. P. Putnam's Sons, 1904), iii.
294. Ibid., iv.
295. Hancock, *Physical Training for Children*, ix.
296. Hancock, *Physical Training for Women*, xi.
297. Sarah K. Fields, *Female Gladiators* (Urbana: University of Illinois Press, 2005), 3.
298. Ying Wushanley, *Playing Nice and Losing: The Struggle for Control of Women's Intercollegiate Athletics, 1960–2000* (Syracuse, NY: Syracuse University Press, 2004), 7.
299. Patricia Campbell Warner, *When the Girls Came Out to Play: The Birth of American Sportswear* (Amherst: University of Massachusetts Press, 2006), 87.
300. "Sporting Miscellany," *Sun* (October 24, 1902).
301. Penny A. Pasque and Shelley Errington Nicholson, *Empowering Women in Higher Education and Student Affairs: Theory, Research, Narratives, and Practice from Feminist Perspectives* (Sterling, VA: Stylus, 2011), 50.
302. Fields, *Female Gladiators*, 3.
303. For an example of a writer encouraging women to learn jujitsu because it was conducive to traditional gender roles, see Teiichi Yamagata, "Jiu-Jitsu: The Art of Self-Defense," *Leslie's Monthly Magazine* LIX, no. I (November 1904): 91–100, p. 100; Fields, *Female Gladiators*, 3; Hancock, *Physical Training for Women*, xi.
304. "Japanese Physical Training," *Independent* (September 1, 1904).
305. "Books of the Week," *Outlook* (June 18, 1904).
306. "Out-of-Door Books," *Critic* (June 1904).
307. Ibid.
308. "Jiu-Jitsu," *New York Times* (September 2, 1905).
309. Ibid.
310. For an example of a woman learning jujitsu from a book, see "Woman Grabs Highwayman," *New York Times* (October 21, 1905).
311. Yamagata, 100.
312. Ibid.
313. "Jiu Jitsu the Feature of Chase's Bill of Vaudeville Novelties," *Washington Post* (April 23, 1905).
314. Hamilton Raymond, "Mysterious Judo Comes to America," *Atlanta Constitution* (September 12, 1920).
315. Hancock, *Jiu-Jitsu Combat Tricks*, 146.
316. "Woman Grabs Highwayman."
317. "Tiny Girl Master Big Cop," *Washington Post* (October 25, 1914).
318. Allan Corstorphin Smith, *The Secrets of Jujitsu: A Complete Course in Self Defense* (Columbus, GA: Stahara, 1920), 1.
319. Hancock, *Physical Training for Women*, xi, xii.
320. "Boxing Girl Arrives," *Washington Post* (October 30, 1904).
321. Frederick William Hackwood, *Old English Sports* (London: T. F. Unwin, 1907), 204, iv.
322. Fredrick Trevor Hill, "The Woman in the Case," *The Century Illustrated Monthly Magazine* 73, no. 3 (January 1907): 408–412, p. 408.
323. Al G. Waddell, "Lady Wrestler Floors a Gent," *LA Times* (June 28, 1916).

324. Beekman, 30.
325. "American Sympathy with the Japanese," *New York Observer and Chronicle* (September 1, 1904).
326. "Japanese Plan Big Coup in Liao-Tung Peninsula," *New York Times* (May 12, 1904).
327. Joseph Cummins, *The War Chronicles, from Flintlocks to Machine Guns: A Global Reference of All the Major Modern Conflicts* (Beverly, MA: Fair Winds Press, 2009), 194.
328. "Reason for Japanese Success," *Washington Post* (September 15, 1904).
329. "Editorial," *New York Observer and Chronicle* (February 25, 1904).
330. Richard Barry, "The Siege of Port Arthur," *Monthly Review* (February 1905): 1–23, p. 13.
331. See, for example, Hancock, *Jiu-Jitsu Combat Tricks*, v.
332. Elise K. Tipton and John Clark, *Being Modern in Japan: Culture and Society from the 1910s to the 1930s* (Honolulu: University of Hawaii Press, 2000), 173.
333. "Self-Defense by Jiu Jitsu," *LA Times* (September 4, 1904).
334. Thomas R. Clark, *Defending Rights: Law, Labor Politics, and the State in California, 1890–1925* (Detroit: Wayne State University Press, 2002), 136.
335. Martin Marger, *Race and Ethnic Relations: American and Global Perspectives* (Belmont, CA: Wadsworth, 1991), 266.
336. United States Bureau of the Census.
337. Ines M. Miyares and Christopher A. Airriess, *Contemporary Ethnic Geographies in America* (Lanham, MD: Rowman & Littlefield, 2007), 35.
338. Nayan Shah, *Contagious Divides: Epidemics and Race in San Francisco's Chinatown* (Berkeley: University of California Press, 2001), 128.
339. "Congress Receives White Slave Report," *New York Times* (December 11, 1909).
340. "East Is East and West Is West," *Duluth Daily Star* (September 26, 1907).
341. Miyares and Airriess, 35.
342. Daniel J. Tichenor, *Dividing Lines: The Politics of Immigration Control in America* (Princeton, NJ: Princeton University Press, 2002), 127.
343. Michael A. Burayidi, *Urban Planning in a Multicultural Society* (Westport, CT: Praeger, 2000), 18.
344. Michael E. McGerr, *A Fierce Discontent: The Rise and Fall of the Progressive Movement in America, 1870–1920* (New York: Free Press, 2003), 213.
345. Ibid.
346. "Ad Santel Here Ready to Wrestle with Miyaki," *LA Times* (April 7, 1916).
347. Joseph R. Svinth, "On the Defeat of Tokugoro Ito in North America," *In Yo* (September 2006), http://ejmas.com/jalt/2006jalt/jcsart_Svinth_0906.html.
348. "Ad Santel Here Ready to Wrestle with Miyaki."
349. See, for example, Edgren, 328; Hancock, *Japanese Physical Training*, 6.
350. "Celebrated Mr. Santel to Wrestle Jap Expert," *LA Times* (March 31, 1916).
351. Ibid.
352. "Ad Santel Here Ready to Wrestle with Miyaki."
353. Joel S. Franks, *Crossing Sidelines, Crossing Cultures: Sport and Asian Pacific American Cultural Citizenship* (Lanham, MD: University Press of America, 2000), 40; Svinth, "On the Defeat of Tokugoro Ito in North America."
354. Svinth, "On the Defeat of Tokugoro Ito in North America."
355. Brian Preston, *Me, Chi, and Bruce Lee: Adventures in Martial Arts from the Shaolin Temple to the Ultimate Fighting Championship* (Berkeley, CA: Blue Snake Books, 2009), 269.
356. Bunasawa and Murray, 210.
357. "Sport Contests Cancelled by War," *Herald Journal* (August 17, 1914).
358. Spencer Tucker and Priscilla Mary Roberts, *World War I: Student Encyclopedia* (Santa Barbara, CA: ABC-CLIO, 2006), 1264.
359. "House Committee Votes for a Call for Volunteers," *New York Times* (April 19, 1917).
360. Robert Sherwood Dillon, *An American Soldier in World War I* (Washington, D.C.: Five and Ten Press, 2005), 15.
361. "Secretaries Baker and Daniels Urge That Colleges of Nation Continue Athletics," *New York Times* (December 29, 1917).
362. Steward Paton, "Conscientious Objectors," *New York Times* (July 13, 1917).
363. Green, *Martial Arts of the World*, 447.
364. Edgren, 322.
365. "Our Letter From Paris," *Medical Record* (March 23, 1918).
366. Green, *Martial Arts of the World*, 447.
367. Ibid.
368. Don W. Farrant, "Vintage Jujitsu: World War 1 Style," *Black Belt* (December 1971): 46–49, p. 46.
369. "1,000 Falls Are Necessary to Win the Black Belt," *Meriden Daily Journal* (February 26, 1916).
370. "Ten Ways to Get a Boche Taught by Jujitsu Experts," *Boston Daily Globe* (June 30, 1918).
371. "Jujitsu Crown Won by Scotsman," *Arizona Republican* (February 26, 1916).
372. Allan Smith, *The Secrets of Jujitsu: A Complete Course in Self Defense* (Columbus, GA: Stahara), 2.
373. "New Secret in Jujitsu Makes You Master of Men," *Popular Science* (August 1921): 9.

374. "Battle in a Poolroom," *New York Times* (October 5, 1902).
375. "Quells Riot with Fists," *LA Times* (September 19, 1908).
376. "Rescues Policeman in Chinese Fight," *New York Times* (March 25, 1909).
377. "Sightseers in Straits," *New York Times* (March 17, 1906).
378. Frank Moss, *The American Metropolis, from Knickerbocker Days to the Present Time* (New York: P. F. Collier, 1897), 415.
379. Fredric J. Masters, "Among the Highbinders," *Californian Illustrated* 1, no. 2 (January 1892): 62–74, p. 72.
380. Arnold Genthe and John Kuo Wei Tchen, *Genthe's Photographs of San Francisco's Old Chinatown* (New York: Dover, 1984), 29.
381. Pierre N. Beringer, "In the Realm of Bookland," *Overland Monthly* 53, no. 1 (January 1909): 52–58, p. 52.
382. For more on Arnold Genthe and his role in documenting Chinatown, see "Photography in the Streets" in Anthony W. Lee, *Picturing Chinatown: Art and Orientalism in San Francisco* (Berkeley: University of California Press, 2001), 101–148.
383. Masters, 72.
384. D. David Dreis, "The Tyrants of the Tongs," *Black Belt* (June 1968): 26–31, p. 27.
385. "Chinatown Tong Wars of the 1920s," Museum of the City of San Francisco http://www.sfmuseum.org/sfpd/sfpd4.html.
386. Carol Green Wilson, *Chinatown Quest: The Life Adventures of Donaldina Cameron* (Stanford, CA: Stanford University Press, 1931), 144; Henry W. Von Morpurgo, "Chinatown Cop," *LA Times* (March 19, 1944).
387. Lee Overman, "How Sergeant Jack Cut Tong Killings," *Sunday Morning Star* (October 19, 1924).
388. David Dreis, "The Kat of Kung Fu," *Black Belt* (December 1968): 44–48, p. 44.
389. Ibid.
390. Dillon, *The Hatchet Men*, 268.
391. Overman.
392. Richard T. Schaefer, *Encyclopedia of Race, Ethnicity, and Society* (Los Angeles: Sage, 2008), 282.
393. Lee Server, *Encyclopedia of Pulp Fiction Writers* (New York: Facts on File, 2002), xiv.
394. Lisa Montanarelli and Ann Harrison, *Strange but True San Francisco: Tales of the City by the Bay* (Guilford, CT: Globe Pequot Press, 2005), 11; "Chinatown Tong Wars of the 1920s."
395. Gary Hoppenstand, *In Search of the Paper Tiger: A Sociological Perspective of Myth, Formula, and the Mystery Genre in the Entertainment Print Mass Medium* (Bowling Green, OH: Bowling Green State University Popular Press, 1987), 97.
396. Hoppenstand, 97.
397. J. Randolph Cox, *The Dime Novel Companion: A Source Book* (Westport, CT: Greenwood Press, 2000), 199.
398. Francis Worcester Doughty, *Hop Lee, the Chinese Slave Dealer, or, Old and Young King Brady and the Opium Fiends: A Story of Shrewd Detective Work in San Francisco* (New York: Frank Tousey, 1899), 25.
399. Francis Worcester Doughty, *The Bradys' Trip to Chinatown: Or, Trailing on Opium Fiend* (New York: Frank Tousey, 1904), 27.
400. Cox, 13.
401. Robert Sampson, *Yesterday's Faces: A Study of Series Characters in the Early Pulp Magazines* (Bowling Green, OH: Bowling Green University Popular Press, 1983), 87.
402. Cox, 13.
403. Jaime Harker, *America the Middlebrow: Women's Novels, Progressivism, and Middlebrow Authorship between the Wars* (Amherst: University of Massachusetts Press, 2007), 112.
404. Paul Eng, *Kungfu Basics* (Boston: Tuttle, 2004), 187.
405. Harker, 112.
406. Harold Schechter, *Savage Pastimes: A Cultural History of Violent Entertainment* (New York: St. Martin's Press, 2005), 114.
407. John Howard Reid, *Silent Films and Early Talkies on DVD: A Classic Movie Fan's Guide* (Morrisville, NC: Lulu Press, 2008), 274.
408. Michael Eury, *Captain Action: The Original Super-Hero Action Figure* (Raleigh, NC: TwoMorrows, 2002), 93.
409. Avi Dan Santo, *Transmedia Brand Licensing Prior to Conglomeration: George Trendle and the Lone Ranger and Green Hornet Brands, 1933–1966* (Austin: University of Texas Libraries, 2006), 235.
410. Jonathan H. X. Lee and Kathleen M. Nadeau, *Encyclopedia of Asian American Folklore and Folklife* (Santa Barbara, CA: ABC-CLIO, 2011), 277.
411. John T. Soister, *Up from the Vault: Rare Thrillers of the 1920s and 1930s* (Jefferson, NC: McFarland, 2004), 12.
412. Sascha Auerbach, *Race, Law, and "the Chinese Puzzle" in Imperial Britain* (New York: Palgrave Macmillan, 2009), 78.
413. Michael Weldon, *The Psychotronic Video Guide* (New York: St. Martin's Griffin, 1996), 99.
414. Hyung-chan Kim, *Distinguished Asian Americans: A Biographical Dictionary* (Westport, CT: Greenwood Press, 1999), 18.
415. Daniel Y. Kim, *Writing Manhood in Black and Yellow: Ralph Ellison, Frank Chin, and the Literary Politics of Identity* (Stanford, CA: Stanford University Press, 2005), 133.
416. Ibid., 134.
417. American Film Institute, *The American Film Institute Catalog of Motion Pictures Pro-*

duced in the United States (Berkeley: University of California Press, 1971), 183.
418. Colleen Lye, *America's Asia: Racial Form and American Literature, 1893–1945* (Princeton, NJ: Princeton University Press, 2005), 205.
419. Yunte Huang, *Charlie Chan: The Untold Story of the Honorable Detective and His Rendezvous with American History* (New York: W. W. Norton, 2010), xvi.
420. Ibid., xvii.
421. United States Bureau of the Census.
422. Dirk Hoerder, *Cultures in Contact: World Migrations in the Second Millennium* (Durham, NC: Duke University Press, 2002), 401.
423. Steven G. Koven and Frank Götzke, *American Immigration Policy Confronting the Nation's Challenges* (New York: Springer, 2010), 132.
424. "Rules Japanese Can't Be Citizens," *New York Times* (November 14, 1922).
425. Don T. Nakanishi and James S. Lai, *Asian American Politics: Law, Participation, and Policy* (Lanham, MD: Rowman & Littlefield, 2003), 51.
426. Pyong Gap Min, *Asian Americans: Contemporary Trends and Issues* (Thousand Oaks, CA: Pine Forge, 2005), 12.
427. "Shortbridge Seeks Ban on All Asiatic Entry to America," *Washington Post* (April 8, 1924).
428. "Japanese Immigration," *Chicago Daily Tribune* (February 16, 1924).
429. "Japan Begins Trade War," *Chicago Daily Tribune* (April 21, 1924).
430. Don T. Nakanishi and James S. Lai, *Asian American Politics: Law, Participation, and Policy* (Lanham, MD: Rowman & Littlefield, 2003), 70; Benson Tong, *Asian American Children: A Historical Handbook and Guide* (Westport, CT: Greenwood Press, 2004), 86; William Francis Deverell, *Whitewashed Adobe: The Rise of Los Angeles and the Remaking of Its Mexican Past* (Berkeley: University of California Press, 2005), 47.
431. See, for example, E. T. Williams, "What Japan Wants," *Political Science Quarterly* 37, no. 2 (June 1922): 333–335, p. 333; Herbert Leslie Stewart, *The Dalhousie Review* 1, no. 1 (April 1921): 104.
432. Daniela De Carvalho, *Migrants and Identity in Japan and Brazil: The Nikkeijin* (London: Routledge Curzon, 2003), 58.
433. T. Z. Tyau, "Educational Comments," *The World's Chinese Students' Journal* 2, no. 1 (July–August 1907): 32–36, p. 34.
434. N. L. Nien, "The Late Professor Arthur S. Mann," *The World's Chinese Students' Journal* 2, no. 1 (July–August 1907): 14–17, p. 16.
435. Katherine Melvina Huntsinger Blackford, *Character Analysis by the Observational Method* (New York: Independent, 1920), 25.

436. *The New International Encyclopedia* (New York: Dodd, Mead, 1922), 584.
437. "Stamps Tell," *Popular Science* (October 1934): 34.
438. "Japan Shows an Astonishing Advance in College Baseball," *Christian Science Monitor* (October 31, 1930).
439. "Japanese Pilot to Be Welcomed," *LA Times* (January 26, 1931).
440. "Japanese Laud Welcome Here," *LA Times* (June 12, 1932).
441. "Church Alarmed for Missionaries," *Washington Post* (January 30, 1932).
442. Jimmy Pedro and William Durbin, *Judo Techniques and Tactics* (Champaign, IL: Human Kinetics, 2001), 16.
443. "Exhibition by Judo Team," *Oxnard Daily Courier* (August 14, 1936).
444. Emil Farkas, *An Illustrated History of Martial Arts in America* (North Hills, CA: Rising Sun, 2007), viii.
445. "Japanese Sailors Vie in Native Sport," *New York Times* (August 29, 1936).
446. Pedro and Durbin, 16.
447. Emil Farkas, *An Illustrated History of Martial Arts in America* (North Hills, CA: Rising Sun, 2007), viii.
448. "Swords and Daggers to Feature Hi-Jinx," *Berkeley Daily Gazette* (March 25, 1933).
449. "Schools for the Man Hunters," *Popular Mechanics* (September 1929): 418–422, p. 420.
450. Diana Rice, "The Crime Bureau's Aid for Young Delinquents," *New York Times* (April 10, 1932).
451. "Police Jiu Jitsuist Gets Better Post," *Christian Science Monitor* (November 20, 1939).
452. "Women Learn Jiu-Jitsu," *New York Times* (December 24, 1926).
453. Pedro and Durbin, 16.
454. David Lee, *Up Close and Personal: The Reality of Close-Quarter Fighting in World War II* (London: Greenhill Books, 2006), 67; W. E. Fairbairn, *Defendu: Scientific Self-Defense* (Shanghai: North China Daily News & Herald, 1926); W. E. Fairbairn, *Scientific Self-Defense, Etc.* (New York: D. Appleton, 1931), viv.

Chapter IV

1. Westbrook Pegler, "It's Dempsey! A Knockout," *Chicago Daily Tribune* (July 22, 1927).
2. "Here's Detail of Shortest Title Fight on Record," *Chicago Daily Tribune* (June 23, 1938).
3. For a more detailed account of the attack on Columbus and its immediate aftermath, see Max Boot, *The Savage Wars of Peace: Small Wars and the Rise of American Power* (New York: Basic Books, 2002), 183–90.

Notes—Chapter IV

4. James W. Hurst, *Pancho Villa and Black Jack Pershing: The Punitive Expedition in Mexico* (Westport, CT: Praeger, 2008), 110.

5. Raymond B. Fosdick, "The Program of the Commission on Training Camp Activities with Relation to the Problem of Venereal Disease," *Social Hygiene* IV, no. 1 (January 1918): 71–76, p. 72.

6. Vladimir Andreff and Stefan Szymanski, *Handbook on the Economics of Sport* (Cheltenham, UK: Edward Elgar, 2006), 284.

7. "YMCA at Work Among Troops on the Mexican Border," *Herald of Gospel Liberty* (July 20, 1916).

8. "Making Vice Unattractive to Soldiers, *Current Opinion* (July 1917).

9. "Muster in Troops," *Spokane Daily Chronicle* (June 28, 1916).

10. "Cavalry Troops in New Camp," *Deseret News* (August 11, 1916).

11. "Capt. William C. Webb Is Here from Border," *Deseret News* (September 23, 1916).

12. "Apache Scouts Hate Peace," *New York Times* (August 11, 1916).

13. "Rufus Williams Army's Champion," *LA Times* (January 3, 1917).

14. "Leo Lomski Passes Up Bout," *Youngstown Vindicator* (May 10, 1828); Colleen Aycock and Mark Scott, *The First Black Boxing Champions: Essays on Fighters of the 1800s to the 1920s* (Jefferson, NC: McFarland, 2010), 228.

15. "Boxing Bout Is Fun for American Army to South of Border," *Eugene Register-Guard* (July 26, 1916).

16. Aycock and Scott, 219.

17. J. Seymour Currey, *Illinois Activities in the World War: Covering the Period from 1914 to 1920* (Chicago: Thomas B. Poole, 1921), 444.

18. "War Will Prevent Carpentier from Appearing in Fight Ring," *Evening News* (August 4, 1914).

19. Robert Sherwood Dillon, *An American Soldier in World War I* (Washington, D.C.: Five and Ten Press, 2005), 15.

20. "Secretaries Baker and Daniels Urge That Colleges of Nation Continue Athletics."

21. Paton, "Conscientious Objectors."

22. Charles N. Wheeler, "Yankees, Minds, and Bodies, Cleanest Army in the World," *Chicago Daily Tribune* (October 13, 1918).

23. "Pershing's Civilian Aide in World War Visitor Here," *St. Petersburg Times* (February 14, 1929).

24. "New York Athletic Club Benefit," *New York Times* (February 24, 1918).

25. "Knights of Columbus War Fund $3,000,000," *Deseret News* (August 8, 1917).

26. "Military Meet," *Youngstown Vindicator* (January 12, 1918).

27. "YMCA Call 4,000 for Work in France," *New York Times* (July 8, 1918).

28. Sol Metzger, "Regards Athletics as Patriotic Duty," *New York Times* (July 22, 1917).

29. "Athletics Help in War," *New York Times* (April 21, 1918).

30. "Athletics among Soldiers and Sailors," *Sunday Chronicle* (December 9, 1917).

31. "Dr. Mott," *Friend* (November 1918).

32. "Urges Training in Gymnasiums," *Gettysburg Times* (September 15, 1917).

33. George Stewart, Jr., and Henry B. Wright, *The Practice of Friendship; Studies in Personal Evangelism with Men of the United States Army and Navy in American Training Camps* (New York: Association Press, 1918), 113.

34. "Be a Nation of Athletes," *Lewiston Morning Tribune* (December 5, 1917).

35. "Police Volunteers Ready for Service," *New York Times* (March 17, 1917).

36. "Make Sports Compulsory," *New York Times* (October 13, 1918).

37. "Wind and Women Missing at Camp," *Galata Journal* (October 4, 1917).

38. "Zbyszko in Draw with Joe Strecher," *New York Times* (November 27, 1918).

39. "Corbett to Teach Soldiers," *New York Times* (August 28, 1917).

40. "More Than 3,000,000 Boxers Developed by System at Army Camps," *Post Express* (May 12, 1919).

41. "Secretaries Baker and Daniels Urge That Colleges of Nation Continue Athletics."

42. Ibid.

43. William J. Jacomb, *Boxing for Beginners, with Chapter Showing Its Relationship to Bayonet Fighting* (Philadelphia: Lea & Febiger, 1918), 51.

44. "Henry Ford Praises YMCA Army Work," *New York Times* (June 30, 1918).

45. "Athletics Help in War," *New York Times* (April 21, 1918).

46. "Soldiers Take to Boxing," *New York Times* (February 18, 1918).

47. "Bouts Boost Recruiting," *New York Times* (May 5, 1918).

48. "Mike Donovan in Ring," *New York Times* (January 13, 1918).

49. "Athletic Events Shown on Screen," *New York Times* (December 9, 1917).

50. "Leonard to Box at Washington," *Telegraph—Herald* (August 14, 1917).

51. Sol Metzger, "Athletics of Past Are Gone Forever in Favor of Those That Will Assist Posterity," *Youngstown Vindicator* (June 29, 1918).

52. Timothy Dowling, *Personal Perspectives: World War I* (Santa Barbara, CA.: ABC-CLIO, 2006), 234.

53. "American Boxers Have Edge in Big Show at London," *Telegraph-Herald* (December 13, 1918).

54. Dowling, 234.

55. "Army School for Boxing," *News and Courier* (January 22, 1920).

56. "Pershing to See Bouts," *New York Times* (March 30, 1920).
57. "Allies Will Meet in Squared Circle," *Border Cities Star* (February 25, 1921).
58. "Sport Recrudescence on Heels of Army Training," *New York Times* (March 2, 1919).
59. Ibid.
60. Ibid.
61. See, for example, "Who Wants These Boxing Lessons?" Advertisement in *Popular Science* 97, no. 4 (October 1920): 126.
62. "Display Ad 201," *New York Times* (November 30, 1919).
63. L. E. Eubanks, "Boxing Pointers for Boys," *Social Progress* 3, no. 3 (March 1919): 154–157, 154.
64. "Wrestling Game in Decline," *Spokesman-Review* (December 17, 1922).
65. "Veterans to Stage Good Boxing Bouts," *Morning Leader* (November 24, 1921).
66. "Veterans to Police Bout," *New York Times* (August 2, 1921).
67. "Boxing Team at Yale," *New York Times* (November 21, 1920).
68. "Maj. Gen. Wood Heads Board to Control Boxing," *Providence News* (March 5, 1919).
69. "Churches Rebuked for Opposing Bout," *New York Times* (May 28, 1919).
70. Ibid.
71. Roberts and Skutt, 103.
72. "Jess Willard," International Boxing Hall of Fame Online, http://www.ibhof.com/pages/about/inductees/oldtimer/willard.html.
73. Roberts and Skutt, 103.
74. "45,000 See Fight in Sizzling Heat," *New York Times* (July 5, 1919).
75. Ray Pearson, "Dempsey Wins World Title with Science as Well as Power," *Chicago Daily Tribune* (July 5, 1919).
76. Ibid.
77. Benny Leonard, "Utah Cyclone Is a Real Champion," *Washington Post* (July 5, 1919).
78. Sugar, *Bert Sugar on Boxing*, 97; Jeremy Schapp, *Cinderella Man: James J. Braddock, Max Baer, and the Greatest Upset in Boxing History* (Boston: Houghton Mifflin, 2005), 24.
79. Robert Anasi, *The Gloves: A Boxing Chronicle* (New York: North Point Press, 2002), 317.
80. Robert D. Mitchell and Paul A. Groves, *North America: The Historical Geography of a Changing Continent* (Totowa, NJ: Rowman & Littlefield, 2001), 285.
81. Ibid., 275.
82. Gorn, *The Manly Art*, 131.
83. Conrad Taeuber, *People of the United States in the Twentieth Century* (Washington, D.C.: Government Printing Office, 1972), 176.
84. Rodriguez, *The Regulation of Boxing*, 35.
85. Ibid., 35.
86. "Well Known Men Back New Measure at Albany for Rigid Boxing Regulation," *New York Times* (March 20, 1919).
87. "Passage of Boxing Bill Urged by War Veterans," *New York Times* (April 13, 1920).
88. "Pastors Advocate Boxing at Hearing," *New York Times* (May 21, 1920).
89. Ibid.
90. Ibid.
91. Rodriguez, *The Regulation of Boxing*, 35.
92. Ibid.
93. Roberts and Skutt, 737.
94. Edward Van Every, *Muldoon, the Solid Man of Sport; His Amazing Story as Related for the First Time by Him to His Friend, Edward Van Every* (New York: Frederick A. Stokes, 1929), 318.
95. "Gov. Miller Names New Athletic Body," *New York Times* (June 7, 1921).
96. Van Every, 328.
97. "New York Gamblers Clean up after Every Bout," *Rochester Evening Journal* (November 1, 1922).
98. "Muldoon Says Ring Champs Are Phony," *Providence News* (April 24, 1929).
99. Roberts and Skutt, 430.
100. Jack Dempsey, "Foreword," in Van Every, vii, viii.
101. "Signing Contracts," *Vancouver Sun* (April 10, 1923).
102. "Bans Dempsey–Wills Bout in this State," *New York Times* (February 3, 1923).
103. "Walker May Try to Abolish Boxing," *New York Times* (February 3, 1923).
104. "Muldoon Extends Ban on Title Bouts," *New York Times* (February 5, 1923).
105. "The Inquiring Reporter," *Chicago Daily Tribune* (February 11, 1923).
106. "Brower Chairman of Boxing Board, *New York Times* (February 9, 1924).
107. Ibid.
108. Roberts and Skutt, 249.
109. Riess, *City Games*, 177.
110. Arthur A. Raney and Jennings Bryant, *Handbook of Sports and Media* (Mahwah, NJ: Lawrence Erlbaum Associates, 2006), 126.
111. Anthony J. Rudel, *Hello, Everybody!: The Dawn of American Radio* (Orlando: Harcourt, 2008), 131.
112. Ibid., 133.
113. Roberts and Skutt, 104; "What the Radio Telephone Means," *Current Opinion* (March 1922).
114. "Second Experiment a Complete Success," *Evening Independent* (August 6, 1921).
115. "What the Radio Telephone Means."
116. "2,000,000 Hear Bout Described by Radio," *New York Times* (July 14, 1923).
117. Raney and Bryant, 126.
118. Ibid., 127.
119. Matthew Lindaman, "Wrestling's Hold on the Western World Before the Great War," *Historian* 62, no. 4 (June 2000): 779–797, p. 796.

120. Keith Elliot Greenberg, *Pro Wrestling: From Carnivals to Cable TV* (Minneapolis, MN: LernerSports, 2000), 14.
121. Beekman, 26; J. Ed Grillo," Sporting Comment," *Washington Post* (April 5, 1908).
122. United States, "Urban and Rural Population: 1900 to 1990," http://www.census.gov/population/censusdata/urpop0090.txt.
123. Rotundo, 222.
124. "Olympic Envoy from Russia Here," *New York Times* (January 22, 1911).
125. "Zbyszko in Draw with Joe Strecher," *New York Times* (November 27, 1918).
126. Lindaman, 796.
127. Morton and O'Brien, 43.
128. "Fight Fans of World Listen in on Title Battle," *Chicago Daily Tribune* (September 24, 1927).
129. Roberts and Skutt, 70.
130. Roger Kahn, *A Flame of Pure Fire: Jack Dempsey and the Roaring '20s* (New York: Harcourt Brace, 1999), 354.
131. "Jack Dempsey Has Nose Remodeled," *Painesville Telegraph* (August 20, 1924).
132. "Kearns Announces Huge Film Offer," *New York Times* (March 25, 1924).
133. "Jack Dempsey a Happy Man," *LA Times* (June 16, 1920); "Soldier Post at Milwaukee Clears Dempsey," *Chicago Daily Tribune* (January 30, 1920).
134. Roberts and Skutt, 143.
135. Rich Westcott, *A Century of Philadelphia Sports* (Philadelphia: Temple University Press, 2001), 70.
136. Thomas Hauser, *The Boxing Scene* (Philadelphia: Temple University Press, 2009), 124.
137. Bruce J. Evensen, *When Dempsey Fought Tunney: Heroes, Hokum, and Storytelling in the Jazz Age* (Knoxville: University of Tennessee Press, 1996), ix; Raney and Bryant, 31.
138. Charles W. Dunkley, "Round-by-Round Story of Heavyweight Title Battle," *LA Times* (September 24, 1926).
139. Hauser, *The Boxing Scene*, 124.
140. John Kieran, "Sports of the Time," *New York Times* (January 13, 1927).
141. Ibid.
142. Jimmy Powers, "Victors Lately," *Evening News* (August 24, 1927).
143. Pegler, "It's Dempsey!"
144. Alan J. Gould, "Dempsey Knocks out Sharkey in Seventh," *LA Times* (July 22, 1927).
145. Pegler, "It's Dempsey!"
146. Ibid.
147. Shirley Povich, "1927: Tunney vs. Dempsey," *Washington Post* (September 22, 1927).
148. Hauser, *The Boxing Scene*, 125.
149. "Seventy Radio Stations Will Broadcast Fight," *Washington Post* (September 22, 1927).
150. Don Maxwell, "Notes from the Ringside," *Chicago Daily Tribune* (September 23, 1927).
151. Povich, "1927: Tunney vs. Dempsey."
152. Frank Loiterzo and Tom Donelson, *Viewing Boxing from Ringside* (San Jose: Writers Club Press, 2002), 58.
153. "The Fight by Rounds," *Chicago Daily Tribune* (September 23, 1927).
154. Loiterzo and Donelson, 58.
155. Bert Randolph Sugar and Teddy Atlas, *The Ultimate Book of Boxing Lists* (Philadelphia: Running, 2010).
156. "Dempsey Is the Hero Despite His Defeat," *New York Times* (September 24, 1927).
157. Kyle Garlett and Patrick O'Neal, *The Worst Call Ever: The Most Infamous Calls Ever Blown by Referees, Umpires, and Other Blind Officials* (New York: Collins, 2007), 225.
158. Hauser, *The Boxing Scene*, 127.
159. Ibid.
160. Kahn, 434.
161. Ibid., 448.
162. Joel S. Franks, *Crossing Sidelines, Crossing Cultures: Sport and Asian Pacific American Cultural Citizenship* (Lanham, MD: University Press of America, 2000), 38.
163. Green, *Martial Arts of the World*, 448.
164. "Pancho Villa Dies on Operating Table," *New York Times* (July 15, 1925).
165. Green, *Martial Arts of the World*, 448.
166. Paul H. Jeffers, *The 100 Greatest Heroes* (New York: Citadel Press, 2003), 227.
167. Roberts and Skutt, 292.
168. Joe Louis Barrow and Barbara Munder, *Joe Louis: 50 Years an American Hero* (New York: McGraw-Hill, 1988), 31.
169. Wilfred Smith, "Watch Mr. Louis If You Want to See a Champion," *Chicago Daily Tribune* (May 8, 1934).
170. Victoria W. Wolcott, *Remaking Respectability: African American Women in Interwar Detroit* (Chapel Hill: University of North Carolina Press, 2001), 196.
171. "Louis' Punches Stop Kracken in First Round," *Chicago Daily Tribune* (July 5, 1934).
172. Roberts and Skutt, 293.
173. Jack Dempsey, "Louis Great Fighter, Writes Jack Dempsey," *LA Times* (June 26, 1935).
174. "Louis' Fists Claim 27th Victim; Review of Week in Sports," *Chicago Daily Tribune* (January 19, 1936).
175. Patrick Myler, *Ring of Hate: Joe Louis vs. Max Schmeling: The Fight of the Century* (New York: Arcade, 2005), 76.
176. Langston Hughes and Joseph McLaren, *Autobiography: I Wonder as I Wander* (Columbia: University of Missouri Press, 2003), 307.
177. Fred Van Ness, "Schmeling to Fight Louis in September," *New York Times* (June 29, 1935).

178. David Margolick, *Beyond Glory: Joe Louis vs. Max Schmeling and a World on the Brink* (New York: A.A. Knopf, 2005), 135, 137.
179. "Louis Plays Golf, Resumes Drill Today," *Chicago Daily Tribune* (June 9, 1936).
180. Margolick, 131.
181. "German Impresses in Sparring Drill," *New York Times* (June 7, 1936).
182. "Presenting Marse Joe Louis and Herr Schmeling," *LA Times* (June 18, 1936).
183. "Joe Louis, Schmeling Impressive," *LA Times* (June 8, 1936).
184. Bill McCormick, "Max Certain He'll Stop Bomber," *Washington Post* (June 17, 1936).
185. "Presenting Marse Joe Louis and Herr Schmeling," *LA Times* (June 18, 1936).
186. Wilfrid Smith, "Schmeling Whips Joe Louis," *Chicago Daily Tribune* (June 20, 1936).
187. Ibid.
188. "Round by Round Story of Louis Schmeling Fight," *Chicago Daily Tribune* (June 20, 1936).
189. Wilfrid Smith, "Schmeling Whips Joe Louis," *Chicago Daily Tribune* (June 20, 1936).
190. "Germany Acclaims Schmeling as National Hero," *New York Times* (June 21, 1936).
191. Westbrook Pegler, "Fair Enough," *Washington Post* (December 15, 1936).
192. "Schmeling Guest of Hitler at Lunch," *New York Times* (June 28, 1936).
193. Thomas R. Hietala, *The Fight of the Century: Jack Johnson, Joe Louis, and the Struggle for Racial Equality* (Armonk, NY: M. E. Sharpe, 2002), 178.
194. "Louis in Seclusion to Take Long Rest," *News-Sentinel* (June 20, 1936).
195. Hughes and McLaren, 308.
196. "Harlem Disorders Mark Louis Defeat," *New York Times* (June 20, 1936).
197. Wilfrid Smith, "Was Louis Fight Fixed? Experts' Analysis of Upset," *Chicago Daily Tribune* (June 22, 1936).
198. Sammons, 109.
199. Hietala, 178.
200. John Kieran, "Sports of the Times," *New York Times* (January 24, 1937).
201. James P. Dawson, "11,000 See Louis Knock out Simms in First for Quickest Victory of Career," *New York Times* (December 15, 1936).
202. Roberts and Skutt, 294.
203. "Fight Facts," *Washington Post* (June 22, 1937).
204. Joseph C. Nichols, "Fans Are Streaming Into Chicago; City Will Reap $5,000,000 Harvest," *New York Times* (June 22, 1937).
205. Arch Ward, "Louis Wins Title Knockout," *Chicago Daily Tribune* (June 23, 1937).
206. Westbrook Pegler, "Joe Louis Is the New Champion of the World, But That's Where the Trouble Starts," *Washington Post* (June 23, 1937).
207. Sammons, 109.
208. "The New Champion," *St. Murice Valley Chronicle* (June 24, 1937).
209. "Louis, Schmeling to Fight June 22; Site Is Undecided," *Chicago Daily Tribune* (March 19, 1938).
210. Sammons, 115.
211. Lewis A. Erenberg, *The Greatest Fight of Our Generation: Louis vs. Schmeling* (Oxford: Oxford University Press, 2007), 138.
212. Frank Deford, "A Clashing Symbol," *Sports Illustrated* (February 14, 2005).
213. "Der Angriff Complains," *New York Times* (June 22, 1938).
214. Westbrook Pegler, *Washington Post* (May 2, 1938).
215. Myler, 120.
216. Joe Louis, Edna Rust, and Art Rust, *Joe Louis: My Life* (New York: Harcourt Brace Jovanovich, 1978), 137.
217. Arch Ward, "Louis Whips Max: 1 Round," *Chicago Daily Tribune* (June 23. 1938).
218. Fred Van Ness, "The Bout Draws 30,000 Visitors," *New York Times* (June 22, 1938).
219. "Here's Detail of Shortest Title Fight on Record," *Chicago Daily Tribune* (June 23, 1938).
220. Ibid.
221. Ward, "Louis Whips Max."
222. Ibid.
223. "Topics of the Times," *New York Times* (June 24, 1938).
224. Sammons, 116.
225. Ibid.
226. "Germany Denies Louis Fight Film Was Doctored," *Chicago Daily Tribune* (July 31, 1938).
227. Shirley Povich, "This Morning," *Washington Post* (December 31, 1938).
228. Mike Vaccaro, *1941, the Greatest Year in Sports: Two Baseball Legends, Two Boxing Champs, and the Unstoppable Thoroughbred Who Made History in the Shadow of War* (New York: Doubleday, 2007), 110.
229. Jack Dempsey, "Joe Fought as Champ Should," *LA Times* (June 23, 1938).
230. "Louis Victory Celebrated," *LA Times* (June 23, 1938).
231. Martin Luther King, *Why We Can't Wait* (New York: Harper & Row, 1964), 100.
232. Richard Bak, *Joe Louis: The Great Black Hope* (Dallas: Taylor, 1996), 173.
233. Sammons, 116.
234. Roberts and Skutt, 686.
235. "Athletic Events Shown on Screen," *New York Times* (December 9, 1917).
236. Sammons, 119.
237. Margolick, 177.
238. Rodriguez, *The Regulation of Boxing*, 38.
239. Streible, 287.
240. Sammons, 119.
241. Streible, 284.
242. Ibid.

Chapter V

1. Jerry Beasley, "The Birth of Competition JKD," *Black Belt* (May 1992, 27).
2. Adrian Gilbert, *The Encyclopedia of Warfare: From Earliest Times to the Present Day* (Guilford, CT: Lyons Press, 2002), 258.
3. Douglas Brinkley and Michael E. Haskew, *The World War II Desk Reference* (New York: Harper Resource, 2004), xiii.
4. "Dempsey Observed Okinawa Invasion," *New York Times* (April 3, 1945).
5. "Rumor of Dempsey Death Circulated along Broadway," *Washington Post* (April 14, 1945).
6. "Louis Signs at $21, Eager to Get Japs," *New York Times* (January 13, 1942).
7. James P. Dawson, "Neil Plaque Goes to 4,019 Boxers in the Service," *New York Times* (December 9, 1943).
8. Milton Brackers, "Joe Louis Spends First Day in Camp," *New York Times* (January 15, 1942).
9. "Dempsey Observed Okinawa Invasion."
10. Randy Roberts, *Joe Louis: Hard Times Man* (New Haven, CT: Yale University Press, 2010), 201.
11. Scott Reynolds Nelson, *Steel Drivin' Man: John Henry, the Untold Story of an American Legend* (Oxford: Oxford University Press, 2006), 144.
12. "Outlook for Boxing Next Year Dreary Says *Ring* Magazine," *Evening Independent* (December 26, 1942).
13. Ibid.
14. "NBA Freezes Boxing Titles," *Miami News* (October 15, 1942).
15. "Outlook for Boxing Next Year Dreary Says *Ring* Magazine."
16. John Kieran, "Sports of the Times," *New York Times* (May 28, 1942).
17. "Army Puts Stress on Mass Athletics," *New York Times* (August 9, 1942).
18. "For Service Men," *New York Times* (September 5, 1942).
19. Joseph C. Nichols, "Boxing Men Form a Training Plan," *New York Times* (April 24, 1944).
20. "Army Puts Stress on Mass Athletics."
21. Allison Danzig, "Football Is Becoming Tough," *New York Times* (June 13, 1942).
22. John Kieran, "Sports of the Times," *New York Times* (November 12, 1942).
23. See, for example, Edgren, 322; Hancock, *Jiu-Jitsu Combat Tricks*, 146.
24. Lee, *Up Close and Personal*, 67; Fairbairn, *Defendu*; Fairbairn, *Scientific Self-Defense, Etc.*, viv.
25. "Briton Here Shows How to Get Tough," *New York Times* (July 15, 1942).
26. Rex Applegate, *Kill or Get Killed; by Major Rex Applegate* (Harrisburg, PA: Military Service Pub.,1943), 4.
27. S. T. Williamson, "The Fine Art of Gouging," *New York Times* (August 15, 1943).
28. Arthur Daley, "Sports of the Times," *New York Times* (March 6, 1944).
29. Ibid.
30. Wanda Ellen Wakefield, *Playing to Win: Sports and the American Military, 1898-1945* (Albany: State University of New York Press, 1997), 93.
31. Arthur Daley, "Sports of the Times," *New York Times* (March 6, 1944).
32. R. J. Overy, *Why the Allies Won* (New York: W. W. Norton, 1995), 177.
33. Sabrina Crewe and Dale Anderson, *The Atom Bomb Project* (Milwaukee, WI: Gareth Stevens, 2005), 24.
34. Joe Garner, *We Interrupt This Broadcast: The Events That Stopped Our Lives—: From the Hindenburg Explosion to the Attacks of September 11* (Naperville, IL: Sourcebooks Media Fusion, 2002), 28.
35. Anni P. Baker, *American Soldiers Overseas: The Global Military Presence* (Westport, CT: Praeger, 2004), 42.
36. Lee, *Up Close and Personal*, 67; Fairbairn, *Defendu*; Fairbairn, *Scientific Self-Defense, Etc.*, viv.
37. Although karate is often considered a Japanese art and many of its most famed experts come from that nation, it was actually a hybrid art with roots in Okinawa and China, with students from many places (Green and Svinth, *Martial Arts of the World*, 240). *Karate* was often used as a generic term to describe an array of arts, much like the Marines' appropriation of the term *judo* to describe their hybrid style.
38. Sergio Ortiz, "Robert Trias: Pioneer of U.S. Karate" *Black Belt* (April 1976): 36–39, p. 38.
39. Ibid.
40. Keith D. Yates, *The Complete Guide to American Karate and Tae Kwon Do* (Berkeley, CA: Blue Snake Books, 2008), 13.
41. Henry Unger, "Karate Gentle Art of Self-Defense," *Popular Mechanics* (July 1959): 125–127, 216, p. 125.
42. Ibid.
43. Haines, 154.
44. Ortiz, 38.
45. Ibid.
46. "School of Hard Knocks," *Sun* (November 25, 1962).
47. Nathan Ligo, "The Living Legend of May Oyama: Kyokushin Karate's Creator Killed Bulls with His Bare Hands," *Black Belt* (April 1994): 40–45, p. 41.
48. Ibid.
49. Yates, *The Complete Guide to American Karate and Tae Kwon Do*, 14.
50. Ibid.
51. Ibid.

52. Larry Wolters, "Television Pins Knockout Hope on Louis Fight," *Chicago Daily Tribune* (June 17, 1946).
53. Rodriguez, *The Regulation of Boxing*, 38.
54. Larry Wolters, "Television Spectator Gets Ringside View and Saves $100," *Chicago Daily Tribune* (June 20, 1946).
55. "Washington to See Bout by Television," *New York Times* (June 15, 1946).
56. Wolters, "Television Spectator Gets Ringside View and Save $100."
57. Larry Wolters, "Video Grows Up! Worth Is Shown by Louis Fight," *Chicago Daily Tribune* (September 29, 1950).
58. "Old and New Louis on TV," *New York Times* (October 27, 1951).
59. Russell Sullivan, *Rocky Marciano: The Rock of His Times* (Urbana: University of Illinois Press, 2002), 199.
60. Marshall Smith, "And New Champion," *Life* (September 22, 1952): 107, 108, 110, 112, 117, 118, p. 112.
61. Sullivan, *Rocky Marciano*, 18.
62. Roberts and Skutt, 299.
63. Sullivan, *Rocky Marciano*, 34, 61; Alan Scott Haft, *Harry Haft: Auschwitz Survivor, Challenger of Rocky Marciano* (Syracuse, NY: Syracuse University Press, 2006), 63.
64. Staff Correspondent, "Blow-by-Blow Description of Championship Fight," *New York Times* (September 24, 1952).
65. Sullivan, *Rocky Marciano*, 177.
66. Ibid., 18.
67. Shirley Povich, "This Morning," *Washington Post* (September 20, 1955).
68. Sullivan, *Rocky Marciano*, 373.
69. Roberts and Skutt, 301.
70. Sullivan, *Rocky Marciano*, 280.
71. Roberts and Skutt, 298.
72. George B. Kirsch, Othello Harris, and Claire Elaine Nolte, *Encyclopedia of Ethnicity and Sports in the United States* (Westport, CT: Greenwood Press, 2000), 243.
73. Lee Wedlake, "The Life and Times of Ed Parker," *Black Belt* (April 1991): 20–23, 96–98, p. 20.
74. Chris Crudelli, *The Way of the Warrior: Martial Arts and Fighting Styles from Around the World* (New York: DK, 2008), 315; Green, *Martial Arts of the World*, 49.
75. Jamie A. Seabrook, *American Kenpo Mastery: A Guide for Students and Instructors* (New York: iUniverse, 2006), 4.
76. Wedlake, 21.
77. Ibid.
78. Ibid.
79. The myth of cultural purity and the interactions of Asian immigrants with Americans, particularly African Americans, stands at the heart of Vijay Prashad's *Everybody Was Kung Fu Fighting* (Boston: Beacon, 2002). Readers interested in this concept should consider examining Prashad's work.
80. John R. Corbett, "Secrets of the Magician of Motion: Ed Parker," *Black Belt* (July 1979): 21–27, p. 26.
81. Jhoon Rhee, *Chon-Ji of Tae Kwon Do Hyung* (Los Angeles: Ohara, 1970), 4.
82. Yates, *The Complete Guide to American Karate and Tae Kwon Do*,14; Haines, 110.
83. Richard Chun, *Tae Kwon Do: Korean Art of Self-Defense* (Santa Clarita, CA: Ohara, 1993).
84. "The Cause of Karate," *Black Belt* (June 1968): 38–41, p. 38.
85. Yates, *The Complete Guide to American Karate and Tae Kwon Do*,15.
86. "Capitol Hill," *Black Belt* (September 1973): 32–34, p. 32.
87. Robert L. Teague, "Via Stolen Bike: The Road to Rome," *New York Times* (August 14, 1960).
88. Ibid.
89. Nick Healy, *Muhammad Ali* (Mankato, MN: Creative Education, 2006), 14.
90. "Five Gloves Champs Win in Olympic Trial," *Chicago Daily Tribune* (May 19, 1960).
91. Shirley Povich, "This Morning," *Washington Post* (August 23, 1960).
92. Arlene Schulman, *Muhammad Ali: Champion* (Minneapolis: Lerner, 1996), 19.
93. "178-Pound Crown Is Taken by Clay," *New York Times* (September 6, 1960); Thomas Hauser, *Muhammad Ali: His Life and Times* (Paradise, CA: Paw Prints, 2008), 24.
94. "Clay Signs for Pro Bout," *New York Times* (October 12, 1960).
95. "LaMotta Confesses He Threw '47 Garden Bout with Billy Fox," *New York Times* (June 15, 1960).
96. Ibid.
97. "Liston Denies Role in Rack Ring Reign," *Chicago Daily Tribune* (December 14, 1960).
98. Tom Wicker, "Underworld Tie of Liston Cited," *New York Times* (December 10, 1960).
99. "Mob or Government," *Sports Illustrated* (October 10, 1960): 16.
100. Sammons, 176.
101. Rodriguez, *The Regulation of Boxing*, 39.
102. Martin Kane, "The End of College Boxing," *Sports Illustrated* (April 25, 1960, 18).
103. Ibid., 19.
104. "Kefauver Favors Tighter Ring Rein," *New York Times* (March 28, 1962); "Should Boxing Be Abolished," *Ebony* (June 1962): 44–46, 48, 50, 52, p. 44.
105. "TV Drops Weekly Boxing Shows," *Washington Post* (December 24, 1963).
106. Rodriguez, *The Regulation of Boxing*, 39.
107. Ibid.
108. Sugar, *Bert Sugar on Boxing*, 189.

109. Leonard Koppett, "Clay Ends Drills, But Not His Talk," *New York Times* (February 22, 1964).
110. Sid Ziff, "Cassius Scared to Death During Weigh In Says Examining Doctor," *LA Times* (February 26, 1964).
111. Shirley Povich, "This Morning," *Washington Times* (November 24, 1963).
112. Elliott J. Gorn, *Muhammad Ali, the People's Champ* (Urbana: University of Illinois Press, 1995), 10.
113. Dave Brady, "Pro Boxing Given Boost," *Washington Post* (January 6, 1964).
114. Ibid.
115. "Cancel 2 TV Casts Over Racial Row," *Chicago Tribune* (February 25, 1964).
116. "Facts, Figures on Title Bout," *LA Times* (February 26, 1964).
117. Ibid.
118. Sugar, *Bert Sugar on Boxing*, 193.
119. For a good blow-by-blow account of the bout, see "Round by Round Summary," *St. Joseph Gazette* (February 26, 1964). For a more colorful description from an excellent writer, see Sugar, *Bert Sugar on Boxing*, 193–198.
120. Wilfrid Smith, "Clay Champ! TKO's Liston," *Chicago Tribune* (February 26, 1964).
121. Robert Lipsyte, "Clay Is Exultant," *New York Times* (February 26, 1964).
122. "Boxing Experts Get Ears Boxed," *New York Times* (February 26, 1964); Lipsyte, "Clay Is Exultant."
123. "Army Insists Clay Didn't Fake Tests," *Washington Post* (April 21, 1964).
124. "Clay and Liston to Get Subpoena," *New York Times* (March 3, 1964).
125. Shirley Povich, "This Morning," *Washington Post* (April 23, 1964).
126. "Florida Finds No Evidence of Fix in Liston–Clay Bout," *New York Times* (March 24, 1964).
127. Gorn, *Muhammad Ali*, 7; Zirin, 146.
128. "Clay Says He Belongs to Muslims," *Chicago Tribune* (February 28, 1964).
129. "Muhammad Ali Clay," *Chicago Tribune* (March 8, 1964).
130. Jim Murray, "The Sheik of Araby," *LA Times* (March 12, 1964); James Roach, "In a Word, 1964 Sports Year Proved Wonderful," *New York Times* (December 20, 1964); Sammons, 183.
131. David K. Wiggins, "Victory for Allah: Muhammad Ali, the Nation of Islam, and American Society," in Gorn, *Muhammad Ali*, 93.
132. Nick Kotz, *Judgment Days: Lyndon Baines Johnson, Martin Luther King, Jr., and the Laws That Changed America* (Boston: Houghton Mifflin, 2005), 125.
133. Russell Baker, "Observer: The Best Men," *New York Times* (May 30, 1965); Sammons, 183.
134. Lacy J. Banks, "The Biggest Fight in History," *Ebony* (March 1971): 134–136, 138, 140–142, p. 135. Jack Johnson, for all the problems he caused for boxing, had whites in opposition to him. He also reigned in an era when boxing did not face any serious competition from a rival sport like football. Ali, in contrast, reigned over a sport already in trouble and faced opposition from rivals within the African American community such as Martin Luther King, Jr., and boxers including Joe Frazier and George Foreman.
135. Bruce Lee and John R. Little, *Words of the Dragon: Interviews 1958–1973* (Boston: C. E. Tuttle, 1997), 76.
136. Ibid.
137. Green, *Martial Arts of the World*, 51.
138. Sid Campbell and Greglon Lee, *Remembering the Master: Bruce Lee, James Yimm Lee, and the Creation of Jeet Kune Do* (Berkeley, CA: Blue Snake Books/Frog, 2006), 172.
139. Ibid., 173.
140. Lee and Little, 27.
141. Bruce Thomas, *Bruce Lee: Fighting Spirit: A Biography* (Berkeley, CA: Frog, 1994), 45.
142. Michael Ferguson, *Idol Worship: A Shameless Celebration of Male Beauty in the Movies* (Sarasota, FL: Star Books Press, 2005), 180; Bruce Lee, *Chinese Gung Fu: The Philosophical Art of Self Defense* (Oakland, CA: Oriental Book Sales, 1963).
143. Greg Roensch, *Bruce Lee* (New York: Rosen, 2002), 11.
144. Ibid.
145. Poshek Fu and David Desser, *The Cinema of Hong Kong: History, Arts, Identity* (Cambridge: Cambridge University Press, 2000), 33.
146. Norman Borine, *King Dragon* (Martinsville, IN: Fideli, 2008), 47.
147. Ibid., 48.
148. Ibid., 50.
149. Borine, 50.
150. "National Karate Finals Set at Coliseum Tonight," *Washington Post* (April 10, 1965).
151. Yates, *The Complete Guide to American Karate and Tae Kwon Do*, 17.
152. Mrs. P.L. Musacchio, "Brickbat for the Gals," *Black Belt* (September 1967): 4.
153. "Storm Clouds over Chicago," *Black Belt* (August 1967): 30–32, p. 30.
154. Ibid.
155. Ibid., 31.
156. Ibid.
157. Ibid., 32.
158. Roger Price, "The Oriental Martial Art of Karatem" *Sports Illustrated* (June 26, 1961): 25–28, p. 28.
159. "Storm Clouds over Chicago," 32.
160. Sarah K. Fields, *Female Gladiators: Gender, Law, and Contact Sport in America* (Urbana: University of Illinois Press, 2005), 34.

161. "Mr. Editor, Why Don't You Print Some Good News," *Modesto Bee* (December 17, 1967).
162. Vaughn, 497.
163. Ibid.
164. Gary R. Edgerton, *The Columbia History of American Television* (New York: Columbia University Press, 2007), 296.
165. Hoyt Harwell, *Tuscaloosa News* (December 8, 1968).
166. Sid Ziff, "Football No. 1 Sport," *LA Times* (September 29, 1967).
167. "Ali May Have to Fight Vietnamese before Terrell," *Jet* (February 24, 1966): 51.
168. Deckle McLean, "The Black Man and the Draft," *Jet* (August 1968): 61–65.
169. "What GI's Think About Ali's Draft Dispute," *Jet* (June 15, 1967): 44–45.
170. Ahmed Shawki, *Black Liberation and Socialism* (Chicago: Haymarket Books, 2006), 8.
171. Roberts and Skutt, 172.
172. "Ali Wins Reversal of Draft Sentence," *LA Times* (June 29, 1971).
173. Ivan C. Brandon, "Violence Won't Win for Negro, Ali Warns," *Washington Post* (May 2, 1968).
174. Gerald Fraser, "Fight at Garden Will Be Picketed, *New York Times* (March 1, 1968).
175. "Could Play Any Sport," *Herald-Journal* (March 24, 1967).
176. Ali Wins Reversal of Draft Sentence."
177. Many scholars expend considerable attention on Ali's popularity, more often emphasizing his role as a political rather than athletic figure. See, for example, Elliot Gorn, "Introduction," in Gorn, *Muhammad Ali*, xiii.
178. Mike Marqusee, *Redemption Song: Muhammad Ali and the Spirit of the Sixties* (London: Verso, 1999), 3.
179. Thomas R. Hietala, "Muhammad Ali and the Age of Bare Knuckle Politics," in Gorn, *Muhammad Ali*, 135.
180. Steve Cady, "A Black Fighter Wins a Big One," *New York Times* (July 4, 1971); Dave Anderson, "The Fight: One of a Kind," *New York Times* (December 19, 1971).
181. Douglas Hartmann, *Race, Culture, and the Revolt of the Black Athlete: The 1968 Olympic Protests and Their Aftermath* (Chicago: University of Chicago Press, 2003), 87, 273.
182. Zirin, 156.
183. Ibid., 156, 159.
184. Harry Edwards, *The Revolt of the Black Athlete* (New York: Free Press, 1969), 38.
185. Vincent Harding, Robin D. G. Kelley, and Earl Lewis, *We Changed the World: African Americans, 1945–1970* (New York: Oxford University Press, 1997), 177.
186. Ibid.
187. James Riordan, *The International Politics of Sport in the Twentieth Century* (London: Spon, 1999), 169.

188. "New York Daily News Reports Ali–Frazier Dream Fight Set for March 8," *Anchorage Daily News* (December 28, 1970): Lacy J. Banks, "The Biggest Fight in History," *Ebony* (March 1971): 134–136, 138, 140–142, p.135.
189. "Ali, Frazier Fright Will Be Seen By 300 Million People," *News-Dispatch* (March 8, 1971).
190. Robert Lipsyte, "Muhammad Ali's Return to the Ring Will Wear Thin," *Edmonton Journal* (September 5, 1970).
191. Dave Anderson, "Police Guard Frazier after Death Threat, Tighten Security at Garden for Ali Fight," *New York Times* (March 8, 1971).
192. Roberts and Skutt, 232.
193. "Can Anybody Beat This Man?," *Jet* (February 18, 1971): 52–56, p. 56.
194. Banks, "The Biggest Fight in History," 135.
195. "Can Anybody Beat This Man?," 56.
196. Ibid.
197. Banks, "The Biggest Fight in History," 135.
198. "Can Anybody Beat This Man?," 54.
199. Roberts and Skutt, 234.
200. Copper Rollow, "It's Frazier by Unanimous Decision," *Chicago Tribune* (March 9, 1971).
201. Lacy Banks, "The Winner, the Loser, the Crowd," *Ebony* (May 1971): 133–134, 136, p. 136.
202. "Turned Away Fans Crash Gates in S.F." *LA Times* (March 9, 1971).
203. "SouthLand Arenas Draw Sellouts," *LA Times* (March 9, 1971).
204. Harold Hobson, "TV: Boxing's Symbolism as Britain Warms to Ali," *Christian Science Monitor* (March 15, 1971).
205. Ali's image appears on the cover of the March 5, 1971, edition. It featured articles on the bout in the March 5, 1971, issue (16–17); issues published on March 19, 1971 (20–25) and March 26, 1971 (3) discussed the results.
206. Copper Rollow, "It's Frazier by Unanimous Decision," *Chicago Tribune* (March 9, 1971).
207. Ibid.
208. Jim Murray, "Feet of Clay," *LA Times* (March 9, 1971).
209. Ibid.
210. "Letters to the Editors," *Life* (April 9, 1971).
211. Lawrence Shainberg, "A Hero on the Screen, a Clown in the Ring," *Village Voice* (March 18, 1971).
212. Front cover, *Sports Illustrated* (May 15, 1971).
213. Ralph Graves, "Some Very Special Help for the Big Fight," *Life* (March 19, 1971): 1.
214. Norman Mailer, "The Ali–Frazier Fight," *Life* (March 19, 1971): 18–30, 32, 36, p. 36.
215. "Letters to the Editor," *Ebony* (May 1971, 16).

216. Ali Dons Karate Gi, Vows to K.O. Frazier," *Black Belt* (August 1972, 11); M. Uyehara, "Bruce Lee: The Final Year," *Black Belt* (October 1976): 13–16, p. 13.
217. Joe Lewis and Jerry Beasley, *The Greatest Karate Fighter of All Time* (Boulder, CO: Paladin Press, 1998), 6.
218. Ibid., 15.
219. Ibid.
220. Ibid.
221. Ibid.
222. Bob MacLaughlin, "The Americanization of Kick-Boxing," *Black Belt* (February 1972): 33–38, p. 33.
223. Ibid.
224. Lloyd Williamsen, "KickBoxing: The Mixture of Mayhem," *Black Belt* (December 1968): 14–21, p. 14.
225. MacLaughlin, 33.
226. Ibid., 33.
227. Jerry Beasley, "The Birth of Competition JKD," *Black Belt* (May 1992): 27.
228. MacLaughlin, 33.
229. Beasley, 27.
230. MacLaughlin, 33.
231. Green, *Martial Arts of the World*, 828.
232. Dan Levin, "Looking for Kicks," *Sports Illustrated* (April 26, 1971): 38–40, 43, 44, p. 39.
233. "TV Revisions," *Chicago Tribune* (May 16, 1970).
234. Don Page, "Back in the Saddle for the Preakness," *LA Times* (May 16, 1970).
235. MacLaughlin, 34.
236. Ibid., 34.
237. "Kick-Boxing Now Legal in Nevada," *Spokesman-Review* (September 19, 1971).
238. MacLaughlin, 34.
239. Ray Valdez, "Southwest Kickboxing Championships: The Verdict Is Favorable," *Black Belt* (December 1971): 52–53, p. 52.
240. *Dear Bruce Lee* (Santa Clarita, CA: Ohara, 1994), 75; Jim Ollhoff, *Martial Arts Movies* (Edina, MN: ABDO, 2008), 6.
241. Sheng-mei Ma, *The Deathly Embrace: Orientalism and Asian American Identity* (Minneapolis: University of Minnesota Press, 2000), 60.
242. Ollhoff, 8.
243. Campbell and Lee, 206.
244. Ibid.
245. Thomas, *Bruce Lee*, 247.
246. Heike Raphael-Hernandez and Shannon Steen, *Afro Asian Encounters: Culture, History, Politics* (New York: New York University Press, 2006), 301.
247. Ollhoff, 8.
248. Robert W. Young, "Can't We Do Anything Right?" *Black Belt* (March 2000): 6.
249. Prashad devotes considerable attention to connections between Asian and African American culture and provides additional insights into Lee's relation to American blacks (Prashad, 126–127, 140, 146–148, 186, 190, 200).
250. John C. Walter and Malina Iida, *Better Than the Best: Black Athletes Speak, 1920–2007* (Seattle: University of Washington Press, 2010), xxxii.
251. Natasa Durovicová and Kathleen Newman, *World Cinemas, Transnational Perspectives* (New York: Routledge, 2008), 196.
252. "Letters," *Black Belt* (February 1975): 9–11, 13–14, p. 10.
253. Prashad, 146.
254. Walter and Iida, 232.
255. Vladimir Bogdanov, *All Music Guide to Soul: The Definitive Guide to R&B and Soul* (San Francisco: Backbeat Books, 2003), 201.
256. Nancy Anderson, "Elvis Gets Top Marks," *Post Daily News* (March 26, 1974); Jerry Hopkins, *Elvis in Hawaii* (Honolulu: Bess Press, 2003), 46.
257. "Karate Teacher Says Kung Fu Movies Do Entertain But Give Fairy Tale View," *Modesto Bee* (March 10, 1974).
258. Chuck Zito and Joseph Layden, *Street Justice* (New York: St. Martin's Press, 2002), 75.
259. Yates, *The Complete Guide to American Karate and Tae Kwon Do*, 13.
260. "Capitol Hill," *Black Belt* (September 1973): 32–34, p. 32.
261. Jhoon Rhee, *Hwa-Rang and Chung-Mu of Tae Kwon Do Hyung* (Los Angeles: Ohara, 1971), 7.
262. Earl Flowers, "Twelve State Political Institutions Squaring Off in North Dakota," *Nashua Telegraph* (October 12, 1974).
263. "Times," *Black Belt* (June 1975): 11.
264. Ali's fight 1976 fight with Antonio Inoki created endless controversies and conflicting accounts that continue today and will probably never be resolved. For the best in-depth look at the fight, see Andy Bull, "The Forgotten Story of … Muhammad Ali v Antonio Inoki," *Guardian* (November 11, 2009), http://www.guardian.co.uk/sport/blog/2009/nov/11/the-forgotten-story-of-ali-inoki.
265. Roberts and Skutt, 173.
266. "People in Sports," *New York Times* (March 25, 1976).
267. David Remnick, *King of the World: Muhammad Ali and the Rise of an American Hero* (New York: Random House, 1998), 90.
268. Bull, "The Forgotten Story of … Muhammad Ali v Antonio Inoki."
269. Ibid.
270. "Morning Briefing," *LA Times* (June 10, 1975).
271. Angelo Dundee and Bert Randolph Sugar, *My View from the Corner: A Life in Boxing* (New York: McGraw-Hill, 2008), 202.
272. Keith Elliot Greenberg, *Pro Wrestling: From Carnivals to Cable TV* (Minneapolis: Lerner Sports, 2000), 74.

273. Robin Herman, "Wrestler's Chin Withstands Ali's Lip," *New York Times* (March 26, 1976).
274. Michael Krugman, *Andre the Giant: A Legendary Life* (New York: Pocket Books, 2008), 20.
275. Ronald Yates, "Inoki Issues Warning for Ali," *Chicago Tribune* (May 16, 1976); Greenberg, *Pro Wrestling*, 73.
276. Green, *Martial Arts of the World*, 487.
277. Ibid.
278. Ibid.
279. Bull, "The Forgotten Story of ... Muhammad Ali v Antonio Inoki."
280. Green, *Martial Arts of the World*, 487.
281. Greenberg, *Pro Wrestling*, 74.
282. Bull, "The Forgotten Story of ... Muhammad Ali v Antonio Inoki."
283. Green, *Martial Arts of the World*, 487.
284. "Ali to Fight Mat Champ," *Chicago Tribune* (March 26, 1976).
285. Herman, "Wrestler's Chin Withstands Ali's Lip."
286. Ibid.
287. Ronald E. Kisner, "Khalilah Says She Doesn't Want Childish Ali Back," *Jet* (July 15, 1976): 44–45, p. 44.
288. Herman, "Wrestler's Chin Withstands Ali's Lip."
289. Yates, "Inoki Issues Warning for Ali."
290. Herman, "Wrestler's Chin Withstands Ali's Lip."
291. Yates, "Inoki Issues Warning for Ali."
292. John Hall, "Around Town," *LA Times* (March 30, 1976).
293. David Condon, "In the Wake of the News," *Chicago Tribune* (June 6, 1976).
294. Herman, "Wrestler's Chin Withstands Ali's Lip."
295. "Inoki Keeps Pounding It Into His Head," *Chicago Tribune* (March 31, 1976).
296. Greenberg, *Pro Wrestling*, 74.
297. Hauser, *Muhammad Ali*, 337.
298. Bull, "The Forgotten Story of ... Muhammad Ali v Antonio Inoki."
299. Ibid.
300. "The Action Was at Shea Stadium," *LA Times* (June 26, 1976).
301. "Ali Pounds Wepner," *Milwaukee Journal* (March 25, 1975).
302. "The Action Was at Shea Stadium."
303. Terry Todd, "To the Giant among Us," *Sports Illustrated* (April 26, 2006): 76–82, 86–90, 92, p. 81.
304. Ibid.
305. "The Action Was at Shea Stadium."
306. Ibid.
307. Daver Anderson, "The Farcical Arts," *New York Times* (June 27, 1976).
308. "The Action Was at Shea Stadium."
309. Krugman, 24.
310. Todd, 81.
311. "Ali, Inoki Rope the Dopes," *LA Times* (June 26, 1976).
312. Joan Ryan, "Down Was Up in Ali–Inoki Farce," *Washington Post* (June 29, 1976).
313. Andrew H. Malcolm, "Ali, Inoki Fight to Draw in a Dull Bout," *New York Times* (June 26, 1976).
314. Ibid.
315. Dundee and Sugar, 202.
316. John Saar, "Ali, Inoki Nonfight to Tokyo Draw," *Washington Post* (June 26, 1976).
317. Malcolm, "Ali, Inoki Fight to Draw in a Dull Bout."
318. Bull, "The Forgotten Story of ... Muhammad Ali v Antonio Inoki."
319. Saar, "Ali, Inoki Nonfight to Tokyo Draw."
320. "Whatever It Was... It's a Draw," *Chicago Tribune* (June 26, 1976).
321. Dave Anderson, "From Ripper to Ripee," *New York Times* (July 4, 1976).
322. Ibid.
323. Anderson, "The Farcical Arts."
324. Dundee and Sugar, 202.
325. "Ali, Inoki Pick and Roll to Standoff Sleeper," *Jet* (July 15, 1976): 52–53, p. 52.
326. Louis Linden, "Mailbox: Ali–Inoki," *New York Times* (July 4, 1976).
327. Bull, "The Forgotten Story of ... Muhammad Ali v Antonio Inoki."
328. Roberts and Skutt, 299.
329. Andrew Malcolm, "Japanese Wrestler, His Prestige Hurt, Has New Thoughts on How to Fight Ali," *New York Times* (February 23, 1977).
330. Ibid.
331. Ibid.
332. Ibid.
333. Bull, "The Forgotten Story of ... Muhammad Ali v Antonio Inoki."
334. Stephen Ducat, *The Wimp Factor: Gender Gaps, Holy Wars, and the Politics of Anxious Masculinity* (Boston: Beacon Press, 2004), 14.
335. Bret E. Carroll, *American Masculinities: A Historical Encyclopedia* (Thousand Oaks, CA: Sage, 2003), 308.
336. Peter J. Ling and Sharon Monteith. *Gender and the Civil Rights Movement* (New Brunswick, NJ: Rutgers University Press, 2004), 156.
337. Judith Lowder Newton, *From Panthers to Promise Keepers: Rethinking the Men's Movement* (Lanham, MD: Rowman & Littlefield, 2005), 169; Early Ofari Hutchinson, *The Assassination of the Black Male Image* (New York: Simon & Schuster, 1996), 30.
338. Judith Kegan Gardiner, *Masculinity Studies and Feminist Theory* (New York: Columbia University Press, 2002), 2.
339. Alexander Macaulay, *Marching in Step:*

Masculinity, Citizenship, and the Citadel in Post-World War II America (Athens: University of Georgia Press, 2009), 133.
  340. Ashyln K. Kuersten, *Women and the Law: Leaders, Cases, and Documenta* (Santa Barbara, CA: ABC-CLIO, 2003), 75.
  341. Fields, *Female Gladiators*, 105.
  342. Valerie Eads, "All Martial Arts Tournament—Second Edition," *Black Belt* (December 1975): 65.
  343. "Male Boxers Don't Want Females in the Boxing Ring," *Jet* (November 9, 1978).
  344. Ossborne, 435.
  345. Sammons, 229.
  346. Sugar, *Bert Sugar on Boxing*, 233.
  347. "It's Holmes' Time to Rule," *Windsor Star* (October 3, 1980).
  348. Ibid.
  349. Sugar, *Bert Sugar on Boxing*, 234.
  350. Jim Nelson, "Holmes Rips Apart the Greatest," *Windsor Star* (October 3, 1980).
  351. Sugar, *Bert Sugar on Boxing*, 234.
  352. Dave Kindred, *Sound and Fury: Two Powerful Lives, One Fateful Friendship* (New York: Free Press, 2006), 241.
  353. Ibid.
  354. Nelson, "Holmes Rips Apart the Greatest."
  355. "Ali Drug Furor," *Edmonton Journal* (October 15, 1980).
  356. "Ali–Berbick Fight Will Go On," *Times-Daily* (December 11, 1981).
  357. Dave Anderson, "Sports of the Times," *New York Times* (December 12, 1981).
  358. Ibid.
  359. Hunter S. Thompson, *The Great Shark Hunt: Strange Tales from a Strange Time* (New York: Summit Books, 1979), 589.

Chapter VI

  1. Kirkpatrick, 66.
  2. "The Solomon Review: UFC 52—Couture vs. Liddell II DVD," http://411mania.com/MMA/video_reviews/82076/The-Solomon-Review:-UFC-52—-Couture-vs.-Liddell-II-DVD.htm.
  3. Michael S. Kimmel, *Manhood in America: A Cultural History* (New York: Free Press, 1996), 270.
  4. Rodriguez, *The Regulation of Boxing*, 39.
  5. Ernest Cashmore, *Making Sense of Sports* (London: Routledge, 2000), 240.
  6. Michael Katz, "Fight Promoter Resurfaces, Says He Fears for His Life, *Pittsburgh Post Gazette* (February 5, 1981).
  7. William Nack, "The Big Bellyache: In a Stunning Fall from Glory, Roberto Duran, the Apostle of Machismo, Blamed Stomach Cramps as He Surrendered His Welterweight Title to Sugar Ray Leonard," *Sports Illustrated* (December 8, 1980): 24–29, p. 29.
  8. "Inquest Planned in Boxer's Death," *Argus Press* (November 6, 1980).
  9. "Do We Really Need Boxing," *The Bulletin* (November 15, 1982).
  10. Anderson, *The Legality of Boxing*, 120.
  11. "Doctor's Vote against Boxing," *Palm Beach Post* (June 24, 1983).
  12. "Ali's Doctor Says Boxer Has Parkinson's," *Times Daily* (September 19, 1984); "Boxing Cited as Cause of Ali's Problems," *Spokane Chronicle* (July 16, 1987).
  13. Gorn, *The Manly Art*, 205.
  14. "Pastors Advocate Boxing at Hearing," *New York Times* (May 21, 1920).
  15. See, for example, Katz, "Fight Promoter Resurfaces"; "Do We Really Need Boxing."
  16. Lindy Lindell, *Metro Detroit Boxing* (Chicago, IL: Arcadia Pub., 2001), 97.
  17. Abby Goodnough, "The Weekend Rocky's Return in Death's Shadow," *New York Times* (September 30, 2003).
  18. Richard Sandomir, "Out of the Barroom onto Pay-per-View," *New York Times* (December 5, 1995).
  19. "Tussle for Title of Toughest," *Sun* (December 23, 1980).
  20. Goodnough, "The Weekend Rocky's Return in Death's Shadow."
  21. Sandomir, "Out of the Barroom Onto Pay-per-View."
  22. "Macho Mayhem," *New York Times* (December 26, 1980).
  23. Goodnough, "The Weekend Rocky's Return in Death's Shadow."
  24. Jim Benagh, "Tough Man Boxing Brings Controversy," *New York Times* (May 18, 1981); Goodnough, "The Weekend Rocky's Return in Death's Shadow."
  25. For more information on Reagan and the welfare queen, see Khiara M. Bridges, *Reproducing Race: An Ethnography of Pregnancy as a Site of Racialization* (Berkeley: University of California Press, 2011), 211.
  26. Peter Heller, *Bad Intentions: The Mike Tyson Story* (New York: New American Library, 1989), 10.
  27. Bert Randolph Sugar, *Boxing's Greatest Fighters* (Guilford, CT: Lyons Press, 2006), 349.
  28. Mike Puma, "Iron Mike Explosive in and out of Ring," http://static.espn.go.com/classic/biography/s/Tyson_Mike.html.
  29. Dave Anderson, "Tyson Era Is Now," *New York Times* (November 24, 1986).
  30. Pat Putnam, "Getting A Belt Out of Life with a Second-Round TKO over Trevor Berbick, 20-Year-Old Mike Tyson Became the Youngest Heavyweight Champion Ever," *Sports Illustrated* (December 1, 1986): 18–21, p. 21.

31. Ibid., 21.
32. Ibid., 21.
33. Anderson, "Tyson Era Is Now."
34. Brett E. Carroll, *American Masculinities: A Historical Encyclopedia* (Thousand Oaks, CA: Sage, 2003), 290.
35. Thomas, *Bruce Lee*, 247.
36. Randy Williams, *Sports Cinema 100 Movies: The Best of Hollywood's Athletic Heroes, Losers, Myths, and Misfits* (Pompton Plains, NJ: Limelight, 2006), 98.
37. Chuck Norris and Ken Abraham, *Against All Odds: My Story* (Nashville, TN: Broadman & Holman, 2004), 33.
38. M. Ray Lott, *The American Martial Arts Film* (Jefferson, NC: McFarland, 2004), 73.
39. Marshall Julius, *Action! The Action Movie A–Z* (Bloomington: Indiana University Press, 1996), 2.
40. Roger Ebert, *Roger Ebert's Four-Star Reviews, 1967–2007* (Kansas City, MO: Andrews McMeel, 2007), 381.
41. Philip C. DiMare, *Movies in American History: An Encyclopedia* (Santa Barbara, CA: ABC-CLIO, 2011), 287.
42. Jose Emiliano Aizona, "Ninja Turtlemania: How Has It Affected the Martial Arts?" *Black Belt* (September 1990): 24.
43. Lott, 226.
44. Aizona, 24. In the interest of full disclosure, I should note that I trained at David Deaton's school and even appeared in a promotional video for him while I lived in Nashville, Tennessee.
45. Horace Newcomb, Cary O'Dell, and Noelle Watson, *Encyclopedia of Television* (Chicago: Fitzroy Dearborn, 2004), 1118.
46. Ibid.
47. The New York Times, *The New York Times Guide to Essential Knowledge: A Desk Reference for the Curious Mind* (New York: St. Martin's Press, 2004), 422.
48. Janet Wasko, *Hollywood in the Information Age: Beyond the Silver Screen* (Austin: University of Texas Press, 1995), 113.
49. Ibid.
50. "Video Tape Will Decide Sumo as Ancient Sport Gets Up to Date," *Black Belt* (August 1969): 12.
51. Sportswriters sometimes ridiculed men who tried to learn unarmed defense from picture books rather than personal instruction; Roger Price, "The Oriental Martial Art of Karatem," *Sports Illustrated* (June 26, 1961): 25–28, p. 25.
52. See, for example, "Spectacular Learning Aids and Products from Kiai Productions," *Black Belt* (February 1985): 39; "Remy Presas Modern Arnis," *Black Belt* (September 1981): 76; "Aiki News Video Tape," *Black Belt* (December 1989): 81; "Gracie Jiu Jitsu in Action," *Black Belt* (December 1988): 78.

53. Guttmann and Thompson, 103.
54. "Summer Theatricals," *Washington Post* (June 25, 1905); "Summer Theatricals," *Washington Post* (June 25, 1905); "President Tries Jiu Jitsu," *New York Times* (December 31, 1904).
55. Ramin Kordi, *Combat Sports Medicine* (London: Springer, 2009), 324.
56. Renzo Gracie and John Danaher, *Mastering Jujitsu* (Champaign, IL: Human Kinetics, 2003), 30.
57. Ibid.
58. Ramin Kordi, *Combat Sports Medicine* (London: Springer, 2009), 324.
59. Gracie and Danaher, 30.
60. L. Jon Wertheim, *Blood in the Cage: Mixed Martial Arts, Pat Miletich, and the Furious Rise of the UFC* (Boston: Houghton Mifflin Harcourt, 2009), 46.
61. Nori Bunasawa and John Murray, *The Toughest Man Who Ever Lived* (Las Vegas: Innovations), 285.
62. Jerry Langton, *Fighter: The Unauthorized Biography of Georges St-Pierre, UFC Champion* (Mississauga, ON J. Wiley & Sons Canada, 2011), 21.
63. Ibid., 23.
64. Liddell and Millman, 61.
65. Langton, 23.
66. "Proving Ground," *Black Belt* (October 2002): 92–97, p. 94.
67. Liddell and Millman, 61.
68. Ken Shamrock, Richard Hanner, and Calixtro Romias, *Inside the Lion's Den* (Boston: Charles E. Tuttle, 1998), 69.
69. "Gracie Jiu Jitsu in Action," *Black Belt* (December 1988): 78.
70. Steven Barnes, "Grappling with Reality," *Black Belt* (February 1989): 13, 103, p. 103.
71. Pat Jordan, "Rorion Gracie Interview," *Playboy* 36, no. 9 (September 1989), http://web.archive.org/web/20060615154821; http://www.bjj.org/interviews/rorion-89-09.html.
72. Carolyn Handler Miller, *Digital Storytelling: A Creator's Guide to Interactive Entertainment* (Boston: Focal Press/Elsevier, 2008), 25.
73. Mark J. P. Wolf, *The Video Game Explosion: A History from Pong to Playstation and Beyond* (Westport, CT: Greenwood Press, 2008), 40.
74. "Karate Champ," http://www.arcade-museum.com/game_detail.php?game_id=8279.
75. Andy Slaven, *Video Game Bible, 1985–2002* (Victoria, BC: Trafford, 2002), 167.
76. Gladys L. Knight, *Female Action Heroes: A Guide to Women in Comics, Video Games, Film, and Television* (Santa Barbara, CA: Greenwood, 2010), 60.
77. Sandra E. Kessler, "*Streetfighter*: A Science-Fiction/Comedy/Fantasy/Action Film," *Black Belt* (February 1995): 45.

78. Russell DeMaria, and Johnny L. Wilson, *High Score!: The Illustrated History of Electronic Games* (Berkeley, CA: McGraw-Hill/Osborne, 2002), 281.
79. Ibid., 281.
80. Sheng-mei Ma, *The Deathly Embrace: Orientalism and Asian American Identity* (Minneapolis: University of Minnesota Press, 2000), 73; Tyler Nagata, "ClassicRadar: Kickass Bruce Lee Clones: We Salute the Great Martial Arts Master and the Lethal Lookalikes He Spawned," *Gamesradar* (September 18, 2008), http://www.gamesradar.com/f/classicradar-kickass-bruce-lee-clones/a-20110324113743589016.
81. "Mortal Kombat Offers Internet Web Site," *Black Belt* (October 1995): 70.
82. "Kid's Gifts: A Nintendo Nightmare Bad-Boy Video Games Have Parents, Makers Talking Moderation," *San Jose Mercury News* (December 20, 1992).
83. Robert E. Hood, "Video Gore: Who Needs It?" *Scouting* (October 1994): 34–35, 58–59, p. 58.
84. Steve L. Kent, *The Ultimate History of Video Games: From Pong to Pokémon and Beyond: The Story Behind the Craze That Touched Our Lives and Changed the World* (Roseville, CA: Prima, 2001), 89.
85. John P. Patton, "Mortal Kombat Comes to the Big Screen," *Black Belt* (October 1995): 67–70, p. 67.
86. Bill Loguidice and Matt Barton, *Vintage Games: An Insider Look at the History of Grand Theft Auto, Super Mario, and the Most Influential Games of All Time* (Boston: Focal Press/Elsevier, 2009), 240.
87. Walt Harrington, *Intimate Journalism: The Art and Craft of Reporting Everyday Life* (Thousand Oaks, CA: Sage, 1997), 50.
88. "UFC's Popularity Grows to Insane," *Dayton Daily News* (June 24, 2007).
89. Peter Meade, "Quines Give Karate Extra Showbiz Kick," *Merced Sun Star* (November 13, 1982).
90. Bob Ottum, "Not Just a Lot of Kicks," *Sports Illustrated* (January 24, 1983): 36–39, 77–79, p. 77.
91. Ibid.
92. Ibid.
93. "A to Z of Alternative Culture," *Spin* (April 1993): 38–52, p. 44.
94. "Storm Clouds over Chicago," *Black Belt* (August 1967): 30–32.
95. "Which Martial Art Will Be the Fad of the '90s," *Black Belt* (October 1994): 49, 52–53, 55, p. 55.
96. "Tae-Bo Guru Billy Blanks Says He Used to Get Teased as a Kid," *Jet* (December 13, 1999): 64; Ron Wiggins, "Cat Woman Clone on a Health Kick," *Palm Beach Post* (May 25, 1997).
97. "Which Martial Art Will Be the Fad of the '90s," 55.

98. Jim Coleman, "World Martial Arts Challenge Does Kickboxing No Favors," *Black Belt* (July 1992): 38–42, p. 38.
99. Ibid., 39.
100. Fleischer, et al., 181.
101. Ibid.
102. "Mike Tyson Marries," *Gainesville Sun* (February 9, 1989).
103. Laura B. Randolph, "Robin: Life After Tyson," *Ebony* (March 1990): 122–124, 127, p. 122.
104. Randolph, 122; Howard Rosenberg, "Abuse Issue Clouded in Tyson–Givens Match," *Pittsburgh Press* (October 15, 1988).
105. "Douglas Kaos Tyson in Tenth Round," *Ellensburg Daily Record* (February 12, 1990).
106. Richard Hoffer, "The Fight," *Sports Illustrated* (February 19, 1990): 14–26, p. 18.
107. "Douglas Kaos Tyson in Tenth Round."
108. "Tyson Says He's Still Champ After Knockout," *Daily Times* (February 12, 1990); "Douglas–Tyson Referee Defends Count in Eighth," *Eugene Register-Guard* (February 14, 1990).
109. Denis Hamill, "Humble Mike Plans Comeback," *Newsday* (February 14, 1990).
110. Carl T. Rowan, "Tyson–Douglas Fiasco Puts Boxing on Ropes," *Chicago Sun-Times* (February 18, 1990).
111. Doug Richardson, "Grand Jury Indicts Mike Tyson for Rape After Investigation," *Daily Union* (September 10, 1991); "Desiree Washington Rape Victim's Photo, Name in Magazine," *Southeast Missourian* (February 14, 1992).
112. "Tyson's Accuser Told Contestants of Alleged Rape," *Eugene Register-Guard* (February 4, 1992).
113. Steve Wulf, "On the Ropes," *Sports Illustrated* (September 9, 1991): 30–35, p. 31.
114. Joyce Carol Oates, "Rape and the Boxing Ring," *Newsweek* (February 23, 1992), http://www.thedailybeast.com/newsweek/1992/02/23/rape-and-the-boxing-ring.html.
115. Ibid.
116. Thomas P. Wyman, "Tyson Ready for Probation After Rape Jail Term," *News Journal* (March 24, 1995).
117. Green, *Martial Arts of the World*, 487.
118. Chris Curdelli, *The Way of the Warrior: Martial Arts and Fighting Styles from Around the World* (New York: D, 2008), 225.
119. Shamrock, et al., 211.
120. Jordan Breen, "A Blood Called Shooto," *Sherdog* (May 8, 2009), http://www.sherdog.com/news/articles/1/A-Blood-Called-Shooto-17377.
121. For example, every fighter at the first professional Shooto event in 1989 was Japanese (http://www.sherdog.com/events/Shooto-Shooto-2377).
122. Alex Marvez, "Karate Instructor Kicks Up His Heels," *Miami Herald* (July 7, 1991).

123. Ibid.
124. "Paulson Wins Title at Shootwrestling Event," *Black Belt* (August 1996): 120, 122, p. 120.
125. Sam Sheridan, *The Fighter's Mind: Inside the Mental Game* (New York: Atlantic Monthly Press, 2010), 171.
126. "Biography," http://www.kenshamrock.com/biography/.
127. Shamrock, et al., 32, 84.
128. Ibid., 46.
129. Jeremy Wall, *UFC's Ultimate Warriors: The Top 10* (Toronto: ECW Press, 2005), 162.
130. Walter and Iida, 230.
131. Shamrock, et al., 56.
132. Langton, 23.
133. Liddell and Millman, 62.
134. Wertheim, 56.
135. Erich Krauss and Bret Aita, *Brawl: A Behind-the-Scenes Look at Mixed Martial Arts Competition* (Toronto: ECW, 2003), 30; Langton, 23.
136. Krauss and Aita, 31. The octagon, while distinctive, bears some similarities to the chicken-wire–enclosed rings used by professional wrestlers since the 1930s. The wrestlers choose chicken wire because it kept wrestlers in and limited the damage that unruly crowds of bottle-throwing patrons might inflict on the performers (Green, *Martial Arts of the World*, 488).
137. Krauss and Aita, 32.
138. Melissa S. Fisher and Greg Downey, *Frontiers of Capital: Ethnographic Reflections on the New Economy* (Durham, NC: Duke University Press, 2006), 116.
139. Liddell and Millman, 63.
140. Brian Scott O'Hara, *The Evolution of Dramatic Storylined in the Packaging, Selling and Legitimizing of Ultimate Fighting Championship* (MA thesis, 2008), 62.
141. Krauss and Aita, 31.
142. Erich Krauss, *Warriors of the Ultimate Fighting Championship* (New York: Citadel, 2004), 9; Don Beu, "The Ultimate Fighting Championship," *Black Belt* (March 1994): 56–60.
143. Jason Probst, "Jason DeLucia: Where Is He Now?" Sherdogwww, http://www.sherdog.com/news/articles/1/Jason-DeLucia-Where-is-He-Now-30670.
144. Shamrock, et al., 61.
145. Krauss and Aita, 59.
146. Wertheim, 56.
147. Shamrock, et al., 62.
148. Beu, 59.
149. Ibid., 60.
150. O'Hara, 24.
151. Kenneth E. Clow and Donald Baack, *Cases in Marketing Management* (Thousand Oaks, CA: Sage, 2012), 112.
152. Ned F. Kock, *Compensatory Adaptation: Understanding How Obstacles Can Lead to Success* (Haverford, PA: Infinity Publishing.com, 2002), 90.
153. Ibid.
154. Bill Wallace, "It's Time Royce Gracie Fought Someone Talented," *Black Belt* (August 1994): 16.
155. Ibid.
156. Shamrock, et al., 65.
157. Krauss, 10.
158. Maarten van Bottenburg and Johan Heilbron, "De-sportization of Fighting Contests: The Origins and Dynamics of No Holds Barred Events and the Theory of Sportization," *International Review for the Sociology of Sport* (May 2006): 259–282, p. 261.
159. Baker, *Playing with God*, 234.
160. Gilles Kepel, *Allah in the West: Islamic Movements in America and Europe* (Stanford, CA: Stanford University Press, 1997), 23.
161. Ibid., 33.
162. Ibid., 33.
163. Wallace Stevens, "Gotham: The Front Page Lynching," *New York Magazine* (October 14, 1996): 21.
164. Daniel O'CTor, *Iron Mike: A Mike Tyson Reader* (New York: Thunder's Mouth Press, 2002), 179.
165. Jill Nelson, "Not Ready for Redemption," *New York Times* (June 17, 1995).
166. Baker, *Playing with God*, 236.
167. "Mike Tyson Greeted as Hero by New York Fans," *Tuscaloosa News* (June 21, 1995).
168. Jim Murray, "The Sheik of Araby," *LA Times* (March 12, 1964); James Roach, "In a Word, 1964 Sports Year Proved Wonderful," *New York Times* (December 20, 1964); Sammons, 183.
169. Jill Nelson, "Not Ready for Redemption," *New York Times* (June 17, 1995).
170. David K. Wiggins, "Victory for Allah: Muhammad Ali, the Nation of Islam, and American Society," in Gorn, *Muhammad Ali*, 93; Douglas Hartmann, *Race, Culture, and the Revolt of the Black Athlete: The 1968 Olympic Protests and Their Aftermath* (Chicago: University of Chicago Press, 2003), 87, 273.
171. Thurston, 266; Riordan, 169.
172. O'CTor, 206.
173. See, for example, Kirkpatrick, 66; "Divorced Mike Tyson," *Time* (February 27, 1989): 69; Frank Hoffmann and William G. Bailey, *Sports & Recreation Fads* (New York: Haworth Press, 1991), 373; Denis Hamill, "Humble Mike Plans Comeback," *Newsday* (February 14, 1990).
174. Kambiz GhaneaBassiri, *A History of Islam in America: From the New World to the New World Order* (New York: Cambridge University Press, 2010), 346.
175. Mohamed Nimer, *The North American Muslim Resource Guide: Muslim Community Life*

in the United States and Canada (New York: Routledge, 2002), 26.

176. United States, *Statistical Abstract of the United States, 2010* (Washington, D.C.: U.S. Census Bureau, 2009), 55.

177. GhaneaBassiri, 346.

178. Paul M. Barrett, *American Islam: The Struggle for the Soul of a Religion* (Paradise, CA: Paw Prints, 2010), 103.

179. Edward L. Queen, Stephen R. Prothero, and Gardiner H. Shattuck, *Encyclopedia of American Religious History* (New York: Facts on File, 2009), 83.

180. Richard Hoffer, "The Big Question. Actually There Are Three: Who Is Mike Tyson These Days? Does He Have Anything Left? Will This Fight Prove Anything?" *Sports Illustrated* (August 21, 1995): 54–68, p. 59.

181. Ibid., 68.

182. "Clay Says He Belongs to Muslims," *Chicago Tribune* (February 28, 1964).

183. Bill Lyon, "Big Fight Should Be Classified as Consumer Fraud," *Boca Raton News* (August 19, 1995).

184. Lowell Cohn, "Fight Won't Be Fixed, But Opponent Is," *Santa Rosa Press Democrat* (August 18, 1995).

185. Fleischer, et al., 413.

186. Jay Pinsonnault, "Tyson–McNeely Fight Was a Joke," *Kingman Daily Miner* (August 21, 1995).

187. Harvey Araton, "Sports of the Times: A Manager Manages to Be Farce's Fall Guy," *New York Times* (August 21, 1995).

188. See, for example, "When They Compare It to Pro Wrestling, It's Not Good for Boxing," *LA Times* (August 26, 1995); Jay Pinsonnault, "Tyson–McNeely Fight Was a Joke"; Lawrence Van Gelder, "Boxing: Fight Fans Are Quick to Voice Displeasure," *New York Times* (August 21, 1995).

189. Jere Longman, "Boxing: Before Facing Tyson, Mathis Takes Punches to His Ego," *New York Times* (December 16, 1995).

190. Bill Lyon, "Tyson, Mathis Set for Human Sacrifice Tonight," *Boca Raton News* (December 16, 1995).

191. "Elsewhere," *Sarasota Herald Tribune* (December 25, 1995).

192. Daver Anderson, "Tyson Is a Champion without a Marquee," *New York Times* (March 18, 1996).

193. Richard Hoffer, *A Savage Business: The Comeback and Comedown of Mike Tyson* (New York: Simon & Schuster, 1998), 175.

194. "Lewis Set to Face McCall for World Title," *Independent* (September 26, 1996); Hoffer, *A Savage Business*, 175.

195. Chris Jenkins, "Tyson Wins in 1:49, but Crowd Cries Foul," *San Diego Union Tribune* (September 8, 1996).

196. Tom Friend, "A Half Hearted Tyson Punch Is Enough to Knock Out Seldon," *New York Times* (September 8, 1996).

197. See, for example, Dave Anderson, "Boxing's Big Need: Spray or Roll-on," *New York Times* (August 4, 1996); Jerry Sullivan, "Boxing Has KO'D Itself in Public Forum," *Buffalo News* (July 21, 1996); Bill Lyon, "Seldon Loss Part of Fraud in Boxing," *Lawrence Journal World* (September 9, 1996).

198. Richard Sandomir, "TV Sports: Death Is Cheap: Maybe It's Just $14.95," *New York Times* (March 8, 1994).

199. Krauss and Aita, 49.

200. Ellen Fitzpatrick, "Does a New Vidmark Release Stand a Fighting Chance?" *Billboard* (April 2, 1994): 57.

201. Tad Friend, "Getting Medieval," *New York Magazine* (February 19, 1996): 38–47, p. 41.

202. James Brooke, "Modern-Day Gladiators Head for Denver, but the Welcome Mat Is Rolled Up," *New York Times* (December 10, 1995).

203. Royce Gracie, "The Superfight: When Is a Draw a Victory?" *Black Belt* (August 1995): 15.

204. Beu, 59.

205. Bill Wallace, "I Tell It Like It Is, Like It or Not," *Black Belt* (December 1996): 24.

206. Clyde Gentry III, *No Holds Barred Evolution* (Richardson, TX: Archon, 2001), 237.

207. Micael Nedderman, "UFC Fights Are Not Realistic," *Black Belt* (February 1996): 6–8, p. 6.

208. Krauss and Aita, 68.

209. Ibid., 68.

210. Susan Murray and Laurie Ouellette, *Reality TV: Remaking Television Culture* (New York: New York University Press, 2004), 129.

211. Annette Hill, *Reality TV: Audiences and Popular Factual Television* (London: Routledge, 2005), 82.

212. See, for example, Rickson Gracie, "Reality Combat Events Must Change If They Are to Survive," *Black Belt* (December 1997): 16; Tami Goldsmith and Jim Coleman, "Extreme Fighting Event an Extreme Disappointment," *Black Belt* (March 1996): 10.

213. Melanie Reid and Kevin O'Sullivan, "Bloody Sick: Ultimate Fighting Makes Wrestling Look Like a Harmless Joke," *Sunday Mail* (August 13, 1995).

214. Chuck Palahniuk, *Fight Club* (New York: W. W. Norton, 1996), 48.

215. Roger Ebert, "Fight Club," Rogerebert.com (October 15, 1999).

216. David Plotz, "Fight Clubbed," *Slate* (November 17, 1999).

217. For quote from Brown, see O'Hara, 62. The comment about boring fights is entirely my own.

Notes—Chapter VI

218. Kevin Flynn, "Promoter Seeks Site for Fight Event Evicted from Stock Show Arena: Could Return to Mammoth," *Rocky Mountain News* (December 6, 1995).
219. Krauss and Aita, 32.
220. Plotz, "Fight Clubbed."
221. "Severn Tops Shamrock, Wins Detroit Superfight," *Black Belt* (September 1996): 70.
222. Jim Coleman, "Inside the Ultimate Fighting Championship," *Black Belt* (January 1996): 6.
223. Friend, 41.
224. Ibid.
225. Bill Wallace, "Lack of Interest Is Killing Reality Combat Shows," *Black Belt* (September 1997): 24.
226. Andrea Stone, "Bare-Knuckle Debate: Fans See Fun in Brawls Where Anything Goes," *USA Today* (December 18, 1995).
227. Reid and O'Sullivan, "Bloody Sick."
228. "TV Violence at Saturation Point," *Ellensburg Daily Record* (January 27, 1990).
229. "Warning Labels Sought on Violent Video Games," *Durant Daily Democrat* (December 12, 1993).
230. Patty Pryor Nolan, "Hot Topics," *Minneapolis Star Tribune* (November 3, 1993).
231. Brooke, "Modern-Day Gladiators Head for Denver."
232. Ibid.
233. Larry King, "Ultimate Fighting," Lexis Nexis transcript of CNN broadcast (December 6, 1995).
234. Plotz, "Fight Clubbed."
235. Fiona Houston, "No Holds Barred," *Scotsman* (April 3, 1996).
236. Dan Barry, "Not Sweet and Not a Science," *New York Times* (November 26, 1995).
237. "Torrid! Torrid! Torrid! 'Ultimate Ultimate' Fighting Championship Set for Dec. 7," *Business Wire* (November 13, 1996).
238. Barry, "Not Sweet and Not a Science."
239. Joseph R. Svinth, "Death Under the Spotlight: The Manuel Velasquez Boxing Fatality Collection: The Data," *Journal of Combative Sport* (November 2007).
240. Leigh Montville, "Requiem for a Super Featherweight: With the Death of Jimmy Garcia, the Brutality of Boxing Is Once Again Exposed," *Sports Illustrated* (May 29, 1995): 98.
241. Hal Bock, "Son Rejected Mom's Pleas to Quit Sport," *Herald Journal* (December 8, 1995).
242. "Golden Gloves Boxer Dies," *Milwaukee Journal Sentinel* (March 2, 1997).
243. Daver Anderson, "Here Is Why Holyfield Was Not Afraid of Tyson," *New York Times* (November 11, 1996).
244. Jeff Jacobs, "New Champion Is a Man of His Word," *Hartford Courant* (November 11, 1996).

245. "Evander Holyfield Retains Title, Mike Tyson Disqualified for Biting," *Jet* (July 14, 1997): 52–57, p. 53.
246. Ibid., 54.
247. "To Many Tacoma Fight Fans, Penalty Too Lenient," *News Tribune* (July 10, 1997).
248. "The Tyson Bite and Boxing," *Post and Courier* (July 2, 1997).
249. Plotz, "Fight Clubbed."
250. Giles Whittell, "Mortal Combat," *Times* (April 4, 1998).
251. Ibid.
252. Plotz, "Fight Clubbed."
253. Bob Minzesheimer, "NY Deals Blow to Extreme Fighting," *USA Today* (February 6, 1997).
254. Paul Cantin and Antonella Artuso, "Canadian Bloodfest?" *Toronto Sun* (March 19, 1998).
255. "Payforview.com Signs Multi-event Deal for Ultimate Fighting Championship Bouts," *Business Wire* (April 24, 2000).
256. "Smith and Severn on Ultimate-Fighting-Championship, 'Collision-Course'; Additional Fighters Announced for October 17 UFC XV," *PR Newswire* (October 8, 1997).
257. Josh Gross, "MMA Vote Takes Place Today in California," *Sheredog* (February 22, 2005), http://www.sherdog.com/news/articles/MMA-Vote-Takes-Place-Today-in-California-2462.
258. Clow and Baack, 112.
259. Thomas Hauser, *The Boxing Scene* (Philadelphia: Temple University Press, 2009), 175.
260. Scott Rosner and Kenneth L. Shropshire, *The Business of Sports* (Sudbury, MA: Jones and Bartlett, 2011), 492.
261. Fields, 120.
262. Sean Callebs and Nick Charles, "Sport or Human Cockfighting," transcript of *CNN Sports* (July 31, 1997).
263. These numbers come from Jack W. Plunkett, *Plunkett's Sports Industry Almanac 2009* (Plunkett Research, 2008), which defines participation in sport as "Age 6 or older; at least once per year."
264. Michelle Tan, "3 Star Army General Earns His Black Belt," *Army Times* (March 17, 2014).
265. L. Jon Wertheim, *Blood in the Cage: Mixed Martial Arts, Pat Miletich, and the Furious Rise of the UFC* (Boston: Houghton Mifflin Harcourt, 2009), 140.
266. Sean Hyson, "Dana White: The Man, the Sport, and the Money," *Men's Fitness*, http://www.mensfitness.com/sports/athletes/dana-white.
267. Ibid.
268. Ibid.
269. Randy Couture and Loretta Hunt, Be-

coming the Natural: My Life In and Out of the Cage (New York: Simon Spotlight Entertainment, 2008), 13; Jonathan Snowden and Kendall Shields, *The MMA Encyclopedia* (Toronto: ECW Press, 2010), 502.

270. "UFC Infographic," June 14, 2010, http://charlesfighttime.files.wordpress.com/2010/06/ufc-infographic.jpg.

271. John Curran, "In the Boxing Doldrums, Atlantic City Seeks to Fill the Breach," *Sports News* (February 22, 2001).

272. Ibid.

273. Clow and Baack, 112.

274. Ibid.

275. Wall, *UFC's Ultimate Warriors*, 71.

276. Leapin Larry L, "Fight Show Not as Stunning as DK's Shirt," *Age* (December 1, 2002), http://www.theage.com.au/articles/2002/11/30/1038386359406.html.

277. Hyson, "Dana White."

278. For an example of this viewpoint, see Hyson, "Dana White."

279. Clow and Baack, 112.

280. Snowden and Shields, 503.

281. Clow and Baack, 112.

282. O'Hara, 26.

283. Ibid., 26.

284. Snowden and Shields, 470.

285. Liddell and Millman, 228.

286. "UFC 52: Couture vs. Liddell 2 Is On!" Sherdog.com (February 3, 2005), http://www.sherdog.com/news/news/UFC-52-Couture-vs-Liddell-2-is-On-2382.

287. Liddell and Millman, 224.

288. Wertheim, 179.

289. Liddell and Millman, 228.

290. Ibid.

291. Ibid.

292. Chuck Liddell, who stood beside White while he delivered the speech, provides a full quote of this speech in his autobiography in which he substitutes the word "bleeping" for "fucking" (Liddell and Millman, 229). I transcribed my own quote directly from the video (http://www.youtube.com/watch?v=0Q8BeT77tVQ). The editors attempted to beep out White's use of the word "fucking," but it is very clear what word he was actually using.

293. Liddell and Millman, 229.

294. Bob Baker, "Reality Television Without Fake Smiles," *New York Times* (August 21, 2005).

295. Thomas Hauser, "Ringside Doctors Duped by Contender," *New York Sun* (July 28, 2005).

296. Kate Aurther, "Arts, Briefly: Strong Ratings for Spike," *New York Times* (April 18, 2005).

297. Clow and Baack, 113.

298. Dave Meltzer, "UFC 52: Chuck Strikes Back," *Yahoo Sports* (May 24, 2005), http://sports.yahoo.com/mma/news?slug=dm-ufcfiftytwo052409.

299. Snowden and Shields, 69.

300. Chuck Liddell biography, http://www.ufc.com/fighter/Chuck-Liddell.

301. Meltzer, "UFC 52."

302. Liddell and Millman, 243.

303. Ibid.

304. "The Solomon Review: UFC 52—Couture vs. Liddell II DVD."

305. Meltzer, "UFC 52."

306. Mike Fagan, "Bloody Elbow Staff Retrospective Event of the Decade," *Bloody Elbow* (January 7, 2011), http://www.bloodyelbow.com/2011/1/7/1921209/bloody-elbow-staff-retrospective-event-of-the-decade.

307. Langton, 100.

308. Clow and Baack, 113.

309. Danny Plyler and Chad Seibert, *The Ultimate Mixed Martial Arts Training Guide: Techniques for Fitness, Self-Defense and Competition* (Cincinnati: Betterway Sports, 2009), 22.

310. Gregory Bledsoe, Edbert Hsu, Jurek George Grabowski, Justin Brill, and Guohua Li, "Incidence of Injury in Professional Mixed Martial Arts Competitions," *Journal of Sports Science and Medicine* (July 1, 2006): 136–142, p. 141.

311. Robert Siegel, "Sport or Spectacle," *National Public Radio* (August 24, 2007).

312. Peter Sanders, "On Vegas Strip, Fast, Brutal Sport Deals Blow to Boxing," *Wall Street Journal* (March 15, 2006).

313. Cheever, 50.

314. For one example of White making this comment, see his interview with TMZ at http://www.tmz.com/videos?autoplay=true&mediaKey=37d12840-e861-4ce2-8fdd-37347f43b949.

315. Pramit Mohapatra, "One-on-One with UFC President Dana White: Q&A with the MMA Executive," *Baltimore Sun* (January 22, 2007).

316. Josh Gross, "Cybor's Upset of Carano Could Bode Well for Women's MMA," *Sports Illustrated* (August 17, 2009), http://sportsillustrated.cnn.com/2009/writers/josh_gross/08/16/strikeforce.women/index.html.

317. Jill Martin, "Rousey Wins First UFC Women's Match," CNN.com (February 24, 2013).

318. Siegel, "Sport or Spectacle."

319. Cheever, 50.

Bibliography

Archival Collections

H. J. Lutcher Stark Center for Physical Culture and Sports at the University of Texas
Library of Congress
Museum of the City of San Francisco
National Archives and Records Administration
Rio Grande Historical Collections, New Mexico State University Library
Southwest Collection at Texas Tech University
Vietnam Center and Archive at Texas Tech University

Newspapers and Magazines

Albion
American Phrenological
American Review
Analectic
Anchorage Daily News
Anderson Intelligencer
Argus Press
Arizona Republican
Atlanta Constitution
Ballou's Pictorial Drawing-Room Companion
Baltimore American
Baltimore Sun
Berkeley Daily Gazette
Billboard
Black Belt
Bloody Elbow
Boston Daily Globe
Boston Evening Transcript
Boston Recorder
Brother Jonathan
Buffalo News
Bulletin
Business Wire
Catholic Telegraph
Chicago Daily Tribune
Chicago Sun-Times
Christian Register
Christian Science Monitor
Christian Secretary
Christian Watchman
Circular
Clinton Morning Age
Columbia Daily Phoenix
Congregationalist
Corsair
Cosmopolitan
Crawfordsville Review
Critic
Current Opinion
Daily News
Daily Union
Dayton Daily News
Democrat's Review
Deseret News
Duluth Daily Star
Durant Daily Democrat
Ebony
Eclectic
Eclectic Review
Edmonton Journal
Ellensburg Daily Record
Eugene Register-Guard
Evangelical Intelligencer
Evening Independent
Evening News
Examiner
Fibre and Fabric
Flag of Our Union
Franklin County Citizen
Free Lance Star
Freeman
Friend
Friends' Weekly Intelligencer

Bibliography

Gainesville Sun
Galata Journal
Gettysburg Times
Gospel Herald
Guardian
Hartford Courant
Harvard Crimson
Herald Journal
Herald of Gospel Liberty
Home Journal
Hudson Independent
Jet
Kingman Daily Miner
Leslie's Monthly Magazine
Life
Lippincott
Littell's Living Age
Los Angeles Times
Medical Mirror
Merced Sun Star
Meriden Daily Journal
Merry's Museum and Parley's
Miami News
Milwaukee Journal
Milwaukee Journal Sentinel
Milwaukee Sentinel
Minneapolis Star Tribune
Modesto Bee
Morning Leader
Munsey's Magazine
Nashua Daily Telegraph
Nashua Telegraph
National Police Gazette
New York Evangelist
New York Magazine
New York Observer and Chronicle
New York Review
New York State Mechanic
New York Sun
New York Times
New Yorker
News-Dispatch
News Journal
News Tribune
Newsday
Niles Weekly Register
North American Miscellany
North Carolina Gazette
Oxnard Daily Courier
Painsville Telegraph
Palm Beach Post
Panoplist and Missionary
Pedagogical Seminary
Philadelphia Daily News
Philadelphia Record
Physical Training
Pittsburgh Post-Gazette
Political Science Quarterly
Popular Mechanics
Popular Science
Post and Courier
Post Daily News
Post Express
Providence News
Reading Eagle
Record Journal
Religious Remembrancer
Remembrancer
Rochester Evening Journal
Rocky Mountain News
St. John Daily Sun
St. Joseph Gazette
St. Murice Valley Chronicle
St. Petersburg Times
San Diego Union Tribune
San Jose Mercury News
Santa Rosa Press Democrat
Sarasota Herald Tribune
Saturday Evening Post
Scientific American
Scotsman
Sheredog
Slate
Smoky Hill and Republican Union
Social Hygiene
Social Progress
Southeast Missourian
Southern Cultivator
Southern Planter
Speculative Philosophy
Spin
Spokane Chronicle
Spokesman-Review
Sporting Magazine
Sports Illustrated
Sports News
Sun
Sunday Chronicle
Sunday Mail
Sunday Morning Star
Te Aroha News
Telegraph-Herald
Time
Toronto Sun
Tuscaloosa News
United Service
USA Today
Vermont Historical Gazetteer
Wall Street Journal
Washington Post
Washington Reporter
Windsor Star
Youngstown Vindicator

Books and Articles

Primary Sources

Adams, John. *A Defence of the Constitutions of Government of the United States of America*. Vol. I. London: John Stockdale, 1794.

Altherr, Thomas L., Larry K. Menna, George B. Kirsch, Gerald R. Gems, Steven A. Riess, and Douglas Owen Baldwin. *Sports in North America: A Documentary History*. Gulf Breeze, FL: Academic International Press, 1992.

Anburey, Thomas. *Travels through the Interior Parts of America in a Series of Letters by an Officer*. London: Lane, 1789.

Applegate, Rex. *Kill or Get Killed*. Harrisburg, PA: Military Service Pub., 1943.

Ashe, Thomas. *Travels in America Performed in 1806: For the Purpose of Exploring the Rivers, Alleghany, Monongahela, Ohio, and Mississippi, and Ascertaining the Produce and Condition of Their Banks and Vicinity*. London: Printed Newburyport, MA. Reprinted for W. Sawyer & Co. by E. M. Blunt, 1808.

Beck, Jacob Christoph, and August Johann Buxtorf. *Supplement zu dem Baselischen allgemeinen historischen Lexicon*. Basel: Bey Johannes Brandmuller Aelter seel. Erben und gedruckt bey Johannes Christ, 1742.

Benedict, George H. *Spalding's Hand Book of Sporting Rules and Training, Containing Full and Authentic Codes of Rules Governing All Popular Games and Sports*. New York: A. G. Spalding & Bros., 1886.

Bibb, Henry, and Lucius C. Matlack. *Narrative of the Life and Adventures of an American Slave*. New York: Author, 1849.

Bristed, John. *America and Her Resources; Or, A View of the Agricultural, Commercial, Manufacturing, Financial, Political, Literary, Moral and Religious Capacity and Character of the American People*. New York: James Eastburn, 1818.

Couture, Randy, and Loretta Hunt. *Becoming the Natural: My Life In and Out of the Cage*. New York: Simon Spotlight Entertainment, 2008.

Delaware, State of, and James Booth. *Laws of the State of Delaware: From the Fourteenth Day of October, One Thousand Seven Hundred, to the Eighteenth Day of August, One Thousand Seven Hundred and Ninety-Seven*. 2 vols. New-Castle: Samuel and John Adams, 1797.

Doughty, Francis Worcester. *The Bradys and the Drug Slaves, or, The Yellow Demons of Chinatown*. New York: Frank Tousey, 1902.

Douglass, Fredrick. *Narrative of the Life of Fredrick Douglass, an American Slave*. London: H. G. Collins, 1851.

Dowling, Fancis. *Fistiana; Or, The Oracle of the Ring*. London: Clement, 1841.

Ducat, Stephen. *The Wimp Factor: Gender Gaps, Holy Wars, and the Politics of Anxious Masculinity*. Boston: Beacon Press, 2004.

Dundee, Angelo, and Bert Randolph Sugar. *My View from the Corner: A Life in Boxing*. New York: McGraw-Hill, 2008.

Eagan, Pierce, and George Cruikshank. *Boxiana, or, Sketches of Ancient and Modern Pugilism: From the Days of the Renowned Broughton and Slack to the Heroes of the Present Milling Era!* London: G. Smeeton, 1818.

Editors of *Black Belt Magazine*. *Dear Bruce Lee*. Santa Clarita, CA: Ohara, 1994.

Fairbairn, W. E. *Defendu Scientific Self-Defence*. Shanghai: North China Daily News & Herald, 1926.

_____. *Scientific Self-Defence*. New York: D. Appleton, 1931.

Ferrell, S. A. *A Ramble of Six Thousand Miles through the United States of America*. London: E. Wilson, Royal Exchange, 1832.

Fox, R. K. *Boxing: With Hints on the Art of Attack and Defense and How to Train for the Prize Ring*. New York: R. K. Fox, 1889.

_____, and Edward Hanlan. *America's Champion Oarsman, with History and Portrait. Also, History and Portrait of Edward A. Trickett, the Great Australian Oarsman*. New York: R. K. Fox, 1880.

Froysell, Thomas. *Sermons Concerning Grace and Temptations*. London: T. Parkhurst, 1637.

Gracie, Renzo, and John Danaher. *Mastering Jujitsu*. Champaign, IL: Human Kinetics, 2003.

Gracie, Royce. *Ultimate Fighting Techniques: Volume 2: Fighting from the Bottom*. Montpelier, VT: Invisible Cities, 2007.

Hancock, H. Irving. *Jiu-Jitsu Combat Tricks; Japanese Feats of Attack and Defence in Personal Encounter*. New York: G. P. Putnam's Sons, 1904.

_____. *Physical Training for Children by Japanese Methods: A Manual for Use in Schools and at Home*. New York: Putnam, 1904.

_____. *Physical Training for Women by Japanese Methods*. New York/London: G. P. Putnam's Sons, 1904.

Jacomb, William J. *Boxing for Beginners, with Chapter Showing Its Relationship to Bayonet Fighting*. Philadelphia: Lea & Febiger, 1918.

Lee, Bruce. *Chinese Gung Fu: The Philosophical Art of Self Defense*. Oakland, CA: Oriental Book Sales, 1963.

_____, and John R. Little. *Words of the Dragon: Interviews 1958–1973*. Boston: C. E. Tuttle, 1997.

Liddell, Chuck, and Chad Millman. *Iceman: My Fighting Life*. New York: Dutton, 2008.

Louis, Joe, and Art Rust. *Joe Louis: My Life*. New York: Harcourt Brace Jovanovich, 1978.

Norris, Chuck, and Ken Abraham. *Against All Odds: My Story*. Nashville, TN: Broadman & Holman, 2004.

North Carolina, State of. *Minutes of the Upper House of the North Carolina General Assembly March 31, 1752–April 15, 1752*. Vol. 4. New Bern, NC: James Davis, 1752.

North Carolina, State of, Samuel Swann, and Edward Moseley. *A Collection of All the Public Acts of Assembly, of the Province of North Carolina: Now in Force and Use. 1715–1752 Together with the Titles of All Such Laws as Are Obsolete, Expir'd, or Repeal'd. And Also, an Exact Table of the Titles of the Acts in Force*. Revised by Commissioners Appointed by an Act of the General Assembly of the Said Province, for That Purpose; and Examined with the Records, and Confirmed in Full Assembly. New Bern, NC: James Davis, 1752.

Rhee, Jhoon. *Chon-Ji of Tae Kwon Do Hyung*. Los Angeles: Ohara, 1970.

Richard K. Fox Publishing Co. *The New Book of Rules: Official and Standard: Together with the Rules of the Amateur Athletic Union*. New York: Richard K. Fox, 1913.

Shamrock, Ken, Richard Hanner, and Calixtro Romias. *Inside the Lion's Den*. Boston: Charles E. Tuttle, 1998.

Sullivan, John Lawrence, and Dudley Allen Sargent. *Life and Reminiscences of a Nineteenth Century Gladiator*. London: Routledge, 1892.

Van Every, Edward. *Muldoon, the Solid Man of Sport: His Amazing Story as Related for the First Time by Him to His Friend, Edward Van Every*. New York: Frederick A. Stokes, 1929.

Watson, Brian. *Judo Memoirs of Jigoro Kano: Early History of Judo*. Victoria, BC: Trafford, 2008.

Secondary Sources

Achebe, Chinua. *Things Fall Apart*. New York: Anchor Books, 1994.

Ackroyd, Marcus. *Advancing with the Army Medicine, the Professions, and Social Mobility in the British Isles, 1790–1850*. Oxford: Oxford University Press, 2006.

Alba, Richard D., Albert J. Raboteau, and Josh DeWind. *Immigration and Religion in America: Comparative and Historical Perspectives*. New York: New York University Press, 2009.

Albanese, Jay S. *Organized Crime in Our Times*. Newark, NJ: LexisNexis Matthew Bender, 2007.

Ambrose, Stephen E. *Duty, Honor, Country: A History of West Point*. Baltimore: Johns Hopkins University Press, 1966.

Anasi, Robert. *The Gloves: A Boxing Chronicle*. New York: North Point Press, 2002.

Anbinder, Tyler. *Five Points: The 19th-Century New York City Neighborhood That Invented Tap Dance, Stole Elections, and Became the World's Most Notorious Slum*. New York: Free Press, 2001.

Anderson, Jack. *The Legality of Boxing: A Punch Drunk Love?* Abingdon, UK: Birkbeck Law Press, 2007.

Anderson, Kristen M., and Christopher W. Kimball. "The Saints on Sunday: Ballparks and Sabatarianism in St. Paul." *Nine* 17, no. 1 (2008).

Andreff, Wladimir, and Stefan Szymanski. *Handbook on the Economics of Sport*. Cheltenham, UK: Edward Elgar, 2006.

Annian, Huang, and Juguo Zhang. *The Silent Spikes: Chinese Laborers and the Construction of North American Railroads*. Beijing: China Intercontinental Press, 2006.

Aycock, Colleen, and Mark Scott. *The First Black Boxing Champions: Essays on Fighters of the 1800s to the 1920s*. Jefferson, NC: McFarland, 2010.

_____, and _____. *Joe Gans: A Biography of the First African American World Boxing Champion*. Jefferson, NC: McFarland, 2008.

Bailey, Beth L. *From Front Porch to Back Seat: Courtship in Twentieth-Century America*. Baltimore: Johns Hopkins University Press, 1988.

Bak, Richard. *Joe Louis: The Great Black Hope*. Dallas, TX: Taylor, 1996.

Baker, Anni P. *American Soldiers Overseas: The Global Military Presence*. Westport, CT: Praeger, 2004.

Baker, William J. *Playing with God: Religion and Modern Sport.* Cambridge, MA: Harvard University Press, 2007.

Barrett, Paul M. *American Islam: The Struggle for the Soul of a Religion.* Paradise, CA: Paw Prints, 2010.

Barrow, Joe Louis, and Barbara Munder. *Joe Louis: 50 Years an American Hero.* New York: McGraw-Hill, 1988.

Bederman, Gail. *Manliness and Civilization: A Cultural History of Gender and Race in the United States, 1880-1917.* Chicago: University of Chicago Press, 1996.

Beekman, Scott. *Ringside: A History of Professional Wrestling in America.* Westport, CT: Praeger, 2006.

Bellesiles, Michael A. *1877: America's Year of Living Violently.* New York: New Press, 2010.

Bledsoe, Gregory, Edbert Hsu, Jurek George Grabowski, Justin Brill, and Guohua Li. "Incidence of Injury in Professional Mixed Martial Arts Competitions." *Journal of Sports Science and Medicine* (July 1, 2006): 136-142.

Block, David. *Baseball before We Knew It: A Search for the Roots of the Game.* Lincoln: University of Nebraska Press, 2005.

Blundell, Sue. *Women in Ancient Greece.* Cambridge, MA: Harvard University Press, 1995.

Boddy, Kasia. *Boxing: A Cultural History.* London: Reaktion, 2008.

Bolelli, Daniele. *On the Warrior's Path: Philosophy, Fighting, and Martial Arts Mythology.* Berkeley, CA: Blue Snake, 2008.

Bolster, Jeffrey W. *Black Jacks: African American Seamen in the Age of Sail.* Cambridge, MA: Harvard University Press, 1997.

Bond, Gregory. "Jim Crow at Play: Race, Manliness, and the Color Line in American Sports, 1876-1916." Ph.D. thesis, University of Wisconsin, Madison, 2008.

Boot, Max. *The Savage Wars of Peace: Small Wars and the Rise of American Power.* New York: Basic Books, 2002.

Bourke, Joanna. *An Intimate History of Killing: Face-to-Face Killing in Twentieth-Century Warfare.* New York: Basic Books, 1999.

Brame, Gloria G., William D. Brame, and Jon Jacobs. *Different Loving: The World of Sexual Dominance and Submission.* London: Century, 1997.

Breen, Jordan. "A Blood Called Shooto." *Sherdog* (May 8, 2009). http://www.sherdog.com/news/articles/1/A-Blood-Called-Shooto-17377

Breen, T. H. "English Origins and New World Development: The Case of the Covenanted Militia in Seventeenth-Century Massachusetts." *Past & Present* 32, no. 57 (November 1972).

Bretelle-Establet, Florence. *Looking at It from Asia: The Processes That Shaped the Sources of History of Science.* Dordrecht: Springer, 2010.

Brettany, G. T. *The People of Asia.* Naga, Delhi: Kalpaz, 2005.

Brewster, Abel. *Free Man's Companion.* Hartford, CT: Canfield Printer, 1827.

Bridges, Khiara M. *Reproducing Race: An Ethnography of Pregnancy as a Site of Racialization.* Berkeley: University of California Press, 2011.

Brinkley, Douglas, and Michael E. Haskew. *The World War II Desk Reference.* New York: Harper Resource, 2004.

Brown, Tom. *Tom Brown's School Days: By an Old Boy.* Cambridge, UK: Macmillan, 1857.

Browne, Ray B., and Pat Browne. *The Guide to United States Popular Culture.* Bowling Green, OH: Bowling Green State University Popular Press, 2001.

Bunasawa, Nori, and John Murray. *The Toughest Man Who Ever Lived.* Las Vegas: Innovations Inc., 2007.

Burayidi, Michael A. *Urban Planning in a Multicultural Society.* Westport, CT: Praeger, 2000.

Burdick, Dakin. "The American Way of Fighting: Unarmed Defense in the United States, 1845-1945," Ph.D. thesis, Indiana University, 1999.

Burke, Victoria E., and Jonathan Gibson. *Early Modern Women's Manuscript Writing: Selected Papers from the Trinity/Trent Colloquium.* Aldershot, UK: Ashgate, 2004.

Butcher, Alex. *Judo: The Essential Guide to Mastering the Art.* London: New Holland, 2001.

Byrd, William, Louis B. Wright, and Marion Tinling. *The Secret Diary of William Byrd of Westover, 1709-1712.* Richmond, VA: Dietz Press, 1941.

Campbell, Sid, and Greglon Lee. *Remembering the Master: Bruce Lee, James Yimm Lee, and the Creation of Jeet Kune Do.* Berkeley, CA: Blue SnakeBooks/Frog, 2006.

Carroll, Bret E. *American Masculinities: A Historical Encyclopedia.* Thousand Oaks, CA: Sage, 2003.

Case, Theresa Ann. *The Great Southwest Railroad Strike and Free Labor.* College Station: Texas A&M University Press, 2010.

Cashmore, Ernest. *Making Sense of Sports.* London: Routledge, 2000.

Cassel, Susie Lan. *The Chinese in America: A History from Gold Mountain to the New Millennium.* Walnut Creek, CA: AltaMira Press, 2002.

Castiglione, Baldassarre, and Leonard Eckstein Opdycke. *The Book of the Courtier.* New York: Scribner's, 1903.

Chae, Youngsuk. *Politicizing Asian American Literature: Towards a Critical Multiculturalism.* New York: Routledge, 2008.

Chan, Jachinson. *Chinese American Masculinities: From Fu Manchu to Bruce Lee.* New York: Garland, 2001.

Cheever, Nancy. "The Uses and Gratifications of Viewing Mixed Martial Arts." *Journal of Sports Media* 4, no. 1 (Spring 2009): 25–53.

Chen, Yong. *Chinese San Francisco, 1850–1943.* Stanford, CA: Stanford University Press, 2002.

Chudacoff, Howard P. *The Age of the Bachelor: Creating an American Subculture.* Princeton, NJ: Princeton University Press, 1999.

Chum, Richard. *Tae Kwon Do: Korean Art of Self-Defense.* Santa Clarita, CA: Ohara, 1993.

Chung, Sue Fawn. *In Pursuit of Gold: Chinese American Miners and Merchants in the American West.* Urbana: University of Illinois Press, 2011.

Clark, Thomas R. *Defending Rights: Law, Labor Politics, and the State in California, 1890–1925.* Detroit: Wayne State University Press, 2002.

Clow, Kenneth E., and Donald Baack. *Cases in Marketing Management.* Thousand Oaks, CA: Sage, 2012.

Coffman, Edward M. *The Regulars: The American Army, 1898–1941.* Cambridge, MA: Belknap Press of Harvard University Press, 2004.

Cohen, Michele. *Fashioning Masculinity: National Identity and Language.* London: Routledge, 1996.

Cohen, Paul A. *China Unbound: Evolving Perspectives on the Chinese Past.* London: Routledge Curzon, 2003.

Cohen, Richard. *By the Sword: A History of Gladiators, Musketeers, Samurai, Swashbucklers, and Olympic Champions.* New York: Random House, 2002.

Collier, Richard. *Masculinity, Law, and the Family.* London: Routledge, 1995.

Collins, Tony, John Martin, and Wray Vamplew. *Encyclopedia of Traditional British Rural Sports.* London: Routledge, 2005.

Conroy, David W. *In Public Houses: Drink and the Revolution of Authority in Colonial Massachusetts.* Chapel Hill, NC: Published for the Institute of Early American History and Culture [Williamsburg, VA] by University of North Carolina Press, 1995.

Constable, Nicole. *Romance on a Global Stage: Pen Pals, Virtual Ethnography, and "Mail-Order" Marriages.* Berkeley: University of California Press, 2003.

Cooke, James J. *Pershing and His Generals: Command and Staff in the AEF.* Westport, CT: Praeger, 1997.

Corber, Robert J. *Homosexuality in Cold War America: Resistance and the Crisis of Masculinity.* Durham, NC: Duke University Press, 1997.

Cox, J. Randolph. *The Dime Novel Companion: A Source Book.* Westport, CT: Greenwood Press, 2000.

Craig, Steve. *Sports and Games of the Ancients.* Westport, CT: Greenwood Press, 2002.

Crego, Robert. *Sports and Games of the 18th and 19th Centuries.* Westport, CT: Greenwood Press, 2003.

Crowther, Nigel B. *Sport in Ancient Times.* Westport, CT: Praeger, 2007.

Curdelli, Chris. *The Way of the Warrior.* London: Dorling Kindersley, 2008.

De Carvalho, Daniela. *Migrants and Identity in Japan and Brazil: The Nikkeijin.* London: Routledge Curzon, 2003.

Desch-Obi, Thomas. *Fighting for Honor: The History of African Martial Art Traditions in the Atlantic World.* Columbia: University of South Carolina Press, 2008.

DeWitt, John. *Early Globalization and the Economic Development of the United States and Brazil.* Westport, CT: Praeger, 2002.

Di Cosmo, Nicola. *Military Culture in Imperial China.* Cambridge, MA: Harvard University Press, 2009.

Dillion, Richard H. *The Hatchet Men: The Story of the Tong Wars in San Francisco's Chinatown.* New York: Coward-McCann, 1962.

Dillon, Robert Sherwood. *An American Soldier in World War I.* Washington, D.C.: Five and Ten Press, 2005.

DiMare, Philip C. *Movies in American History: An Encyclopedia.* Santa Barbara, CA: ABC-CLIO, 2011.

Dirlik, Arif, and Malcolm Yeung. *Chinese on the American Frontier.* Lanham, MD: Rowman & Littlefield, 2001.

Durovicová, Natasa, and Kathleen Newman.

World Cinemas, Transnational Perspectives. New York: Routledge, 2008.

Duus, Peter, and Kenji Hasegawa. *Rediscovering America: Japanese Perspectives on the American Century*. Berkeley: University of California Press, 2011.

Edwards, Harry. *The Revolt of the Black Athlete*. New York: Free Press, 1969.

Eng, David L. *Racial Castration: Managing Masculinity in Asian America*. Durham, NC: Duke University Press, 2001.

Erenberg, Lewis A. *The Greatest Fight of Our Generation: Louis vs. Schmeling*. Oxford: Oxford University Press, 2007.

España-Maram, Linda. *Creating Masculinity in Los Angeles's Little Manila: Working-Class Filipinos and Popular Culture, 1920s–1950s*. New York: Columbia University Press, 2006.

Fields, Armond. *James J. Corbett: A Biography of the Heavyweight Boxing Champion and Popular Theater Headliner*. Jefferson, NC: McFarland, 2001.

Fields, Nic. *Soldier of the Pharaoh: Middle Kingdom Egypt 2055–1650 BC*. Oxford, UK: Osprey, 2007.

Fields, Sarah K. *Female Gladiators: Gender, Law, and Contact Sport in America*. Urbana: University of Illinois Press, 2005.

Fleischer, Nat, Sam Andre, and Don Rafael. *An Illustrated History of Boxing*. New York: Citadel Press/Kensington, 2001.

Franklin, John Hope. *The Militant South, 1800–1861*. Cambridge, MA: Belknap Press of Harvard University Press, 1956.

Franks, Joel S. *Crossing Sidelines, Crossing Cultures: Sport and Asian Pacific American Cultural Citizenship*. Lanham, MD: University Press of America, 2000.

Gallicchio, Marc S. *The African American Encounter with Japan and China: Black Internationalism in Asia, 1895–1945*. Chapel Hill: University of North Carolina Press, 2000.

Gardiner, Judith Kegan. *Masculinity Studies and Feminist Theory*. New York: Columbia University Press, 2002.

Gardiner, Norman E. *Athletics of the Ancient World*. Oxford, UK: Clarendon Press, 1930.

Gardiner, Simon. *Sports Law*. London: Cavendish, 2004.

Garlett, Kyle, and Patrick O'Neal. *The Worst Call Ever: The Most Infamous Calls Ever Blown by Referees, Umpires, and Other Blind Officials*. New York: Collins, 2007.

Garner, Joe. *We Interrupt This Broadcast: The Events That Stopped Our Lives: From the Hindenburg Explosion to the Attacks of September 11*. Naperville, IL: Sourcebooks Media Fusion, 2002.

Gems, Gerald R., Linda J. Borish, and Gertrud Pfister. *Sports in American History: From Colonization to Globalization*. Champaign, IL: Human Kinetics, 2008.

Gentry, Clyde. *No Holds Barred Evolution*. Richardson, TX; Archon, 2001.

Gilfoyle, Timothy J. *City of Eros: New York City, Prostitution, and the Commercialization of Sex, 1820–1920*. New York: W. W. Norton, 1992.

Golden, Mark. *Sport and Society in Ancient Greece*. Cambridge: Cambridge University Press, 1998.

Gorn, Elliot. "Gouge and Bite, Pull Hair and Scratch": The Social Significance of Fighting in the Southern Backcountry." *American Historical Review* 90, no. 1 (February 1985): 18–43.

———. *The Manly Art: Bare-Knuckle Prize Fighting in America*. Ithaca: Cornell University Press, 2010.

Gorn, Elliot J. *Muhammad Ali, the People's Champ*. Urbana: University of Illinois Press, 1995.

———, Warren Goldstein, and Eric Foner. *A Brief History of American Sports*. New York: Hill and Wang, 1993.

Green, Thomas. "Dambe: Traditional Nigerian Boxing." *Journal of Combative Sport* (September 2005). http://ejmas.com/jalt/2005jalt/jcsart_Green_0905.html

Green, Thomas A., and Joseph R. Svinth. *Martial Arts in the Modern World*. Westport, CT: Praeger, 2003.

Greenberg, Amy S. *Manifest Manhood and the Antebellum American Empire*. Cambridge: Cambridge University Press, 2005.

Greenberg, Keith Elliot. *Pro Wrestling: From Carnivals to Cable TV*. Minneapolis, MN: Lerner Sports, 2000.

Grossman, Dave. *On Killing: The Psychological Cost of Learning to Kill in War and Society*. Boston: Little, Brown, 1996.

Guttmann, Allen. "Puritans at Play? Accusations and Replies." In David Kenneth Wiggins, *Sport in America: From Wicked Amusement to National Obsession*. Champaign, IL: Human Kinetics, 1995.

———. *Sports: The First Five Millennia*. Amherst: University of Massachusetts Press, 2004.

———. *Women's Sports: A History*. New York: Columbia University Press, 1991.

———, and Lee Thompson. *Japanese Sports:*

A History. Honolulu: University of Hawaii Press, 2001.

Hackwood, Frederick William. *Old English Sports.* London: T. F. Unwin, 1907.

Haft, Alan Scott. *Harry Haft: Auschwitz Survivor, Challenger of Rocky Marciano.* Syracuse: Syracuse University Press, 2006.

Hauser, Thomas. *The Boxing Scene.* Philadelphia: Temple University Press, 2009.

_____. *Muhammad Ali: His Life and Times.* Paradise, CA: Paw Prints, 2008.

Isenberg, Michael T. *John L. Sullivan and His America.* Urbana: University of Illinois Press, 1988.

Jeffords, Susan. *Hard Bodies: Hollywood Masculinity in the Reagan Era.* New Brunswick, NJ: Rutgers University Press, 1994.

Johnson, Marilynn S. *Street Justice: A History of Police Violence in New York City.* Boston: Beacon Press, 2003.

Jordan, D., and Joseph Herrera. *Medical Aspects of Boxing.* London: Springer Verlag, 2008.

Kahn, Roger. *A Flame of Pure Fire Jack Dempsey and the Roaring '20s.* New York: Harcourt Brace, 1999.

Kelley, Robin D. G. "But a Local Phase of a World Problem: Black History's Global Vision, 1883–1950." *Journal of American History* 86, no. 3 (December 1999): 1045–1077.

Kimmel, Michael S. *The Gender of Desire: Essays on Male Sexuality.* Albany, NY: State University of New York Press, 2005.

_____. *The History of Men: Essays in the History of American and British Masculinities.* New York: State University of New York Press, 2005.

_____. *Manhood in America.* New York: Oxford University Press, 2006.

Krauss, Erich. *Warriors of the Ultimate Fighting Championship.* New York: Citadel, 2004.

_____, and Bret Aita. *Brawl: A Behind-the-Scenes Look at Mixed Martial Arts Competition.* Toronto: ECW, 2003.

Krugman, Michael. *Andre the Giant: A Legendary Life.* New York: Pocket Books, 2008.

Kuersten, Ashlyn K. *Women and the Law: Leaders, Cases, and Documents.* Santa Barbara, CA: ABC-CLIO, 2003.

Kyle, Donald G. *Sport and Spectacle in the Ancient World.* Malden, MA: Blackwell, 2007.

Laver, Harry S. *Citizens More Than Soldiers: The Kentucky Militia and Society in the Early Republic.* Lincoln: University of Nebraska Press, 2007.

Lee, David. *Up Close and Personal: The Reality of Close-Quarter Fighting in World War II.* London: Greenhill Books, 2006.

Lee, Robert G. *Orientals: Asian Americans in Popular Culture.* Philadelphia: Temple University Press, 1999.

Leen, Jeff. *The Queen of the Ring: Sex, Muscles, Diamonds, and the Making of an American Legend.* New York: Atlantic Monthly Press, 2009.

Lender, Mark Edward, and James Kirby Martin. *Drinking in America: A History.* New York: Free Press, 1982.

Lovatt, Helen. *Statius and Epic Games: Sport, Politics, and Poetics in the Thebaid.* Cambridge: Cambridge University Press, 2005.

Margolick, David. *Beyond Glory: Joe Louis vs. Max Schmeling and a World on the Brink.* New York: A. A. Knopf, 2005.

Marqusee, Mike. *Redemption Song: Muhammad Ali and the Spirit of the Sixties.* London: Verso, 1999.

Morton, Gerald W., and George M. O'Brien. *Wrestling to Rasslin: Ancient Sport to American Spectacle.* Bowling Green, OH: Bowling Green State University Popular Press, 1985.

O'Hara, Brian Scott. "The Evolution of Dramatic Storylines in the Packaging, Selling and Legitimizing of Ultimate Fighting Championship." MA thesis, Colorado State University, 2008.

Ownby, Ted. *Subduing Satan: Religion, Recreation, and Manhood in the Rural South, 1865–1920.* Chapel Hill: University of North Carolina Press, 1993.

Poliakoff, Michael. *Combat Sports in the Ancient World: Competition, Violence, and Culture.* New Haven: Yale University Press, 1987.

Pollack, Adam J. *John L. Sullivan: The Career of the First Gloved Heavyweight Champion.* Jefferson, NC: McFarland, 2006.

Pomeroy, Sarah B. *Spartan Women.* Oxford: Oxford University Press, 2002.

Prashad, Vijay. *Everybody Was Kung Fu Fighting.* Boston: Beacon, 2002.

Putney, Clifford. *Muscular Christianity: Manhood and Sports in Protestant America, 1880–1920.* Cambridge, MA: Harvard University Press, 2001.

Reel, Guy. *The National Police Gazette and the Making of the Modern American Man, 1879–1906.* New York: Palgrave Macmillan, 2006.

Remnick, David. *King of the World: Muhammad Ali and the Rise of an American Hero.* New York: Random House, 1998.

Roberts, James B., and Alexander G. Skutt. *The Boxing Register: International Boxing Hall of Fame Official Record Book.* Ithaca, NY: McBooks Press, 2006.

Roberts, Randy. *Jack Dempsey, the Manassa Mauler.* Baton Rouge: Louisiana State University Press, 1979.

———. *Joe Louis: Hard Times Man.* New Haven: Yale University Press, 2010.

———. *Papa Jack: Jack Johnson and the Era of White Hopes.* New York: Free Press, 1985.

Rodriguez, Robert G., and George Kimball. *The Regulation of Boxing: A History. A Comparative Analysis of Policies Among American States.* Jefferson, NC: McFarland, 2009.

Roensch, Greg. *Bruce Lee.* New York: Rosen, 2002.

Rotundo, Anthony E. *American Manhood: Transformations in Masculinity from the Revolution to the Modern Era.* New York: Basic Books, 1993.

Sales, William W. *From Civil Rights to Black Liberation: Malcolm X and the Organization of Afro-American Unity.* Boston: South End Press, 1994.

Salisbury, Joyce E. *Encyclopedia of Women in the Ancient World.* Santa Barbara, CA: ABC-CLIO, 2001.

Sammons, Jeffrey. *Beyond the Ring: The Role of Boxing in American Society.* Urbana: University of Illinois Press, 1990.

Seigel, Micol. *Uneven Encounters: Making Race and Nation in Brazil and the United States.* Durham, NC: Duke University Press, 2009.

Server, Lee. *Encyclopedia of Pulp Fiction Writers.* New York: Facts on File, 2002.

Snowden, Jonathan, and Kendall Shields. *The MMA Encyclopedia.* Toronto: ECW Press, 2010.

Soister, John T. *Up from the Vault: Rare Thrillers of the 1920s and 1930s.* Jefferson, NC: McFarland, 2004.

Somers, Dale A. *The Rise of Sports in New Orleans; 1850–1900.* Baton Rouge: Louisiana State University Press, 1972.

Somrack, Daniel. *Boxing in San Francisco.* Charleston, SC: Arcadia, 2005.

Stott, Richard Briggs. *Jolly Fellows: Male Milieus in Nineteenth-Century America.* Baltimore: Johns Hopkins University Press, 2009.

Strible, Dan. *Fight Pictures: A History of Boxing and Early Cinema.* Berkeley: University of California Press, 2008.

Struna, Nancy. "Puritans and Sport: The Irretrievable Tide of Change." In Steven A. Reiss, *The American Sporting Experience: A Historical Anthology of Sport in America.* New York: Leisure Press, 1984.

Struna, Nancy L. *People of Prowess: Sport, Leisure, and Labor in Early Anglo-America Sport and Society.* Urbana: University of Illinois Press, 1996.

Svinth, Joseph R. "Death Under the Spotlight: The Manuel Velasquez Boxing Fatality Collection." *Journal of Combative Sport* (November 2007). http://ejmas.com/jcs/jcsart_svinth_a_0700.htm.

———. "Japanese Professional Wrestling Pioneer: Sorakichi Matsuda." *In Yo: Journal of Alternative Prospectives* (November 2000; updated January 2005). http://ejmas.com/jalt/jaltart_Svinth1_1100.htm.

———. "On the Defeat of Tokugoro Ito in North America." *In Yo: Journal of Alternative Prospectives* (September 2006). http://ejmas.com/jalt/2006jalt/jcsart_Svinth_0906.html.

———. "Professor Yamashita Goes to Washington." *Journal of Combative Sport* (October 2000). http://ejmas.com/jcs/jcsart_svinth1_1000.htm

Takaki, Ronald T. *Strangers from a Different Shore: A History of Asian Americans.* Boston: Little, Brown, 1989.

Terrill, Robert. *Malcolm X: Inventing Radical Judgment.* East Lansing: Michigan State University Press, 2004.

Thomas, Bruce. *Bruce Lee: Fighting Spirit.* Berkeley, CA: Frog, 1994.

Thompson, Hunter S. *The Great Shark Hunt: Strange Tales from a Strange Time.* New York: Summit Books, 1979.

Thurston, Robert W. *Lynching: American Mob Murder in Global Perspective.* Farnham, UK: Ashgate, 2011.

Tichenor, Daniel J. *Dividing Lines: The Politics of Immigration Control in America.* Princeton, NJ: Princeton University Press, 2002.

van Botteburg, Maarten. *Global Games.* Urbana: University of Illinois Press, 2001.

———, and Johan Heilbron. "De-sportization of Fighting Contests: The Origins and Dynamics of No Holds Barred Events and the Theory of Sportization." *International Review for the Sociology of Sport* (May 2006): 259–282.

Wertheim, L. Jon. *Blood in the Cage: Mixed Martial Arts, Pat Miletich, and the Furious Rise of the UFC*. Boston: Houghton Mifflin Harcourt, 2009.

Wiggins, David Kenneth. *Sport in America: From Wicked Amusement to National Obsession*. Champaign, IL: Human Kinetics, 1995.

Wolf, Mark J. P. *The Video Game Explosion: A History from Pong to PlayStation and Beyond*. Westport, CT: Greenwood Press, 2008.

Wyatt-Brown, Bertram. *Honor and Violence in the Old South*. New York: Oxford University Press, 1986.

Yates, Keith D. *The Complete Guide to American Karate & Tae Kwon Do*. Berkeley, CA: Blue Snake Books, 2008.

Zinn, Howard. *The Twentieth Century: A People's History*. New York: Harper & Row, 1984.

Zirin, Dave. *A People's History of Sports in the United States: 250 Years of Politics, Protest, People, and Play*. New York: New Press, 2008.

Zito, Chuck, and Joseph Layden. *Street Justice*. New York: St. Martin's Press, 2002.

Index

Aiyaruk 23
Alexander the Great 19
Ali, Muhammad (Cassius Clay) 9, 176, 178–179, 184, 188, 197, 201, 211, 218
American kickboxing 187–189, 209–211, 215, 232
American Revolutionary War 6, 39–46, 51, 64
archery 25

bare knuckle 34, 41, 48, 58, 85–86, 89, 201–202, 216, 222–224
barea athla 17
Barnum, P.T. 75, 77, 88, 227
Beowulf 25
Bible 104, 144
biting 18, 37, 42, 51, 58, 60
Black Belt 207–208, 217, 221
black power 184–185, 188, 195
boxing 1–11, 15, 16–19, 22–24, 27, 33–42, 45, 47–50, 52–73, 75–83, 85–89, 90–95, 97–98, 102, 104, 114, 118, 121–123, 128–129, 132–133, 138, 140–235
Brazilian jujitsu 10–11, 206–207, 214–215, 228

capoeira 21
cestus 19
Chan, Charlie 136
Chinatowns 133–135
Civil War, United States 66–67, 70–71, 73–75, 78–79
collar and elbow wrestling 62, 67, 69, 82, 205
comic books 204
Couture, Randy 231–232
Cribb, Tom 49, 51–52, 58
crisis of masculinity 17, 195–196
cudgeling 34, 36–37

dambe 22
Davie, Art 214
Dempsey, Jack 140, 147, 149–157, 164–165, 168, 211
dueling 7

elbow strikes 187, 222, 224

fencing 30, 55, 63, 71, 80, 93, 121, 141
Figg, James 35, 55, 60
Filipino Martial Arts 119–120
Fox, Richard 81–83
frontier, American 6–7, 32, 38, 42–50, 53, 56, 59, 62

Gilgamesh 14
Gotch, Karl 191
gouging 3, 6–8, 18, 30, 37–39, 42–48, 60, 62, 71, 170
Gracie, Royce 215–217, 221–222
Greco-Roman Wrestling 11, 75, 78, 80, 82, 85, 117–118, 154, 231

Harry Hill's 77–78, 81
head butting 51, 210
hunting 27

Iliad 16–17
Inoki, Antonio 9, 191–195, 212, 218

"Jacob Wrestling the Angel" 6, 14, 25, 33, 56, 62, 143
Johnson, Jack 3, 9, 63, 95–98, 132, 147, 150, 160, 180, 185
jousting 30
judo 8–11, 115, 121–122, 126, 130–131, 138, 167, 170–171, 175, 187, 191–192, 206, 213, 234

Kano, Jigoro 8, 115–116, 138
kara 22

karate 5, 9, 10, 24, 138, 139, 166, 171–173, 175, 176, 180–182, 187–192, 204–210, 212, 215–217, 232
kendo 187
King's Book of Sport 27
knee strikes 15–16, 187, 224
kung fu 9, 20, 102, 108, 133–134, 166, 175, 189–190, 209, 216

Las Vegas, Nevada 196–197, 200, 210, 220, 227–229, 233
Lee, Bruce 9, 113, 134, 180–181, 187, 204, 208–209
Lewis, Joe 166, 187–189, 204
Liddell, Chuck 5, 198–199, 228, 230–232
Lincoln, Abraham 62, 68, 71, 73
London Rules 60, 63–64
Long, Kathy 215
Louis, Joe 9, 140, 156–164, 168, 173, 183–185
Lua 24
Luther, Martin 25, 164, 180
Lycurgus the Lawgiver 17, 39, 43

McCain, John 224–226, 233
militia 6–7, 27, 31–32, 36, 40, 43, 48, 50–51, 71, 226
Milius, John 214
Molineaux, Tom 49–53, 63, 70
Morrill Act 70
Mortal Combat (video game) 209, 224
muay thai 187, 210
Muhammad 23
Muldoon, William 78–79, 82–83, 85, 87, 94, 116–117, 122, 130, 150–151
muscular Christianity 66–67, 78–79, 90, 116, 143, 150

Native American fight sports 21, 24, 31, 56, 62
New England Galaxy 30
New York Athletic Club 77, 80, 143, 146
New York City 51, 54–56, 58, 60–63, 68, 77–78, 80–81, 92, 108–109, 114, 121, 124–126, 132–133, 138, 154, 158, 162, 169, 186, 188, 190

octagon 215, 221, 222–225, 233, 235
Odyssey 16–17
Olympic Games 7, 16, 19, 22, 25, 80, 89, 92, 126, 131, 142, 176–177, 184–185, 190–192, 200, 232, 234

pankration 17–19, 215
pay per view television 215–216, 220, 226, 229, 231–233
Plato 16, 19
Playboy 208
police 117, 122, 124–126, 128–129, 132–134, 138, 143, 169, 170, 176, 201, 225

Police Gazette 65, 81, 83, 113–114, 117, 125
Puritans 27–28, 30, 32–33

Queensbury Rules 3, 5, 60, 71–74, 85, 89, 129, 169

revolt of the black athlete 184, 218
Richmond, Bill 51–52, 63
Die Ringer-Kunst 26
Roosevelt, Theodore 8, 79, 92–94, 122–123, 130
Rousey, Rhonda 234

Santel, Ad 8, 130–131
savate 171, 215–216
Second Great Awakening 47, 61–62, 119
Severn, Dan 222–223
Shakespeare, William 25
Shamrock, Ken 213–214, 216, 223
Shaolin Monastery 20, 102
shoot fighting 212–213
slavery 6, 37, 42, 50, 51, 62–63, 67–68, 95, 98, 100, 109, 157–158, 163
Spirit of the Times 60, 65, 81, 107
Sports Illustrated 1, 177, 182, 186, 188, 212, 219, 225
stomp 34
Streetfighter (video game) 209
suffragettes 116–117
Sukune, Nomi No 20–21
Sullivan, John L. 5, 78, 83–92, 94, 118, 150, 153, 185, 227
sumo wrestling 20–21, 23–24, 63, 104, 206, 216, 221

taekwondo 171, 176, 190, 210, 213
Thompson, Hunter S. 197
Tonawanda, Jackie 196
tongs 113–114, 133–135
tough man contests 201
Twain, Mark 77
Tyson, Mike 2, 198, 202–203, 208, 211–213, 218–221, 225, 233

The Ultimate Fighter 230–231
Ultimate Fighting Championship (UFC) 10–11, 199, 214–217, 221–226, 228–234

vaudeville 75, 83, 121
Vietnam War 183–185, 195–196, 214, 218

Wallace, Bill 215–217, 221
War of 1812 3, 53–55
Washington, George 40, 62
White, Dana 198, 227–228, 232–234
World War I 131, 142–145
World War II 168–172

Young Men's Christian Association (YMCA) 80, 116, 121, 141, 143–145, 175, 180

www.ingramcontent.com/pod-product-compliance
Ingram Content Group UK Ltd.
Pitfield, Milton Keynes, MK11 3LW, UK
UKHW041926140426
5217IPUK00014B/342